/ 06

THE
100 BEST
STOCKS
TO OWN IN
AMERICA

★★★ **2nd Edition** ★★★

Gene Walden

Dearborn
Financial Publishing, Inc.

For Laurie, Whitney and Ryan

While a great deal of care has been taken to provide accurate and current information, the ideas, suggestions, general principles and conclusions presented in this book are subject to local, state and federal laws and regulations, court cases and any revisions of same. The reader is thus urged to consult legal counsel regarding any points of law—this publication should not be used as a substitute for competent legal advice.

Publisher: Kathleen A. Welton
Associate Editor: Karen A. Christensen
Senior Project Editor: Jack L. Kiburz

© 1989, 1991 by Dearborn Financial Publishing, Inc.

Published by Dearborn Financial Publishing, Inc.

Printed in the United States of America

91 92 93   10 9 8 7 6 5 4 3 2 1

Library of Congress Cataloging-in-Publication Data

Walden, Gene.
    The 100 best stocks to own in America / Gene Walden—2nd ed.
        p.   cm.
    Includes index.
    ISBN 0-79310-264-2 (cloth)
    1. Stocks—United States.   I. Title.   II. Title: One hundred best stocks to own in America.
HG4963.W35   1991   91-24491
332.63'22'0973—dc20   CIP

TABLE OF CONTENTS

Acknowledgments   vii

Preface   ix

Introduction   xi

How To Use This Book   xxiii

 1. Philip Morris Companies, Inc.   1
 2. UST, Inc.   5
 3. Rubbermaid Inc.   9
 4. Wm. Wrigley Jr. Company   13
 5. Anheuser-Busch Companies, Inc.   16
 6. The Limited, Inc.   21
 7. Giant Food, Inc.   24
 8. Sara Lee Corporation   28
 9. Torchmark Corporation   32
10. H.J. Heinz Company   35
11. The J.M. Smucker Company   39
12. ConAgra, Inc.   42
13. Waste Management, Inc.   46
14. Liz Claiborne, Inc.   50
15. Stanhome, Inc.   54
16. Fifth Third Bancorp   57
17. Merck & Company   60
18. Bristol Myers Squibb Company   64
19. Abbott Laboratories   68
20. Wal-Mart Stores, Inc.   72
21. Food Lion, Inc.   76
22. Albertson's, Inc.   80
23. Valspar Corp.   84
24. Alberto-Culver Company   87
25. Universal Foods Corp.   91
26. Bemis Company, Inc.   94

27. Carter-Wallace, Inc.   97
28. Sherwin-Williams Company   100
29. Kellogg Company   103
30. Borden, Inc.   107
31. Dean Foods Company   111
32. The Interpublic Group of Companies, Inc.   115
33. H&R Block, Inc.   118
34. Safety-Kleen Corp.   122
35. Sonoco Products Company   126
36. Hubbell Incorporated   129
37. Browning-Ferris Industries   132
38. Shaw Industries, Inc.   135
39. Newell Co.   138
40. Ralston Purina Company   141
41. Hershey Foods Corporation   145
42. Crompton & Knowles Corp.   149
43. Walgreen Company   152
44. Sysco Corporation   156
45. Banc One Corp.   159
46. Kimberly-Clark Corp.   162
47. The Quaker Oats Company   166
48. Bandag, Inc.   170
49. Syntex Corp.   173
50. Deluxe Corp.   176
51. PepsiCo, Inc.   180
52. John H. Harland Company   184
53. Dillard Department Stores, Inc.   187
54. Tyson Foods, Inc.   190
55. The Coca-Cola Company   194
56. Bruno's, Inc.   198
57. Warner-Lambert Company   202
58. General Mills, Inc.   206
59. Jostens, Inc.   210
60. Eli Lilly and Company   213

61. Pitney Bowes, Inc. — 217
62. Schering-Plough Corporation — 221
63. Luby's Cafeterias, Inc. — 225
64. A. Schulman, Inc. — 228
65. The Gillette Company — 231
66. The Walt Disney Company — 235
67. Kelly Services, Inc. — 239
68. The May Department Stores Company — 242
69. Loctite Corp. — 245
70. National Service Industries — 248
71. McDonald's Corporation — 251
72. American Home Products Corp. — 255
73. General Electric Company — 260
74. Johnson & Johnson — 265
75. RPM, Inc. — 269
76. The Procter & Gamble Company — 273
77. Sigma-Aldrich Corp. — 277
78. R.R. Donnelley & Sons Company — 280
79. Automatic Data Processing, Inc. — 283
80. Premier Industrial Corp. — 286
81. Genuine Parts Company — 289
82. Microsoft Corp. — 292
83. International Dairy Queen, Inc. — 296
84. Stryker Corp. — 299
85. PPG Industries, Inc. — 302
86. Melville Corp. — 305
87. Westinghouse Electric Corp. — 308
88. Gannett Co., Inc. — 312
89. Super Valu Stores, Inc. — 316
90. Wallace Computer Services, Inc. — 319
91. National Medical Enterprises, Inc. — 322
92. Pall Corporation — 325
93. American Brands, Inc. — 328
94. Rite Aid Corp. — 332

95. Medtronic, Inc.   335
96. Emerson Electric Co.   338
97. Becton Dickinson and Co.   341
98. GTE Corp.   344
99. Martin Marietta Corp.   348
100. McGraw-Hill, Inc.   352

100 Best by State   355
100 Best by Industry   361
Index   365

ACKNOWLEDGMENTS

This book was made possible through the efforts of a long list of people. My special thanks goes to:

- The Council on Economic Priorities—particularly Ben Corson and Leslie Gottlieb, who did an extraordinary job of compiling the social responsibility sections on many of the companies featured in this book;
- The dozens of financial and corporate relations officers who double-checked financial figures and provided updated information on their companies;
- John Hogan, who served as a research assistant on both this book and *The 100 Best Stocks To Own in the World*. He dug through piles of financial records, crunched numbers, sent letters, made last minute fact-checking calls to scores of corporations, and helped maintain some semblance of order in this otherwise overwhelming undertaking.

PREFACE

A little more than two years have passed since the first edition of this book was published in 1989.

In that short span, the country has gone to war twice—in Panama and Iraq. The Iron Curtain has fallen, Germany has united, and much of the Eastern Bloc was moved closer to a free market economy.

At home, the country has endured a series of economic setbacks. The savings and loan industry has continued its decline, and the insurance industry has stepped dangerously closer to a similar crisis. Housing prices on both coasts have suffered severe declines, the booming junk bond market has gone bust, and the United States has experienced its first full-blown recession since the early 1980s.

Yet through it all, America's best-run corporations have continued to chalk up record sales and earnings, continued to expand their market share—both here and abroad—and continued to deliver bigger dividends and higher stock prices for their shareholders. The best of those companies are profiled in this book.

In this edition, I have added a couple of features designed to give investors a more complete picture of the 100 companies. Included with each profile is a six-year financial history with annual revenues, earnings per share, net earnings, dividends, stock prices and book value per share.

I have also included information on the social and ethical practices of many of the companies on the list. The information, provided by the Council on Economic Priorities, gives investors yet another element to consider in making their investment selections. Ethical concerns played no part in the selection process of the *100 Best* list. As before, the companies were chosen strictly on the basis of their financial performance.

About one-third of the stocks are new to the list in this edition. In all, 35 stocks were dropped from the original 100, either because they were acquired by another company or because their financial performance did not meet the high standards necessary to be included on the *100 Best* list. Those companies were replaced by 35 others that have had superior performance over the past several years.

I have also updated and rewritten the profiles of the 65 original companies that were again included in the top 100 list.

With all the updates, changes and new features, I think, you'll find this edition of *The 100 Best Stocks To Own in America* to be one sequel that's better than the original.

INTRODUCTION

It is America's most profitable product. It weighs just under a gram and is just 3¹/₂ inches in length and half an inch in diameter. To use it, you have to burn it—which Americans do nearly 600 billion times a year.

Welcome to Marlboro country.

Despite years of negative publicity, mounting health concerns and a congressional ban that has kept cigarette advertising off the airwaves for the past 20 years, tobacco continues to be the country's most lucrative commodity.

Philip Morris, the world's largest consumer products company and the maker of Marlboro, Virginia Slims, Merit, Benson & Hedges, Miller Beer and dozens of well-known food products, ranks as the number one stock to own in America.

Following closely behind at number two is UST (formerly U.S. Tobacco), maker of Skoal, Bandits and Copenhagen smokeless tobaccos and several pipe and rolling tobaccos.

Rounding out the top five picks on this honor roll of America's best stocks are Rubbermaid, Wm. Wrigley and Anheuser-Busch.

Philip Morris and UST made it to the top of the list by compiling a remarkable record of earnings, dividend growth and stock price growth. Both companies have raised their earnings per share and dividends for more than 30 consecutive years. Over the past ten years, shareholders of each company have reaped an average return on their investment of about 30 percent per year. In dollar terms, a $10,000 investment in either stock ten years ago would now be worth well over $100,000.

How could a pair of tobacco producers waft to the top of corporate America in an era of rising antismoking sentiment generated by the roughly 400,000 U.S. deaths attributed each year to tobacco-related ailments?

"Very simple," says John Schultz, president of the board of the Social Investment Forum. "They have an addicted clientele who are willing to pay whatever they have to to buy their products." That enables cigarette producers to set their prices at an artificially high level. While profit margins for most consumer goods average about 12 percent, tobacco products command about a 44 percent profit margin.

"The tobacco cartel has also been very successful in luring youngsters into the tobacco habit," adds Schultz. "Kids under 18 spend an estimated $1.3 billion a year on cigarettes. More than 3 million youngsters are daily smokers." In all, about 50 million Americans smoke 1.5 billion cigarettes a day.

As controversial as its chief product may be, however, Philip Morris is still widely recognized as one of the most well-managed companies in the world. Through its astute marketing, the company has elevated Miller Beer from near bankruptcy to the second most successful brewery in America (behind Anheuser-Busch). And it has used the profits from its cigarette sales to acquire a vast empire of name brand foods, including Kraft, Jell-O, Oscar Mayer, Post and Maxwell House. In fact, Philip Morris and UST have flourished while other tobacco companies have struggled. The next best cigarette firm, American Brands, ranks only 93rd out of the top 100 stocks. And Loews, which made the list in the last edition of this book, has dropped entirely off the list after a couple of years of subpar performance.

While tobacco companies occupy the top two spots in the top 100, several other industries are also well represented. The list includes 16 foods producers (led by Sara Lee at number 8), five grocery store chains (led by Giant Food at number 7), seven retailers (led by The Limited at number 6) and 14 medical products manufacturers (led by Merck at number 17).

On the other hand, a few industries that fared well in the first edition of this book have hit upon hard times and are poorly represented in this edition. One of the more battered sectors is the publishing industry. The New York Times, Dow Jones and Paramount (formerly Gulf & Western) were all dropped from the list after some lean years, while McGraw-Hill slid from number 58 to number 100. Gannett, the only other survivor from the publishing business, moved from 87 to 88.

The aerospace and defense industry has also taken some lumps. Four of the five entries in the first edition—Rockwell, Lockheed, Kaman and Precision Castparts—have been deleted, while Martin Marietta is barely hanging on at number 99.

The financial sector has had some casualties as well. Absent from this edition are MNC Financial, Dreyfus, CoreStates Financial and PNC Financial. On the other hand, Fifth Third Bancorp, Torchmark and Banc One are still going strong.

The other beleaguered sector is lodging. The two entries from the first edition, Marriott and Prime Motor Inns, have both been axed. In fact, Prime was the top 100's biggest loser, falling from a high of about $35 a share in 1989 to low of under $1 a share in 1991.

On the bright side, 65 companies have performed well enough to stay in the top 100. In fact, overall the 100 stocks from the first edition performed remarkably well. During the two-and-a-half-year period from January 1, 1989, through June 1, 1991, the 100 stocks were up, on average, 40 percent (including dividends). The strong showing came in spite of the war, the recession and a disastrous 1990 stock market, when U.S. stocks dropped an average of more than 10 percent.

In this edition, we've added some outstanding new companies: J.M. Smucker at number 11, Liz Claiborne at number 14 and Alberto-Culver at number 24. Other familiar names making their first appearance in the top 100 include Coca-Cola, General Electric, General Mills, Johnson & Johnson, Procter & Gamble, Microsoft and Gillette.

FUTURE PROSPECTS

This book makes no pretense of projecting the future performance of any security. The rankings are based strictly on the past performance of the companies.

But while there is no assurance that any of these companies will outperform the market in the years to come, they do have a couple of strong points in their favor. For one, each company featured here has proven its ability to compete as a market leader in one or more areas. Their concepts are working. Their products or services have made an impact in the marketplace and have been highly profitable for ten years or more. Each of these companies has a management team that has also proven capable of turning a profit on a consistent basis. They have ridden the ups and downs of the economy over the past decade, survived the rash of mergers and acquisitions (and probably made a few of their own), weathered the crash of 1987 and have still come away with an outstanding record of earnings and stock price growth. Presumably, most of these companies will continue their success into the next decade.

While it is certainly possible that companies like McDonald's (more than 100 consecutive quarters of record earnings), Automatic Data Processing (116 consecutive quarters of double-digit growth in both earnings and revenues), Torchmark (39 consecutive years of record earnings), Deluxe (51 consecutive years of record sales) and RPM (44 consecutive years of record sales and earnings) could slip into a sudden free-fall, after decades of uninterrupted growth, the odds are against it.

THE CASE FOR STOCKS

While an individual's first investment priority should be money in the bank—everyone needs a cash cushion to fall back on—stocks should be a key component of any well-balanced portfolio.

Why buy stocks rather than collecting that safe, consistent flow of interest earnings a bank account would offer? Here are some numbers to reflect on.

On average, over the 66 years for which records are available—which includes both the crash of '29 and the crash of '87—stocks have paid an average annual return of about 10 percent, roughly double the return of bonds and three times the return of money market funds. The difference is even more dramatic when put in inflation-adjusted terms. A dollar invested in a money market account 66 years ago would have grown (inflation-adjusted) to about $2.60 today. That same dollar invested in the broad stock market would have grown to about $78 (inflation-adjusted) today. Stocks may have their ups and downs, but if you can live with the volatility, you're going to be a far richer investor by keeping your money in the stock market.

Sometimes stock market investing requires great patience. Stock performance can vary dramatically from one ten-year period to another. An investor entering the market in 1965, for instance, would have experienced an agonizing 1.2 percent average annual return over the next ten years. But an investor in the market from 1949 to 1958 would have reaped a 20 percent average annual return. Over the past ten years, stocks have paid an average annual return of about 15 percent—which is higher than any other commonly traded form of investment, including corporate bonds, T-bills, stamps, coins, oil, housing and precious metals.

Stocks or Mutual Funds?

The other issue for many investors is whether to invest in individual stocks or stock mutual funds. The fact is, mutual funds probably should be the investment of choice for many investors—particularly those who haven't the time, the expertise or the resources to invest in a well-diversified selection of stocks.

But if you have an interest in the market, the time to spend researching it and the money to diversify your portfolio, individual stocks can offer several advantages that mutual funds can't.

First, buying stocks can be challenging, stimulating and, at times, fulfilling. You pit your wits against the market and against the millions of other unseen investors who are also scouring the market for a bargain. It is a test of your insight, your shrewdness and—during downturns in the market—your courage as you hold fast to your position in anticipation of that next market rally.

When you pick a winner, the results can be exhilarating. You watch the price move up, you see the stock split two for one. Your investment grows to a multiple of your initial outlay. You've won at the age-old game of picking stocks. And the victory is a boon not only to your pocketbook, but to your ego as well. It's that psychic reward of picking a winner that motivates so many investors to set aside mutual funds and test their hand in the stock market.

There's another important—though less publicized—reason to choose stocks over mutual funds. Money, they say, is power, but it's only power if you use it powerfully. That means controlling it yourself and deciding exactly where each dollar is put to work. Socially conscious individuals who wouldn't dream of investing in companies that pollute the environment, produce tobacco products or build weapons of mass destruction unwittingly invest in all those types of companies when they invest in stock mutual funds. Most mutual funds pay little heed to social concerns.

There are, of course, mutual funds that take an ethical approach and avoid investing in companies with questionable ethical connections. The problem is, when you invest in those funds you're still letting someone else decide the fate of your money. After all, you may not necessarily agree with all the fund's ideals. You might, for instance, enjoy a beer on a hot afternoon and see no reason to avoid investing in alcoholic beverage producers. You may prefer not to invest in a weapons manufacturing company, but you may think nuclear power is the best thing since windmills. You may oppose the racist tactics of the South African regime but still believe American businesses can have a positive influence there. So a mutual fund that invests according to all the popular ethical issues of our time may not be exactly the investment for you.

Stocks give you the freedom to make those choices for yourself.

That's one area in which this book can help you. In addition to the statistical information on earnings, revenues, dividends and stock price growth included in each of the 100 company profiles, the book provides a basic overview of each company's operations. And in this edition we've also addressed a variety of ethical concerns. By reading through the profile of a given company, you can decide whether it's the type of business you would feel comfortable investing your money in, based on your own values, principles and prejudices.

RATING THE COMPANIES

In selecting the 100 companies for this book, I looked at a wide range of financial factors, the most important of which was earnings performance. I wanted companies with a long history of annual increases in earnings per share because if a company is able to raise its earnings year after year, the stock price will ultimately follow.

Other factors such as revenue growth, stock price performance and dividend yield also played into the screening process, but none carried the same weight as earnings growth.

I made my selections after reviewing the financial histories of about 2,000 major U.S. companies. After narrowing the list to the final 100, the next step was to rank them 1 to 100 based on a six-part rating system. Each category is worth up to four points for a maximum of 24 points.

The categories are earnings per share growth, stock growth, dividend yield, dividend growth, consistency and shareholder perks. I've also tried to bridge the long-term performance with the short-term performance. Earnings and stock growth are judged on the most recent ten-year performance record. The dividend growth rating is based on the most recent five-year period, and the dividend yield is averaged out over the past two years. That gives the rating system a blend of the long term and the short term.

Accompanying each company profile, you will see a ratings chart similar to this:

ABCDE Corp.

EARNINGS GROWTH	★ ★ ★
STOCK GROWTH	★ ★ ★ ★
DIVIDEND YIELD	★
DIVIDEND GROWTH	★ ★
CONSISTENCY	★ ★ ★
SHAREHOLDER PERKS	★ ★
NYSE—ABE	**15 points**

Each star represents one rating point. This company scored the maximum (4 points) for stock growth and somewhat less for other categories. The total score is shown at the lower right, and the exchange the stock is traded on is shown at the lower left (NYSE = New York Stock Exchange; OTC = over-the-counter exchange; ASE = American Stock Exchange) along with the stock trading symbol ("ABE" in this case).

The following charts offer an exact breakdown of the point system for each category.

Earnings Growth

10-year Growth Rate	Average Annual Rate	Points Awarded
125%–224%	9%–12%	★ (1 point)
225%–349%	13%–16%	★ ★
350%–499%	17%–19%	★ ★ ★
500% & up	20% & up	★ ★ ★ ★

Stock Growth

10-year Growth Rate	Average Annual Rate	Points Awarded
160%–249%	10%–13%	★ (1 point)
250%–399%	14%–17%	★ ★
400%–599%	18%–21%	★ ★ ★
600% & up	22% & up	★ ★ ★ ★

Dividend Yield

(Based on dividend yield average over past two years)

0.5% to 1.4%	★
1.5% to 2.4%	★ ★
2.5% to 3.9%	★ ★ ★
4.0% and above	★ ★ ★ ★

Dividend Growth

In one sense, dividend growth may be even more important than the dividend yield. As the dividend grows, the current return on your original investment grows with it. Here's an example:

A stock yielding 2 percent when you bought it ten years ago at $10 a share may still be yielding a current return of only 2 percent, but if the stock has appreciated in value to $100 a share, than that 2 percent yield has now grown from its original 20 cents a share on a $10 stock to $2 per share on the $100 stock—the equivalent of a very generous 20 percent yield on your original $10 investment.

The rating scale is based on dividend growth over the most recent five-year period.

39% to 59%	★
60% to 99%	★ ★
100% to 159%	★ ★ ★
160% and above	★ ★ ★ ★

Consistency

Consistency is a fairly subjective category that takes into account a wide range of factors.

- A company that has had a flawless run of increases in earnings per share, revenue, operating income, book value and dividend for the past ten years would score four points. The consistency of the stock price growth is not taken into account here because the volatility in a stock price can often be dictated by market factors beyond the control of the company. But if the company is strong and growing steadily, the stock price, over time, should reflect that.
- A company that has had a nearly flawless run of increases in the primary fundamental growth categories would score three points.
- A company that has had a fairly consistent growth record, with occasional lapses in the key categories, would score two points.
- A company that has been somewhat inconsistent, with several ups and downs in the basic growth categories, would score one point in this category.
- Theoretically, a company with a very volatile growth record would score no points here, although the more volatile companies have been weeded out of the top 100 list.

Shareholder Perks

General speaking, the grading was very tough in the perks category. Only a couple of the 100 companies scored a perfect four, and many scored no perk points at all.

Without question, this has been both the most admired and the most criticized category of the rating system. Investment purists question its validity, while others who want a little extra zip in their portfolios have raved about it.

The most common perk is dividend reinvestment and stock purchase plan, offered by about 75 of the 100 companies in the book. These programs enable shareholders not only to reinvest their dividends in additional shares automatically, but also to buy more stock in the company either commission-free or for a nominal fee (usually under $5).

For example, Ralston Purina and Coca-Cola shareholders may buy up to $60,000 a year in additional shares through the company plan, and McDonald's shareholders may make up to $75,000 a year in commission-free stock purchases. A handful of companies even offer a 5 percent discount to the market on the stocks they buy for shareholders through the dividend reinvestment plan. The discount does not apply to voluntary stock purchases.

The only drawback to such plans is that the shareholder has no control over when the stocks are purchased. Most companies have a date set each month or each quarter (depending on how the plan is set up) to make all shareholder stock purchases. (Note also that shareholders must pay income taxes on their dividends, even though the dividends are automatically reinvested in additional stock.)

These programs are perfect for investors who want to build a position in three or four companies at a time with relatively small monthly contributions (under most plans, investors can contribute from $25 to several thousand dollars per month or per quarter). The savings can be immense. For instance, commission costs even through a discount broker would run, on average, at least $40 per stock purchase per month—a total of $160 per month for four stocks. That adds up to $1,920 per year. With the free reinvestment plans, you can either put that $1,920 into your pocket or invest it in additional stock. Either way, the commission-free programs are a great perk, and well worth the two points my system awards to each company that offers such a program.

Many companies offer other interesting perks as well. Some firms send welcome kits with free samples of their products to new shareholders of record. Others serve a free lunch at the annual meeting and give away packages of their products. Anheuser-Busch shareholders who attend the annual meeting are welcome to sample the brewer's full line of beers and snacks. Shareholders are also offered a discount on admission to Busch Gardens. Walt Disney gives discounts on admission to its amusement parks, on accommodations at its lodges and on purchases made at Disney stores. Wrigley sends shareholders about 20 packs of gum each Christmas.

Hershey is one of several companies that put together Christmas gift boxes their shareholders may buy (at discount prices) to send to friends or business clients. Shareholders simply send in their money along with the name and address of their friends, and the company does the rest.

While shareholder perks may not contribute to an investor's total return, they can bring some other benefits. One investor called me to report that he had great success with several stocks from the book except Marriott (which fell prey to hard times in the lodging industry). "But," he added,

"I've used Marriott's 50 percent shareholder discount on lodging rates on several business trips, and it has already saved me a couple hundred dollars."

Bizarre as it may seem, there may even be a correlation between shareholder perks and stock price performance. In tracking the 100 stocks from the first edition of this book, I found that the companies that scored higher in the shareholder perks category, in general, outperformed companies with lower perks scores.

The companies that continued to perform well enough to remain in the top 100 scored, on average, 2.1 points in the perks category. Those that dropped off the list because of subpar performance scored, on average, 30 percent lower at 1.5 perks points. Nearly one-third (31 percent) of the stocks that dropped off the list scored a zero in the perks category, while only 17 percent of the companies that remained in the top 100 were shut out in the perks category.

If there is any logical explanation for this, it might be that companies that offer perks tend to be stronger, more stable and more well established than those that don't. Or perhaps they are simply better managed. Firms that are progressive enough to understand the importance of maintaining good relationships with their shareholders may also have a better understanding of how to maintain good relationships with their employees and with their customers.

Breaking Ties

The 100 companies are ranked in order by points, with the highest-scoring company ranked first (Philip Morris with 21 points) and the company with the fewest points (McGraw-Hill with 9) ranked last. When two companies have identical point scores, the company with the higher total return on shareholder investment gets the higher ranking. When two companies tie on both total points and return on shareholder investment, the company with the higher total revenue gets the higher ranking.

Corporate Responsibility

One more category added in this edition is corporate responsibility. The category carries no points, and thus has no bearing on the screening process nor the rankings, but may be very useful for investors in making their stock investment decisions. Social responsibility information was available only on about half of the 100 companies in the book.

The information was prepared by the Council on Economic Priorities (CEP). CEP has been monitoring corporations for 22 years, and researches company performance in the areas of the environment, South Africa, women's advancement, minority advancement, charitable giving, animal testing, community outreach, family benefits, nuclear power, workplace issues, military contracts and disclosure information.

The social responsibility profiles for this book are based on research done for CEP's publications, its Corporate Conscience Awards, its Corporate Environmental Data Clearinghouse and its Institutional Investor Research Service.

The profiles are based on information current as of August 1990 or later. The information was gathered from:

1. extensive data from the companies themselves
2. existing public information available in government agencies, libraries and specialized centers, or from citizens groups
3. advisors who are experts in the chosen categories

CEP claims no predictive value for its ratings or profiles; a company may change its behavior tomorrow. CEP claims no knowledge of programs or problems not in the public domain or voluntarily submitted by the companies themselves or other sources. CEP is a nonpartisan organization that does not endorse any company. If a company receives a high rating, it does not mean CEP approves of all of its policies—it is merely a recognition of the company's accomplishments in that specific area.

The social responsibility profiles in this book highlight company policies or practices that CEP felt ethical investors would be interested in. They are not to be construed as comprehensive analyses of corporate social performance.

Investors interested in more information on social issues may wish to order CEP's books, *The Better World Investment Guide* (Prentice-Hall, 1991, $19.95 plus $3 shipping), a comprehensive 528-page book covering "100 companies whose policies you should know before you invest your money," and *Shopping for a Better World* (Ballantine, 1991, $4.95 plus $1.50 shipping). The books are available through CEP at 1-800-822-6435.

HOW TO USE THIS BOOK

Think of this book as a sales catalog for investment shoppers. You can page through it, look over the merchandise and make your selections.

Let's assume that you have $20,000 to invest in stocks. Here is the process I would recommend you use to select the best stocks for you based on the entries in this book.

Read through all the 100 profiles and narrow your choices to 10 to 12 stocks by asking these questions:

- Are they companies that you like, that are involved in business activities you think have a strong future?
- Are they located in your part of the country? This is not essential, but it is easier to follow companies based close to home because the local press tends to give them fuller coverage.
- Do they represent a diverse cross-section of industries? Spread your choices around. You might select a food company, a medical products firm, a heavy manufacturer, perhaps a publisher, a retailer, or a computer or data processing company. Choose no more than two or three companies from the same industrial segment. By making a broad selection, you can minimize your losses if one sector goes sour.

Narrow your initial list of favorites to the four or five companies you will ultimately invest in. If you wish to use a stockbroker or financial advisor, call your advisor, read your list of choices and ask if he or she has any current research on those stocks. Find out which ones the broker recommends, and buy the stocks through your broker. If you are interested in enrolling in the dividend reinvestment plan or in receiving the special perks your chosen companies might offer, instruct your broker to put your stocks in your name rather than holding them at the brokerage office in "street name." Most dividend reinvestment plans and perks programs are available only to shareholders of record.

GOING IT ALONE

If you have no broker, or wish to go it alone through a discount broker, here are some steps you can use to narrow down your initial list to the four or five companies you will ultimately invest in:

- Write or call those companies to request their annual report and their 10-K report, then skim through the reports. (The phone numbers and addresses of all 100 companies are listed in this book along with their corporate profiles.)

- Go to the library and look up recent articles on those stocks and any other information the library may have on your selections. If it's a local company, there's a good chance your library will have an entire file on the company. Make sure the company hasn't become involved in any major scandals or business problems. The library may also have two or three investment research books you can use to check up on your stock selections. *Value Line Investment Survey* and the Standard & Poor's report both offer up-to-date information and recommendations on hundreds of companies.
- Keep an eye on the stock prices of the companies you are interested in. Find out what range each stock has been trading in over the past few months. Then select the four or five stocks that appear at present to be the best values. Timing can be very important in your overall success. All stocks fluctuate greatly in price, tugged along by the current of the overall market. But some stocks vacillate more than others.

For instance, you could have bought Walt Disney stock in 1973 for $27 a share (split-adjusted) and sold it for a mere $4 a share a year later. You could have reinvested in the stock in 1976 at $15 a share and sold out in disgust in 1984 at $11.50 a share. On the other hand, you might have bought the stock for that same $11.50 a share in 1984 and sold out with a smile for more than ten times that price ($136 a share) in 1990. So even with stocks such as Disney, which qualified as a *100 Best* entry, timing can make a significant difference.

WHEN TO BUY

Volumes have been written on this topic. But the best advice may have come from Baron Von Rothchild in the mid-1800s. He said, "Buy when the enemy has your city surrounded, and sell when you hear your calvary's bugle sounding charge."

Wall Street has a popular adage that reinforces that concept: "Pessimism is always most rampant just before the market hits bottom."

There have been two extraordinary buying opportunities in the past five years. The first came in 1987 following the October Black Monday crash. The crash frightened many investors out of the market, but those who bought when everyone else was selling got in on the bottom of a market that grew more than 50 percent over the next 18 months.

The second great opportunity came during Iraq's occupation of Kuwait, when oil prices were rising and the world was transfixed on the Middle East crisis. The market dropped about 15 percent in the months after Iraq invaded Kuwait, then roared back more than 20 percent in a three-month span that began the day the allies began the bombing.

But barring war or disaster, the best strategy for most investors is a steady, persistent, long-term investment program.

One of the easiest and most effective investment strategies is called dollar cost averaging, and it's as simple as this: Pick a number, any number—$100 for instance—and invest that amount every month (or every quarter or every year) in the same stock.

Elementary as it is, however, the dollar cost averaging method is also a very effective technique for beating the market. By sticking to a set sum each time you invest, you automatically buy fewer shares when the stock price is high and more shares when the price is low.

The following table illustrates the advantages of dollar cost averaging. The table assumes that the stock price fluctuates somewhat each month and lists the monthly price of the stock. The table compares the number of shares purchased through a dollar cost averaging strategy with the number of shares purchased through a method in which the investor buys a set number of shares each month.

Dollar Cost Averaging vs. Set Quantity Investment

Month	Jan.	Feb.	Mar.	Apr.	May	June	July	Aug.	Sept.	Oct.	Nov.	Dec.	Totals
Stock Price*	$10	9	12	13	9	10	8	7	9	12	10	11	
Dollar cost averaging**	$100	100	100	100	100	100	100	100	100	100	100	100	$1,200
Shares	10	11.1	8.3	7.7	11	10	12.5	14.3	11	8.3	10	9.1	123.5 shrs.
Set quantity investment†	$100	90	120	130	90	100	80	70	90	120	100	110	$1,200
Shares	10	10	10	10	10	10	10	10	10	10	10	10	120 shrs.

  * Indicates price of the stock each month.
 ** Assumes investor invests $100 a month in the stock.
  † Assumes investor buys ten shares of the stock per month.

As the table indicates, the investor using the dollar cost averaging method would have purchased 3½ more shares than the investor who bought a set amount of shares each month, even though both spent a total of $1,200 during the year.

It should be emphasized that the dollar cost averaging method is most effective when you can make your purchases at no commission (or minimal commissions) through a company's dividend reinvestment and voluntary stock purchase plan. Such plans are ideal for dollar cost averaging because they enable the investor to buy fractional shares and to make regular contributions (some companies offer stock purchase options once per month, others once per quarter). However, if the company you're interested in has no stock purchase plan, the brokerage commissions you would have to pay to make regular investments in the company's stock would greatly diminish the advantages of a dollar cost averaging plan. Most of the companies listed in this book offer a dividend reinvestment and voluntary stock purchase plan.

PICKING WINNERS

There is no infallible system for predicting tomorrow's market winners—only ratios and theories and computer-generated formulas that seem foolproof, but aren't. For investors who trade actively in stocks, the key to beating the market is not so much which stocks to buy, but when to buy them and when to sell them. And that's about as easy to predict as next month's weather.

Even Wall Street's finest can't consistently outfox the market. Stock mutual funds offer an interesting example. Despite being actively managed by some of the sharpest, most well-supported analysts in the investment industry, the average rate of return on stock mutual funds traditionally trails the overall market averages. Generally speaking, history has shown that you can do better just buying and holding a representative sample of stocks—without ever making a single trade—than most mutual fund managers do with their wealth of investment research, their finely honed trading strategies and all of their carefully calculated market maneuvers.

Nor do investment newsletters, on average, fare any better than the mutual fund managers at timing their trade recommendations, according to Mark Hulbert, publisher of the *Hulbert Financial Digest.* "Most newsletters have not kept up with the Standard & Poor's 500," says Hulbert. In fact, in tracking the seven-year performance of a sampling of investment newsletters, Hulbert found that the ones that recommended the greatest number of buys and sells (switches) were the ones that did the worst.

"We've also conducted some studies that show that in the case of most newsletters, if you had bought and held the stocks they recommended at the first of the year, you would have done better than if you had followed all of their trading recommendations throughout the year."

The moral? For sustained, long-term growth, it's hard to beat a buy-and-hold strategy. Buy good companies with the intention of holding onto them for many years.

The Theory of Benign Neglect

Most of us know someone who bought a few shares of a stock many years ago, stashed the certificates in a drawer and then discovered years later that the stock had grown to a multiple of the original cost. A great example is Food Lion, the North Carolina grocery store chain. If you had bought $1,000 of Food Lion stock in 1957 when it was first issued, held onto it and reinvested the dividends, your investment would now be worth $23 million. Benign neglect is often the smartest policy for stock market investors.

Besides avoiding the difficulties of making timely buying and selling decisions, the buy-and-hold approach offers some other excellent advantages:

No commission costs.   Let's assume that you turn over your stock portfolio just once a year. You sell out all the stocks you own and buy stocks that you think have greater short-term potential. Typically, you would incur about a 2 percent commission to sell the old stocks and a 2 percent commission to buy new ones—a total of 4 percent in round trip commissions. That means, for instance, that a respectable 12 percent gain on your investments would suddenly shrink to 8 percent after you've paid off your broker. That commission may not seem like much at the time, but over the long term, it can add up to a significant amount.

Tax-sheltered earnings.   A buy-and-hold strategy is one of the best tax-advantaged investments available today. You pay no taxes on the price appreciation of your stocks until you sell them—no matter how long you keep them. (You are taxed, however, on any stock dividend income.)

However, every time you sell a stock, the federal government taxes you up to 29 percent on your gains (for most working professionals). And state taxes would very likely nibble away another 5 percent or so. That means each year Uncle Sam bites off about one-third of your investment profits. So you're looking at losing 34 percent of your gains, plus the brokerage house commission, every time you sell a stock at a profit. How does that translate into real dollars?

Assume that (1) you start with an investment of $10,000, (2) your portfolio of stocks appreciates at a rate of 12 percent per year and (3) you sell your stocks, take the profit and buy new stocks once a year. The chart on the next page compares your performance with that of a buy-and-hold investor with an identical 12 percent compounded average annual appreciation rate.

As you can see, over a 20-year period, the buy-and-hold portfolio could earn more than four times the profit of a buy-and-sell approach even though both portfolios earn an average annual return of 12 percent.

Less emotional wear and tear.   By adhering to a buy-and-hold strategy you also avoid the high anxiety of trying to buy and sell stocks actively—of watching the financial pages each day to see how your stocks have fared, and of the inevitable disappointment of watching them rise and fall, then

The Hidden Costs of a Buy-and-Sell Approach

$10,000 investment @ 12% annual growth	*Buy and hold* (no commission, no taxes)	*Buy-and-sell results** (with commission)**	(with taxes)†
Opening balance	$10,000	$10,000	$10,000
After 1 year	11,200	10,800	10,540
After 5 years	17,600	14,700	13,000
After 10 years	31,000	21,600	17,000
After 20 years	90,000	47,000	29,000

* Assumes investor sells all stocks in portfolio one time per year (and reinvests in new stocks).
** Assumes commission of 2 percent to buy and 2 percent to sell (an annual total of 4 percent of total portfolio price).
† Assumes 28 percent federal and 5 percent state tax (an annual total of 33 percent of profits).

rise and fall again. Every stock goes through many ups and downs each year. There are no exceptions. The market ebbs and flows, and every time it moves, it carries with it the broad market of individual stocks. Typically, about 70 percent of the movement of a stock is attributable to the stock market itself. If the broad market is moving up, almost any stock you pick will also rise, but if the market is in a tailspin, almost any stock you pick—even those with record earnings—will fall with it. The remaining 30 percent of the movement of a stock is attributable to its industry group and to the performance of the company that issued the stock.

You skirt much of the emotional pressure the market inflicts if you invest with a buy-and-hold approach. You don't have to concern yourself with the daily and yearly ups and downs of the market because if you have bought stocks of good solid growing companies, the value of your portfolio will eventually reflect the strong performance of those companies. That's why it is crucial to select your stocks carefully. Because these are "one decision stocks," that one decision takes on much greater importance.

When Not To Buy

The easiest way to narrow your list to your four or five final selections may be through the process of elimination: Weed out the stocks that appear to be overvalued, and invest in the others.

Here are two common don'ts to assist you in that process.

Don't buy when a stock is at an all-time high. Stocks constantly rise and fall. There's an adage in the securities industry that says, "The market always gives you a second chance." In almost every case, when a stock reaches an all-time high, it will eventually drop back in price, bounce back, then drop back again. Nothing goes in a straight line. If a stock is at its all-time high, it probably is not a very good value at that time. Prior to the October 1987 crash, most stocks were at or near their all-time highs, which is why many investment experts claimed that there were few good values in the market.

Don't buy when the price-earnings ratio is unusually high. It sounds complicated, but the price-earnings ratio is actually a very simple formula that offers yet another barometer of a stock's relative value. And best of all, the price-earnings ratio (or P/E ratio, as the pros call it) is listed along with the company's stock price in the financial section of most newspapers, so you don't have to calculate it yourself.

Specifically, the price-earnings ratio is the current price of the stock divided by the company's earnings per share. For example: ABC Corporation's stock price is $30. Its earnings per share is $3.

stock price	earnings per share	P/E ratio
$30	÷ $3	= 10.0

P/E ratios are like golf scores—the lower the better. Generally speaking, the P/Es of most established companies are in the 10 to 20 range (although, a handful of the stocks listed in this book have P/Es over 20, and a few have P/Es under ten). The real key, however, is not how the P/E of one company compares to the P/E of another, but how a company's current P/E compares to its P/E ratios of the past.

At the end of each company profile in this book, you will see a six-year financial summary that lists the company's annual revenues, earnings, stock price, dividends, book value per share and P/E ratio. You can use that P/E ratio as a guidepost to provide a relative point of comparison. The P/E ratios in this book were calculated based on the earnings of the company's most recent four quarters (just as they are in the daily newspaper).

If you find in comparing the company's current P/E (as listed in your morning newspaper) with its previous P/E (as listed in this book) that the P/E has risen significantly, that could indicate that the stock is relatively overvalued.

One More Way To Save

Once you decide which stocks to buy, you may be able get more for your money by taking one more step.

Call several discount brokerage firms to find out which has the lowest minimum, then buy your stocks through that discounter. Have the broker put the stocks in your name (rather than street name) and mail the certificates to you. If you feel the stock is at a particularly good price or the company has no dividend reinvestment plan, you might decide to go a little above the minimum in your initial order. Otherwise, buy a few shares— whatever you feel comfortable with, enroll in the company's dividend reinvestment and stock purchase plan, and make your subsequent stock purchases through the company. You may never have to pay commissions again.

WHEN—IF EVER—TO SELL

The most common mistake investors make in selling their stocks is that they tend to sell their winners to take a fully taxable profit and hold onto their losers in hopes that those stocks will someday rebound. That's an excellent way to assemble a portfolio full of losers. Prevailing wisdom in the investment business calls for just the opposite approach: "Cut your losses and let your profits run."

With that in mind, there are a couple of basic strategies for selling stocks that you might consider.

Sell when news is grim.   If a company you own stock in comes under legal siege or becomes involved in a disaster or health controversy (as happened with Union Carbide, A.H. Robbins, Manville Corp., Exxon), take your lumps and get out as fast as you can.

Sell when the stock price drops relative to the market.   You might also want to set up some other type of safety valve for your stocks. For instance, if the stock drops 15 to 20 percent while the market in general is moving up, it might be time to move on to something more promising. Some investors use a 10%/10% rule in which they sell a stock when it drops 10 percent from its recent high and also drops 10 percent relative to the market. For example, if your stock drops 10 percent from $100 to $90, it meets the first criterion. But if the market has gone down with it, then the stock still hasn't met the second criterion. If, on the other hand, the broad market stays the same or moves up while your stock drops 10 percent, then it's time to sell—based on the 10%/10% rule.

More patient investors might lean toward a 20%/20% rule. If your stock drops 20 percent and drops 20 percent relative to the market, then sell it and move onto something more promising.

Mark Hulbert addresses the sell timing issue this way: "You need to approach those decisions realizing that more than half the time you're inclined to sell you would be better off holding than selling. Look at the Crash of 1987. A lot of people sold right after the Crash, and missed out on a gain in the market of more than 20 percent in the following months. So you better make sure there's a preponderance of evidence in your favor before you sell."

1

PHILIP MORRIS COMPANIES, INC.

120 Park Avenue
New York, NY 10017
212-880-5000
Chairman and CEO: Hamish Maxwell
President: John A. Murphy

EARNINGS GROWTH	★ ★ ★ ★
STOCK GROWTH	★ ★ ★ ★
DIVIDEND YIELD	★ ★ ★
DIVIDEND GROWTH	★ ★ ★ ★
CONSISTENCY	★ ★ ★ ★
SHAREHOLDER PERKS	★ ★
NYSE—MO	**21 points**

A funny thing happened to Philip Morris on its way to becoming a major world foods conglomerate. With signs of a declining market for cigarette sales growing more apparent every year, the New York manufacturer began a corporate acquisition binge designed to assemble a diversified stable of foods that would fill the profit void when cigarette sales stumbled.

By all accounts, its efforts have been entirely successful. The company now puts more than 3,000 separate products on retailers' shelves.

But for Philip Morris, the funny thing that happened along the way is that cigarette sales never stumbled. In spite of the powerful antismoking campaign of the past two decades, Philip Morris sells more cigarettes now—at greater profit—than ever before. The company has bolstered its foreign cigarette sales significantly while consistently hiking profit margins on its domestic sales.

As a result, Philip Morris has become one of the world's most profitable corporations. It has annual revenues of $51 billion and operating earnings of about $8 billion. The company is the largest consumer products producer in America and the third largest producer in Europe, thanks to its August 1990

1

acquisition of Switzerland-based chocolates and coffee giant Jacobs Suchard.

Philip Morris has enjoyed 36 consecutive years of record earnings per share.

The company's long string of acquisitions has brought in an array of recognizable brands, including Kraft, Oscar Mayer, Post, Tang, Jell-O, Miracle Whip, Cool Whip and Kool-Aid. It also owns Maxwell House and Sanka coffees, Frujsen Gladjen and Breyers ice creams, Stove Top Stuffing, Velveeta cheese and Parkay margarine.

The company's foods group accounts for about 51 percent of revenue and 30 percent of operating income.

Another one of Philip Morris's recent successes has been its ability to breathe new life into yet another of its acquisitions, Miller Beer. Miller has continued to pick up market share in the beer industry and now accounts for about 23 percent of all beer sold in the U.S. Beer sales make up 8 percent of the company's revenue and 3 percent of operating income.

But stack all of its beer and food products into one grocery sack and the company's lineup of consumer staples still doesn't measure up to the profit power of its tobaccos. Led by Marlboro and Marlboro Lights, the more than $5 billion a year in operating profit the company pockets off its cigarette sales is roughly double its earnings from all of its other consumer products combined.

As the country's and the world's largest-selling cigarette, Marlboro alone earns about $3 billion a year. It accounts for 26 percent of the 523 billion cigarettes sold in the U.S. each year. Marlboro Lights, the leading low-tar brand, accounts for another 10 percent of all U.S. sales. Philip Morris, which also makes Merit, Virginia Slims, Benson & Hedges, Parliament and Cambridge, is the world's leading cigarette manufacturer, holding about a 7 percent share of the 5 trillion-unit world market.

In terms of profit margin, cigarettes continue to be well ahead of all of the company's other products. While Philip Morris earns, on average, 10 cents on every dollar of goods it sells from its nontobacco segment, cigarette sales bring in a hefty 30–40 cents on the dollar—three to four times the average profit margin from its other products.

How long can Philip Morris continue to increase its profits in the face of mounting opposition to cigarettes? Since 1971, when cigarette ads were banned from TV, the company has racked up record earnings year after year. With increased restrictions on smoking in offices and public places, and with new measures pending that could put cigarette vending machines out of business, the tobacco industry could face further erosion in cigarette sales.

But tobacco companies have been down this road before, and they have always survived by maintaining high profit margins on the cigarettes they sell.

Philip Morris is also compensating for falling U.S. sales by increasing its cigarette sales abroad. Eastern and Western Europe, Japan and the Soviet Union are all booming markets for Marlboro and other Philip Morris brands.

The company's other segments have been very successful and have contributed to its recent growth.

EARNINGS GROWTH

Philip Morris has had excellent long-term growth. Over the past ten years, its earnings per share increased 560 percent (an average of 21 percent per year).

The company has about 170,000 employees and 100,000 shareholders.

STOCK GROWTH

The company has had exceptional stock growth the past ten years, increasing 845 percent (25 percent per year) during the period.

Including reinvested dividends, a $10,000 investment in Philip Morris stock at its closing stock price in 1980 would have grown to about $133,000 ten years later. Average annual compounded rate of return (including stock growth and reinvested dividends): about 29.5 percent.

DIVIDEND YIELD

Philip Morris generally pays a good yield, averaging about 3.3 percent over the past five years. During the most recent two-year rating period (fiscal 1990 and 1991) the stock paid an average annual current return (dividend yield) of 2.9 percent.

DIVIDEND GROWTH

Philip Morris typically raises its dividend every year. The dividend increased 210 percent (25 percent per year) from 1985 to 1990.

CONSISTENCY

With 36 consecutive years of record earnings, Philip Morris has been one of the most consistent companies in America. Its price-earnings ratio of 14 to 17 is high for a cigarette company but about average for a foods company.

SHAREHOLDER PERKS

The company offers an excellent dividend reinvestment and voluntary stock purchase plan. There are no fees or commissions, and shareholders of record may buy $10 to $60,000 per year in additional shares through the voluntary payment plan.

CORPORATE RESPONSIBILITY

As the U.S. surgeon general has repeatedly emphasized, cigarettes are highly addictive and are linked with cancer and heart disease. An estimated 400,000 Americans die each year of smoking-related lung and heart ailments. Environmentalists also charge that the tobacco-curing process is a major cause of deforestation. For details on the environmental implications of growing tobacco, see the American Brands profile (p. 330).

Philip Morris has a good record for promoting women and minorities. A minority male and four women, two of whom are minorities, serve on its 21-member board of directors.

According to an Environmental Protection Agency report analyzing 1988 Toxics Release Inventory (TRI) data, Philip Morris is one of the companies with the most TRI facilities. In that year, the company had 71 facilities that reported releasing a total of 5,942,397 pounds of toxics into the air, water and land. (Source: Council on Economic Priorities)

SUMMARY

Fiscal year ended: Dec. 31
(Revenue and net income in millions)

	1991*	1990	1989	1988	1987	1986	1985	5-year growth, %† (annual/total)
Revenue		51,169	44,080	31,273	27,650	25,542	16,158	26/216
Net income		3,540	2,946	2,337	1,842	1,478	1,255	23/182
Earnings/share		3.83	3.18	2.51	1.94	1.55	1.31	24/192
Dividend/share		1.55	1.25	1.01	0.79	0.62	0.50	25/210
Dividend yield, %	2.5	3.3	3.0	3.8	3.8	3.4	4.5	—/—
Stock price	68.75	52.00	42.00	26.00	21.00	18.00	11.00	37/372
P/E ratio	17.0	14.0	13.0	10.0	11.0	11.0	8.0	—/—
Book value/share		12.90	10.30	8.30	7.20	5.95	4.95	21/160

* Stock price as of 5–1–91
† 1985–90
Source: Company sources

2

UST

UST, INC.

100 West Putnam Avenue
Greenwich, CT 06830
203-661-1100
Chairman and CEO: Louis F. Bantle
President and COO: Vincent A. Gierer, Jr.

EARNINGS GROWTH	★ ★ ★
STOCK GROWTH	★ ★ ★ ★
DIVIDEND YIELD	★ ★ ★
DIVIDEND GROWTH	★ ★ ★ ★
CONSISTENCY	★ ★ ★ ★
SHAREHOLDER PERKS	★ ★
NYSE—UST	**20 points**

Americans have been puffing less in recent years and chewing more. And with each "pinch between the cheek and gum," UST moves a chaw closer to yet another year of record sales and earnings.

The world leader in smokeless tobacco sales, UST has posted 31 consecutive years of increased earnings per share. It has been one of the stock market's most consistent performers over the past decade, reaching new highs ten of the past 11 years—while paying an average annual dividend yield of about 5 percent.

With its Skoal, Bandits, Copenhagen and other tobacco products, the Greenwich, Connecticut manufacturer commands an 85 percent share of all U.S. moist smokeless tobacco sales. In all, UST sells half a billion cans a year of its tobaccos.

Tobacco products account for 85 percent of the company's $765 million in annual revenue and about 97 percent of operating income. In addition to its Skoal and Copenhagen brands, UST (formerly United States Tobacco) produces Red Seal, Rooster, Standard, Bruton, CC and Devoe dry tobaccos, WB Cut chewing tobacco, Borkum Riff, Amphora and

Alsbo pipe tobaccos and Don Tomas and La Regenta cigars. Copenhagen is UST's oldest product, introduced in 1822.

UST also produces a line of wines (8 percent of revenue and 1 percent of operating earnings) through its International Wines and Spirits, Ltd. subsidiary. Most of its wines are made in the state of Washington and sold under the labels of Chateau Ste. Michelle, Columbia Crest, Conn Creek and Villa Mt. Eden.

UST's other segment, which includes Dr. Grabow presmoked pipes, Mastercraft imported pipes, Dill pipe cleaners, National Pen and Pencil Company writing instruments and Zig-Zag cigarette papers, accounts for about 8 percent of revenue and 2 percent of operating income.

EARNINGS GROWTH

UST has had consistent long-term growth. Over the past ten years, its earnings per share increased 460 percent (an average of 19 percent per year).

The company has about 3,500 employees and 10,500 shareholders.

STOCK GROWTH

The company has had exceptional stock growth the past ten years, increasing 1,094 percent (28 percent per year) during the period.

Including reinvested dividends, a $10,000 investment in UST stock at its closing stock price in 1980 would have grown to about $170,000 ten years later. Average annual compounded rate of return (including stock growth and reinvested dividends): about 33 percent.

DIVIDEND YIELD

UST generally pays a very good dividend yield, averaging just over 4 percent over the past five years. During the most recent two-year rating period (fiscal 1990 and 1991) the stock paid an average annual current return (dividend yield) of 3.3 percent.

DIVIDEND GROWTH

UST has paid a dividend each year since 1912, with increases each of the past 20 years. The dividend rose 206 percent (25 percent per year) from 1985 to 1990.

CONSISTENCY

The company has had 31 consecutive years of increased revenue and earnings per share. Its price-earnings ratio of around 16 to 22 is very high for a tobacco company but not unusual for a company with UST's outstanding growth record.

SHAREHOLDER PERKS

UST provides an excellent dividend reinvestment and voluntary stock purchase plan for its shareholders. There are no fees or service charges, and shareholders may contribute $10 to $10,000 per month to the stock purchase plan.

At its annual meeting, the company hands out samples of its products, such as cigars and smokeless tobacco, and small gifts such as UST potholders and keychains.

CORPORATE RESPONSIBILITY

The U.S. surgeon general has warned that smokeless tobacco users are subject to a higher risk of cancer and other diseases—an assessment augmented in a recent study of 1,109 major and minor league baseball players and coaches.

The study, conducted by the University of California–San Francisco School of Dentistry, concluded that those who use smokeless tobacco are at an increased risk of oral leukoplakia and periodontal disease. The study found oral leukoplakia in 46 percent of current users, as well as a higher than normal level of gum recession and bone loss. The use of smokeless tobaccos, for many years a mainstay in professional baseball, has been banned in some minor leagues.

Since 1987, the government has banned TV and radio ads for chewing tobaccos and requires tobacco producers to print warnings on their packages informing consumers that "This product is not a safe alternative to cigarettes," or, more bluntly, "This product may cause mouth cancer." Further restrictions in the promotion and sale of UST's products may be imposed.

SUMMARY

Fiscal year ended: Dec. 31
(Revenue and net income in millions)

	1991*	1990	1989	1988	1987	1986	1985	5-year growth, %† (annual/ total)
Revenue		765	682	618	576	517	480	10/59
Net income		223	191	162	130	103	93	19/139
Earnings/share		1.96	1.63	1.41	1.13	.92	.82	19/139
Dividend/share		1.32	.92	.74	.60	.49	.43	25/206
Dividend yield, %	3.0	3.6	4.6	4.6	5.1	4.9	4.0	—/—
Stock price	44.63	37.00	31.00	21.00	13.50	11.16	8.72	32/300
P/E ratio	22	16	11	12	11	11	13	—/—
Book value/share		4.40	4.10	3.65	3.35	2.90	2.55	12/74

* Stock price as of 5–1–91
† 1985–90
Source: Company sources

3

RUBBERMAID INC.

1147 Akron Road
Wooster, OH 44691
216-264-6464
Chairman and CEO: Walter W. Williams
President: Wolfgang R. Schmitt

EARNINGS GROWTH	★ ★ ★ ★
STOCK GROWTH	★ ★ ★ ★
DIVIDEND YIELD	★
DIVIDEND GROWTH	★ ★ ★ ★
CONSISTENCY	★ ★ ★ ★
SHAREHOLDER PERKS	★ ★ ★
NYSE—RBD	**20 points**

There's nothing like success to gain the admiration of your contemporaries—which may be one good reason that Rubbermaid has made *Fortune* magazine's list of the ten most admired companies for six years running.

The Wooster, Ohio housewares manufacturer, which ranked second in *Fortune*'s 1991 rankings, has posted 39 consecutive years of record sales and 13 straight years of record earnings. It has raised its dividend to shareholders for 36 consecutive years.

Long known for its plastic housewares, Rubbermaid's product line now goes well beyond soap dishes and dustpans. The company manufactures more than a thousand products, including toys, office computer stands, lawn furniture, mops, brooms, buckets and waste bins.

Rubbermaid opened its doors in 1920 as a balloon manufacturer called the Wooster Rubber Company. In the 1930s it began producing its first houseware products—rubber dustpans, drainboard mats and soap dishes. Rubbermaid has grown rapidly the past decade and now has annual revenue of about $1.5 billion.

Its rapid growth is due in part to a number of key acquisitions, including Little Tikes (toys) in 1984, Gott (leisure products) in 1985, SECO Industries (floor maintenance products) and MicroComputer Accessories in 1986, Viking Brush (Canada's leading maker of brushes, brooms and other cleaning aids) in 1987, and Eldon Industries (office supplies and soldering tools) in 1989.

The company's products are geared to both consumers (77 percent of sales) and institutional customers (23 percent of sales). In addition to its U.S. sales, Rubbermaid also does a good foreign business and recently agreed to a joint venture with the Curver Group of the Netherlands, which will give Rubbermaid a prominent role in the European housewares market. Foreign sales account for about 15 percent of the company's revenue.

Rubbermaid breaks its U.S. operations into five divisions:

- Housewares. The oldest and largest of Rubbermaid's divisions manufactures such products as sinkware, space organizers, household containers, trash cans, cookware, food storage containers, rubber gloves, casual dinnerware, shelf liner and vacuum cleaner bags.
- Specialty products. This division makes lawn furniture, planters, bird feeders, thermos jugs, insulated food chests, canteens and water coolers.
- Commercial products. Products geared to the commercial, industrial and institutional markets include brooms, mops, brushes, trash cans, trays, pitchers, cups, food storage containers, housekeeping carts and other maintenance, food service and office products.
- Office products. The company makes modular desk systems, floor mats, and accessories for personal computers, word processors and data terminals, including plastic molded stands for computers and printers, storage racks and disk files.
- Toys. Through its Little Tikes subsidiary, the company makes pedal cars, children's furniture and other children's recreational equipment.

EARNINGS GROWTH

Rubbermaid has enjoyed outstanding long-term growth. Over the past ten years, its earnings per share increased 683 percent (an average of 23 percent per year).

The company has about 13,000 employees and 9,000 shareholders.

STOCK GROWTH

The company has had exceptional stock price appreciation the past ten years, increasing 1,255 percent (30 percent per year) during the period.

Including reinvested dividends, a $10,000 investment in Rubbermaid stock at its closing stock price in 1980 would have grown to about $160,000 ten years later. Average annual compounded rate of return (including stock growth and reinvested dividends): about 32 percent.

DIVIDEND YIELD

Rubbermaid generally pays a fairly modest yield, averaging about 1.3 percent over the past five years. During the most recent two-year rating period (fiscal 1990 and 1991), the stock paid an average annual current return (dividend yield) of 1.3 percent.

DIVIDEND GROWTH

Rubbermaid has raised its dividend for 36 consecutive years. The dividend increased 160 percent (21 percent per year) from 1985 to 1990.

CONSISTENCY

The company has had 10 consecutive years of record earnings per share, and 39 consecutive years of record revenues. Its recent price-earnings ratio of about 28 is very high—even for a growing manufacturer.

SHAREHOLDER PERKS

Shareholders who attend Rubbermaid's annual meeting usually receive a free Rubbermaid product. One year it was a file case, another year it was a set of food storage containers, and one year it was a dip and snack tray. On the day of the annual meeting shareholders may shop in the company store, where they receive discounts on dozens of Rubbermaid products.

The company also offers a dividend reinvestment and voluntary stock purchase plan. There are no fees or commissions, and shareholders may contribute $10 to $3,000 per quarter toward the purchase of additional shares through the voluntary stock purchase plan.

CORPORATE RESPONSIBILITY

Rubbermaid often appears in socially screened portfolios. Its labor relations have been relatively peaceful, and it has no involvement in South Africa or weapons manufacturing. In fact, Rubbermaid's Little Tikes toy subsidiary does not even make toy guns because the company has an explicit policy against doing so. Little Tikes does not advertise directly to children and stopped its membership in the Toy Manufacturers of America after the trade organization came out in favor of advertising to children.

Rubbermaid has two women serving on its 12-member board of directors, which is quite impressive for a company of its size.

Last fall, officials at Rubbermaid said the firm was increasing its commitment to recycling as it prepared to take part in a $16 million program with eight polystyrene manufacturers who have formed the National Polystyrene Recycling Company (NPRC). Rubbermaid will use recycled polystyrene materials provided by the NPRC to produce a number of consumer goods, including fast-food serving trays, refuse containers and office supplies. The NPRC's stated goal is to recycle 25 percent of all disposable polystyrene products by 1995. (Source: Council on Economic Priorities)

SUMMARY

Fiscal year ended: Dec. 31
(Revenue and net income in millions)

	1991*	1990	1989	1988	1987	1986	1985	5-year growth, %† (annual/ total)
Revenue		1,534	1,452	1,291	1,096	864	747	15/105
Net income		143	124	106	90	75	62	18/130
Earnings/share		1.80	1.57	1.34	1.15	.95	.79	18/127
Dividend/share		.60	.46	.38	.32	.26	.23	21/160
Dividend yield, %	1.1	1.4	1.5	1.6	1.1	1.2	1.7	—/—
Stock price	52.25	42.00	36.75	25.13	24.88	24.25	17.25	19/143
P/E ratio	28.0	20.0	19.8	17.7	24.2	23.1	16.7	—/—
Book value/share		9.60	8.10	6.95	5.94	4.91	4.20	17/123

* Stock price as of 5–1–91
† 1985–90
Source: Company sources

4

WM. WRIGLEY JR. COMPANY
410 North Michigan Avenue
Chicago, IL 60611
312-644-2121
President and CEO: William Wrigley

EARNINGS GROWTH	★ ★ ★
STOCK GROWTH	★ ★ ★ ★
DIVIDEND YIELD	★ ★ ★
DIVIDEND GROWTH	★ ★ ★ ★
CONSISTENCY	★ ★ ★
SHAREHOLDER PERKS	★ ★ ★
NYSE—WWY	**20 points**

Around the world, the most recognizable name in chewing gum is Wrigley's. Consumers are "doubling their pleasure" in more than 100 countries—while Wrigley doubles and redoubles its sales and profits.

The largest share of Wrigley's gum—65 percent—is sold in the U.S. (The company claims that 47 percent of all gum chewed in the U.S. is Wrigley's.) European sales make up about 20 percent of the company's total revenue, while other foreign sales account for about 15 percent.

Part of Wrigley's success has come through product line expansion. Over the past several years, the Chicago-based company has added about 15 new brands and flavors to its longstanding favorites. For most of the company's 99-year history, Wrigley was known for its Juicy Fruit, Spearmint, Doublemint and Big Red gums.

Now the company offers Freedent (spearmint, peppermint, icemint and cinnamon), Extra (bubble, spearmint, peppermint, cinnamon and wintergreen), Hubba Bubba (original, cola, strawberry, raspberry, blueberry, grape) and Sugarfree Hubba Bubba (original and grape). Wrigley's Extra is the top selling sugarless gum in America.

Wrigley also owns Amurol Products, which manufactures children's novelty bubble gum and other confectionery products, including Big League Chew and baseball trading cards. One of the company's newest offerings, Bubble Tape, has been a growing favorite in the bubble gum market.

Founder William Wrigley, Jr. (grandfather of current president William Wrigley, 57) was a baking soda salesman who first offered gum in 1891 as a premium to customers for buying the baking soda. But the gum quickly became more in demand than the baking soda, so in 1893 he introduced his first flavors of Wrigley's gum, Spearmint and Juicy Fruit.

EARNINGS GROWTH

Wrigley has enjoyed excellent long-term growth. Over the past ten years, its earnings per share increased 360 percent (16.5 percent per year).

The company has about 6,000 employees, 10,000 common shareholders and 6,500 Class B shareholders.

STOCK GROWTH

The company's stock has soared 925 percent (26 percent per year) over the past ten years. Including reinvested dividends, a $10,000 investment in Wrigley stock at its closing stock price in 1980 would have grown to about $150,000 ten years later. Average annual compounded rate of return (including stock growth and reinvested dividends): about 31 percent.

DIVIDEND YIELD

Wrigley traditionally pays a very good yield, averaging about 3 percent over the past five years. During the most recent two-year rating period (fiscal 1989 and 1990) the stock paid an average annual current return (dividend yield) of 3 percent.

DIVIDEND GROWTH

Wrigley has raised its dividend for ten consecutive years. The dividend increased 190 percent (24 percent per year) from 1985 to 1990.

CONSISTENCY

The company has had increased earnings per share and revenue nine of the past ten years, and increased book value per share for more than 15 consecutive years. Its price-earnings ratio of about 17 to 20 is in line with other growing companies.

SHAREHOLDER PERKS

Wrigley sends out a gift package to all its shareholders each Christmas that includes about 20 packs of Wrigley's gum, personally selected by company chairman and president, William Wrigley. All shareholders who attend the annual meeting receive a gift box of about 20 packs of gum.

The company also offers its shareholders of record a good dividend reinvestment and voluntary stock purchase plan. There are no fees or commissions, and shareholders of record may purchase $50 to $5,000 per month in additional shares through the voluntary stock purchase plan.

SUMMARY

Fiscal year ended: Dec. 31
(Revenue and net income in millions)

	1991*	1990	1989	1988	1987	1986	1985	5-year growth, %† (annual/ total)
Revenue		1,111	993	891	781	698	620	12/79
Net income		117	106	87	70	54	43	22/172
Earnings/share		2.99	2.70	2.18	1.68	1.27	1.03	24/190
Dividend/share		1.48	1.36	1.09	.85	.64	.51	24/190
Dividend yield, %		2.9	3.0	3.0	3.1	3.0	4.1	—/—
Stock price	62.00	51.25	53.63	36.13	34.50	22.58	15.50	27/230
P/E ratio	20	17	17	17	16	17	12	—/—
Book value/share		10.25	8.73	7.76	7.18	6.93	6.13	11/67

* Stock price as of 5-1-91
† 1985-90
Source: Company sources

5

ANHEUSER-BUSCH COMPANIES, INC.

One Busch Place
St. Louis, MO 63118
314-577-2000
Chairman, President and CEO: August A. Busch III

EARNINGS GROWTH	★ ★ ★
STOCK GROWTH	★ ★ ★ ★
DIVIDEND YIELD	★ ★
DIVIDEND GROWTH	★ ★ ★
CONSISTENCY	★ ★ ★ ★
SHAREHOLDER PERKS	★ ★ ★ ★
NYSE—BUD	**20 points**

The age of moderation has taken a bite out of the nation's beer business, and a 1991 increase in excise taxes promised to dampen suds sales still further. But even in a beer market gone flat, the "king of beers" has managed to keep the brews flowing and the profits growing.

Anheuser-Busch, the world's largest brewer, has continued to knock down record revenues and earnings by soaking up a larger share of the U.S. beer market. Some 42 percent of all beer consumed in the U.S. is produced by Anheuser-Busch. And if the shakeout in the beer market continues, Busch could emerge with an even larger stake.

Busch is the maker of Budweiser, Michelob, Bud Light, Busch and half a dozen other brews. It produces about 87 million barrels of beer a year. It also imports two European-brewed beers, Carlsberg and Elephant Malt Liquor. The company recently discontinued its LA beer after the low-alcohol brew failed to attract a following.

Beer and beer-related products account for about 76 percent of the company's $10.7 billion a year in total revenue.

Internationally, the company's beer is sold in 40 countries.

Busch's brewing business is fully integrated. It operates a dozen breweries in the U.S., and it owns a beverage can manufacturer, a barley processing plant, a label printing operation and a refrigerated rail car transportation subsidiary.

Bud has maintained its throne as the king of beers through relentless marketing muscle. The company spends hundreds of millions of dollars each year on advertising and promotional campaigns. In addition to its many TV and radio advertising campaigns ("This Bud's for you," "Why ask why?" "Know when to say when," Spuds McKenzie, "Nothing beats a Bud," "Keep your Bud light shining," "Everything else is just a light," "The night belongs to Michelob," "the original Bud man," and "Head for the mountains of Busch"), the company is an active sponsor in golf, bowling, horse racing, auto racing, soccer, pool, track and field and other competitions.

The company's other segments include:

- Food products (20 percent of revenues). Campbell Taggart, one of the country's largest bakery operations, has 43 bakeries and several other related production facilities. It markets its baked goods primarily under the Grant's Farm, Colonial Rainbo or Kilpatrick's label. The company also supplies sandwich buns to some of the major fast-food chains.

    Eagle Snacks produces peanuts, pretzels, potato chips and other snack foods.
- Family entertainment (3 percent of revenues). Busch Entertainment operates theme parks throughout the U.S., including The Dark Continent (Busch Gardens) and Adventure Island in Tampa, Florida, The Old Country in Williamsburg, Virginia, and Sesame Place in Langhorne, Pennsylvania. In 1989 it acquired four Sea World parks and two other theme parks from Harcourt Brace Jovanovich.

    Anheuser-Busch also owns the St. Louis Cardinals National League baseball team, which has been one of the most successful franchises in sports history.

Anheuser-Busch traces its roots to a small St. Louis brewery started in 1852. After a few years of lackluster results, the original owner, George Schneider, sold out the struggling operation to an investment group headed by St. Louis soap tycoon Eberhard Anheuser. Anheuser ultimately turned the business over to his son-in-law, a portly, gregarious man by the name of Adolphus Busch.

Mr. Busch, who converted the small brewery into a national force, is generally recognized as the founder of Anheuser-Busch. Budweiser, which Mr. Busch helped develop in 1876, was one of the first beers to achieve widespread distribution. Michelob, the company's "premium" beer, was first brought to market in 1896. When Adolphus Busch died in 1913, his son, August A. Busch, assumed control of the business. The reins have since been passed through two more generations of the Busch family. August A. Busch III, 53, now directs the company as its chairman of the board, president and CEO.

EARNINGS GROWTH

Anheuser-Busch has had 14 consecutive years of record earnings. Over the past ten years, its earnings per share increased 368 percent (an average of 17 percent per year).

The company has about 47,000 employees and 67,000 shareholders.

STOCK GROWTH

The company has had exceptional stock growth the past ten years, increasing 856 percent (25 percent per year) during the period.

Including reinvested dividends, a $10,000 investment in Anheuser-Busch stock at its closing stock price in 1980 would have grown to about $110,000 ten years later. Average annual compounded rate of return (including stock growth and reinvested dividends): about 27 percent.

DIVIDEND YIELD

Busch generally pays a fairly good yield, averaging just over 2 percent over the past five years. During the most recent two-year rating period (fiscal 1990 and 1991) the stock paid an average annual current return (dividend yield) of 2.2 percent.

DIVIDEND GROWTH

The company raises its dividend every year. The dividend increased 154 percent (20 percent per year) from 1985 to 1990.

CONSISTENCY

The company has had very consistent growth in its earnings, revenue and book value per share, including 14 consecutive years of record sales and earnings. Its price-earnings ratio of about 16 is about average for sound, growing U.S. companies.

SHAREHOLDER PERKS

New shareholders of record are sent a letter of welcome, a fact book on the company and a pamphlet on its dividend reinvestment plan.

The company makes a point of moving its annual meetings around the country. In recent years, meetings have been held in Tampa, Florida, Williamsburg, Virginia, and Fort Collins, Colorado. Those who attend get to sample all of the company's brews, including Budweiser, Busch, Bud Light, Michelob, Michelob Light, Michelob Classic Dark, LA and Natural Light.

Shareholders are also entitled to a discount on admission to the company's amusement parks.

The company's dividend reinvestment plan allows investors to have all or part of their dividends reinvested in Anheuser-Busch stock. Shareholders may also contribute $25 to $5,000 per quarter to the company's voluntary stock purchase plan—all without fees or commissions.

CORPORATE RESPONSIBILITY

Studies have shown that drinking may cause as many as 100,000 deaths a year in the U.S., although Anheuser-Busch points out that moderate consumption of beer may actually have some health benefits. (Studies have shown that those who drink small amounts of alcoholic beverages are in the lowest risk groups for coronary disease.)

Legislation has been proposed that would ban beer and wine advertising from radio and television. If enacted, such legislation could have an adverse effect on the company's sales and earnings.

Anheuser-Busch has no involvement in South Africa, does no animal testing and has a good charitable giving record. In 1988, Anheuser-Busch gave nearly $20 million to charity, which represented an impressive 1.9 percent of the company's average pretax income. Two of the company's top 25 officers are minorities.

Anheuser-Busch has an environmental compliance record that is free of significant problems. Its breweries recycle and reuse much of their process materials, including containers. However, the company has a history of opposing bottle-deposit bills and laws that have helped reduce litter and collect recyclable materials. (Source: Council on Economic Priorities)

SUMMARY

Fiscal year ended: Dec. 31
(Revenue and net income in millions)

	1991*	1990	1989	1988	1987	1986	1985	5-year growth, %† (annual/ total)
Revenue		10,744	10,283	9,705	9,110	8,478	7,756	7/38
Net income		842	767	716	615	518	444	14/89
Earnings/share		2.95	2.68	2.45	2.04	1.69	1.42	16/107
Dividend/share		.94	.80	.66	.54	.44	.37	20/154
Dividend yield, %	1.9	2.3	2.2	2.2	1.7	1.8	2.4	—/—
Stock price	53.75	43.00	39.00	31.00	33.38	26.13	20.88	16/106
P/E ratio	18.0	16.0	14.0	12.0	17.0	15.0	11.0	—/—
Book value/share		13.00	12.50	11.00	9.00	9.00	7.80	11/66

* Stock price as of 5–1–91
† 1985–90
Source: Company sources

6

THE LIMITED, INC.

THE LIMITED, INC.
Two Limited Parkway
P.O. Box 16000
Columbus, OH 43230
614-479-4000
Chairman, President and CEO: Leslie H. Wexner

EARNINGS GROWTH	★ ★ ★ ★
STOCK GROWTH	★ ★ ★ ★
DIVIDEND YIELD	★
DIVIDEND GROWTH	★ ★ ★ ★
CONSISTENCY	★ ★ ★ ★
SHAREHOLDER PERKS	★ ★
NYSE—LTD	**19 points**

In 1982, The Limited acquired a struggling four-unit chain of women's lingerie stores called Victoria's Secret. Profits from the business, which also included a catalog operation, were as scant as the lingerie on the retailers' racks.

But since then, under the guiding hand of The Limited founder and chairman, Leslie Wexner, Victoria's Secret has become one of the greatest success stories in the retailing trade. The chain now includes about 400 stores, plus a catalog mailing list of millions. Its earnings growth and profit margins are among the best in the clothing business. Even during the economic slowdown of the past couple of years, Victoria's Secret continued to rack up record sales. Wexner says the business now has annual sales potential of $2 billion.

The success of Victoria's Secret has helped The Limited keep its corporate earnings climbing while profits slide at other retailers.

The Limited, which the 53-year-old Wexner founded in 1963, has total annual revenue of $5.3 billion. It operates about 3,800 retail clothing stores, primarily for women, and has continued an aggressive expansion program that includes both acquisitions and internal expansion. The company has also been growing by making its stores larger. While many of its shops are still in the range of 3,000 square feet, some of its newer shops are as large as 20,000 to 30,000 square feet.

Says Wexner: "In 1985, our stores occupied perhaps 5 percent of the gross leasable space in a typical regional mall. Today, when we locate all of our retail businesses in a single mall, we will occupy up to 25 to 30 percent of the gross leasable space—100,000 to 125,000 square feet."

In addition to Victoria's Secret, the major chains operated by The Limited include:

- **The Limited.** The original Limited clothing store chain has grown to more than 760 stores.
- **Lerner.** Lerner is geared to the "off-price" customer. With 770 stores, Lerner is the largest women's apparel business under one name in the country. The Limited acquired Lerner in 1985.
- **Lane Bryant.** The chain of apparel stores for large-size women has grown from 222 stores in 1982 to more than 720 stores by 1991.
- **Brylane.** This is the second largest fashion catalog retailer in the U.S.
- **Limited Express.** The Express has more than 470 women's apparel stores.
- **Structure.** A new chain of men's stores. Approximately 150 shops are either freestanding or located in Express stores.
- **Abercrombe & Fitch.** Acquired in 1988, the chain of 26 stores sells sportswear for men and women.

EARNINGS GROWTH

The Limited has had spectacular long-term growth. Over the past ten years, its earnings per share increased 3,567 percent (43 percent per year).

The company has about 63,000 employees and 19,000 shareholders.

STOCK GROWTH

The company has also enjoyed spectacular stock price appreciation the past ten years, soaring 3,500 percent (43 percent per year) during the period.

Including reinvested dividends, a $10,000 investment in The Limited stock at its closing stock price in 1980 would have grown to about $375,000 ten years later. Average annual compounded rate of return (including stock growth and reinvested dividends): about 44 percent.

DIVIDEND YIELD

The Limited generally pays a fairly modest yield, averaging about 1 percent over the past five years. During the most recent two-year rating period (fiscal 1990 and 1991) the stock paid an average annual current return (dividend yield) of 1.2 percent.

DIVIDEND GROWTH

The Limited has raised its dividend for just three consecutive years. The dividend increased 380 percent (37 percent per year) from 1985 to 1990.

CONSISTENCY

The company has had 11 consecutive years of record revenue, earnings and book value per share. Its recent price-earnings ratio of about 25 is high even for a growing retailer, but not unusual considering the company's spectacular growth record.

SHAREHOLDER PERKS

The Limited offers an excellent dividend reinvestment and voluntary stock purchase plan. There are no fees or commissions, and shareholders of record may buy $30 to $6,000 per quarter in additional shares through the voluntary stock purchase program.

SUMMARY

Fiscal year ended: Jan. 31*
(Revenue and net income in millions)

	1991**	1990	1989	1988	1987	1986	1985	5-year growth, %† (annual /total)
Revenue		5,254	4,647	4,070	3,527	3,142	2,387	17/120
Net income		398	346	245	235	227	145	22/174
Earnings/share		1.10	.96	.68	.63	.61	.40	22/175
Dividend/share		.24	.16	.12	.12	.08	.05	37/380
Dividend yield, %	1.0	1.3	0.9	1.1	0.7	0.5	0.6	—/—
Stock price	27.63	18.00	18.00	13.63	8.63	16.12	10.42	12/73
P/E ratio	25	17	17	17	29	25	21	—/—
Book value/share		4.30	3.45	2.64	2.04	2.07	1.12	31/284

* Refers to previous year (example: Fiscal year ended Jan. 31, 1991, is listed under 1990), except stock price: Dec. 31, 1985–1990
** Stock price as of 5-1-91
† 1985–90
Source: Company sources

GIANT FOOD, INC.

6300 Sheriff Road
Landover, MD 20785
301-341-4100
Chairman, President and CEO: Israel Cohen

EARNINGS GROWTH	★ ★ ★ ★
STOCK GROWTH	★ ★ ★ ★
DIVIDEND YIELD	★ ★
DIVIDEND GROWTH	★ ★ ★ ★
CONSISTENCY	★ ★ ★
SHAREHOLDER PERKS	★ ★
ASE—GFS "A"	**19 points**

In and around the nation's capital, Giant Food is well known for its large, bright stores and bountiful selection of grocery staples. But its secret weapon—and its single greatest asset in the highly competitive grocery business—is its cozy relationship with its principal supplier.

The Washington, D.C. grocery store chain gets the bulk of its baked goods, dairy products, soft drinks, floral arrangements, tobacco products, ice cream, produce and ice cubes from the same supplier—itself.

Giant owns its own 173,000-square-foot bakery, its own dairy, soft drink bottling plant, ice cream plant and ice cube plant. It also owns its own produce, tobacco and flower wholesale operations. By producing many of its own grocery goods itself, Giant is able not only to control the quality of its goods, but also to keep profit margins at a premium. The company also sells to other retailers. Its nonretail operations account for about 30 percent of Giant's profits.

Giant's quest for self-reliance stretches into other areas as well. The company owns its own construction subsidiary, which builds its stores and often wins the contracts to build the shopping centers where its stores are located. In nine of the company's store locations, Giant owns not only its store buildings, but also the shopping centers in which they are located.

Giant is the dominant grocer in Washington, D.C., where it holds about a 45 percent market share. About 100 of the company's 150 stores are located within the D.C. metropolitan area. Giant is also big in Baltimore, where its 37 stores comprise about a 25 percent market share. The rest of Giant's stores are located in relatively close proximity to the company's Landover, Maryland, headquarters. It operates stores in Fredericksburg, Warrenton and Charlottesville, Virginia, and in Salisbury, Annapolis and Frederick, Maryland.

Giant's stores, as the name implies, are spacious emporiums of foods and other consumer goods. Its largest new stores cover 65,000 square feet— an acre and a half—and carry everything from basic grocery products to fresh seafood, floral arrangements, prescriptions and "Gourmet-to-Go." About 95 of its stores have full-line pharmacies.

Founded in 1935, Giant has built its empire through steady, controlled growth. It added five new stores in fiscal 1988, three in 1989, four in 1990 and is scheduled to add four more in 1991.

Of the company's $3.4 billion in annual sales, about 25 percent comes from meat, delicatessen, dairy and seafood; 66 percent from grocery and nonfood items; and 9 percent from fresh produce.

EARNINGS GROWTH

Giant has had excellent long-term growth. Over the past ten years, its earnings per share jumped 618 percent (22 percent per year).

The company has about 26,000 employees and 11,000 shareholders.

STOCK GROWTH

The company has had exceptional stock growth the past ten years, increasing 1,800 percent (34 percent per year) during the period.

Including reinvested dividends, a $10,000 investment in Giant stock at its closing stock price in 1980 would have grown to about $230,000 ten years later. Average annual compounded rate of return (including stock growth and reinvested dividends): about 37 percent.

DIVIDEND YIELD

Giant generally pays a fairly good yield, averaging about 2 percent over the past five years. During the most recent two-year rating period (fiscal 1990 and 1991) the stock paid an average annual current return (dividend yield) of 2.0 percent.

DIVIDEND GROWTH

Giant has raised its dividend for more than 15 consecutive years. The dividend increased 200 percent (25 percent per year) from 1985 to 1990.

CONSISTENCY

The company's earnings per share has increased eight of the past ten years, and its revenue and book value per share have gone up for more than 15 consecutive years. Its price-earnings ratio of around 15 is in line with other growing companies.

SHAREHOLDER PERKS

The company offers a dividend reinvestment and voluntary stock purchase plan. There are no fees or commissions, and shareholders of record may buy $10 to $1,000 per dividend period in additional shares.

CORPORATE RESPONSIBILITY

Giant Food rates well across the board on social responsibility issues. In Maryland, the company has participated in the Montgomery County Housing Opportunities Commission for five years. As part of the commission, Giant Food teamed up with two local banks to invest $3.2 million in housing for low- and moderate-income families. The agreement allows businesses to take a 9 percent tax credit each year for ten years; houses are held available to low- and moderate-income workers for 15 years.

Giant has taken some positive environmental steps as well. The company has an environmental task force; is testing natural gas for its fleet of trucks; makes cloth diapers available in its stores; and recycles its plastic grocery bags. (Source: Council on Economic Priorities)

SUMMARY

Fiscal year ended: Feb. 28*
(Revenue and net income in millions)

	1991**	1990	1989	1988	(53 wks) 1987	1986	1985	5-year growth, %† (annual /total)
Revenue	3,350	3,249	2,987	2,721	2,528	2,247	2,138	9/56
Net income	119	108	98	76	46	57	45	21/164
Earnings/share	2.01	1.80	1.63	1.26	.77	.95	.77	21/161
Dividend/share	.60	.50	.40	.33	.30	.25	.20	25/200
Dividend yield, %	2.1	1.9	1.8	1.9	2.1	2.1	2.1	—/—
Stock price	28.75	25.00	29.00	21.00	16.50	14.30	10.15	19/146
P/E ratio	14.4	16.1	15.7	13.0	13.6	18.4	11.5	—/—
Book value/share	9.42	8.25	7.11	5.91	4.99	4.53	3.84	19/145

 * Except stock price, which states stock price average for calendar years 1985–90
** Stock price as of 5–1–91
 † 1986–91
Source: Company sources

8

SARA LEE CORPORATION

SARA LEE CORPORATION
Three First National Plaza
Chicago, IL 60602-4260
312-726-2600
Chairman and CEO: John H. Bryan, Jr.
President: Paul Fulton

EARNINGS GROWTH	★ ★
STOCK GROWTH	★ ★ ★ ★
DIVIDEND YIELD	★ ★ ★
DIVIDEND GROWTH	★ ★ ★
CONSISTENCY	★ ★ ★ ★
SHAREHOLDER PERKS	★ ★ ★
NYSE—SLE	**19 points**

One-fourth of all frozen baked goods sold in the U.S. are prepared in the kitchens of Sara Lee. But baked goods are not the only market the Chicago-based bakery dominates. Sara Lee is also the nation's leader in women's hosiery (Hanes, L'eggs, Isotoner), the second leading manufacturer of brassieres, men's and boys' underwear and printed T-shirts, and it ranks number one in hot dogs, smoked sausage and breakfast sausage.

Sara Lee has operations in more than 30 countries and distribution in nearly 150 countries. It is well established in Europe and is the leading coffee distributor in the Netherlands and Belgium. Of its $12 billion in total annual sales, 73 percent comes from within the U.S. and 27 percent from abroad.

Sara Lee has had 16 consecutive years of record earnings.

The company divides its operations into five key segments:

- Packaged foods (29 percent of revenue). Sara Lee's meats, desserts and other frozen baked goods make up its largest corporate segment. With its Hillshire Farm and Jimmy Dean meats, the company is the leading producer of sausage and hot dogs.

- Packaged consumer products (25 percent of sales). The firm's fastest growing area, this segment includes Hanes (underwear, T-shirts, Isotoner and Silk Reflection hosiery) and L'eggs (Sheer Energy and Sheer Elegance), Fuller Brush, Coach Leatherware (a nationwide chain of leather goods stores) and Socks Galore & More, a retail and mail order socks business.
- Food service (22 percent of sales). Sara Lee's PYA/Monarch is one of the largest food service operations in the U.S. It supplies food and non-food items to institutional dining facilities (at hospitals, schools, factories, etc.).
- Household and personal care products (10 percent of revenue). Based in Utrecht, the Netherlands, Sara Lee's household goods and personal care products division does most of its business outside the U.S. About 69 percent of its revenue comes from Europe and the United Kingdom. The company makes shoe care products (Kiwi and Esquire shoe polish), toiletries, over-the-counter medications, specialty detergents and insecticides.
- Coffee and grocery products (15 percent of sales). Sara Lee owns Douwe Egberts, one of Europe's leading brands of coffee and tea, and several other European coffee and tea lines. It also owns Duyvis nuts, the leading marketer of nuts in both the Netherlands and France.

EARNINGS GROWTH

Sara Lee has had strong, sustained long-term growth. Over the past ten years, its earnings per share increased 267 percent (14 percent per year).

The company has about 110,000 employees and 65,000 shareholders.

STOCK GROWTH

The company has had outstanding stock price appreciation the past ten years, increasing 967 percent (25.5 percent per year) during the period.

Including reinvested dividends, a $10,000 investment in Sara Lee stock at its closing stock price in 1980 would have grown to about $142,000 ten years later. Average annual compounded rate of return (including stock growth and reinvested dividends): about 30.5 percent.

DIVIDEND YIELD

Sara Lee generally pays a very good yield, averaging about 2.8 percent over the past five years. During the most recent two-year rating period (fiscal 1990 and 1991) the stock paid an average annual current return (dividend yield) of 2.6 percent.

DIVIDEND GROWTH

Sara Lee has raised its dividend for 13 consecutive years. The dividend increased 131 percent (18 percent per year) from 1985 to 1990.

CONSISTENCY

The company has had 15 consecutive years of increased earnings and book value per share. Its revenue has gone up eight of the past ten years. Its price-earnings ratio of around 15 to 19 is well in line with other growing foods companies.

SHAREHOLDER PERKS

Each year at the annual meeting, Sara Lee shareholders receive a gift box of Sara Lee products, including such items as Kiwi shoe polish and L'eggs or Hanes hosiery, plus a handful of coupons for foods such as Jimmy Dean and Hillshire Farm meats and Sara Lee frozen desserts.

The company also offers its shareholders of record a dividend reinvestment and voluntary stock purchase plan. There are no fees or commissions, and shareholders of record may purchase $5 to $1,500 per quarter in additional shares through the voluntary stock purchase plan.

CORPORATE RESPONSIBILITY

Sara Lee's record for corporate responsibility is quite good in most areas. The company has two women and two minorities on its 18-member board of directors and two women among its top 25 paid officers. Sara Lee was one of the founding members of the Chicago Equity Fund, in which it invested $1 million over three years to rehabilitate houses for low-income residents in Chicago neighborhoods. The company has a strong charitable giving program and donates millions of pounds of food each year to the Second Harvest food bank.

Sara Lee's record is not so good in terms of workplace safety and health. In 1989, its Hillshire Farm plant in New London, Wisconsin, was cited by OSHA for four allegedly willful violations for exposing employees to cumulative trauma disorders (CTDs). Sara Lee reached an agreement with the government agency by paying $40,000 in penalties and establishing a plan to reduce CTDs in its meat processing plants around the nation.

Cumulative trauma disorders are not unique to Sara Lee's meat processing plants. Members of the local Bakery, Confectionery and Tobacco Workers Union in New Hampton, Iowa, who, according to the head of the international union, were "driven to the breaking point by cumulative trauma, inhumane working conditions and disrespect," went on strike in March of 1990. A contract was reached in June that called for addressing CTDs. (Source: Council on Economic Priorities)

SUMMARY

Fiscal year ended: July 1*
(Revenue and net income in millions)

	1991**	1990	1989	1988	1987	1986	1985	5-year growth, %† (annual /total)
Revenue		11,606	11,718	10,424	9,155	7,938	8,117	8/43
Net income		470	399	325	267	223	206	18/128
Earnings/share		1.91	1.70	1.42	1.18	1.01	.90	16/112
Dividend/share		.81	.69	.58	.48	.39	.35	18/131
Dividend yield, %	2.4	2.8	3.0	2.9	2.5	3.0	4.1	—/—
Stock price	39.25	32.00	33.50	28.00	24.00	14.33	12.72	19/137
P/E ratio	19.0	15.4	13.6	14.0	16.3	12.7	9.4	—/—
Book value/share		9.95	8.42	7.12	6.39	5.41	4.63	16/14

  * Except stock price 12/31/85–90
 ** Stock price as of 5-1-91
  † 1985–90
Source: Company sources

9

TORCHMARK CORPORATION

2001 Third Avenue South
Birmingham, AL 35233
205-325-4200
Chairman and CEO: R. K. Richey
President: Jon W. Rotenstreich

EARNINGS GROWTH	★ ★ ★
STOCK GROWTH	★ ★ ★ ★
DIVIDEND YIELD	★ ★ ★
DIVIDEND GROWTH	★ ★ ★
CONSISTENCY	★ ★ ★ ★
SHAREHOLDER PERKS	★ ★
NYSE—TMK	**19 points**

The banking, financial and insurance industries have been hit with one crisis after another over the past decade, but Torchmark has never flickered. The Birmingham-based parent company of Liberty National Insurance and Waddell & Reed (W&R) financial services continues to chalk up impressive returns, including a remarkable string of 39 consecutive years of record earnings.

The company's exceptional record of success—both over the long term and during the past few years—has made Torchmark the best performing company in America's financial services sector.

Liberty National is the largest of Torchmark's small battery of insurance companies, with $20 billion of life insurance in force and annual total premiums of more than $400 million. The company employs 2,500 agents in 101 sales offices throughout the Southeast and sells a complete line of life and health insurance and annuity policies.

Liberty's casualty insurance arm, Liberty National Fire, offers a range of fire, property and casualty insurance for individuals and businesses.

About 29 percent of Liberty's premium distribution comes from individual life insurance policies, 58 percent comes from health policies and 13 percent from property-casualty and other types of policies.

Waddell & Reed (which is a branch of United Investors Management Company, a Torchmark subsidiary) offers financial planning services for individual investors and investment management services for large institutional investors. The company manages 16 mutual funds with assets of $7.5 billion and offers other investment products.

Waddell & Reed has 3,500 financial services representatives in 190 offices across all 50 states. They serve 900,000 customers nationwide. In addition to mutual funds and financial planning assistance, W&R reps sell life and health insurance policies from another Torchmark subsidiary, United Investors Life, and oil and gas limited partnerships managed by another subsidiary, Torch Energy.

W&R's sales force attracts its client base, in large part, through public seminars on money management aimed at individual investors. The company's representatives conduct nearly 4,000 seminars a year, which draw about 100,000 prospective clients.

Torchmark's other two major subsidiaries are United American Insurance, which sells Medicare supplement insurance through some 61,000 independent agents nationwide, and Globe Life and Accident Insurance, which markets health insurance through 1,400 agents in 76 branch offices. Globe also sells life insurance through 300 agents.

EARNINGS GROWTH

Torchmark has enjoyed excellent long-term growth. Over the past ten years, its earnings per share increased 410 percent (18 percent per year).

The company has about 6,000 employees and 8,000 shareholders.

STOCK GROWTH

The company has had exceptional stock price appreciation the past ten years, increasing 833 percent (25 percent per year) during the period.

Including reinvested dividends, a $10,000 investment in Torchmark stock at its closing stock price in 1980 would have grown to about $132,000 ten years later. Average annual compounded rate of return (including stock growth and reinvested dividends): about 29.5 percent.

DIVIDEND YIELD

Torchmark traditionally pays a very good yield, averaging about 3.3 percent over the past five years. During the most recent two-year rating period (fiscal 1990 and 1991) the stock paid an average annual current return (dividend yield) of 3.0 percent.

DIVIDEND GROWTH

Torchmark has raised its dividend for 39 consecutive years. The dividend increased 155 percent (21 percent per year) from 1985 to 1990.

CONSISTENCY

The company has had 39 consecutive years of record earnings per share. Its price-earnings ratio of about 12 is very low for a growing company.

SHAREHOLDER PERKS

The company offers its shareholders of record a dividend reinvestment and voluntary stock purchase plan. For a nominal fee, shareholders of record may purchase up to $3,000 per quarter in additional shares through the voluntary purchase plan.

SUMMARY

Fiscal year ended: Dec. 31
(Revenue and net income in millions)

	1991*	1990	1989	1988	1987	1986	1985	5-year growth, %† (annual/ total)
Revenue		1,796	1,633	1,611	1,532	1,459	1,297	7/38
Net income		229**	211	185	189	205	165	7/39
Earnings/share		4.28**	3.88	3.20	2.80	2.72	2.17	15/97
Dividend/share		1.40	1.25	1.15	1.00	.90	.55	21/155
Dividend yield, %	3.1	2.9	3.0	3.8	3.5	3.0	2.5	—/—
Stock price	52.38	49.00	56.00	31.00	24.50	26.00	22.00	18/127
P/E ratio	12.0	11.0	11.0	9.5	10.0	11.0	10.0	—/—
Book value/share		16.70	15.03	13.23	13.47	12.52	12.29	6/36

  * Stock price as of 5–1–91
** After one-time charge of $12,693,000 pretax, or $.16 per share after tax, in connection with efforts to acquire American General Corp.
  † 1985–90
Source: Company sources

10

H.J. HEINZ COMPANY

600 Grant Street
P.O. Box 57
Pittsburgh, PA 15230-0057
412-456-5700
Chairman, President and CEO: Anthony J.F. O'Reilly

EARNINGS GROWTH	★ ★
STOCK GROWTH	★ ★ ★ ★
DIVIDEND YIELD	★ ★ ★
DIVIDEND GROWTH	★ ★ ★
CONSISTENCY	★ ★ ★ ★
SHAREHOLDER PERKS	★ ★ ★
NYSE—HNZ	**19 points**

Never have so many spent so much to gain so little.

Dieters around the world have turned Weight Watchers, Inc., a multi-faceted international diet concern owned by H.J. Heinz, into a $1.5 billion a year business. More than a million members a week attend Weight Watchers meetings. The Weight Watchers brand of frozen dinners, with sales of about $900 million a year, has overtaken Lean Cuisine as the top-selling reduced-calorie frozen entree brand in America.

Heinz acquired Weight Watchers a dozen years ago for about $100 million. Now the division's annual operating earnings alone exceed the $100 million mark, making it Heinz's second most profitable division behind its ketchups and related Heinz brand foods.

Weight Watchers operates branches in more than 20 countries, hosting about 25,000 meetings a week for diet-conscious members. Its frozen foods division produces a wide range of low-calorie entrees and desserts. Weight Watchers frozen desserts hold about a 20 percent share of the frozen desserts market. The company also markets more than 50 dry and canned products such as salad dressings, sauces, and dinner and dessert mixes.

Heinz's other food groups also continued to perform well in recent years, helping propel the company to 26 consecutive years of record earnings. The Pittsburgh manufacturer has sales and operations worldwide. About 40 percent of its annual earnings are generated abroad.

The company's most famous product is its ketchup. When Americans reach for the ketchup, the name on the bottle is usually Heinz. The company holds slightly more than a 50 percent share of the U.S. consumer ketchup market. Heinz brand sales account for about 16 percent of the company's $6.1 billion in total revenue.

Heinz also produces Star-Kist ("Sorry, Charlie") tuna, which holds about a 40 percent share of the U.S. tuna market and accounts for about 15 percent of the company's total revenue.

Heinz has achieved a growing presence in the pet food market. With its 9-Lives brand cat food (Morris's personal favorite) and its Vets, Recipe and Skippy Premium dog foods, Heinz holds a 13 percent share of the U.S. pet food market, including a 22 percent share of the cat food market.

Heinz is also a leading producer of baby food, canned soup, desserts, beans, sauces and condiments, pasta, candy, pickles, chilled salads, rice cakes, frozen meats, vinegar, flavored rice products and other processed foods. Its Ore-Ida frozen potatoes group is one of the nation's top selling brands.

The company's strongest areas outside the U.S. and Canada include the United Kingdom, Europe, Australia, Venezuela and Japan.

EARNINGS GROWTH

Heinz has enjoyed strong, sustained long-term growth. Over the past ten years, its earnings per share increased 273 percent (14 percent per year).

The company has about 37,000 employees and 47,000 shareholders.

STOCK GROWTH

The company has had exceptional stock growth the past ten years, increasing 800 percent (25 percent per year) during the period.

Including reinvested dividends, a $10,000 investment in Heinz stock at its closing stock price in 1980 would have grown to about $124,000 ten years later. Average annual compounded rate of return (including stock growth and reinvested dividends): about 28.7 percent.

DIVIDEND YIELD

Heinz traditionally pays a good yield, averaging about 2.6 percent over the past five years. During the most recent two-year rating period (fiscal 1990

and 1991) the stock paid an average annual current return (dividend yield) of 2.7 percent.

DIVIDEND GROWTH

Heinz has raised its dividend each year since 1967. The dividend increased 107 percent (16 percent per year) from 1985 to 1990.

CONSISTENCY

The company has had 26 consecutive years of record sales, earnings and book value per share. Its price-earnings ratio of about 18 is well in line with other growing foods companies.

SHAREHOLDER PERKS

Shareholders who attend the annual meeting receive a gift package of some of the company's newer products.

The company puts out one of corporate America's best quarterly reports, packed with new product information and company developments. They also occasionally carry special offers or product discounts for Heinz shareholders.

Heinz provides a good dividend reinvestment and voluntary stock purchase plan for its shareholders. There are no fees or commissions, and shareholders of record may purchase $25 to $1,000 per quarter in additional shares through the voluntary stock purchase plan.

CORPORATE RESPONSIBILITY

Heinz has responded to public outcry (and a boycott led by Earth Island Institute) by promising to catch tuna for its Star-Kist brand in a dolphin-safe way. On April 12, 1990, Heinz's Star-Kist brand stopped buying tuna from suppliers that use methods that also harm dolphins. After Heinz announced its decision, the other major tuna companies, Bumble Bee and Chicken of the Sea, followed suit within hours.

Heinz was once one of 16 companies and trade associations in the Coalition for Food Irradiation that lobbied for legislation supporting food irradiation. Food irradiation is a federally approved production process some companies use to lengthen the shelf life of vegetables and other foods. Critics are concerned because the process exposes food to radioactive sources. At a shareholders meeting in September of 1989, Heinz responded to questions by announcing that neither the company nor its suppliers use irradiated ingredients or the food irradiation process. According to Sister Patricia

Daly, who represented the Interfaith Center for Corporate Responsibility and Food & Water at that meeting, Heinz's decision was followed by the announcement of similar policies at dozens of other companies.

In 1990, Heinz announced plans to develop a recyclable squeezable ketchup bottle that would be available in 1991. The new bottle is made of 98.5 percent polyethylene terephthalate (PET), which is the easiest form of plastic to recycle. At the same time, Heinz is attempting to encourage recycling programs through the National Recycling Awards. At the 1991 U.S. Conference of Mayors, the H.J. Heinz Company Foundation honored communities that were most active in developing recycling programs.

While Heinz does not invest or operate in South Africa, it is one of the few companies that invest and manufacture in other sub-Saharan countries, taking risks and providing employment, but also taking advantage of access to new markets and valuable raw materials. Heinz purchased a 51 percent interest in Ilivine Industries, Inc., Zimbabwe's top brand food products company, and entered Botswana by purchasing Kgalagadi Soap Industries, the sole producer there of toilet and laundry soaps. (Source: Council on Economic Priorities)

SUMMARY

Fiscal year ended: Apr. 30*
(Revenue and net income in millions)

	1991**	1990	1989	1988	1987	1986	1985	5-year growth, %† (annual /total)
Revenue		6,086	5,800	5,244	4,639	4,366	4,047	8/50
Net income		504	440	386	338	301	266	14/89
Earnings/share		1.90	1.67	1.45	1.24	1.10	.96	15/98
Dividend/share		.81	.70	.61	.51	.44	.39	16/107
Dividend yield, %	2.5	2.8	2.4	3.1	2.7	2.3	2.9	—/—
Stock price	38.00	34.88	35.00	23.38	20.19	20.25	16.19	17/115
P/E ratio	18.0	18.4	20.9	16.1	16.2	18.4	16.9	—/—
Book value/share		7.45	6.90	6.25	5.40	5.08	4.50	11/65

  * Except stock price 12/31/85–90
 ** Stock price as of 5–1–91
  † 1985–90
Source: Company sources

11

THE J.M. SMUCKER COMPANY

Strawberry Lane
Orville, OH 44667-0280
216-682-3000
CEO: Paul H. Smucker
Chairman: Tim Smucker
President: Richard K. Smucker

EARNINGS GROWTH	★ ★ ★
STOCK GROWTH	★ ★ ★ ★
DIVIDEND YIELD	★ ★
DIVIDEND GROWTH	★ ★ ★
CONSISTENCY	★ ★ ★ ★
SHAREHOLDER PERKS	★ ★ ★
NYSE—SJM	**19 points**

It was in 1897 that J.M. Smucker first began preparing his jams, jellies and preserves for public consumption. He named the famous fruit spreads for himself, reasoning, no doubt, that "with a name like Smucker's, it has to be good."

Today the company, which is still run by the Smucker family, sells nearly half a billion dollars a year worth of fruit spreads, toppings, fillings and beverages. It markets its foods in several countries around the world, and it has production plants or offices in eight U.S. states, plus Canada, England and Australia.

Smucker's sales have been growing consistently for many years. Its fiscal 1991, ended April 30, marked the company's 15th consecutive year of record earnings per share. Its total annual revenue is about $475 million.

While fruit spreads continue to be Smucker's primary breadwinner, the firm has launched some related products recently. Its Knudsen & Sons subsidiary introduced a line of Santa Cruz Natural organic juices in 1990. One of Smucker's newer products, Simply Fruit all-fruit spread, has been one of its fastest-growing products over the past two years. In 1990, the company introduced another new line of organic fruit spreads under the Mary Ellen label.

The company sells fruit spreads and butters under several brand names, including Elsenham, Dickinson, Lost Acres, Purely Fruit, Autumn Harvest, Summer Harvest, Slenderella, Dutch Girl, Good Morning, IXL, Shirriff, Schwartau and Goober peanut butters.

Smucker also offers several brands of fruit juices (including Very Veggie, Vita Juice, Nice & Natural, Recharge, Hibiscus Cooler and Rich-n-Fiber) and ice cream toppings (Magic Shell and Special Recipe).

In addition to its retail products, Smucker markets spreads, syrups and juices to the institutional, food services, restaurant and food processing trades.

EARNINGS GROWTH

Smucker has enjoyed excellent long-term growth. Over the past ten years, its earnings per share increased 388 percent (17 percent per year). The company has about 2,000 employees and 4,000 shareholders.

STOCK GROWTH

The company has had exceptional stock price appreciation the past ten years, rising 1,050 percent (26.5 percent per year).

Including reinvested dividends, a $10,000 investment in Smucker's stock at its closing stock price in 1980 would have grown to about $130,000 ten years later. Average annual compounded rate of return (including stock growth and reinvested dividends): about 29 percent.

DIVIDEND YIELD

Smucker generally pays a fairly modest yield, averaging about 1.5 percent over the past five years. During the most recent two-year rating period (fiscal 1990 and 1991) the stock paid an average annual current return (dividend yield) of 1.7 percent.

DIVIDEND GROWTH

Smucker generally raises its dividend every year. The dividend increased 108 percent (16 percent per year) from 1985 to 1990.

CONSISTENCY

The company has had 15 consecutive years of record revenue, book value and earnings per share. Its price-earnings ratio of around 20 is a bit higher than most growing food production companies.

SHAREHOLDER PERKS

The company hands out a gift box of some of its fruit spreads, toppings, fillings and newer products to shareholders who attend the annual meeting.

The company offers its shareholders a good dividend reinvestment and voluntary stock purchase plan. Shareholders of record may purchase $20 to $1,500 per month in additional shares through the voluntary stock purchase plan.

CORPORATE RESPONSIBILITY

Smucker has a clean environmental record, is not involved in South Africa, does not test its products on animals and has a good charitable giving record. In 1989 Smucker gave close to half a million dollars to charity. This represented a sizable 1.3 percent of its average pretax income. (Source: Council on Economic Priorities)

SUMMARY

Fiscal year ended: Apr. 30*
(Revenue and net income in millions)

	1991**	1990	1989	1988	1987	1986	1985	5-year growth, %† (annual /total)
Revenue		422	367	314	288	263	231	13/82
Net income		30	28	23	18	16	16	14/87
Earnings/share		2.05	1.88	1.56	1.21	1.08	1.07	14/91
Dividend/share		.52	.46	.38	.32	.30	.25	16/108
Dividend yield, %	1.7	1.6	1.6	1.5	1.5	1.5	2.1	—/—
Stock price	44.75	46.38	36.28	29.75	25.00	24.75	25.13	12/78
P/E ratio	21	17	15	16	18	19	11	—/—
Book value/share		11.35	9.82	8.51	7.32	6.43	5.94	14/91

 * Except stock price 12/31/85–90
** Stock price as of 5–1–91
 † 1985–90
Source: Company sources

CONAGRA, INC.

ConAgra Center
One ConAgra Drive
Omaha, NE 68102
402-595-4000
Chairman and CEO: Charles M. Harper
President: Philip B. Fletcher

EARNINGS GROWTH	★ ★ ★
STOCK GROWTH	★ ★ ★ ★
DIVIDEND YIELD	★ ★
DIVIDEND GROWTH	★ ★ ★
CONSISTENCY	★ ★ ★ ★
SHAREHOLDER PERKS	★ ★ ★
NYSE—CAG	**19 points**

With operations in virtually every link of the food chain—from feeds and fertilizers to fresh fish and frozen dinners—ConAgra has become the nation's second largest food processor.

Much of the company's growth has come through acquisitions, including the buyout of the financially troubled Beatrice group in August 1990. The addition of Beatrice, with its complement of name brands including Hunt's tomato products, Wesson cooking oils, Orville Redenbacher's popcorns and Swiss Miss puddings and cocoa mixes, was expected to push ConAgra's total 1991 revenues to over $20 billion.

The bread and butter of ConAgra's operations is its meats—ham, poultry and beef—fresh, frozen and packaged. The Omaha-based conglomerate owns a number of meat subsidiaries, including Banquet, Armour, Morton, Monfort, E.A. Miller, Country Pride, Decker, Golden Star, Pfaelzer, Cook Family Food, ConAgra Fresh Meats and ConAgra Poultry.

ConAgra divides its operations into three primary segments:

- Prepared foods (63 percent of revenue). In addition to its meats, the company has other prominent holdings in the prepared foods market including Banquet (frozen dinners, pot pies, chicken, etc.), Morton dinners, Home Brand peanut butter and Chun King dinners. The company also operates some specialized subsidiaries such as its pet products group.
- Agri-products (20 percent of revenue). The company sells a wide range of fertilizers, insecticides and crop protection chemicals. It also sells animal feeds and nutrient additives for feeds and livestock health care products.

    ConAgra owns a chain of 91 Country General Stores that carry merchandise targeted to country living such as boots, clothing, housewares, lawn and garden supplies, farm and ranch supplies, hardware, animal care products and sporting goods. It also owns a chain of 86 Northwest Fabric & Crafts stores.
- Trading and processing (17 percent of revenue). The company trades agricultural commodities and foodstuffs worldwide with offices in 26 nations. It has food processing facilities throughout the U.S., Canada, Europe and Latin America. Among its leading subsidiaries in the food trading and processing business are Berger and Company, Camerican International and Woodward & Dickerson. It also owns Peavey Grain Co. and recently acquired Pillsbury's grain merchandising division.

In all, ConAgra operates more than 40 different companies with locations throughout North and South America, Europe, Asia and Australia.

EARNINGS GROWTH

ConAgra has had steady growth, with its earnings per share climbing 444 percent (18.5 percent per year) over the past ten years.

The company has 75,000 employees and 40,000 shareholders of record.

STOCK GROWTH

The company's stock price has had outstanding appreciation, increasing 640 percent over the past ten years through 1990 (22 percent per year). ConAgra has had two 2-for-1 and two 3-for-2 stock splits since 1980.

Including reinvested dividends, a $10,000 investment in ConAgra stock at the close of 1980 would have grown to about $97,000 ten years later. Average annual compounded rate of return (including stock growth and reinvested dividends): about 25.5 percent.

DIVIDEND YIELD

The company generally pays a fairly good yield, averaging about 2.3 percent over the past three years.

DIVIDEND GROWTH

ConAgra has raised its dividend 15 consecutive years. The dividend has increased 107 percent (16 percent per year) from 1986 to 1990.

CONSISTENCY

Over the past ten years, ConAgra has had a string of increases in earnings, revenues, dividends and book value per share.

SHAREHOLDER PERKS

At its annual meetings, ConAgra passes out a gift pack of some of its foods. The company also includes discount offers in some of its quarterly earnings reports.

ConAgra has a good dividend reinvestment and voluntary cash contribution plan that is free to shareholders of record. Shareholders can contribute $10 to $3,000 per quarter to the stock purchase plan.

CORPORATE RESPONSIBILITY

ConAgra's record on food safety in the workplace is not an enviable one. Monfort, Inc., which is owned by ConAgra, has been the primary advocate for and participant in a U.S. Department of Agriculture (USDA) pilot program for a plan known as the Streamlined Inspection System-Cattle (SIS-C). SIS-C is essentially an honor system in which the largest cattle slaughter operations are deputized to inspect themselves as the main basis for USDA approval. According to the Government Accountability Project (GAP), USDA inspectors and processing customers have found that Monfort SIS-C beef has had visible and microbial contamination rates eight to ten times higher than the norm at plants under traditional USDA inspection.

More recently, the Occupational Safety and Health Administration (OSHA) proposed fines against a Monfort plant totaling $1.09 million for 197 violations of OSHA's new standard governing the control of hazardous energy sources. The citations followed the death of an employee that was linked to improper lockout procedures.

In January 1990, OSHA cited the ConAgra Turkey Company in Carthage, Missouri a second time in six months, this time for ''willfully'' violating agency safety and health standards and for "flagrant failure to protect their workers from cumulative trauma disorders" such as carpal tunnel syndrome. The previous citation was in June 1989, when the company was asked to pay a penalty of more than $1 million in connection with record-keeping violations.

In October 1987, ConAgra agreed to pay $6.6 million in back pay and related costs to answer National Labor Relations Board charges in a hiring discrimination case related to ConAgra's takeover of the Armour Food Company in 1983.

In April 1990, the National Labor Relations Board found Monfort guilty of a pattern of "numerous, pervasive and outrageous" violations of labor law. (Source: Council on Economic Priorities)

SUMMARY

Fiscal year ended: May 31
(Revenue and net income in millions)

	1991*	1990	1989	1988	1987	1986	1985	5-year growth, %† (annual/ total)
Revenue		15,501	11,340	9,474	9,001	5,911	5,498	13/181
Net income		230	198	155	149	105	91	20/152
Earnings/share		1.85	1.63	1.29	1.23	1.02	.88	16/110
Dividend/share		.58	.50	.43	.37	.33	.28	16/107
Dividend yield, %	1.6	2.2	2.4	2.3	1.9	2.4	3.1	—/—
Stock price	43.75	31.00	22.84	18.50	17.83	18.58	11.33	21/173
P/E ratio	21.0	14.0	13.0	15.0	16.0	14.0	10.0	—/—
Book value/share		8.95	7.85	6.95	6.15	5.15	4.60	14/93

* Stock price as of 5–1–91
† 1985–90
Source: Company sources

13

WASTE MANAGEMENT, INC.

3003 Butterfield Road
Oak Brook, IL 60521
708-572-8800
Chairman: Dean L. Buntrock
President: Phillip B. Rooney

EARNINGS GROWTH	★ ★ ★ ★
STOCK GROWTH	★ ★ ★ ★
DIVIDEND YIELD	★
DIVIDEND GROWTH	★ ★ ★ ★
CONSISTENCY	★ ★ ★ ★
SHAREHOLDER PERKS	★ ★
NYSE—WMX	**19 points**

Over the past 20 years, America's waste disposal problems have continued to grow, and so has Waste Management's bottom line. With landfill space at a premium, and waste disposal standards becoming increasingly complex, demand for the company's services has never been stronger. The Chicago operation—whose very name has become synonymous with the gritty yet gainful business of waste control—is the world's largest provider of solid and hazardous waste management and recycling services.

Waste Management has established itself as one of America's most profitable companies, posting increased earnings and revenue every year since it went public in 1971. It has more than 450 subsidiaries and divisions in North America and a dozen more overseas. It manages 125 landfills in the U.S., with more under development, and provides trash collection services for 8 million homes and apartments and 700,000 commercial and industrial customers in some 600 North American communities.

The company's recently launched Recycle America program now serves more than a million households in 130 North American cities.

Waste Management has also been making swift progress in its waste-to-energy program. The company has about a dozen facilities in operation that convert landfill gases to electrical energy, with several more facilities now under construction. In all, the company's operating facilities provide the energy equivalent of about 2 million barrels of oil a year.

Through its Chemical Waste Management subsidiary (of which Waste Management owns 78 percent), the company provides disposal and treatment of hazardous chemical wastes and low-level radioactive wastes. Its Chem-Nuclear Systems subsidiary is the largest provider of low-level radioactive waste management services in the U.S.

Waste Management has also made major inroads into the medical waste business through its Medical Services subsidiary. The company operates nine medical waste incinerators.

The firm is also involved in several related ventures. It provides street-sweeping services for municipal and commercial customers, operates municipal water and wastewater treatment plants, markets Port-O-Let portable lavatories, and has built a thriving business in lawn care and pest control through the acquisition of several small regional firms.

Waste Management expanded its solid waste services beyond North America with several key acquisitions in Europe in 1989. The firm also has operations in Argentina, Australia, New Zealand and Saudi Arabia.

The company owns a 55 percent stake in Wheelabrator Technologies, which builds and operates waste-to-energy facilities. Wheelabrator, a publicly traded company, reported revenue in 1990 of about $1.2 billion.

EARNINGS GROWTH

Waste Management has enjoyed outstanding long-term growth. Over the past ten years, its earnings per share increased 728 percent (23.5 percent per year).

The company has about 43,000 employees and 30,000 shareholders.

STOCK GROWTH

The company has had exceptional stock price appreciation the past ten years, climbing 775 percent (24 percent per year) for the period.

Including reinvested dividends, a $10,000 investment in Waste Management stock at its closing stock price in 1980 would have grown to about $93,000 ten years later. Average annual compounded rate of return (including stock growth and reinvested dividends): about 25 percent.

DIVIDEND YIELD

Waste Management generally pays a modest yield, averaging about 1 percent over the past five years. During the most recent two-year rating period (fiscal 1990 and 1991) the stock paid an average annual current return (dividend yield) of 1.0 percent.

DIVIDEND GROWTH

Waste Management has raised its dividend for 16 consecutive years. The dividend jumped 227 percent (27 percent per year) from 1985 to 1990.

CONSISTENCY

The company has increased its revenue and earnings every year since it went public in 1971. Its price-earnings ratio of around 24 to 27 is quite a bit higher than most growing companies.

SHAREHOLDER PERKS

Waste Management offers its shareholders a good dividend reinvestment and voluntary stock purchase plan. There are no fees or commissions, and shareholders of record may purchase $25 to $2,000 per month in additional shares through the voluntary stock purchase plan.

CORPORATE RESPONSIBILITY

Although the company appears in some environmental funds because of its line of business, Waste Management's environmental record is spotty at best. According to its 1990 annual report, at the end of 1990, Waste Management, Inc. and its subsidiaries had been notified that they are potentially responsible parties in connection with 105 Superfund sites.

In Southeast Chicago, where the company operates the largest toxic waste incinerator in the U.S., whistle blowers from People for Community Recovery (PCR) and others prompted the federal EPA to investigate alleged violations at the incinerator. As a result, the company was fined $3.75 million (the largest fine ever against Waste Management) in May 1989 for falsification of monitoring records, illegal burning of PCBs and other violations. Waste Management officials claim that the violation was reported by the company itself and that the fines stemmed from the actions of two employees who were dismissed as a result.

Waste Management was voted one of the "Ten Worst Corporations of 1989" by the *Multinational Monitor* based on its environmental record and history of antitrust law violations. (Source: Council on Economic Priorities)

SUMMARY

Fiscal year ended: Dec. 31
(Revenue and net income in millions)

	1991*	1990	1989	1988	1987	1986	1985	5-year growth, %† (annual/ total)
Revenue		6,034	4,458	3,565	2,757	2,017	1,625	30/271
Net income		709	562	464	327	370	171	33/315
Earnings/share		1.49	1.22	1.02	.73	.88	.43	28/246
Dividend/share		.36	.29	.23	.18	.14	.11	27/227
Dividend yield, %	0.9	1.0	1.1	1.2	.9	1.1	1.6	—/—
Stock price	40.50	35.00	35.00	20.00	18.81	13.91	8.88	31/294
P/E ratio	27	24	22	18	27	23	17	—/—
Book value/share		8.00	5.88	4.82	4.16	3.67	2.79	23/187

* Stock price as of 5–1–91
† 1985–90
Source: Company sources

14

Liz claiborne, inc.

LIZ CLAIBORNE, INC.

1441 Broadway
New York, NY 10018
212-354-4900
Chairman: Jerome A. Chazen
President and Vice Chairman: Harvey Falk

EARNINGS GROWTH	★ ★ ★ ★
STOCK GROWTH	★ ★ ★ ★
DIVIDEND YIELD	★
DIVIDEND GROWTH	★ ★ ★ ★
CONSISTENCY	★ ★ ★
SHAREHOLDER PERKS	★ ★
NYSE—LIZ	**18 points**

Elisabeth Claiborne Ostenberg retired in 1989 as chairman, president and chief executive officer of the company that has carried her name since 1976. The femme phenom of fashion is most renowned for bringing style to the nine-to-five set. Claiborne officially entered the apparel business 14 years ago with her personal line of upbeat designer clothes for the largely untapped professional women's market. Over the next decade and a half, she fashioned the enterprise into the nation's third largest clothing manufacturer.

The company reports total sales of $1.7 billion a year. It has posted record earnings per share for 10 of its 11 years as a publicly traded corporation.

The New York-based manufacturer offers a wide range of women's clothing for both work and leisure. It is one of the nation's leading sportswear manufacturers. About 59 percent of the company's annual revenue is generated by its women's sportswear division. Better sportswear is offered under a variety of labels, including Claiborne, Lizsport, Lizwear, Elisabeth and Liz & Co. Its higher-end lines are offered under the Dana Buchman label.

Other areas include accessories (12 percent of revenue), dresses (10 percent), men's sportswear (9 percent), cosmetics (4 percent), outlet stores (3 percent), retail specialty stores (3 percent) and all other operations (5 percent).

The company began producing men's sportswear (under the Claiborne trademark) in 1985 and now sells well over $100 million a year in men's sportswear. It began offering women's fragrances in 1986 and men's fragrances in 1989.

The company opened its first retail specialty store in 1989 under the First Issue trademark and had 25 stores up and running by the end of the year. The company also operates more than 20 Liz Claiborne outlet stores that sell surplus or prior season's merchandise.

One of its newest retail concepts is the Liz Claiborne "store-within-a-store." Under the program, in about a dozen large department stores, Liz Claiborne products are allocated an area of approximately 7,000 square feet where its women's apparel is sold along with Liz accessories, shoes, hosiery, eyewear and fragrances.

EARNINGS GROWTH

Liz Claiborne has had exceptional growth throughout the 12 years for which public records are available. Over the past ten years, its earnings per share increased 2,863 percent (40.5 percent per year).

The company has about 5,400 employees and 16,000 shareholders.

STOCK GROWTH

The company has had explosive stock growth since its shares first became publicly traded in 1981. Over the past nine years, the stock has surged 2,900 percent (45 percent per year).

Including reinvested dividends, a $10,000 investment in Liz Claiborne stock at its average stock price in 1981 would have grown to about $310,000 nine years later. Average annual compounded rate of return (including stock growth and reinvested dividends): about 45.5 percent.

DIVIDEND YIELD

Liz pays a modest yield, averaging just under 1 percent over the past five years. During the most recent two-year rating period (fiscal 1990 and 1991) the stock paid an average annual current return (dividend yield) of 0.8 percent.

DIVIDEND GROWTH

Liz Claiborne has been paying a dividend for seven years, and has raised it each year. The dividend jumped 212 percent (26 percent per year) from 1985 to 1990.

CONSISTENCY

The company has had consistent growth, with increased earnings per share 11 of its 12 years, plus increased revenue and book value all 12 years. Its recent price-earnings ratio of about 18 is relatively high for Liz Claiborne, but well in line with other growing manufacturers.

SHAREHOLDER PERKS

Liz Claiborne offers a good dividend reinvestment and voluntary stock purchase plan. There are no fees or commissions, and shareholders of record may purchase $25 to $1,000 per month in additional shares through the voluntary stock purchase plan.

CORPORATE RESPONSIBILITY

The most obvious note to make about Liz Claiborne, Inc. is that its CEO, until her 1989 retirement, was the only woman among the three in the *Fortune* 1,000 who did not inherit her post. The company has built a reputation for promoting women into important posts, providing top-notch benefits for nonmanagerial women, and, through the Liz Claiborne Foundation, offering scholarship aid to up-and-coming designers.

The 1990 annual report lists more than 40 women among the 97 people in company management. This includes five women who head up divisions of the company (Claiborne, Inc. has a total of 12 divisions). There is one woman among the seven officers listed as senior management.

Liz Claiborne, Inc.'s many benefits and programs for nonmanagerial women are noteworthy because about 65 percent of the company's workforce is female. These benefits include flextime, job sharing, parental leave, child and dependent care assistance and profit sharing for nonunionized workers. (About half of Liz Claiborne, Inc., employees are union members.) The company offers 60 days leave at full pay for mothers of newborn and newly adopted children. A separate leave policy for fathers allots two weeks at full pay.

The company offers many on-site courses, including English as a second language and high school equivalency, as well as courses in management development. It also offers financial assistance for employees pursuing higher education. (Source: Council on Economic Priorities)

SUMMARY

Fiscal year ended: Dec. 31
(Revenue and net income in millions)

	1991*	1990	1989	1988	1987	1986	1985	5-year growth, %† (annual/ total)
Revenue		1,729	1,411	1,184	1,053	813	557	25/210
Net income		206	164	110	114	86	61	27/237
Earnings/share		2.37	1.87	1.26	1.32	1.00	0.71	27/233
Dividend/share		.25	.19	.18	.16	.12	.08	26/212
Dividend yield, %	0.8	0.8	0.8	1.1	0.6	0.6	0.6	—/—
Stock price	44.75	29.75	24.00	18.00	17.50	24.00	12.13	20/145
P/E ratio	18	11	12	13	21	20	14	—/—
Book value/share		8.60	6.95	5.22	4.10	2.85	1.90	35/352

* Stock price as of 5–1–91
† 1985–90
Source: Company sources

15

STANHOME, INC.

333 Western Avenue
Westfield, MA 01085
413-562-3631
Chairman: H.L. Tower
President and CEO: Alejandro Diaz Vargas

EARNINGS GROWTH	★ ★
STOCK GROWTH	★ ★ ★ ★
DIVIDEND YIELD	★ ★ ★
DIVIDEND GROWTH	★ ★ ★ ★
CONSISTENCY	★ ★
SHAREHOLDER PERKS	★ ★ ★
NYSE—STH	**18 points**

They are tiny figurines of cherub-faced boys and girls, smiling, praying, dancing and generally looking "precious." Together, they make up the core of Stanhome's Precious Moments collection, which, over the past 13 years, has soared to phenomenal success with the collectibles crowd.

The Precious Moments collection, introduced in 1978 by Stanhome's Enesco subsidiary, is the number one collectibles collection in the U.S. The company markets 7,000 separate items—brassware, tinware, music boxes, dolls and ornaments—sold in more than 50,000 retail outlets.

So popular are its porcelain dolls that more than half a million collectors have joined the company's Precious Moments collectors and birthday clubs.

In all, the company sells more than $300 million a year in giftware and collectibles (45 percent of the company's $676 million in annual revenue).

Stanhome also has two other key segments:

- Direct selling (46 percent of revenue). Stanhome operates a Tupperware-style direct sales venture for homemakers called the Famous Stanley Hostess Party Plan. The business, which is worldwide, has had excellent success in Europe. The company uses its direct selling network to market a wide line of household and personal care products including brooms, brushes, mops, pesticides, cosmetics, toiletries, weight loss products and vitamins.

Most of the sales are made through the Famous Stanley Hostess parties in which homemakers invite friends and neighbors to their homes for a demonstration of the products by an independent Stanley dealer. The sponsoring hostess generally receives prizes or gifts from the dealer for organizing the gathering.

- Direct response (9 percent of revenue). Through its Hamilton Group subsidiary (acquired in 1989), Stanhome sells a line of collectible plates, dolls and figurines directly to consumers through print advertising and direct mail. The company has expanded sales to Canada and the United Kingdom.

EARNINGS GROWTH

Stanhome has had strong growth for the past seven years. Over the past ten years, its earnings per share increased 265 percent (14 percent per year).

The company has about 4,000 employees and 4,000 shareholders.

STOCK GROWTH

The company has had exceptional stock growth the past ten years, increasing 667 percent (22.5 percent per year) during the period.

Including reinvested dividends, a $10,000 investment in Stanhome stock at its closing stock price in 1980 would have grown to about $120,000 ten years later. Average annual compounded rate of return (including stock growth and reinvested dividends): about 28 percent.

DIVIDEND YIELD

Stanhome generally pays a good dividend yield, averaging about 2.8 percent over the past five years. During the most recent two-year rating period (fiscal 1990 and 1991) the stock paid an average annual current return (dividend yield) of 2.7 percent.

DIVIDEND GROWTH

Stanhome has raised its dividend for seven consecutive years. The dividend jumped 176 percent (22 percent per year) from 1985 to 1990.

CONSISTENCY

The company has had seven consecutive years of increased earnings and book value per share. Its revenue has increased eight of the past ten years. Its price-earnings ratio of about 13 to 14 is somewhat low for a fast-growing company.

SHAREHOLDER PERKS

Stanhome offers a good dividend reinvestment and voluntary stock purchase plan for its shareholders. There are no fees or service charges, and shareholders may contribute $10 to $5,000 per quarter to the stock purchase plan.

The company also hands out a gift pack of product samples to all shareholders who attend the annual meeting.

SUMMARY

Fiscal year ended: Dec. 31
(Revenue and net income in millions)

	1991*	1990	1989	1988	1987	1986	1985	5-year growth, %† (annual/total)
Revenue		676	571	480	433	381	328	12/76
Net income		51	45	41	33	26	18	23/183
Earnings/share		2.54	2.23	1.96	1.58	1.17	.86	24/193
Dividend/share		.83	.71	.61	.47	.40	.30	22/176
Dividend yield, %	2.8	2.5	2.5	3.1	3.0	3.9	5.1	—/—
Stock price	32.75	33.75	25.875	18.375	15.00	11.375	7.1875	30/369
P/E ratio	14.0	13.3	12.2	9.4	10.0	8.7	6.9	—/—
Book value/share		10.82	8.80	7.93	6.68	5.31	5.17	18/109

* Stock price as of 5–1–91
† 1985–90
Source: Company sources

16

FIFTH THIRD BANK

FIFTH THIRD BANCORP

38 Fountain Square Plaza
Cincinnati, OH 45263
513-579-5300
Chairman: Clement L. Buenger
President and CEO: George A. Schaefer

EARNINGS GROWTH	★ ★
STOCK GROWTH	★ ★ ★ ★
DIVIDEND YIELD	★ ★ ★
DIVIDEND GROWTH	★ ★ ★
CONSISTENCY	★ ★ ★ ★
SHAREHOLDER PERKS	★ ★
OTC—FITB	18 points

Someone forgot to tell Fifth Third Bancorp that there's a recession under way in the banking industry. The Cincinnati-based bank holding company continues to open new branches, make acquisitions and find new ways to bolster its bottom line. Despite the turbulence in the savings business, Fifth Third has posted 17 consecutive years of record earnings per share.

Bancorp operates 214 branches in Ohio, Kentucky and Indiana, and it is constantly scouring the market for new acquisitions. One of its most recent purchases was a group of nine Ohio branch offices the company acquired from Chase Manhattan.

Not all of its growth comes as a result of acquisitions, however. The company has been opening about 20 to 25 branch offices per year for its existing systems.

Part of Fifth Third's success has been a matter of location. Its home base in the Midwest has not been affected by the housing and banking crisis as much as most other areas of the country.

Fifth Third has also introduced several new services designed to increase its customer base, including the company's popular "bank mart" concept. Bank marts are small, full-service, seven-day-a-week banking centers located in grocery stores. Since 1986, the company has opened 29 bank marts in Kroger stores in three states.

Fifth Third operates Midwest Payment Systems (MPS), which is one of the nation's largest processors of electronic funds transfers through automatic teller machines. MPS works with a wide range of ATM services, including Jeanie (an ATM system owned by MPS that operates with 108 participating financial institutions in the Ohio, Kentucky, Indiana area), CIRRUS, Plus System, VISA, MasterCard and Money Station.

Fifth Third got its unusual name early in this century as the result of a merger of the Fifth National and the Third National Banks of Ohio. "Bancorp" was added in the late 1970s. Fifth Third Bancorp officials now refer to the company as "Bancorp."

EARNINGS GROWTH

Fifth Third has enjoyed strong, consistent long-term growth. Over the past ten years, its earnings per share increased 270 percent (an average of 14 percent per year).

The company has 4,000 employees and 10,000 shareholders of record. Cincinnati Financial Corp. owns about 20 percent of the company stock, and Western-Southern Life Insurance Company owns 8 percent.

STOCK GROWTH

The company has had exceptional stock growth the past ten years, jumping 676 percent (23 percent per year) for the period.

Including reinvested dividends, a $10,000 investment in Fifth Third stock at its closing stock price in 1980 would have grown to about $110,000 ten years later. Average annual compounded rate of return (including stock growth and reinvested dividends): about 27 percent.

DIVIDEND YIELD

Fifth Third traditionally pays a good dividend yield, averaging about 3 percent over the past five years. During the most recent two-year rating period (fiscal 1990 and 1991) the stock paid an average annual current return (dividend yield) of 2.7 percent.

DIVIDEND GROWTH

Fifth Third has raised its dividend for more 15 consecutive years. The dividend increased 108 percent (18 percent per year) from 1985 to 1990.

CONSISTENCY

The company has had 17 consecutive years of increased earnings and book value per share. Its price-earnings ratio of 10 to 15 is in line with other banking organizations.

SHAREHOLDER PERKS

Fifth Third provides a dividend reinvestment and voluntary stock purchase plan for its shareholders of record. Shareholders, who are assessed a small fee not to exceed $3 per month for the voluntary cash purchase plan, may purchase $25 to $1,000 per month in additional shares.

SUMMARY

Fiscal year ended: Dec. 31
(Loans and net income in millions)

	1991*	1990	1989	1988	1987	1986	1985	5-year growth, %† (annual/total)
Loans¹		5,497	5,164	4,542	3,685	3,009	2,463	18/123
Net income		120	108	91	83	71	62	14/93
Earnings/share		3.07	2.79	2.41	2.22	1.92	1.73	12/77
Dividend/share		1.02	.90	.78	.68	.59	.49	18/108
Dividend yield, %	2.3	3.3	2.6	2.7	3.1	3.2	2.8	—/—
Stock price	47.25	33.00	37.00	30.17	23.00	20.22	19.04	12/73
P/E ratio	15.0	10.7	13.3	12.5	10.4	10.5	11.0	—/—
Book value/share		19.87	17.86	15.89	14.19	12.69	11 00	13/81

* Stock price as of 5–1–91
† 1985–90
1 net of unearned, gross of reserve
Source: Company sources

MERCK & COMPANY

126 E. Lincoln Avenue
P.O. Box 2000
Rahway, NJ 07065
201-574-4000
Chairman, President and CEO: P. Roy Vagelos

EARNINGS GROWTH	★ ★ ★
STOCK GROWTH	★ ★ ★
DIVIDEND YIELD	★ ★
DIVIDEND GROWTH	★ ★ ★ ★
CONSISTENCY	★ ★ ★ ★
SHAREHOLDER PERKS	★ ★
NYSE—MRK	**18 points**

Merck & Company has won the hearts of many admirers and saved the hearts of others. The Rahway, New Jersey manufacturer is one of the world's leading producers of cardiovascular medications.

Merck is arguably America's most celebrated corporation. It has been *Fortune*'s "most admired company" five years running (through 1991) and *Forbes*' "most innovative pharmaceutical company." It has made lists for being among the best managed (*Business Week* and *Business Month*), best for working women (*New Woman*), best for black employees (*Black Enterprise*) and best in public service (*Business Week*).

Over the years, Merck & Company has developed medications for everything from swollen prostates to dry-eye syndrome. In all, it produces about 150 different medications and vaccines. Merck has operations in about 20 countries and sells its products in more than 100 countries. Roughly half of its $6.6 billion in annual revenue comes from foreign sales.

Among the company's pharmaceutical sales, heart-related medications constitute its largest profit center, accounting for 34 percent of its total revenue. Its leading drug is Vasotec, a blood pressure medication that has been one of the world's hottest sellers, with revenues of about $1 billion a year.

The company reports that Vasotec is the only drug in its class proven to reduce the death rate of patients with severe heart failure.

Mevacor, a cholesterol-lowering medication, has also been a leading seller for Merck, setting a U.S. sales record for new drugs in 1987, the year it was released. A single daily dose of Mevacor reportedly helps normalize cholesterol levels even among patients with extremely high levels. The company says the development of Mevacor came after 35 years of study and testing. The drug was named one of *Fortune*'s products of the year in 1987.

In addition to its list of successful cardiovascular-related medications, Merck has developed some leading prescription drugs in several other fields. Antibiotics account for 15 percent of the company's revenues, anti-inflammatories account for 14 percent, ophthalmologicals (eye treatments) account for 7 percent, and ulcer medications and vaccines account for about 5 percent each. Merck has also been on the leading edge of AIDS research.

In addition to its human health focus, the company has a strong interest in animal medications (9 percent of revenue), and specialty chemicals for water treatment, oil field drilling, food processing, cleaning, disinfecting and skin care (8 percent of revenue).

One of the keys to Merck's success has been its outstanding research program. The company employs about 5,000 people in its research activities and spends about $900 million a year in research and development.

EARNINGS GROWTH

Merck has enjoyed outstanding sustained growth. Over the past ten years, its earnings per share increased 396 percent (an average of 17.5 percent per year).

The company has about 37,000 employees and 82,000 shareholders.

STOCK GROWTH

The company has had exceptional stock growth the past ten years, jumping 532 percent (20 percent per year) during the period.

Including reinvested dividends, a $10,000 investment in Merck stock at its closing stock price in 1980 would have grown to about $80,000 ten years later. Average annual compounded rate of return (including stock growth and reinvested dividends): about 23 percent.

DIVIDEND YIELD

Merck generally pays a good yield, averaging just over 2 percent over the past five years. During the most recent two-year rating period (fiscal 1990

and 1991) the stock paid an average annual current return (dividend yield) of 2.4 percent.

DIVIDEND GROWTH

Merck has raised its dividend for seven consecutive years. The dividend increased 322 percent (33 percent per year) from 1985 to 1990.

CONSISTENCY

The company has had nine straight years of increased earnings per share, and more than ten consecutive years of increased revenue and book value per share. Its price-earnings ratio of around 17 to 23 is higher than average, but not out of line considering the company's recent growth record.

SHAREHOLDER PERKS

Merck provides a good dividend reinvestment and voluntary stock purchase plan for its shareholders of record. There are no fees or service charges, and shareholders may contribute $25 to $5,000 per quarter to the stock purchase plan.

CORPORATE RESPONSIBILITY

Perhaps Merck's best-known expression of its corporate social responsibility occurred in 1988, when the company made a huge donation of the drug Ivermectin—used to treat river blindness disease—for use by people in West Africa, Guatemala and the Middle East. River blindness afflicts about 18 million people and threatens another 85 million. Merck also has a model affirmative action training program that has been widely imitated. Phase III, as the program is known, aims at making employees aware of sexism, racism and other barriers to equality by having managers lead small discussion groups.

Despite these positive programs, those concerned with animal testing may want to avoid Merck. In a recent update of a study they did in 1990, the Investor Responsibility Research Center found that, according to federal data, Merck is one of the largest corporate users of animals. In 1989, the company used 25,785 animals (excluding rats and mice) in testing at its in-house laboratories, an increase of almost 11 percent over 1988.

Although Merck was the first major U.S. pharmaceutical firm to sell its South African operations, the company does maintain licensing and distribution agreements in that country. (Source: Council on Economic Priorities)

SUMMARY

Fiscal year ended: Dec. 31
(Revenue and net income in millions)

	1991*	1990	1989	1988	1987	1986	1985	5-year growth, %† (annual/total)
Revenue		7,672	6,550	5,939	5,061	4,128	3,547	17/116
Net income		1,781	1,495	1,206	906	675	539	18/230
Earnings/share		4.56	3.78	3.05	2.23	1.62	1.26	23/185
Dividend/share		2.24	1.64	1.28	.82	.63	.53	33/322
Dividend yield, %		2.5	2.3	2.2	1.5	2.0	2.9	—/—
Stock price	111.50	90.00	78.00	58.00	52.80	41.28	34.00	30/276
P/E ratio	23	17	19	18	25	20	15	—/—
Book value/share		11.00	8.90	7.20	5.37	6.28	6.26	12/76

* Stock price as of 5–1–91
† 1985–90
Source: Company sources

18

BRISTOL-MYERS SQUIBB COMPANY

345 Park Avenue
New York, NY 10154-0037
212-546-4000
Chairman and CEO: Richard L. Gelb

EARNINGS GROWTH	★ ★
STOCK GROWTH	★ ★ ★
DIVIDEND YIELD	★ ★ ★
DIVIDEND GROWTH	★ ★ ★
CONSISTENCY	★ ★ ★ ★
SHAREHOLDER PERKS	★ ★ ★
NYSE—BMY	**18 points**

It's the name brands—Excedrin, Bufferin, Ban, Clairol, Windex, among others—that get the fanfare at Bristol-Myers Squibb. But the bulk of the company's business—some 65 percent of revenue—comes from its pharmaceutical and health care products divisions.

Its 1989 merger with Squibb made Bristol-Myers the nation's second largest pharmaceuticals manufacturer (behind Johnson & Johnson), with annual revenues of about $10 billion. The company has been a steady performer for many years, posting record earnings the past 17 consecutive years.

Bristol-Myers Squibb divides its operations into several key segments:

- Nonprescription health aids (18 percent of revenue). Along with Excedrin and Bufferin, the company makes Nuprin, No Doz, Ban deodorant, Comtrex cold medicine and a number of other over-the-counter remedies.
- Toiletries, beauty aids and household products (18 percent of revenue). Bristol-Myers makes Balsam, Clairol, Body on Tap, Final Net and Vitalis hair care products and Keri Lotion. Among its line of household products are Behold, Drano, Endust, Vanish bowl cleaner and Windex window cleaner.

- Pharmaceuticals (51 percent of revenue). Bristol-Myers produces the broadest range of anticancer agents in the U.S. It also produces drugs for the treatment of cardiovascular ailments, high cholesterol, infections, congestion and nervous disorders. The company is currently developing treatments for the AIDS virus.
- Medical products (14 percent of revenue). Bristol-Myers manufactures a wide range of medical products, including artificial hips and knees, implantable hearing devices, compression garments for burn treatments and a range of other patient care products. The firm also manufactures equipment used for implant and reconstructive surgery.

Bristol-Myers does a strong international business, bolstered by its merger with Squibb. The company markets its products in more than 100 countries. Foreign sales account for about 39 percent of its total revenue.

EARNINGS GROWTH

Bristol-Myers has had consistent long-term growth. Over the past ten years, its earnings per share increased 226 percent (an average of 12.5 percent per year).

The company has about 53,000 employees and 90,000 shareholders.

STOCK GROWTH

The company has had exceptional stock growth the past ten years, increasing 448 percent (18.5 percent per year) during the period.

Including reinvested dividends, a $10,000 investment in Bristol-Myers stock at its closing stock price in 1980 would have grown to about $67,000 ten years later. Average annual compounded rate of return (including stock growth and reinvested dividends): about 21 percent.

DIVIDEND YIELD

Bristol-Myers generally pays an excellent yield, which has averaged about 3.4 percent over the past five years. During the most recent two-year rating period (fiscal 1990 and 1991) the stock paid an average annual current return (dividend yield) of 3.4 percent.

DIVIDEND GROWTH

Bristol-Myers has raised its dividend for more than 18 consecutive years. The dividend increased 126 percent (18 percent per year) from 1985 to 1990.

CONSISTENCY

The company has had very consistent growth in its earnings and revenue, including 17 consecutive years of record earnings per share. Its price-earnings ratio of about 20 is fairly high for blue-chip companies.

SHAREHOLDER PERKS

Bristol-Myers sends all of its new shareholders of record a welcome packet of its consumer products, including small bottles of Excedrin, Bufferin, Nuprin, Clairol, Ban and Vanish bowl cleaner.

The company also offers its shareholders an excellent dividend reinvestment and voluntary stock purchase plan. There are no fees or commissions, and shareholders of record may purchase $10 to $2,500 per month in additional shares through the voluntary stock purchase plan.

CORPORATE RESPONSIBILITY

Since 1975, Bristol-Myers has published an equal opportunity report that describes recruiting and employment programs, minority purchasing, community involvement, initiatives for disabled employees and in-house career development programs for minorities and women. Bristol-Myers' merger with Squibb in 1989 has not affected this impressive initiative. The company's 1990 equal opportunity report indicates that 10.3 percent of its officials and managers are minorities, and nearly 25 percent are women.

The company maintains a presence in South Africa, employing 550 people and selling mainly pharmaceutical and health care products. In addition, Bristol-Myers Squibb is one of the infant formula makers under investigation by the Federal Trade Commission (FTC) for alleged price fixing. Infant formula price increases resulting from the alleged collusion are of particular concern because the formula is an important element of the federal food program for poor women and children. Bristol-Myers Squibb has an agreement with Gerber Products to market Gerber baby formula. The two companies have angered medical and consumer activist groups by marketing their formula directly to new mothers in their homes; in the past, they marketed to doctors only. According to the American Association of Pediatrics, this practice is "in direct opposition to the WHO (World Health Organization) code that prohibits direct advertising of breast milk substitutes to the consumer." Bristol-Myers Squibb is also involved in controversial marketing practices in the Third World. See the Abbott Laboratories entry for details.

Bristol-Myers Squibb is a major animal tester. The Investor Responsibility Research Center listed the company as one of "the top 50 companies reporting the highest number of animals used in research and testing in fiscal year 1989.'' According to the report, Bristol-Myers Squibb tested on 16,195 animals at its in-house laboratories, excluding rats and mice. However, the company has made significant efforts to reduce the number of animals it uses in testing. Bristol-Myers Squibb has given money to research nonanimal tests, including a grant of $800,000 to the Johns Hopkins Center for Alternatives to Animal Testing and a $150,000 grant to the United Kingdom's Fund for the Replacement of Animals in Medical Experiments (FRAME). The company's in-house investigative toxicology unit, founded in 1973, is devoted to finding in vitro (nonanimal) methods to screen new drugs for toxicity and was among the first of its kind in the industry. (Source: Council on Economic Priorities)

SUMMARY

Fiscal year ended: Dec. 31
(Revenue and net income in millions)

	1991*	1990	1989	1988	1987	1986	1985	5-year growth, %† (annual/total)
Revenue		10,300	9,189	8,558	7,558	6,620	5,849	12/76
Net income		1,748	1,440	1,254	1,068	785	732	19/138
Earnings/share		3.33	1.43	2.39	1.98	1.44	1.35	20/146
Dividend/share		2.12	2.00	1.68	1.40	1.06	.94	18/126
Dividend yield, %	3.1	3.6	3.5	3.7	2.9	2.8	3.2	—/—
Stock price	78.25	67.00	56.00	45.00	46.00	40.00	32.13	16/108
P/E ratio	22	18	18	15	19	18	15	—/—
Book value/share		11.00	9.67	9.49	8.88	7.84	7.30	9/50

* Stock price as of 5–1–91
† 1985–90
Source: Company sources

19

ABBOTT LABORATORIES

One Abbott Park Road
Abbott Park, IL 60064-3500
708-937-6100
Chairman and CEO: Duane L. Burnham
President and COO: Thomas R. Hodgson

EARNINGS GROWTH	★ ★ ★
STOCK GROWTH	★ ★ ★
DIVIDEND YIELD	★ ★
DIVIDEND GROWTH	★ ★ ★
CONSISTENCY	★ ★ ★ ★
SHAREHOLDER PERKS	★ ★ ★
NYSE—ABT	**18 points**

Abbott's knack for diagnosing deadly illnesses has kept the 103-year-old Chicago-area medical products manufacturer on a healthy roll, with 20 consecutive years of record sales, earnings and dividends.

Diagnostic equipment is Abbott's specialty. Its Vision desk-top blood analyzer tests for 25 different conditions on-site—printing out the results in minutes. Its AIDS antibody test was the first on the market in the world. The company has also been a forerunner in diagnostic testing for cancer, hepatitis, strep throat, high cholesterol and other conditions.

Foreign sales account for 35 percent of the company's $6.1 billion in annual revenue. The firm has sales or operations in 130 countries.

The company divides its operation into two segments:

- Pharmaceutical and nutritional products (49 percent of revenue). While most of Abbott's products are specialized for the medical profession, the company produces a handful of consumer products such as Murine eye drops, Selsun Blue dandruff shampoo, Tronolane hemorrhoid medication and Isomil and Similac nutritional formulas for infants.

Among its leading prescription medications are treatments for anxiety, epilepsy and hypertension. It is a leading producer of antibiotics and it manufactures a broad line of cardiovascular products, cough and cold formulas and vitamins.

The company also manufactures a stable of agricultural products such as plant growth regulators and herbicides. It is the world's leading supplier of biological pesticides.

- Hospital and laboratory (51 percent of revenue). Abbott is among the world leaders in the sale of diagnostic and testing equipment. It controls about 10 percent of the massive AIDS testing market worldwide and is a leader in the burgeoning (although controversial) drug testing market.

Abbott was founded in 1888 by Dr. Wallace C. Abbott, who began the business as a sideline to his physician's practice. Working in his small Chicago apartment, he made pills from the alkaloid of plants.

EARNINGS GROWTH

Abbott Labs has had strong, consistent long-term growth. Over the past ten years, its earnings per share increased 416 percent (an average of 18 percent per year).

The company has about 44,000 employees and 50,000 shareholders.

STOCK GROWTH

Abbott has had very good stock growth the past ten years, increasing 400 percent (17.5 percent per year).

Including reinvested dividends, a $10,000 investment in Abbott stock at its closing stock price in 1980 would have grown to about $62,000 ten years later. Average annual compounded rate of return (including stock growth and reinvested dividends): about 20 percent.

DIVIDEND YIELD

The company pays a fairly good yield, averaging about 2.5 percent over the past ten years. During the most recent two-year rating period (fiscal 1990 and 1991) the stock paid an average annual current return (dividend yield) of 2 percent.

DIVIDEND GROWTH

Abbott has raised its dividend every year since 1971. The dividend increased 140 percent (19 percent per year) from 1985 to 1990.

CONSISTENCY

The company has had very consistent growth in its earnings, revenue, operating income and book value per share, including 20 consecutive years of record sales and earnings. Its price-earnings ratio of about 18 is normal for growing U.S. companies.

SHAREHOLDER PERKS

Shareholders who attend the annual meeting receive a sampling of Abbott's consumer products such as Selsun Blue, Murine, Tronolane, an ice pack and a bottle of vitamins.

The company also provides a dividend reinvestment and voluntary stock purchase plan for its shareholders of record. There are no fees or commissions, but shareholders are limited to $10 to $1,000 per quarter in additional shares through the voluntary stock purchase plan.

CORPORATE RESPONSIBILITY

The Federal Trade Commission (FTC) has begun an investigation of Abbott and other infant formula makers for alleged price fixing. Infant formula price increases resulting from the alleged collusion are of particular concern because the formula is an important element of the federal food program for poor women and children.

Abbott has also been criticized for its formula marketing practices in the Third World. Although donating products to new mothers seems harmless enough, the health implications can be severe. If breast feeding is stopped in the early stages of postnatal care, the production of breast milk ceases. When the new mother leaves the hospital she becomes dependent on the costly formula and may mix it with contaminated water or dilute it to make it last longer. These practices often result in bottle baby disease, which can lead to death. In 1981, the World Health Organization and UNICEF set up an international code to regulate the marketing of breast milk substitutes. While the companies maintain that they are not in violation of this code, certain religious and activist groups disagree.

Abbott maintains operations in South Africa, has made no significant reductions in its animal testing, has a poor charitable giving record, and operates one of the largest Political Action Committees in the pharmaceutical industry with 1987–1988 contributions to political campaigns of over $200,000. (Source: Council on Economic Priorities)

SUMMARY

Fiscal year ended: Dec. 31
(Revenue and net income in millions)

	1991*	1990	1989	1988	1987	1986	1985	5-year growth, %†(annual/total)
Revenue		6,159	5,380	4,937	4,387	3,807	3,360	13/83
Net income		966	860	752	633	541	465	16/107
Earnings/share		2.22	1.93	1.67	1.39	1.16	.97	18/128
Dividend/share		.84	.70	.60	.50	.42	.35	19/140
Dividend yield, %	1.9	1.9	2.4	2.6	1.7	1.9	2.6	—/—
Stock price	51.38	45.00	34.00	24.00	24.13	22.81	17.09	20/150
P/E ratio	22	17	15	14	21	19	14	—/—
Book value/share		6.60	6.16	5.48	4.62	3.89	3.91	11/69

* Stock price as of 5-1-91
† 1985-90
Source: Company sources

WAL-MART

WAL-MART STORES, INC.
702 S.W. 8th Street
Bentonville, AR 72716
501-273-4000
Chairman: Sam M. Walton
President and CEO: David D. Glass

EARNINGS GROWTH	★ ★ ★ ★
STOCK GROWTH	★ ★ ★ ★
DIVIDEND YIELD	★
DIVIDEND GROWTH	★ ★ ★ ★
CONSISTENCY	★ ★ ★ ★
SHAREHOLDER PERKS	(no points)
NYSE—WMT	**17 points**

Almost since its inception in 1962, Wal-Mart has been the nation's fastest-growing department store chain. The company has never had a year in which it didn't set new records for sales and earnings. In fact, since 1969, when the company went public, its stock has outperformed every other major blue-chip stock in America.

Now Wal-Mart can claim one more distinction: it is the nation's most profitable retail chain. For the first time ever, Wal-Mart's 1990 profit of $1.3 billion (on total revenue of $33 billion) exceeded that of the long-established Sears, Roebuck & Co., which posted 1990 earnings of $902 million (on total revenue of $56 billion).

For most of its incredibly successful 29-year history, Wal-Mart has avoided the major markets, settling instead on smaller, less competitive rural markets. Most of the company's 1,500 stores are located in towns like Grapevine, Texas, and Blue Earth, Minnesota.

But now that Wal-Mart has begun to saturate America's heartland, the company is taking aim at major metropolitan markets. That's good news for urban area shoppers, bad news for Sears, K mart, Target and Wal-Mart's other discount competitors.

Wal-Mart opens a new store, on average, about every three days. In 1980 there were 330 Wal-Mart stores in 11 states. Now the 1,500-store chain stretches through 29 states.

In addition to its namesake stores, Wal-Mart also operates about 135 Sam's Wholesale Club stores, which tend to be located in larger metropolitan markets, and four Hypermart ★ USA stores, which are essentially an expanded version of Wal-Mart that includes both groceries and general merchandise. The company acquired 27 Wholesale Club stores in 1990 and sold its chain of 14 dot Discount Drug stores.

The first Wal-Mart store (called Wal-Mart Discount City) was opened in Rogers, Arkansas, in 1962 by Samuel M. Walton. By the time he opened his first Wal-Mart, Walton was already well schooled in the art of operating discount department stores. His original foray into retailing came in 1945, when he opened a Ben Franklin variety store franchise in Newport, Arkansas. He's been in the discount retailing business ever since and still serves as Wal-Mart's chairman of the board.

The company achieved its early success largely by opening stores in locations where there was little competition from other discounters. Its other key to success has been its low prices. Wal-Mart buys its merchandise in large volume and, through discount pricing, turns it over quickly, incurring a minimum of overhead in the process.

Aside from their rural locations, Wal-Mart stores are much the same as any other discount department stores. Each store sells a wide range of merchandise, including apparel, housewares, hardware, appliances, automotive accessories, cameras, toys, sporting goods, health and beauty aids, jewelry and other high-demand products.

EARNINGS GROWTH

Wal-Mart has enjoyed extraordinary long-term growth. Over the past ten years, its earnings per share increased 2,180 percent (37.5 percent per year).

The company has about 275,000 employees and 80,000 shareholders.

STOCK GROWTH

The company had had phenomenal stock price appreciation the past ten years, surging 3,233 percent (41.5 percent per year) during the period.

Including reinvested dividends, a $10,000 investment in Wal-Mart stock at its closing stock price in 1980 would have grown to about $350,000 ten years later. Average annual compounded rate of return (including stock growth and reinvested dividends): about 42 percent.

DIVIDEND YIELD

Wal-Mart generally pays a very modest yield, averaging about 0.5 percent over the past five years. During the most recent two-year rating period (fiscal 1990 and 1991) the stock paid an average annual current return (dividend yield) of 0.5 percent.

DIVIDEND GROWTH

Wal-Mart has raised its dividend every year since it began paying a dividend in 1977. The dividend jumped 250 percent (28 percent per year) from 1985 to 1990.

CONSISTENCY

The company has never had a year when it didn't set new records for sales and earnings since going public in 1969. Its price-earnings ratio of about 30 to 36 is among the highest of all U.S. blue-chip stocks, but then Wal-Mart has traditionally been among the fastest growing of all major companies.

SHAREHOLDER PERKS   (no points)

Wal-Mart does not offer a dividend reinvestment plan, nor does it offer any other shareholder perks.

CORPORATE RESPONSIBILITY

Wal-Mart frequently appears on socially screened portfolios. The company has been pushing its manufacturing partners to produce more environmentally responsible products. Letters to existing vendors and full-page advertisements in the *Wall Street Journal* and *USA Today* encouraged the marketing of green products and said that the company would feature environmentally improved products with special signs in its stores. Wal-Mart also asked manufacturers, employees and customers to pool their ideas to develop the program further. Today, more than 70 products are identified with flags that proclaim: "CFCs no longer used in this product"; "packaging made of recycled/recyclable material"; "nontoxic cleaner"; and "this product's packaging is refillable/reusable." Not every product identified by suppliers as environmentally friendly qualifies for the special labeling; for instance, Wal-Mart does not include controversial biodegradable plastics in the program. According to Thomas Rauh, director of retail consulting at Ernst & Young, "Wal-Mart is extremely influential and a consistent leader in the industry. It's really a kick in the pants to manufacturers for them to take up this [environmental] issue." (Source: Council on Economic Priorities)

SUMMARY

Fiscal year ended: Jan. 31*
(Revenue and net income in millions)

	1991**	1990	1989	1988	1987	1986	1985	5-year growth, %† (annual/total)
Revenue	32,602	25,811	20,649	15,960	11,909	8,451	6,400	31/286
Net income	1,291	1,076	837	628	450	327	270	32/295
Earnings/share	1.14	.95	.74	.56	.40	.29	.24	32/293
Dividend/share	.14	.11	.08	.06	.04	.04	.03	28/250
Dividend yield, %	0.4	0.6	0.5	0.4	0.4	0.5	0.5	—/—
Stock price	41.13	30.00	22.50	15.50	13.00	11.63	7.97	28/253
P/E ratio	36	21	20	28	28	23	20	—/—
Book value/share	4.50	3.50	2.66	2.00	1.50	1.14	.88	32/295

* Except stock price 12/31/85–90
** Stock price as of 5-1-91
† 1986–91
Source: Company sources

21

FOOD LION, INC.
2110 Executive Drive
P.O. Box 1330
Salisbury, NC 28145-1330
704-633-8250
Chairman, President and CEO: Tom E. Smith

EARNINGS GROWTH	★ ★ ★ ★
STOCK GROWTH	★ ★ ★ ★
DIVIDEND YIELD	★
DIVIDEND GROWTH	★ ★ ★ ★
CONSISTENCY	★ ★ ★ ★
SHAREHOLDER PERKS	(no points)
OTC—FDLN	**17 points**

When Food Lion's 69-year-old cofounder, Ralph W. Ketner, stepped down recently as chairman of the North Carolina-based grocery chain, the man tapped to succeed him was Tom E. Smith. If for no other reason, Smith was the logical choice because he had already held virtually every other job in the organization—from bag boy to CEO.

Smith, 49, a Tarheel native, started with the company while in high school in 1958, bagging groceries at the new Salisbury Food Town. After high school, he managed the store, using the money to pay his tuition at nearby Catawba College. Smith later became a buyer for Food Lion, was promoted to vice president of distribution and then to executive vice president. He was appointed president in 1981, CEO in 1986 and chairman in May 1990.

As CEO, Smith staked a strategy of rapid store expansion—a policy he promises to continue as chairman. Food Lion, which has nearly 800 stores primarily in the southeastern U.S., has been adding 100 to 125 new stores a year. One of its latest expansion drives is in the Dallas/Fort Worth area, where it is building 40 to 50 new supermarkets.

Most of Food Lion's stores are what you would call self-service, cash-and-carry, no-frills groceries. They offer no trading stamps, no pharmacy, no video rental, no floral boutique; just a solid selection of groceries with prices slashed to the nub. The low prices have helped Food Lion roll to 23 consecutive years of record sales and earnings. Scant margins and high volume have long been a trademark of the company, which champions the philosophy: "We'd rather make five fast pennies than one slow nickle."

Food Lion's basic format calls for conventional 25,000-square-foot groceries, which are relatively small compared with many of the new grocery superstores other chains are now building. By comparison, Albertson's (another *100 Best* entry) is now building stores of 40,000 to 73,000 square feet—two to three times the size of Food Lion's standard stores.

Although Food Lion is slowly moving to expand its offerings (and increase its per store margins), the real draw for consumers continues to be its low prices. The company has been able to trim costs even more by operating its own truck fleet and building its own food warehouse distribution centers in North and South Carolina, Virginia, Tennessee, Florida and Pennsylvania.

Founded as Food Town in the 1950s, the firm's rapid growth has been legend. When the stock was first issued in 1957, its value was $10 a share; $1,000 would buy 100 shares. Food Lion trades now at about $18 a share, but the stock has gone through so many splits over the years that by 1991 that original 100 shares would have ballooned to 1.3 million shares, and the original $1,000 investment would be worth about $23 million.

EARNINGS GROWTH

Food Lion has had outstanding long-term growth. Over the past ten years, its earnings per share increased 980 percent (27 percent per year).

The company has about 45,000 employees and 14,000 shareholders. Its stock is evenly divided between Class A (nonvoting) and Class B (voting). Class B stock generally trades about 5 to 10 percent higher than Class A stock. The Belgian supermarket company, Establissements Delhaize Freres et Cie, S.A., controls about 45 percent of all Food Lion stock.

STOCK GROWTH

The company has had exceptional stock growth the past ten years, increasing 2,600 percent (39 percent per year) for the period (B stock).

Including reinvested dividends, a $10,000 investment in Food Lion stock at its closing stock price in 1980 would have grown to about $280,000 ten years later. Average annual compounded rate of return (including stock growth and reinvested dividends): about 39.5 percent.

DIVIDEND YIELD

Food Lion has traditionally paid a very modest yield, averaging well under 1 percent over the past five years. During the most recent two-year rating period (fiscal 1990 and 1991) the stock paid an average annual current return (dividend yield) of 0.9 percent.

DIVIDEND GROWTH

Food Lion generally raises its dividend every year. The dividend leaped 1,200 percent (68 percent per year) from 1985 to 1990.

CONSISTENCY

The company has had 20 consecutive years of record earnings per share, book value per share and revenue. Its recent price-earnings ratio of about 30 is very high, even for a quickly growing company.

SHAREHOLDER PERKS   (no points)

The company offers no dividend reinvestment plan, nor does it offer any other shareholder perks.

CORPORATE RESPONSIBILITY

The United Food and Commercial Workers Union (UFCW) filed a class action suit against Food Lion in 1990, accusing the supermarket chain of cheating thousands of nonunion workers out of health and retirement benefits. The UFCW alleged that Food Lion executives deliberately fired workers just before they had been working long enough to be vested in or eligible for full benefits from the company's $200 million profit sharing plan. According to the UFCW, only 81 of the company's 21,000 workers were vested in the profit sharing plan. The case is still pending with the National Labor Relations Board.

Back in 1984, the National Association for the Advancement of Colored People (NAACP) targeted 22 companies in the Southeast, including Food Lion, that it wanted to sign a "fair share" agreement. The companies were asked to increase the numbers of minorities in management and to do more business with minority-owned businesses. According to Fred Rasheed, who negotiated for the NAACP, "Food Lion was the only supermarket chain that wouldn't even meet with us until we staged a two-month boycott." Food Lion eventually agreed to become part of the fair share program. (Source: Council on Economic Priorities)

SUMMARY

Fiscal year ended: Dec. 31
(Revenue and net income in millions)

		1991*	1990	1989	1988	1987	1986	1985	5-year growth, %† (annual/total)
Revenue			5,584	4,717	3,815	2,954	2,407	1,866	25/199
Net income			173	140	113	86	62	48	29/260
Earnings/share[1]			.54	.43	.35	.27	.19	.15	29/260
Dividend/share[1]			.13	.10	.07	.04	.02	.01	68/1,200
Dividend yield, %	A	0.8	1.00	.92	.75	.33	.35	.27	—/—
	B	0.8	.96	.89	.70	.31	.33	.28	—/—
Stock price	A	18.38	13.00	10.88	9.38	12.00	5.63	3.67	28/254
Stock price	B	18.75	13.50	11.25	10.00	12.88	6.06	3.63	30/271
P/E ratio	A	32	24.07	25.29	26.78	44.44	29.63	24.47	—/—
P/E ratio	B	33	25.00	26.16	28.57	47.70	31.89	24.20	—/—
Book value/share			2.08	1.67	1.34	1.06	.83	.65	26/220

* Stock price as of 5–1–91
† 1985–90
1 Amounts are based upon the weighted average number of the Class A and Class B common shares outstanding.
Source: Company sources

ALBERTSON'S, INC.
250 Parkcenter Boulevard
P.O. Box 20
Boise, ID 83726
208-385-6200
Chairman and CEO: Gary G. Michael
President and COO: John B. Carley

EARNINGS GROWTH	★ ★ ★
STOCK GROWTH	★ ★ ★ ★
DIVIDEND YIELD	★ ★
DIVIDEND GROWTH	★ ★ ★
CONSISTENCY	★ ★ ★ ★
SHAREHOLDER PERKS	★
NYSE—ABS	**17 points**

In an age of grocery superstores, Albertson's is making small potatoes of the competition. The company's no-frills discount "warehouses" are a full 73,000 square feet. That's three times the size of most grocery stores, and twice the size of many grocery superstores.

Albertson's new warehouse stores are part of a trend in the grocery business—where acres of groceries coexist with floral centers, pharmacies, video rentals and full-scale bakeries. The move to bigger stores helped the Boise, Idaho-based grocer raise its sales and earnings in 1990 for the 21st consecutive year.

Albertson's conventional stores average 27,000 square feet—nearly three times the size of the original Albertson's grocery, which founder Joe Albertson opened in Boise in 1939. Albertson's stores also come in three other sizes, including its 42,000-square-foot superstores, its 58,000-square-foot combination stores and its 73,000-square-foot discount warehouse stores.

Of the company's 531 stores, 157 are conventional groceries, 200 are superstores, 140 are combination stores and 33 are warehouse stores.

Most Albertson's stores are located in 15 western states, although it also has some stores in Florida and Louisiana. Albertson's is strongest on the West Coast. Nearly half its stores are located in California, Washington and Oregon.

The company is now the sixth largest food and drug chain in the United States. Albertson's consistent, sustained growth may be due in part to its commitment to updating, remodeling and expanding its stable of stores.

In 1990, the company began a five-year $1.9 billion expansion and re-modeling program. Plans call for the opening of 230 new stores, with primary emphasis on California, Texas and Arizona. The company will also remodel, and in some cases expand, 175 of its existing stores.

Albertson's pins much of its growth not only on its expanding store base, but also on its expanding product base. In addition to its standard grocery offerings, many of its larger stores have five special service departments:

- Pharmacy. Low-cost pharmacies are available in more than 200 Albertson's stores.
- Lobby departments. Many of its stores provide customer services such as money orders, bus passes, lottery tickets, stamps, camera supplies, film developing and video rental.
- Service deli. Delicatessens in 441 of its stores offer take-home foods, meats, cheeses, fresh salads and fried chicken. Salad bars have been added in about 200 Albertson's stores.
- Service fish and meat departments. Most of the larger Albertson's stores have specialty departments with an array of fresh fish, shell fish, premium cuts of meat and semiprepared items such as stuffed pork chops.
- Bakeries. The company is moving towards a partial self-service concept in which customers may pick out freshly baked breads, pastries, cakes and cookies on their own (or request personal service).

EARNINGS GROWTH

Albertson's has enjoyed strong, consistent long-term growth. Its earnings per share increased 400 percent (an average of 17.5 percent per year) over the past ten years.

Albertson's has about 55,000 employees and 11,500 shareholders.

STOCK GROWTH

The company has had exceptional stock growth the past ten years, increasing 1,380 percent (31 percent per year) for the period.

Including reinvested dividends, a $10,000 investment in Albertson's stock at its closing stock price in 1980 would have grown to about $180,000 ten years later. Average annual compounded rate of return (including stock growth and reinvested dividends): about 33.5 percent.

DIVIDEND YIELD

The company generally pays a modest yield, averaging about 1.8 percent over the past five years. During the most recent two-year rating period (fiscal 1990 and 1991) the stock paid an average annual current return (dividend yield) of 1.5 percent.

DIVIDEND GROWTH

Albertson's has raised its dividend every year for 19 consecutive years. The dividend increased 152 percent (20 percent per year) from 1986 to 1991.

CONSISTENCY

The company has had very consistent growth in its earnings, revenue, operating income and book value per share, including 22 consecutive years of record sales and earnings. Its recent price-earnings ratio of about 18 is normal for growing U.S. companies.

SHAREHOLDER PERKS

Shareholders who attend the annual meeting receive some of Albertson's private label groceries, including canned vegetables, napkins, paper towels and other household products.

CORPORATE RESPONSIBILITY

Albertson's has sent letters to 13,000 suppliers asking them to reduce packaging waste. It also recycles its plastic bags and shipping shrink wrap. It sells reusable bags, offers rebates to customers using their own bags and has a corporate officer who focuses solely on environmental affairs.

The company has one woman, Kathryn Albertson, on its 14-member board of directors. (Source: Council on Economic Priorities)

SUMMARY

Fiscal year ended: Jan. 31*
(Revenue and net income in millions)

	1991**	1990	1989	1988	1987	1986	1985	5-year growth, %† (annual/total)
Revenue	8,219	7,423	6,773	5,869	5,380	5,060	4,736	10/62
Net income	234	197	163	125	100	85	80	22/175
Earnings/share	1.75	1.47	1.22	.94	.75	.64	.61	22/173
Dividend/share	.48	.40	.28	.24	.21	.19	.17	20/152
Dividend yield, %	1.3	1.6	1.7	1.8	2.0	2.5	2.6	—/—
Stock price	45.63	37.00	28.00	19.00	12.68	10.75	8.13	35/348
P/E ratio	18	17	14	14	14	12	11	—/—
Book value/share	8.15	6.90	6.00	5.00	4.45	3.90	3.45	19/136

* Except stock price Dec. 31, 1985–90
** Stock price as of 5-1-91
† 1986–91 Except stock price 1985–90
Source: Company sources

23

The Valspar Corporation

VALSPAR CORP.

1101 Third Street South
Minneapolis, MN 55415
612-332-7371
Chairman and CEO: Angus Wurtele
President: Robert E. Pajor

EARNINGS GROWTH	★ ★ ★ ★
STOCK GROWTH	★ ★ ★ ★
DIVIDEND YIELD	★ ★
DIVIDEND GROWTH	★ ★ ★
CONSISTENCY	★ ★ ★ ★
SHAREHOLDER PERKS	(no points)
ASE—VAL	**17 points**

Take a splash of latex, a dab of acrylics, a stroke of stain and a canvas that covers the world, and you've got a fair portrait of Valspar Corp.

Valspar is one of the five largest manufacturers of paints and coatings in North America. The company, now headquartered in Minneapolis, has 24 manufacturing plants in the U.S. and Canada, and licensees throughout the world.

Through an aggressive policy of acquisitions, Valspar has acquired a patchwork of about 50 smaller paints and coatings companies over the past 20 years and blended them into a well-integrated corporate operation.

Valspar's consumer group is the largest of its four product segments, accounting for 32 percent of the firm's $571 million in annual revenue. Valspar's latex and oil-based paints, wood stains, industrial maintenance coatings and marine coatings are sold primarily to do-it-yourself consumers through home centers, paint and wallcovering stores, hardware stores, farm stores and lumberyards.

The company's major consumer brands include Colony, Enterprise, Valspar, McCloskey, Minnesota, Masury and Magicolor. It also supplies the paint for private label brands such as Target, Cenex, Courtesy and Lowe's.

Valspar's other three segments include:

- Industrial metal coatings (22 percent of total revenue). The company produces a variety of industrial coatings such as high solids, epoxies, acrylics, electrocoats and powders for use by manufacturers in the appliance, automotive, railcar, farm, industrial, construction and fabricated metal products industries.
- Special products (22 percent of revenue). The company produces resins and emulsions for coatings, heavy-duty maintenance and marine coatings, high-performance floor coatings for industrial and commercial use, colorants and colorant systems. Major markets include oil structures, utilities, nuclear plants, paper mills, food processing and pharmaceutical plants waste facilities and the marine industry.
- Packaging (21 percent of revenue). Valspar makes coatings for food and beverage cans, and flexible packaging materials (paper, paperboard, plastic film and aluminum foil).

Valspar traces its origins to a Boston paint shop called Color and Paint, which opened in 1806. That business eventually became Valentine & Co., which introduced a line of "Valspar" quick-drying varnishes and stains in 1906. Valspar was touted as "the varnish that won't turn white." Its claim to fame was a boiling water test that Valspar-varnished woods could endure with no apparent ill effects.

EARNINGS GROWTH

Valspar has enjoyed exceptional long-term growth. Over the past ten years, its earnings per share jumped 545 percent (20.5 percent per year).

The company has about 2,500 employees and 2,000 shareholders.

STOCK GROWTH

The company has had outstanding stock price appreciation the past ten years, soaring 1,500 percent (31 percent per year) during the period.

Including reinvested dividends, a $10,000 investment in Valspar stock at its closing stock price in 1980 would have grown to about $180,000 ten years later. Average annual compounded rate of return (including stock growth and reinvested dividends): about 33.5 percent.

DIVIDEND YIELD

Valspar generally pays a fairly modest yield, averaging almost 1.5 percent over the past five years. During the most recent two-year rating period (fiscal 1990 and 1991) the stock paid an average annual current return (dividend yield) of 1.5 percent.

DIVIDEND GROWTH

Valspar has raised its dividend for 12 consecutive years. The dividend increased 172 percent (22 percent per year) over the five-year period from 1985 to 1990.

CONSISTENCY

The company has had 16 consecutive years of record earnings and book value per share. It has had increased sales eight of the past ten years. Its price-earnings ratio of around 14 to 19 is well in line with other growing manufacturers.

SHAREHOLDER PERKS   (no points)

Valspar provides no dividend reinvestment plan, nor does it offer any other special perks for its shareholders.

SUMMARY

Fiscal year ended: Oct. 31*
(Revenue and net income in millions)

	1991**	1990	1989	1988	1987	1986	1985	5-year growth, %† (annual/total)
Revenue		571	528	482	449	348	350	10/63
Net income		27	23	18	18	15	12	17/125
Earnings/share		2.45	2.08	1.63	1.61	1.26	.97	20/152
Dividend/share		.52	.44	.40	.32	.26	.22	22/172
Dividend yield, %	1.4	1.5	1.6	1.6	1.1	1.4	1.9	—/—
Stock price	43.50	36.00	36.00	24.00	25.63	21.25	15.25	22/176
P/E ratio	19	14	13	16	18	15	12	—/—
Book value/share		11.84	10.22	8.92	7.70	6.41	6.30	14/88

 * Except stock price Dec. 31, 1985–90
** Stock price as of 5–1–91
† 1985–90
Source: Company sources

24

ALBERTO CULVER

ALBERTO-CULVER COMPANY

2525 Armitage Avenue
Melrose Park, IL 60160
708-450-3000
Chairman and CEO: Leonard H. Lavin
President: Howard B. Bernick

EARNINGS GROWTH	★ ★ ★ ★
STOCK GROWTH	★ ★ ★ ★
DIVIDEND YIELD	★
DIVIDEND GROWTH	★ ★ ★
CONSISTENCY	★ ★ ★ ★
SHAREHOLDER PERKS	★
NYSE—ACV	**17 points**

Alberto-Culver has turned hair care into a multinational initiative. The company's growing line of VO5 products now tint, tease, clean, curl and condition hair in more than 100 countries worldwide.

The hair care market has kept the Chicago manufacturer's sales and earnings growing steadily. Annual revenue is up to nearly $800 million, and its earnings per share has increased 14 of the past 15 years.

But unlike many of the past decade's high flying young companies, Alberto-Culver has achieved most of its growth by developing its product base from within, not by pursuing a steady diet of acquisitions. The company has not made an acquisition since 1983, when it bought Indola, an Italian professional hair products manufacturer. Company chairman Leonard Lavin says he wouldn't rule out further acquisitions, "but only when the price is right and the business fits. We've made some mistakes and have learned some lessons. If we aren't entirely confident in our ability to manage and grow the target company's business, or if the asking price goes awry, we go away."

Unquestionably, Alberto-Culver's most successful acquisition was its 1969 purchase of the Sally Beauty Company. At the time, the company operated ten Texas-based beauty products stores for barbers and stylists. Alberto-Culver has since opened nearly 900 Sally shops throughout the U.S. and Great Britain. The Sally stores now account for 41 percent of Alberto-Culver's total revenue.

But the company's leading segment continues to be mass marketed personal use products, which generate 47 percent of revenue. Among its leading products are its Alberto VO5 line of shampoos and conditioners, Bold Hold, Consort men's hair spray, Clean 'n Gentle and TCB hair care products for Blacks and Hispanics.

The company also produces a line of foods and household products including Molly McButter, Mrs. Dash, Baker's Joy, Static Guard and Kleen Guard.

Alberto-Culver's institutional products segment accounts for 12 percent of sales. The company sells hair care products for professionals through beauty and barber distributors. It also sells a line of specialty foods to restaurants and institutions.

EARNINGS GROWTH

Alberto-Culver has enjoyed accelerated growth over the past decade. Its earnings per share increased 584 percent over the most recent ten-year period (an average of 21 percent per year).

The company has about 5,600 employees.

Alberto-Culver lists two stocks on the New York Stock Exchange, A and B. Both stocks have the same par value and pay the same dividend, but the B stock, which has ten times the voting clout of the A shares, tends to trade as much as 20 to 30 percent higher than the A stock. Analysts and company officials generally recommend the A stock because of its discount. "The only logical explanation we can think of for the spread in price between our A and B stocks," says company spokesman Steve Crews, "is that our B stock is listed on the Standard & Poor's 500, so it's included in a lot of index funds. In fact, the 11 largest B stock shareholders are index funds."

STOCK GROWTH

The company has had exceptional stock price appreciation. Over the past ten years, the stock has 1,400 percent (30 percent per year) for the period.

Including reinvested dividends, a $10,000 investment in Alberto-Culver stock at its closing stock price in 1980 would have grown to about $165,000 ten years later. Average annual compounded rate of return (including stock growth and reinvested dividends): about 32.5 percent.

DIVIDEND YIELD

Alberto-Culver generally pays a modest yield, averaging about 1 percent over the past five years. During the most recent two-year rating period (fiscal 1990 and 1991) the stock paid an average annual current return (dividend yield) of 0.9 percent.

DIVIDEND GROWTH

Alberto-Culver has raised its dividend most years. The dividend increased 100 percent (15 percent per year) from 1985 to 1990.

CONSISTENCY

The company has had increased revenue, book value and earnings per share 14 of the past 15 years. Its price-earnings ratio of about 18 is normal for growing U.S. companies.

SHAREHOLDER PERKS

Alberto-Culver provides no dividend reinvestment plan, but it does offer a nice gift package for shareholders who attend the annual meeting. The package includes VO5 shampoos, moisturizers, mousses and other hair treatments, along with a selection of the company's food products.

CORPORATE RESPONSIBILITY

The Council on Economic Priorities reports that Alberto-Culver has not been very open concerning its deeds in the area of social responsibility, although some information was available. Women have advanced to high levels at the company. Two of the company's nine board members are women as are four of the company's top 23 officers.

Although it is difficult to rate the company's overall environmental performance, certain incidents are noteworthy. Alberto-Culver has been involved in what some environmentalists are calling "eco-pornography." The company's Alberto VO5 hair spray is labelled as "ozone friendly." Alberto-Culver says that this term means that the product contains no chlorofluorocarbons (CFCs), which deplete the earth's protective ozone layer. Although the label is new, the product is not. Alberto-Culver, along with all commercial aerosol product manufacturers, was forced to stop using CFCs by a federal ban in 1978. Not only is the company's timing suspect, but the substituted materials—hydrocarbon propellants—are as well. These propellants are known to exacerbate smog pollution in many urban areas. The problem is so bad in Southern California that the California Air Resources Board ruled in 1989 that deodorant aerosols could not contain hydrocarbons known to contribute to smog. (Source: Council on Economic Priorities)

SUMMARY

Fiscal year ended: Sept. 30*
(Revenue and net income in millions)

	1991**	1990	1989	1988	1987	1986	1985	5-year growth, %† (annual/total)
Revenue		796	717	605	515	435	387	15/105
Net income		35	29	25	18	13	8	34/337
Earnings/share		1.30	1.13	.92	.64	.53	.34	31/282
Dividend/share		.20	.18	.15	.12	.11	.10	15/100
Dividend yield, %	0.9	0.8	0.9	1.1	1.1	1.1	2.3	—/—
Stock price	25.30	33.25	22.31	18.38	10.38	9.75	7.34	35/353
P/E ratio	19	18	18	15	17	17	12	—/—
Book value/share		8.10	6.10	5.15	4.75	4.20	3.00	22/170

  * Except stock price Dec. 31, 1985–90
 ** Stock price as of 5–1–91
 † 1985–90
Source: Company sources

25

UNIVERSAL FOODS CORP.

433 E. Michigan Street
Milwaukee, WI 53202
414-271-6755
Chairman, President and CEO: Guy A. Osborn

EARNINGS GROWTH	★ ★
STOCK GROWTH	★ ★ ★ ★
DIVIDEND YIELD	★ ★
DIVIDEND GROWTH	★ ★ ★
CONSISTENCY	★ ★ ★
SHAREHOLDER PERKS	★ ★ ★
NYSE—UFC	**17 points**

Universal Foods, with sales of less than $1 billion a year, may be small potatoes compared with many of its multibillion dollar competitors in the foods industry. But the Milwaukee-based manufacturer is no small fry in the fried potatoes business. The company's new seasoned, battered Crispy Q and Curly Q frozen fries have suddenly caught fire, turning Universal into the world leader in the fast-growing specialty french fries market.

Universal first entered the frozen fries business in 1985, with the acquisition of Idaho Frozen Foods. It has since developed its popular Curly Q and Crispy Q frozen fries, which quickly became its fastest-growing segment. Frozen fries now account for nearly 40 percent of Universal's annual revenue. About 85 percent of its sales are to the food services industry (restaurants and institutions), and the other 15 percent to the retail trade.

Universal has operations in about 20 countries around the world. The company has been a steady performer in recent years with earnings per share increases nine of the past ten years. It has annual revenue of about $840 million.

In addition to its frozen foods division, Universal divides its business into four other key segments:

- Flavors (19 percent of revenue). Thanks to some recent acquisitions, Universal has become the leading U.S. producer of beverage and dairy flavors. It has also begun to expand into the food flavors segment.

- Colors (10 percent of revenue). With its acquisition in 1984 of Warner-Jenkinson, Universal became the leading producer of food colors in North America. Its products are used for soft drinks, bakery products, processed foods, confections, pet foods, alcoholic beverages and pharmaceuticals.
- Dehydrated products (9 percent of sales). Universal produces dehydrated onion and garlic, chili powder, chili pepper, paprika, and dehydrated vegetables such as parsley, celery and spinach. Its customers are primarily food manufacturers.
- Yeast (25 percent of sales). Universal is the leading supplier of baker's yeast to commercial bakeries. It is also establishing a growing presence in the pizza yeast market. Its yeast is sold under the Red Star label in dry, compressed and liquid form.

EARNINGS GROWTH

Universal has enjoyed strong, steady long-term growth. Over the past ten years, its earnings per share increased 322 percent (15.5 percent per year).

The company has about 6,000 employees and 5,500 shareholders.

STOCK GROWTH

The company has had exceptional stock growth the past ten years, increasing 818 percent (25 percent per year) for the period.

Including reinvested dividends, a $10,000 investment in Universal stock at its closing stock price in 1980 would have grown to about $135,000 ten years later. Average annual compounded rate of return (including stock growth and reinvested dividends): about 30 percent.

DIVIDEND YIELD

Universal generally pays a good yield, averaging about 2.5 percent over the past five years. During the most recent two-year rating period (fiscal 1990 and 1991) the stock paid an average annual current return (dividend yield) of 2.3 percent.

DIVIDEND GROWTH

Universal has raised its dividend for five consecutive years. The dividend increased 112 percent (16 percent per year) from 1985 to 1990.

CONSISTENCY

The company has had increased earnings per share nine of the past ten years, and increased book value per share for the past 16 consecutive years.

Its price-earnings ratio of about 18 is normal for growing food production companies.

SHAREHOLDER PERKS

Universal offers an excellent dividend reinvestment plan, providing shareholders with a 5 percent discount off the market price for all dividend reinvestment stock purchases. Shareholders may also make cash contributions of $25 to $1,000 a month to buy additional shares (at full share price).

At its annual meeting, the company distributes products such as Curly Qs, Red Star Yeast, food flavorings and other foods to all of its shareholders.

CORPORATE RESPONSIBILITY

In the book *Shopping for a Better World,* Universal Foods appears on the Council on Economic Priorities' dishonor roll. The company received bottom ratings on four of the 12 issues rated by CEP. Universal has a poor record for advancing both women and minorities, has no significant programs designed to benefit the communities in which it operates and offers working parents only minimal family-related benefits. (Source: Council on Economic Priorities)

SUMMARY

Fiscal year ended: Sept. 30*
(Revenue and net income in millions)

	1991**	1990	1989	1988	1987	1986	1985	5-year growth, %† (annual/total)
Revenue		839	837	721	711	604	493	11/70
Net income		48	40	28	25	15	17	23/182
Earnings/share		1.90	1.60	1.23	.93	.82	.75	20/153
Dividend/share		.68	.53	.41	.36	.34	.32	16/112
Dividend yield, %	2.0	2.5	2.4	3.3	3.1	3.6	4.3	—/—
Stock price	37.25	32.13	23.88	23.17	11.56	10.44	8.82	29/264
P/E ratio	18.0	14.5	14.0	11.9	12.8	11.5	9.9	—/—
Book value/share		9.59	8.12	7.21	6.87	6.27	5.52	12/73

* Except stock price Dec. 31, 1985–90
** Stock price as of 5–1–91
† 1985–90
Source: Company sources

BEMIS COMPANY, INC.
625 Marquette Avenue
Minneapolis, MN 55402
612-340-6000
Chairman: Howard Curler
President and CEO: John H. Roe

EARNINGS GROWTH	★ ★
STOCK GROWTH	★ ★ ★ ★
DIVIDEND YIELD	★ ★
DIVIDEND GROWTH	★ ★ ★ ★
CONSISTENCY	★ ★ ★
SHAREHOLDER PERKS	★ ★
NYSE—BMS	**17 points**

With roots that extend back more than 150 years, Bemis is one of America's oldest packaging producers. It began with grain bags in 1858 and has evolved to shrink wraps, double-play bags, plastic pouches and coated cardboard boxes.

Packaging products (and packaging machinery) account for 72 percent of the company's $1.1 billion in annual revenue. The range of packaging products Bemis produces is almost as broad as the foods business itself.

The Minneapolis manufacturer produces the packaging for paper towels and toilet tissues, soap, cereals, chips, cheese, coffee, candies, cookies, crackers, cake mix, meat, milk and molded microwavable trays for frozen foods.

Bemis also manufactures packaging machinery for the foods industry to use on-site to package tissues, candy, frozen vegetables, meats, fertilizer, insulation materials, detergent, pharmaceuticals and other products.

Bemis has more than 30 manufacturing plants in 18 states and two foreign countries that specialize in wrapping foods in flexible plastic or paper packages. Among its specialties are Monofilm packaging, which includes shrink wraps and stretchfilms, printed roll stock and molded plastic containers, and multiwall and small paper bags for seed, feed, fertilizer, flour, cement, chemicals, sugar, rice and pet food.

The company's specialty coated and graphics products group accounts for 28 percent of total revenue. Bemis has about 16 manufacturing plants that produce specially coated and printed products for the packaging industry, including pressure-sensitive labels for product containers, adhesive products used for mounting and bonding, roll labels and laminates for graphics and photography. The company also produces vinyl materials, wall coverings and specialized padding for furniture and automobiles.

EARNINGS GROWTH

Bemis has had eight consecutive years of increased earnings per share. Over the past ten years, its earnings per share increased 315 percent (an average of 15 percent per year).

The company has about 8,000 employees and 4,500 shareholders.

STOCK GROWTH

The company has had strong consistent stock growth the past ten years, increasing 887 percent (25.5 percent per year) during the period.

Including reinvested dividends, a $10,000 investment in Bemis stock at its closing stock price in 1980 would have grown to about $133,000 ten years later. Average annual compounded rate of return (including stock growth and reinvested dividends): about 29.5 percent.

DIVIDEND YIELD

Bemis generally pays a moderate yield, averaging about 2.2 percent over the past five years. During the most recent two-year rating period (fiscal 1990 and 1991) the stock paid an average annual current return (dividend yield) of 2.4 percent.

DIVIDEND GROWTH

Bemis has raised its dividend for seven consecutive years. The dividend increased 188 percent (24 percent per year) from 1985 to 1990.

CONSISTENCY

The company has had consistent growth in its earnings, revenue and book value per share over the past seven years, but it had drops in earnings and revenue prior to that. Its price-earnings ratio of about 18 is normal for growing U.S. companies.

SHAREHOLDER PERKS

The company offers a good dividend reinvestment and voluntary stock purchase plan. Shareholders may contribute $25 to $10,000 per quarter to the stock purchase plan with no fees or commissions.

SUMMARY

Fiscal year ended: Dec. 31
(Revenue and net income in millions)

	1991*	1990	1989	1988	1987	1986	1985	5-year growth, %† (annual/total)
Revenue		1,128	1,077	1,069	930	865	787	8/43
Net income		51	47	40	32	26	23	17/121
Earnings/share		1.98	1.80	1.48	1.18	.93	.82	19/141
Dividend/share		.72	.60	.44	.36	.30	.25	24/188
Dividend yield, %	2.4	2.3	2.0	2.0	2.1	2.3	3.1	—/—
Stock price	35.25	29.63	34.38	23.25	19.19	14.13	11.16	22/165
P/E ratio	18	15	17	15	15	14	10	—/—
Book value/share		11.61	10.45	9.48	8.66	7.73	7.14	10/62

* Stock price as of 5–1–91
† 1985–90
Source: Company sources

27

CARTER-WALLACE, INC.

1345 Avenue of the Americas
New York, NY 10105
212-339-5000
Chairman and CEO: Henry H. Hoyt, Jr.
President and COO: Daniel J. Black

EARNINGS GROWTH	★ ★ ★
STOCK GROWTH	★ ★ ★ ★
DIVIDEND YIELD	★ ★
DIVIDEND GROWTH	★ ★ ★ ★
CONSISTENCY	★ ★ ★ ★
SHAREHOLDER PERKS	(no points)
NYSE—CAR	**17 points**

The thrust toward "safe sex" made condoms one of the great boom industries of the past decade, and no company benefited more than Carter-Wallace. Its Trojan brand condoms account for about 50 percent of all condoms sold in the U.S. and generate about $50 million a year in sales worldwide. And with its acquisition in 1989 of the Mentor and Magnum condom lines (from Mentor Corp.), Carter-Wallace stands to gain still more from America's sudden passion for safe passion.

The New York health care concern manufactures an array of personal care products and prescription drugs. Its biggest single seller is Arrid Extra Dry deodorant, which accounts for 23 percent of the company's $555 million a year in total revenue. Arrid is among the nation's leading deodorants, controlling an estimated 11 percent of the total U.S. antiperspirant market.

Its other consumer products (which account for 29 percent of revenue) include Pearl Drops dental polish, Answer at-home pregnancy tests, Carter's Little Pills (laxative), Nair (hair remover), H-R lubricating jelly, Regident denture adhesives, Triple X pediculicide (for lice) and Deoped foot care products.

In the pet care market, Carter-Wallace produces Color Guard flea and tick collars, Chirp vitamins for birds, Evict liquid wormers, Bar Flies and

Boundary mosquito repellent, Femalt hairball remover, Ear Rite miticide, Victory Veterinary Formula insecticides, Fresh 'n Clean grooming products and stain and odor remover, Medi-Cleen, Huggin' Clean, Snowy Coat and Good Bye Dry shampoos, Shield and Head to Tail flea and tick products, and the "Lassie" line of pet products.

Carter's other key segment is health care products, which accounts for 48 percent of revenue. The company manufactures tranquilizers, muscle relaxants, antibiotics, laxatives, expectorants, antibacterials and antihypertensive drugs. Carter-Wallace also makes Rynatan and Rynatuss cough and cold products, Bentasil medicated throat lozenges, Aspro aspirins, Peptol antiulcer medication, Diovol and Univol antacid products, Butisol sedative-hypnotic drugs, Atasol analgesics and Jordan toothbrushes.

Its other products include antinauseants, topical analgesics, nasal decongestants and antispasmodics. The company also markets a line of medical testing kits.

Outside the U.S., Carter-Wallace has manufacturing plants in Canada, England, France, Italy, Mexico, Puerto Rico and New Zealand. Foreign sales account for about 15 percent of its operating income.

EARNINGS GROWTH

Carter-Wallace has had excellent long-term growth. Over the past ten years, its earnings per share increased 367 percent (an average of 17 percent per year).

The company has about 4,000 employees and 3,600 shareholders.

STOCK GROWTH

The company has had exceptional stock growth the past ten years, increasing 980 percent (27 percent per year) during the period.

Including reinvested dividends, a $10,000 investment in Carter-Wallace stock at its closing stock price in 1980 would have grown to about $130,000 ten years later. Average annual compounded rate of return (including stock growth and reinvested dividends): about 29 percent.

DIVIDEND YIELD

Carter-Wallace generally pays a modest yield, averaging about 1.3 percent over the past five years. During the most recent two-year rating period (fiscal 1990 and 1991) the stock paid an average annual current return (dividend yield) of 1.5 percent.

DIVIDEND GROWTH

Carter-Wallace has raised its dividend for nine consecutive years. The dividend jumped 216 percent (26 percent per year) from 1985 to 1990.

CONSISTENCY

The company has had very consistent growth in its earnings, revenue and book value per share, including 15 consecutive years of record earnings per share and book value per share. Its price-earnings ratio of about 16 to 19 is normal for growing U.S. companies.

SHAREHOLDER PERKS   (no points)

Carter-Wallace offers no dividend reinvestment plan, nor does it provide any other perks for its shareholders.

CORPORATE RESPONSIBILITY

Carter-Wallace was among the lowest-rated companies in the Council on Economic Priorities' 1991 edition of *Shopping for a Better World*. The company has no women on its board or among its officers, provides only limited family benefits to its employees and tests its products on animals. Carter-Wallace provided no information that demonstrated either significant reductions in the company's use of animals in testing or a significant commitment to researching nonanimal tests. (Source: Council on Economic Priorities)

SUMMARY

Fiscal year ended: Mar. 31*
(Revenue and net income in millions)

	1991**	1990	1989	1988	1987	1986	1985	5-year growth, %† (annual/total)
Revenue		555	515	483	451	400	348	10/60
Net income		50	45	38	32	28	21	19/138
Earnings/share		3.30	2.97	2.50	2.20	1.82	1.33	20/148
Dividend/share		.79	.65	.51	.38	.29	.25	26/216
Dividend yield, %	1.4	1.5	1.7	1.2	0.9	1.3	1.9	—/—
Stock price	65.88	54.00	58.00	39.00	37.50	40.13	25.25	16/113
P/E ratio	19	16	13	17	18	12	10	—/—
Book value/share		22.55	19.80	17.45	15.25	13.35	11.70	14/93

 * Except stock price Dec. 31, 1985–90
** Stock price as of 5–1–91
† 1985–90
Source: Company sources

28

SHERWIN-WILLIAMS COMPANY

101 Prospect Avenue Northwest
Cleveland, OH 44115-1075
216-566-2000
Chairman and CEO: John G. Breen
President: Thomas A. Commes

EARNINGS GROWTH	★ ★ ★
STOCK GROWTH	★ ★ ★ ★
DIVIDEND YIELD	★ ★
DIVIDEND GROWTH	★ ★
CONSISTENCY	★ ★ ★ ★
SHAREHOLDER PERKS	★ ★
NYSE—SHW	**17 points**

For 125 years, Sherwin-Williams paints have been "covering the earth." Today, the Cleveland-based manufacturer is the nation's largest producer of paints and varnishes, with paint stores in 48 states and licensees, joint ventures and subsidiaries in 35 countries.

Sherwin-Williams, which produces Dutch Boy, Martin-Senour, Dupli-Color, Krylon and Kem-Tone paints, has always sold its consumer paints almost exclusively through its national network of paint stores. But in 1990, for the first time ever, the company began selling its paints in two of the nation's largest retail chains.

Sears began selling Dutch Boy paints nationally in all of its stores, and Wal-Mart began selling Kem-Tone paints in 400 of its stores. The new marketing agreements give Sherwin-Williams a huge new window into the consumer market.

But the company certainly has no plans of abandoning its paint center concept. Sherwin-Williams currently has about 1,935 paint and wall covering stores, and has been adding about 50 new stores a year. The stores sell paints, wall and floor coverings, industrial finishes, window treatments, brushes, scrapers, rollers, spray equipment and other products and tools.

Its primary customers are professional painters, contractors and maintenance people, do-it-yourself homeowners and small to medium sized manufacturers of products requiring a factory finish.

The paint stores account for about 63 percent of the company's $2.3 billion in total revenue and 44 percent of its total profit.

Sherwin-Williams' other key segment, coatings, accounts for 36 percent of revenue and 58 percent of sales. The company recently acquired DeSoto's consumer paint operation, which was expected to add nearly $200 million a year in additional revenue to Sherwin-Williams' bottom line. The coatings segment is divided into four primary U.S. divisions:

- Consumer division. Manufactures the company's line of consumer paints, such as Dutch Boy and Sherwin-Williams brands, as well as a number of private label paints for independent dealers, mass merchandisers and home improvement centers. Sherwin-Williams also manufactures industrial maintenance products, labels, adhesives and color cards.
- Automotive division. Makes auto finishes and refinishing coatings for body shops and other refinishers. The company operates 150 distribution branches throughout the U.S. and Canada.
- Chemical coatings. Makes finishes for original equipment manufacturers of metal, plastic and wood products. Its major markets include automotive, building products, furniture and construction and farm equipment.
- Spray-on division. Makes custom and industrial aerosols for paints and coatings, and automotive, sanitary supply, institutional, pest control and industrial products.

EARNINGS GROWTH

Sherwin-Williams has enjoyed strong, steady growth. Over the past ten years, its earnings per share increased 422 percent (an average of 18 percent per year).

The company has about 12,000 employees and 16,000 shareholders.

STOCK GROWTH

The company's stock price appreciation was flat from 1986 through 1990, following five years of spectacular growth. Over the ten-year period through 1990, the stock price jumped 911 percent (26 percent per year).

Including reinvested dividends, a $10,000 investment in Sherwin-Williams stock at its closing stock price in 1980 would have grown to about $123,000 ten years later. Average annual compounded rate of return (including stock growth and reinvested dividends): about 28.5 percent.

DIVIDEND YIELD

Sherwin-Williams generally pays a moderate yield, which has averaged about 2 percent over the past five years. During the most recent two-year rating period (fiscal 1990 and 1991) the stock paid an average annual current return (dividend yield) of 1.9 percent.

DIVIDEND GROWTH

Sherwin-Williams has raised its dividend for 12 consecutive years. The dividend increased 65 percent (11 percent per year) from 1985 to 1990.

CONSISTENCY

The company has had 13 consecutive years of increased earnings and book value per share. It has had revenue gains nine of the past ten years. The firm's price-earnings ratio of about 15 is normal for a growing manufacturer.

SHAREHOLDER PERKS

Sherwin-Williams offers a very good dividend reinvestment and voluntary stock purchase plan. There are no fees or commissions, and shareholders of record may buy $10 to $2,000 per month in additional shares through the voluntary cash purchase plan.

SUMMARY
Fiscal year ended: Dec. 31
(Revenue and net income in millions)

	1991*	1990	1989	1988	1987	1986**	1985	5-year growth, %† (annual/total)
Revenue		2,267	2,123	1,950	1,801	1,558	1,526	8/48
Net income		123	109	101	97	86	75	10/64
Earnings/share		1.41	1.26	1.15	1.08	.94	.81	12/74
Dividend/share		.38	.35	.32	.28	.25	.23	11/65
Dividend yield, %	1.8	2.0	2.0	2.5	2.3	1.8	2.1	—/—
Stock price	22.75	18.75	17.25	12.75	12.25	13.88	11.13	11/68
P/E ratio	15.0	13.3	13.7	11.1	11.3	14.8	13.7	—/—
Book value/share		8.77	7.73	6.85	6.13	5.37	5.03	12/74

  * Stock price as of 5-1-91
** Excludes unusual item of $19.6 million from net income in 1986
† 1985–90
Source: Company sources

Kellogg's

KELLOGG COMPANY

P.O. Box 3599
Battle Creek, MI 49016-3599
616-961-2000
Chairman and CEO: William E. LaMothe
President: Arnold G. Langbo

EARNINGS GROWTH	★ ★
STOCK GROWTH	★ ★ ★ ★
DIVIDEND YIELD	★ ★
DIVIDEND GROWTH	★ ★ ★
CONSISTENCY	★ ★ ★
SHAREHOLDER PERKS	★ ★ ★
NYSE—K	**17 points**

Around the world, more people wake up each day to Kellogg's than any other breakfast cereal. In fact, outside the U.S., Kellogg's cereals outsell all other ready-to-eat cereals combined.

Since its founding in 1906, the Kellogg Company has been one of the most successful corporations in American industry. The company has had 46 consecutive years of increased sales and 34 years of increased dividends. Its string of 37 straight years of increased earnings per share ended in 1989 when earnings dropped 12 percent. But the Battle Creek, Michigan manufacturer was back on track in 1990 with an earnings increase of 20 percent.

Kellogg holds a 38 percent share of the U.S. cold cereals market and a 51 percent share of the non-U.S. market. Its cereals are sold in about 130 countries. Of the company's $5.2 billion a year in revenue, 42 percent comes from foreign sales.

Through the years, Kellogg has remained primarily a breakfast foods company. In addition to its original favorites—Corn Flakes, Rice Krispies, Bran Flakes and All-Bran—Kellogg produces almost 30 other varieties, including Froot Loops, Frosted Flakes, Frosted Mini-Wheats, Nutri-Grain, Nut & Honey Crunch, Special K, Apple Jacks, Cracklin' Oat Bran, Balance and Fruity Marshmallow Krispies.

Kellogg also owns Mrs. Smith's frozen foods, Eggo and Nutri-Grain frozen waffles, Whitney's yogurt, Salada teas, LeGout soups and Pop Tarts.

The company has production operations on six continents and 16 countries, including Canada, Australia, Japan, Mexico, the United Kingdom and South Africa.

The company was founded by W.K. Kellogg, who first test-marketed his toasted flake cereals in the late 1880s on the patients of the Battle Creek Sanitarium. The cereal was such a hit that many patients wrote the sanitarium after their release to ask where they might buy more of it.

Mr. Kellogg, recognizing a classic market opportunity when he saw one, founded the Battle Creek Toasted Corn Flake Company in 1906, and, as one fabled Kellogg's spokesman would put it, business has been "Grrrreat" ever since.

While W.K. Kellogg will be remembered most for his pioneering efforts in the development of cold cereals, it was his shrewd, aggressive marketing efforts that set his company apart from the competition. A full-page ad in the *Ladies Home Journal* shortly after the company opened in 1906 helped propel Corn Flakes sales to 2,900 cases a day. By 1911, Kellogg's advertising budget had swelled to more than $1 million a year. And in 1912, the company erected the world's largest sign on Times Square in New York City—an 80-foot-high, 100-foot-wide "Kellogg's."

Kellogg introduced 40% Bran Flakes in 1915 and All-Bran in 1916. Rice Krispies first began to snap, crackle and pop on American breakfast tables in 1928.

EARNINGS GROWTH ★ ★

Kellogg has enjoyed strong long-term growth. Over the past ten years, its earnings per share increased 244 percent (13 percent per year).

The company has about 17,000 employees and 24,000 shareholders.

STOCK GROWTH ★ ★ ★ ★

The company has had exceptional stock growth the past ten years, jumping 660 percent (22.5 percent per year) for the period.

Including reinvested dividends, a $10,000 investment in Kellogg stock at its closing stock price in 1980 would have grown to about $110,000 ten years later. Average annual compounded rate of return (including stock growth and reinvested dividends): about 27 percent.

DIVIDEND YIELD

Kellogg generally pays a good dividend yield, averaging about 2.4 percent over the past five years. During the most recent two-year rating period (fiscal 1990 and 1991) the stock paid an average annual current return (dividend yield) of 2.4 percent.

DIVIDEND GROWTH

Kellogg has raised its dividend for 34 consecutive years. The dividend increased 113 percent (16 percent per year) from 1985 to 1990.

CONSISTENCY

The company has had 46 consecutive years of record sales, but its string of 37 straight years of increased earnings per share came to an end in 1989 when earnings dropped 12 percent. Its price-earnings ratio of about 16 to 19 is well in line with other growing foods companies.

SHAREHOLDER PERKS

All new shareholders of record receive a welcome kit with brochures and reports on the company along with a pair of coupons for free grocery products such as cereal, frozen waffles or one of Kellogg's newer products.

Those attending the annual meetings in Battle Creek, Michigan, also receive product samples and discount coupons. The company sometimes hands out special gifts such as the decorative Kellogg's plates that were given to shareholders at one meeting.

Kellogg has a good dividend reinvestment and stock purchase plan. There are no fees or commissions, and shareholders may contribute $25 to $25,000 per year to the stock purchase plan.

CORPORATE RESPONSIBILITY

Kellogg was one of the top-rated companies in the 1991 edition of CEP's *Shopping for a Better World*. However, Kellogg has 294 employees in South Africa, where it sells cereals, drinks and jellies. Kellogg's business in South Africa represents less than 1 percent of the company's sales and brings in less than 1/2 percent of its profits. In 1990, Kellogg was recognized by the Union Label & Service Trades Department of the AFL-CIO with the Labor-Management Award.

Environmentally, Kellogg states that it has used recycled packaging for its products since the company was founded in 1906. Currently, 100 percent of all "U.S.-produced, ready-to-eat cereal and convenience food cartons and shipping cases are made from recycled paper." Kellogg says that it used more than 360 million pounds of recycled paper in more than 2 billion packages in 1989. In recognition of its recycling efforts, the company was chosen as the Michigan Recycler of the Year in 1987.

Kellogg also says that it has implemented waste management and recycling programs in recent years across the country. These efforts have led to more than 15 million pounds of scrap paper and carton board being recycled, more than 50,000 gallons of used machine and motor oil recycled to refiners, more than 90 million pounds of unusable pet food made available to pet food processors and farmers for animal feed, and more than half a million pounds of wooden pallets and scrap metal recycled. At the Battle Creek Plant, Kellogg's largest facility, such efforts have decreased the total landfill scrap volume by 60 percent.

The company has also converted its printing from solvent-based to nontoxic water-based inks, reducing organic emissions in the process. (Source: Council on Economic Priorities)

SUMMARY

Fiscal year ended: Dec. 31
(Revenue and net income in millions)

	1991*	1990	1989	1988	1987	1986	1985	5-year growth, %† (annual/total)
Revenue		5,181	4,651	4,358	3,793	3,340	2,930	12/76
Net income		503	470	480	396	319	281	12/79
Earnings/share		4.16	3.85	3.90	3.20	2.58	2.28	13/82
Dividend/share		1.92	1.72	1.52	1.29	1.02	.90	16/113
Dividend yield, %	2.3	2.5	2.5	2.4	2.2	2.2	3.2	—/—
Stock price	90.75	76.00	68.00	64.00	52.38	51.75	34.75	16/111
P/E ratio	19	16	20	14	19	18	12	—/—
Book value/share		15.00	13.40	12.07	9.80	7.27	5.54	22/170

* Stock price as of 5-1-91
† 1985-90
Source: Company sources

BORDEN, INC.
277 Park Avenue
New York, NY 10172
212-573-4000
Chairman and CEO: R.J. Ventres
President: Anthony S. D'Amato

EARNINGS GROWTH	★
STOCK GROWTH	★ ★ ★ ★
DIVIDEND YIELD	★ ★ ★
DIVIDEND GROWTH	★ ★ ★
CONSISTENCY	★ ★ ★
SHAREHOLDER PERKS	★ ★ ★
NYSE—BN	**17 points**

Milk, for many years the mainstay of Borden, is suddenly spilling into the background of the Park Avenue conglomerate. While Borden still pours more milk than any other American producer, the company has been scaling back its dairy division, inching Elsie out to pasture.

"In 1989, our dairy division was still our largest in sales," Borden president Anthony D'Amato told shareholders at the company's 1991 annual meeting. "By 1990 it was the smallest of our four operating divisions. We project that 1991 dairy sales will account for less than 20 percent of total sales, compared with 34 percent four years ago."

The company cites competitive pressures and lower margins for its decision to shut down or sell out its dairy facilities in several regions. However, Borden is continuing to maintain a strong presence in the South and West where it claims to have the greatest brand strength.

Borden's new focus, says Borden spokesman Nicholas Iammartino, is on "becoming a low-cost producer in every business segment through construction of new plants as well as expansions, consolidations and modernizations of existing ones."

The company has also made a concerted effort the past few years to develop a broader international business. Its foreign sales have grown from 17 percent of total revenue in 1987 to 28 percent of the company's $7.6 billion in total revenue in 1990.

Borden breaks its operation into four divisions:

- Grocery and specialty products (27 percent of revenue). Borden is the world's largest pasta producer and controls 34 percent of the U.S. pasta market. Its flagship brand is Creamette. The company also produces a range of niche grocery products, including specialty cheeses, soups, seafoods, Cracker Jack, ReaLemon lemon juice, canned seafood and fruit jams and pie fillings.

  Among its nonfood consumer products are Elmer's glue, Krazy Glue, and Accent and Country Colors artist and craft paints.
- Snacks and international (26 percent of revenue). Borden is the nation's second largest "salty snack" producer and has made major inroads into the European market. In Germany, Borden is the leader in sweet baked snacks. Borden produces Seyfert's chips, Jays chips, Krunchers!, Cheez Doodles and a long list of regional chips and snack foods.
- Dairy (23 percent of revenue). Borden produces a full range of dairy products (milk, cottage cheese, sour cream, whipping cream, egg nog, ice cream) under the labels of Borden, Meadow Gold and a number of regional brands.
- Packaging and industrial products (24 percent of revenue). Borden is the world leader in wall coverings and is a major competitor in spray paints and household glues. It manufactures Rally Car Wash, Rain Dance Glass Cleaner and Krylon paints. Borden also produces packaging, plastic films and specialty resins and coatings.

EARNINGS GROWTH   ★

Borden has had consistent long-term growth. Over the past ten years, its earnings per share increased 208 percent (an average of 12 percent per year).

The company has about 47,000 employees and 39,000 shareholders.

STOCK GROWTH   ★ ★ ★ ★

The company has had excellent stock growth the past ten years, increasing 603 percent (21.5 percent per year) during the period.

Including reinvested dividends, a $10,000 investment in Borden stock at its closing stock price in 1980 would have grown to about $100,000 ten years later. Average annual compounded rate of return (including stock growth and reinvested dividends): about 26 percent.

DIVIDEND YIELD

Borden generally pays a moderate yield, averaging about 2.8 percent over the past five years. During the most recent two-year rating period (fiscal 1990 and 1991) the stock paid an average annual current return (dividend yield) of 3.3 percent.

DIVIDEND GROWTH

Borden has raised its dividend for more than 15 consecutive years. The dividend increased 112 percent (16 percent per year) from 1985 to 1990.

CONSISTENCY

The company has had eight consecutive years of increased revenue and earnings per share, plus increased book value per share nine of the past ten years. Its price-earnings ratio of about 15 is normal for blue chip companies.

SHAREHOLDER PERKS

Shareholders who attend the annual meeting receive a grab bag of Borden products. The samples change each year, but in 1991 the treats included Elmer's glue, Creamette pasta, Classico pasta sauce, Krunchers! potato chips, Wise Choice popcorn, Orleans canned shrimp, Cremora Lite nondairy creamer and Mrs. Grass soup mix.

The company offers its shareholders of record a good dividend reinvestment and voluntary stock purchase plan. There are no fees or commissions, and shareholders of record may purchase up to $10,000 per quarter in additional shares through the voluntary stock purchase plan.

CORPORATE RESPONSIBILITY

Borden's social responsibility record has improved steadily over the years, and the company has even created the position of vice president of social responsibility. Borden has two women and one minority male on its nine-member board of directors, as well as two women, one of whom is a minority, among the 17 employees at the vice presidential level or higher at corporate headquarters. These women are both among the 25 highest-paid officers at Borden.

The company does maintain a presence in South Africa, where it employs about 300 employees. Borden's subsidiaries in South Africa sell mostly milk products and in 1989 had sales of $40 million.

In 1988, Borden settled a civil antitrust action filed by the Florida attorney general. A complaint was filed on behalf of school boards in 32 counties, which alleged that a Borden unit and six other milk processors overcharged for milk that was distributed to Florida school children. The company paid $10.4 million to settle the case, which was the largest antitrust action ever brought against the milk industry. (Source: Council on Economic Priorities)

SUMMARY

Fiscal year ended: Dec. 31
(Revenue and net income in millions)

	1991*	1990	1989	1988	1987	1986	1985	5-year growth, %† (annual/total)
Revenue		7,633	7,653	7,304	6,574	5,058	4,770	10/60
Net income		364	344	312	267	223	194	13/87
Earnings/share		2.46	.41	2.11	1.81	1.50	1.25	15/97
Dividend/share		1.04	.90	.75	.62	.55	.49	16/112
Dividend yield, %	3.1	3.5	2.6	2.5	2.5	2.3	2.8	—/—
Stock price	37.38	29.88	34.38	29.63	24.75	23.50	17.25	12/73
P/E ratio	15	14	14	13	15	14	11	—/—
Book value/share		12.50	11.12	12.50	11.25	9.75	9.15	6/36

* Stock price as of 5–1–91
† 1985–90
Source: Company sources

DEAN FOODS COMPANY

3600 N. River Road
Franklin Park, IL 60131
312-625-6200
Chairman and CEO: Howard M. Dean
President and CEO: William D. Fischer
Vice Chairman: Kenneth J. Dovacas

EARNINGS GROWTH	★ ★
STOCK GROWTH	★ ★ ★ ★
DIVIDEND YIELD	★ ★
DIVIDEND GROWTH	★ ★
CONSISTENCY	★ ★ ★ ★
SHAREHOLDER PERKS	★ ★ ★
NYSE—DF	**17 points**

Even in an industry as mature as the dairy business, Dean Foods has managed to serve up a steady stream of earnings gains for 17 consecutive years. The company's growth has come primarily through a well-tested strategy of acquisitions. It skims off the cream of the crop of the small, well-managed regional foods companies and integrates them into its own well-homogenized dairy empire.

Among its more recent acquisitions have been Bluhill-American of Arvada, Colorado; Hart's Dairy of Ft. Myers, Florida; Richard Shaw, Inc., a California frozen foods producer; Big Stone, Inc., a Minnesota canned foods processor; Ryan Milk of Murray, Kentucky; Reiter Dairy of Akron, Ohio; Modern Dairy of Elgin, Illinois; Fairmont Products of Bellville, Pennsylvania; and VeriFine Dairy of Sheboygan, Wisconsin. Through a stock merger agreement, Dean also absorbed Larsen Company, a large producer of canned and frozen vegetables.

Typically, Dean continues to market the products of its subsidiaries under the original names. Among its leading regional dairy brands are Creamland, Fieldcrest, Gilt Edge, McArthur, Hart's, Bowman, Bell,

Gandy's, Carnival, Calypso and Fitzgerald. Dean also owns McCadam, the New York State cheese maker.

About 53 percent of the Chicago producer's $2 billion in annual revenue is generated by milk sales, 7 percent comes from ice cream, 3 percent from cheeses, 4 percent from powdered drinks and creamers, 18 percent from canned and frozen vegetables (Veg-All, Freshlike and Larsen brands), 9 percent from pickles (Peter Piper, Heifetz, Pesta, Atkins and Bond pickles), 3 percent from sauces and 3 percent from its refrigerated trucking subsidiary.

Many Dean products are sold under private label brands at grocery chains across the country. Jewel stores, for example, carries Dean products under its own Jewel label. Jewel, a subsidiary of American Store, is Dean's largest customer, accounting for about 9 percent of its total annual sales.

Dean sold its chain of 425 Baskin-Robbins ice cream franchises in 1989.

EARNINGS GROWTH

Dean has enjoyed very solid, consistent long-term growth. Over the past ten years, its earnings per share increased 275 percent (an average of 14 percent per year).

The company has about 9,000 employees and 8,000 shareholders.

STOCK GROWTH

The company's stock growth has been slow but steady the past five years, following five years of exceptional growth. Over the past ten years the stock price has jumped 700 percent (23 percent per year).

Including reinvested dividends, a $10,000 investment in Dean stock at its closing stock price in 1980 would have grown to about $93,000 ten years later. Average annual compounded rate of return (including stock growth and reinvested dividends): about 25 percent.

DIVIDEND YIELD

Dean generally pays a modest yield, averaging about 1.7 percent over the past five years. During the most recent two-year rating period (fiscal 1990 and 1991) the stock paid an average annual current return (dividend yield) of 1.8 percent.

DIVIDEND GROWTH

Dean has raised its dividend for 16 consecutive years. The dividend rose 83 percent (13 percent per year) from 1985 to 1990.

CONSISTENCY

The company has had very consistent growth in its earnings, revenue and book value per share, including 17 consecutive years of record sales and earnings. Its price-earnings ratio of about 15 to 19 is in line with other growing foods companies.

SHAREHOLDER PERKS

No one goes home hungry from a Dean Foods annual meeting. The company passes out a small grab bag of groceries that might include such items as cans of fruits and vegetables, sauces, mixes and coupons.

Dean offers a good dividend reinvestment and voluntary stock purchase plan. There are no fees, and shareholders of record may buy $25 to $3,000 per quarter in additional shares.

CORPORATE RESPONSIBILITY

Dean Foods has been implicated in two bid-rigging schemes in the last five years. In 1988, Dean Foods settled a civil antitrust action filed by the Florida attorney general. A complaint was filed, on behalf of school boards in 32 counties, which alleged that a Dean Foods unit and six other milk processors overcharged for milk that was distributed to Florida school children. Dean Foods paid $7 million to settle the case, which was the largest antitrust action ever brought against the milk industry. In 1990, two subsidiaries of Dean Foods, again in Florida, were charged with conspiring to rig school milk bids. Both subsidiaries entered a plea agreement under which they agreed to plead guilty and pay fines of $1 million each. The companies also paid an additional $175,000 each to settle potential civil claims.

Women and minorities are not well represented in the top levels of management at Dean Foods. The company has one woman on its board of directors, but that is the extent of its diversity. (Source: Council on Economic Priorities)

SUMMARY

Fiscal year ended: May 31*
(Revenue and net income in millions)

	1991**	1990	1989	1988	1987	1986	1985	5-year growth, %† (annual/total)
Revenue		1,988	1,684	1,552	1,435	1,269	1,034	14/92
Net income		61	55	51	41	41	32	14/91
Earnings/share		2.28	2.07	1.90	1.54	1.53	1.39	10.5/64
Dividend/share		.66	.60	.54	.48	.40	.36	13/83
Dividend yield, %	1.6	2.0	2.1	1.8	1.6	1.4	1.5	—/—
Stock price	47.25	40.00	33.00	30.00	25.13	30.75	30.00	6/33
P/E ratio	19	15	14	15	20	18	15	—/—
Book value/share		13.40	11.15	9.90	8.83	7.76	7.47	12/79

  * Except stock price Dec. 31, 1985–90
 ** Stock price as of 5–1–91
 † 1985–90
 Source: Company sources

32

THE INTERPUBLIC GROUP OF COMPANIES, INC.
1271 Avenue of the Americas
New York, NY 10020
212-399-8000
Chairman, President and CEO: Philip H. Geier, Jr.

EARNINGS GROWTH	★ ★
STOCK GROWTH	★ ★ ★ ★
DIVIDEND YIELD	★ ★
DIVIDEND GROWTH	★ ★ ★
CONSISTENCY	★ ★ ★ ★
SHAREHOLDER PERKS	★ ★
NYSE—IPG	**17 points**

It gave Chevrolet the "heartbeat of America," deemed Coke "the real thing" and made UPS the "tightest ship in the shipping business." It has developed marketing campaigns for Exxon, Dristan, Nabisco, Alka-Seltzer, IBM and Johnson & Johnson, among others. With 240 offices spread through 75 countries, and annual revenue of $1.37 billion, the Interpublic Group is one of the world's largest advertising agencies.

The New York-based corporation is made up of several agencies that operate more or less independently, including McCann-Erickson, Lintas, Cambell-Ewald (a division of Lintas), Fahlgren & Swink, Daily & Associates and the Lowe Group plc., a British agency acquired by Interpublic in late 1990.

Interpublic has grown quickly and consistently over the past decade, with nine consecutive years of increased earnings per share.

The company is truly global in scope. Just 37 percent of its commission and fee income is generated by U.S. accounts. Its European accounts provide 39 percent of the company's income, the Far East brings in 13.5 percent, and operations elsewhere around the world provide the other 10 percent.

Interpublic's three biggest clients are General Motors, Coca-Cola and Unilever, the British/Dutch conglomerate.

Among its long list of other clients are GMAC, Snuggle fabric softener, Lipton tea, Inter-Continental Hotels, Princess cruises, Friskies cat food, Birds Eye frozen foods, Levi Strauss, L'Oreal cosmetics, Texas Instruments, Camel cigarettes and Del Monte fruits.

The agencies create advertising campaigns, place print and broadcast advertising and produce direct response mailers.

Interpublic was founded in 1902 by A.W. Erickson (and in 1911 by Harrison K. McCann). It was first incorporated in 1930 as McCann-Erickson and has been operating under the name Interpublic Group since 1961.

EARNINGS GROWTH

Interpublic has had solid, steady long-term growth. Over the past ten years, its earnings per share increased 226 percent (an average of 12.5 percent per year).

The company has about 16,000 employees and 4,200 shareholders.

STOCK GROWTH

The company has enjoyed excellent stock growth the past ten years, rising 600 percent (21.5 percent per year) for the period.

Including reinvested dividends, a $10,000 investment in Interpublic stock at its closing stock price in 1980 would have grown to about $86,000 ten years later. Average annual compounded rate of return (including stock growth and reinvested dividends): about 24 percent.

DIVIDEND YIELD

Interpublic generally pays a moderate yield, averaging just over 2 percent over the past five years. During the most recent two-year rating period (fiscal 1990 and 1991) the stock paid an average annual current return (dividend yield) of 2.0 percent.

DIVIDEND GROWTH

Interpublic has raised its dividend for seven consecutive years. The dividend increased 111 percent (16 percent per year) from 1985 to 1990.

CONSISTENCY

The company has had nine consecutive years of increased earnings per share and more than 15 consecutive years of increased revenue and book value per share. Its recent price-earnings ratio was about 20. A price-earnings ratio in the 14 to 16 range would be more in line with its track history.

SHAREHOLDER PERKS

Interpublic offers its shareholders a good dividend reinvestment and voluntary stock purchase plan. Shareholders may contribute $10 to $3,000 per quarter toward the purchase of additional shares.

SUMMARY

Fiscal year ended: Dec. 31
(Revenue and net income in millions)

	1991*	1990	1989	1988	1987	1986	1985	5-year growth, %† (annual/total)
Revenue		1,368	1,257	1,165	971	814	691	15/97
Net income		80	70	60	47	41	37	17/116
Earnings/share		2.38	2.10	1.82	1.50	1.25	1.11	16/114
Dividend/share		.76	.64	.51	.44	.40	.36	16/111
Dividend yield, %	1.7	2.2	2.1	2.3	1.9	2.2	2.7	—/—
Stock price	45.75	35.00	33.00	36.75	31.75	27.38	21.44	19/135
P/E ratio	20	14	15	12	15	14	12	—/—
Book value/share		12.00	10.65	9.55	8.10	7.25	6.35	14/89

* Stock price as of 5–1–91
† 1985–90
Source: Company sources

H&R BLOCK®

H&R BLOCK, INC.
4410 Main Street
Kansas City, MO 64111
816-753-6900
Chairman and CEO: Henry W. Bloch
President and COO: Thomas M. Bloch

EARNINGS GROWTH	★ ★
STOCK GROWTH	★ ★ ★
DIVIDEND YIELD	★ ★ ★
DIVIDEND GROWTH	★ ★ ★
CONSISTENCY	★ ★ ★ ★
SHAREHOLDER PERKS	★ ★
NYSE—HRB	**17 points**

Since H&R Block first began preparing tax returns in 1955, the company has exhibited an uncanny knack for consistent growth. Year in and year out, its ability to increase its corporate earnings and revenues has become as inevitable as...well...death and taxes.

The company has raised its revenue each of its 35 years of operation. It has raised its earnings for 19 consecutive years and 34 of its 35 years.

H&R Block prepares tax returns for about 11 million Americans each year—roughly 11 percent of all returns filed with the Internal Revenue Service. Outside the U.S., the company prepares another 2 million returns in Canada and about half a million returns in Australia, New Zealand and Europe.

In all, the company has 8,850 offices, about 4,000 of which are owned and operated by the company, and 4,850 of which are owned and operated by independent franchisees.

The company also offers related services, including an "executive tax service" for clients with more complicated returns. This service has about a quarter million clients.

One of its most popular new services is "rapid refund," in which the company files tax returns electronically with the IRS, expediting the time it takes for taxpayers to receive their refunds. The company filed about 3 million returns electronically in 1990.

The company has gone one step further with a "refund anticipation loan service." After filing the returns, H&R Block, through a participating bank, will loan clients the amount of their return, minus a bank transaction fee (and interest), giving the clients almost instant access to their money. The IRS then issues the returns directly to the participating bank. Some 2.4 million taxpayers used the refund anticipation loan service in 1990—up roughly 200 percent from 1989.

Tax preparation services account for 52 percent of the company's $1.05 billion in annual revenue.

The company has three other key business segments:

- Computer services (20 percent of revenue). The company's CompuServe computer information service provides on-line services and information to just over half a million computer owners. The company acquired its chief competitor, the Source, in 1989 and merged its operations into CompuServe.

  CompuServe also offers a credit card validation system that allows merchants to pass a customer's card through a computer terminal and determine almost instantly whether the card is valid. The company also offers computer information networking services for business applications.
- Supplemental personnel services (22 percent of revenue). The company's Personnel Pool of America subsidiary has 510 offices, including 150 company-owned offices, 350 franchisee-owned offices and 13 licensed operations. The company specializes in two areas: temporary health care personnel and general temporary workers for both industrial and office jobs.
- Business education services (5.5 percent of revenue). H&R Block's Path Management Industries subsidiary provides a range of business and management training programs. It offers about 8,000 seminars a year in more than 400 cities in six countries.

EARNINGS GROWTH

H&R Block has had solid long-term growth. Over the past ten years, its earnings per share increased 225 percent (an average of 12.5 percent per year).

The company has about 3,600 permanent employees and 25,000 shareholders.

STOCK GROWTH

The company has had exceptional stock growth the past ten years, increasing 438 percent (18.5 percent per year) during the period.

Including reinvested dividends, a $10,000 investment in H&R Block stock at its closing stock price in 1980 would have grown to about $80,000 ten years later. Average annual compounded rate of return (including stock growth and reinvested dividends): about 23 percent.

DIVIDEND YIELD

H&R Block pays a good yield, averaging almost 5 percent over the past ten years. During the most recent two-year rating period (fiscal 1990 and 1991) the stock paid an average annual current return (dividend yield) of 3.4 percent.

DIVIDEND GROWTH

The company has raised its dividend every year for more than 15 consecutive years. The dividend increased 110 percent (16 percent per year) from 1985 to 1990.

CONSISTENCY

The company has had very consistent growth in its earnings, revenue and book value per share, including 35 consecutive years of record sales and 19 straight years of record earnings. Its price-earnings ratio of about 18 is normal for growing U.S. companies.

SHAREHOLDER PERKS

The company offers its shareholders a dividend reinvestment and voluntary stock purchase plan. There are minimal commissions, and shareholders of record may purchase $10 to $2,500 per quarter in additional shares through the voluntary stock purchase plan.

SUMMARY

Fiscal year ended: Apr. 30*
(Revenue and net income in millions)

	1991**	1990	1989	1988	1987	1986	1985	5-year growth, %† (annual/total)
Revenue		1,053	900	813	722	615	497	16/112
Net income		124	100	90	75	62	55	18/125
Earnings/share		2.31	1.90	1.72	1.43	1.21	1.08	16/114
Dividend/share		1.22	1.00	.85	.73	.66	.58	16/110
Dividend yield, %	3.0	3.7	3.6	3.0	3.2	3.9	5.2	—/—
Stock price	52.38	43.25	36.00	28.38	31.00	22.50	19.25	18/125
P/E ratio	24	14	14	17	16	14	10	—/—
Book value/share		9.53	8.49	7.35	6.76	5.79	4.99	14/91

 * Except stock price Dec. 31, 1985–90
** Stock price as of 5–1–91
† 1985–90
Source: Company sources

34

SAFETY-KLEEN CORP.

777 Big Timber Road
Elgin, IL 60123
708-697-8460
Chairman and CEO: Donald W. Brinckman
President: Joseph F. Knott

EARNINGS GROWTH	★ ★ ★
STOCK GROWTH	★ ★ ★ ★
DIVIDEND YIELD	★
DIVIDEND GROWTH	★ ★ ★
CONSISTENCY	★ ★ ★ ★
SHAREHOLDER PERKS	★ ★
NYSE—SK	**17 points**

For 20 years now, Safety-Kleen has proven that saving the environment *and* raking in big corporate profits actually *can* go hand-in-hand.

The Elgin, Illinois operation, which recycles millions of gallons of cleaning solvent, paint thinner and motor oil each year, has had record earnings every year since 1974, when it was spun off from its original parent company (Chicago Rawhide).

Safety-Kleen's primary clients include auto repair and body shops, manufacturing facilities and dry cleaning services. The company already claims more than half a million customers. It and its licensees operate more than 275 branches in the U.S., 11 solvent recycling centers, three fuel-blending facilities and three waste oil processing plants. It has wholly owned subsidiaries in Canada, Puerto Rico and the United Kingdom; joint ventures in France and Spain; licensees in Australia, Japan, New Zealand and West Germany.

The company's largest segment is its parts cleaner service, which accounts for 59 percent of Safety-Kleen's $589 million a year in revenue. The company provides parts cleaning services for more than 200,000 automotive businesses such as service stations, car dealers, small engine repair shops and fleet maintenance shops. It leases and services parts cleaning equipment designed to remove the buildup of gum and varnish from carburetors, fuel injection parts, transmission parts and other engine components.

Safety-Kleen makes regular service visits to clean and maintain the cleaning equipment, to empty the spent material and to replace it with fresh solvent. The spent solvent is then returned to one of Safety-Kleen's recycling centers, where it is cleaned and prepared for use again. The company provides a similar service for nearly 20,000 dry cleaning shops that use the company's recycled cleaning solution.

Another Safety-Kleen sideline is a paint refinishing service the company offers for automotive body shops, dealerships and manufacturing plants. As part of the service, the company supplies cleaned buffing pads, offers spray gun cleaning assistance, and removes and recycles used paint thinner.

Its fastest-growing segment is its oil recovery service, which collects and cleans used lubricating oil and resells it for repeated use. As more stringent standards are placed on the disposal of used motor oil, Safety-Kleen anticipates additional demand for its recycling services.

EARNINGS GROWTH

Safety-Kleen has had excellent, sustained long-term growth. Over the past ten years, its earnings per share increased 483 percent (19 percent per year).

The company has about 5,000 employees and 5,000 shareholders.

STOCK GROWTH

The company has enjoyed outstanding stock price appreciation the past ten years, surging 643 percent (22 percent per year) during the period.

Including reinvested dividends, a $10,000 investment in Safety-Kleen stock at its closing stock price in 1980 would have grown to about $80,000 ten years later. Average annual compounded rate of return (including stock growth and reinvested dividends): about 23 percent.

DIVIDEND YIELD

Safety-Kleen generally pays a modest yield, averaging about 1 percent over the past five years. During the most recent two-year rating period (fiscal 1990 and 1991) the stock paid an average annual current return (dividend yield) of 1.1 percent.

DIVIDEND GROWTH

Safety-Kleen has raised its dividend for 11 consecutive years. The dividend increased 125 percent (18 percent per year) from 1985 to 1990.

CONSISTENCY

The company has had 20 consecutive years of record revenue and earnings per share. Its recent price-earnings ratio of more than 30 is very high, even for a quickly growing company.

SHAREHOLDER PERKS

Safety-Kleen offers an excellent dividend reinvestment and stock purchase plan. There are no fees or commissions, and shareholders may contribute $25 to $5,000 per month toward the purchase of additional stock.

CORPORATE RESPONSIBILITY

Safety-Kleen's business, recycling of cleaning solvents, often gets it on to socially screened portfolios. Although the company is undeniably providing an environmental service, its own record in terms of the environment is not without blemishes. In 1990, the California Department of Health Services charged Safety-Kleen with numerous violations of the state Hazardous Waste Control Law. The company settled the suit by paying $725,000, although it admitted no wrongdoing. Many of the alleged violations were the result of faulty paperwork, although others involved actual groundwater contamination. More recently, the EPA proposed fines of $495,000 against Safety-Kleen for violations of the Resource Conservation and Recovery Act. The EPA alleges that, among other things, the company "spilled solvents on the ground, failed to report the spills, and did not take actions to remove the spilled wastes." Safety-Kleen is contesting the charges. (Source: Council on Economic Priorities)

SUMMARY

Fiscal year ended: Dec. 31
(Revenue and net income in millions)

	1991*	1990	1989	1988	1987	1986	1985	5-year growth, %† (annual/total)
Revenue		589	478	417	333	255	221	22/166
Net income		55	46	39	35	26	24	18/129
Earnings/share		1.05	.91	.77	.71	.52	.48	17/118
Dividend/share		.27	.24	.20	.16	.14	.12	18/125
Dividend yield, %		1.0	1.2	1.1	0.8	0.9	1.2	—/—
Stock price	33.25	26.00	20.33	16.00	21.80	15.00	11.44	18/127
P/E ratio	32	23	22	24	29	28	21	—/—
Book value/share		7.80	5.13	4.33	3.66	2.83	2.36	27/230

* Stock price as of 5–1–91
† 1985–90
Source: Company sources

35

SONOCO PRODUCTS COMPANY

P.O. Box 160
Hartsville, SC 29550
803-383-7000
Chairman and CEO: Charles W. Coker
President: Russell C. King, Jr.

EARNINGS GROWTH	★ ★
STOCK GROWTH	★ ★ ★ ★
DIVIDEND YIELD	★ ★ ★
DIVIDEND GROWTH	★ ★ ★ ★
CONSISTENCY	★ ★
SHAREHOLDER PERKS	★ ★
OTC—SONO	**17 points**

From its headquarters in Hartsville, South Carolina, where Sonoco began as a yarn cone manufacturer in 1899, the company has spun its influence around the world. The diversified packaging manufacturer has operations in more than 200 locations across America and in 19 foreign countries.

Sonoco has grown largely through an aggressive policy of acquisitions both in the U.S. and abroad.

The company manufactures a range of packages and packaging material from plastic motor oil containers and Ajax tubes to fibre drums and industrial wire spools. Sonoco has annual income of $1.66 billion.

The company divides its domestic business into three key segments:

- Converted products (56 percent of total revenue). In addition to its trademark cones, tubes and cores, Sonoco Products also makes cans and plastic bottles for packaging snack foods, frozen juice concentrates, solid shortening, motor oil, Ajax scouring powder and other consumer products. It manufactures fibre and plastic drums for packaging products such as chemicals, pharmaceuticals and foods, and it makes fibre partitions and packaging forms for shipping cartons.

- Paper (15 percent of revenue). Sonoco produces more than half a million tons of cylinderboard from recycled waste paper (the company recycles nearly a million tons of waste paper each year). Most of the cylinderboard is converted to paperboard packaging products such as tubes, cones and drums for Sonoco's own operations. The company also produces about 150,000 tons per year of corrugated material.
- Miscellaneous (14 percent of revenue). The company also makes metal beams for the textile industry; wood and metal reels for the wire and cable industries; adhesives and coating; wood chips for pulping; railroad crossties and hardwood lumber. Plastic grocery sacks, produced by Sonoco's Polysack division, are one of the company's fastest-growing products.

    Sonoco's international segment, with operations in England, Canada, Mexico, Australia and 14 other nations, accounts for about 16 percent of the company's total revenue.

EARNINGS GROWTH

Sonoco has had strong, steady long-term growth. Over the past ten years, its earnings per share increased 235 percent (13 percent per year).

    The company has about 15,000 employees and 14,000 shareholders.

STOCK GROWTH

The company has enjoyed excellent stock price appreciation the past ten years, increasing 627 percent (22 percent per year) during the period.

    Including reinvested dividends, a $10,000 investment in Sonoco stock at its closing stock price in 1980 would have grown to about $92,000 ten years later. Average annual compounded rate of return (including stock growth and reinvested dividends): about 25 percent.

DIVIDEND YIELD

Sonoco generally pays a good yield, averaging about 2.5 percent over the past five years. During the most recent two-year rating period (fiscal 1990 and 1991) the stock paid an average annual current return (dividend yield) of 2.9 percent.

DIVIDEND GROWTH

Sonoco has raised its dividend for eight consecutive years. The dividend increased 158 percent (21 percent per year) from 1985 to 1990.

CONSISTENCY

The company has had increased earnings per share nine of the past ten years, although it appeared to be headed for a drop in earnings in 1991 because of the slow economy. Sonoco has had increased revenue and book value per share for more than 15 consecutive years. Its price-earnings ratio of about 15 is in line with other manufacturers.

SHAREHOLDER PERKS

The company offers its shareholders of record a dividend reinvestment and voluntary stock purchase plan. There is just a nominal fee for participants, who may contribute $10 to $500 per month toward the purchase of additional stock.

SUMMARY

Fiscal year ended: Dec. 31
(Revenue and net income in millions)

	1991*	1990	1989	1988	1987	1986	1985	5-year growth, %† (annual/total)
Revenue		1,669	1,656	1,600	1,312	964	870	14/92
Net income		105	104	96	72	55	49	16/114
Earnings/share		2.41	2.36	2.20	1.53	1.25	1.13	16/113
Dividend/share		.93	.81	.64	.50	.41	.36	21/158
Dividend yield, %		2.8	2.9	2.3	2.3	2.0	2.2	—/—
Stock price	36.25	32.00	37.00	34.00	21.25	19.00	15.38	16/109
P/E ratio		13	15	13	17	15	11	—/—
Book value/share		11.90	11.70	10.36	8.27	7.60	6.75	12/76

* Stock price as of 5–1–91
† 1985–90
Source: Company sources

36

HUBBELL INCORPORATED

584 Derby Milford Road
Orange, CT 06477-4024
203-799-4100
Chairman, President and CEO: G. J. Ratcliffe

EARNINGS GROWTH	★ ★
STOCK GROWTH	★ ★ ★
DIVIDEND YIELD	★ ★ ★
DIVIDEND GROWTH	★ ★ ★
CONSISTENCY	★ ★ ★ ★
SHAREHOLDER PERKS	★ ★
ASE—HUB "B"	**17 points**

Hubbell has been making electrical devices since 1888. The company's product line (connectors, outlets, adaptors, floor boxes, switches, lights and the whole range of electrical devices) has never produced spectacular financial returns—just a steady current of increased earnings.

The Connecticut-based manufacturer has had 30 consecutive years of increased operating income and increased dividends. With subsidiaries in Canada, England and Puerto Rico, Hubbell has annual revenue of $720 million.

Hubbell divides its product line into three segments:

- Low-voltage products. The company makes thousands of electrical devices such as fuses, switches, wall plates, cables, plugs, surge suppressor units, connectors, adaptors and wall outlets. The company's lighting division sells lights for athletic fields, service stations, outdoor display signs, parking lots, shopping centers and roadways. It manufactures indoor lights for gymnasiums, industrial plants and commercial buildings.

    Other low-voltage products include industrial controls such as motor speed controls, power and grounding resistors and overhead crane controls.

129

- High-voltage products. Through its Kerite Company subsidiary, Hubbell makes insulated electric power and signal cable for electric utilities, major industries and railroads. Its Ohio Brass Company subsidiary manufactures polymer insulators and high-voltage surge arresters used in the construction of electrical transmission and distribution lines and substations.
- Other electronics products. Hubbell's Raco, Inc. and Killark subsidiaries manufacture steel and plastic boxes used at outlets, switch locations and junction points. They also make fittings, tubing and enclosures.

     Hubbell's Pulse Communications division manufactures voice and data signal processing equipment used primarily by the telephone and telecommunications industry.

EARNINGS GROWTH

Hubbell has had strong, steady long-term growth. Over the past ten years, its earnings per share increased 274 percent (an average of 14 percent per year).

     The company has about 6,000 employees, 1,600 class A shareholders and 6,000 class B shareholders.

STOCK GROWTH

The company has enjoyed outstanding stock price appreciation the past ten years, rising 407 percent (18 percent per year) for the period.

     Including reinvested dividends, a $10,000 investment in Hubbell stock at its closing stock price in 1980 would have grown to about $70,000 ten years later. Average annual compounded rate of return (including stock growth and reinvested dividends): about 21.5 percent.

DIVIDEND YIELD

Hubbell generally pays a very good dividend yield, averaging just over 3 percent over the past five years. During the most recent two-year rating period (fiscal 1990 and 1991) the stock paid an average annual current return (dividend yield) of 3.3 percent.

DIVIDEND GROWTH

Hubbell has hiked its dividend for 30 consecutive years. The dividend increased 116 percent (17 percent per year) from 1985 to 1990.

CONSISTENCY

The company has had 30 consecutive years of increased operating income. Its revenue has increased nine of the past ten years, and its book value and earnings per share have increased more than 15 consecutive years. The company's price-earnings ratio of around 13 to 17 is well in line with other manufacturers.

SHAREHOLDER PERKS

Hubbell's modest dividend reinvestment and stock purchase plan allows shareholders to contribute $100 to $1,000 per quarter (plus dividends) toward the purchase of additional stock.

SUMMARY

Fiscal year ended: Dec. 31
(Revenue and net income in millions)

	1991*	1990	1989	1988	1987	1986	1985	5-year growth, %† (annual/total)
Revenue		720	669	614	581	559	521	7/38
Net income		86	79	71	63	55	48	13/79
Earnings/share		2.88	2.65	2.37	2.06	1.83	1.65	12/75
Dividend/share		1.38	1.18	.94	.79	.71	.64	17/116
Dividend yield, %	3.1	3.4	3.4	3.2	2.6	2.7	3.4	—/—
Stock price	47.88	44.38	45.75	35.75	32.13	30.25	24.88	15/103
P/E ratio	17	13.9	13.2	12.5	14.8	14.3	11.2	—/—
Book value/share		15.87	14.49	13.19	11.94	10.96	9.91	10/60

* Stock price as of 5–1–91
† 1985–90
Source: Company sources

BROWNING-FERRIS INDUSTRIES

Browning-Ferris Building
757 N. Eldridge
P.O. Box 3151
Houston, TX 77253
713-870-8100
Chairman and CEO: William D. Ruckelshaus

EARNINGS GROWTH	★ ★ ★ ★
STOCK GROWTH	★ ★ ★
DIVIDEND YIELD	★ ★
DIVIDEND GROWTH	★ ★ ★
CONSISTENCY	★ ★ ★
SHAREHOLDER PERKS	★ ★
NYSE—BFI	**17 points**

Solid waste has brought solid growth for many years to Houston-based Browning-Ferris Industries. America's second largest waste handler has posted 15 consecutive years of record earnings. But suddenly analysts are beginning to question the company's ability to keep the dollars growing. Public recycling efforts have cut back its volume, and tighter municipal landfill laws have made it tougher on BFI to open new facilities. In 1990, the company's stock price fell by more than 50 percent.

But in a world still swimming in plastic wrappers, disposable diapers and chemical toxins, business continues to look promising for BFI. With annual revenue of $3 billion, Browning-Ferris ranks just behind industry leader Waste Management, Inc.

BFI provides waste collection and disposal services for homes, businesses and factories in 600 communities in 43 states—plus operations in Canada and several other countries. It operates 105 solid waste landfills and manages hazardous waste disposal sites in several states. In all, it provides solid waste disposal service for 5.4 million U.S. households and 622,000 commercial and industrial customers.

The company's commercial and industrial solid waste business accounts for 58 percent of its revenue, its residential service accounts for 16 percent of revenue, solid waste processing and disposal brings in another 16 percent of revenue, and special services accounts for 8 percent of the company's revenue.

Among its special services is a recycling program that entails 130 curbside collection programs serving nearly a million households. BFI also serves a number of commercial and industrial customers and operates 34 recycling centers.

Among its other more successful specialized services is its Medical Waste Systems, which operates 23 processing sites, including 18 incinerators. It serves medical clients in 42 states plus Canada.

BFI is also expanding its recently established garbage-to-energy resource recovery services. American Ref-Fuel Company, which BFI owns jointly with Air Products and Chemicals, Inc., has a new facility in Long Island. The plant burns 2,300 tons of garbage a day to generate electricity.

The company has two other similar facilities under construction, two more under contract and two more in the planning stages. Construction costs range from $100 million to $350 million per plant, with plant capacities of 600 to 3,000 tons per day.

Browning-Ferris also has subsidiaries involved in street and parking lot sweeping, portable restroom rental and bus and van transportation services.

EARNINGS GROWTH

BFI has had excellent growth. Over the past ten years, its earnings per share increased 529 percent (20 percent per year).

The company has about 25,000 employees and 20,000 shareholders.

STOCK GROWTH

In spite of its large drop in 1990, BFI stock has had excellent long-term gains, including an increase over the past ten years of 450 percent (18.5 percent per year).

Including reinvested dividends, a $10,000 investment in BFI stock at its closing stock price in 1980 would have grown to about $67,000 ten years later. Average annual compounded rate of return (including stock growth and reinvested dividends): about 21 percent.

DIVIDEND YIELD

BFI has been paying a modest yield. During the most recent two-year rating period (fiscal 1990 and 1991) the stock paid an average annual current return (dividend yield) of 2.3 percent.

DIVIDEND GROWTH

BFI has raised its dividend for at least 15 consecutive years. The dividend rose 137 percent (19 percent per year) from 1985 to 1990.

CONSISTENCY

The company has had 15 consecutive years of record earnings per share, although some analysts projected a slight decline for 1991. Its revenues increased for at least 15 straight years, but its book value per share dropped 9.4 percent in 1990. Its price-earnings ratio of about 19 is a little higher than most major companies.

SHAREHOLDER PERKS

BFI offers its shareholders an excellent dividend reinvestment and voluntary stock purchase plan. There are no fees or commissions, and shareholders of record may purchase $25 to $60,000 per year in additional shares through the voluntary stock purchase plan.

SUMMARY

Fiscal year ended: Sept. 30
(Revenue and net income in millions)

	1991*	1990	1989	1988	1987	1986	1985	5-year growth, %† (annual/total)
Revenue		2,967	2,550	2,067	1,656	1,328	1,144	21/159
Net income		256	262	226	172	136	111	18/130
Earnings/share		1.68	1.74	1.51	1.15	.95	.80	16/110
Dividend/share		.64	.56	.48	.40	.32	.27	19/137
Dividend yield, %	2.4	2.1	1.4	1.7	1.2	1.7	2.2	—/—
Stock price	28.63	30.75	41.25	27.88	33.25	19.00	12.22	20/151
P/E ratio	19	18	24	19	29	20	15	—/—
Book value/share		7.61	8.33	7.05	5.93	5.11	3.90	14/95

* Stock price as of 5–1–91
† 1985–90
Source: Company sources

38
❄ Shaw Industries, Inc.

SHAW INDUSTRIES, INC.
P.O. Drawer 2128
Dalton, GA 30722-2128
404-278-3812
Chairman: J.C. Shaw
President and CEO: Robert E. Shaw

EARNINGS GROWTH	★ ★ ★ ★
STOCK GROWTH	★ ★ ★ ★
DIVIDEND YIELD	★ ★
DIVIDEND GROWTH	★ ★ ★ ★
CONSISTENCY	★ ★
SHAREHOLDER PERKS	(no points)
NYSE—SHX	**16 points**

It has been a wild carpet ride for Shaw shareholders over the past decade. The high-flying Georgia carpet king has seen its stock price dip and soar half a dozen times in recent years. But the altitude keeps getting higher before each dip. The long-term result has been a spectacular ten-year return to shareholders of about 2,000 percent.

Shaw, the nation's leading carpet manufacturer, can blame its volatility on its commitment to stick strictly to its knitting. Carpet is not only Shaw's principal business, it's its only business. The company sells more than $1 billion a year in carpeting throughout the United States.

Shaw should not be faulted for concentrating solely on its carpeting business, but its lack of diversity tends to tie the company's fortunes to the cyclical construction industry. When the construction business begins to boom again, look for Shaw stock to take another leap up the charts.

Shaw Industries is a relatively young company, formed in 1967 by brothers J.C. and Robert E. Shaw. The brothers, now in their late fifties, still serve as chairman and president, respectively, and control about 16 percent of the company's stock.

Shaw's carpeting is marketed under the Magee, Philadelphia, Cabin Craft and Stratton labels, as well as some private labels for distributors and retailers. The company sells carpeting through about 25,000 retail stores and 150 wholesale distributors in the United States. Foreign business accounts for less than 1 percent of the company's total revenue.

Like 95 percent of the U.S. carpeting industry, Shaw makes tufted carpet from nylon yarn. Shaw is vertically integrated, handling every step of the carpet-making process—spinning the fibre, dyeing it, weaving the rug and cutting it to size. In all, Shaw makes about 500 styles of tufted carpet for residential and commercial customers.

Through its rather aggressive acquisitions program, the company has been able to bring some of the best-known carpet brands into its fold. By integrating those operations and marketing them through one sales force, it has been able to reduce overhead and sales costs. It also attempts to provide more efficient and timely distribution through its 11 regional distribution centers.

EARNINGS GROWTH

Shaw has enjoyed outstanding long-term growth. Over the past ten years, its earnings per share increased 905 percent (26 percent per year).

The company has about 11,000 employees and 1,500 shareholders.

STOCK GROWTH

The company has had exceptional stock growth the past ten years, jumping 1,900 percent (34 percent per year) for the period.

Including reinvested dividends, a $10,000 investment in Shaw stock at its closing stock price in 1980 would have grown to about $230,000 ten years later. Average annual compounded rate of return (including stock growth and reinvested dividends): about 37 percent.

DIVIDEND YIELD

Shaw generally pays a moderate yield, averaging about 2.5 percent over the past five years. During the most recent two-year rating period (1989 and 1990) the stock paid an average annual current return (dividend yield) of 2.1 percent.

DIVIDEND GROWTH

Shaw has raised its dividend for seven consecutive years. The dividend increased 221 percent (26 percent per year) from 1985 to 1990.

CONSISTENCY

The company has been among the most erratic of the *100 Best* stocks. Its earnings per share have gone up eight of the past ten years (through 1990), but Shaw was headed for a sharp earnings drop in fiscal 1991, primarily because of the recession and the weak construction industry. Its price-earnings ratio of around 13 to 17 is well in line with other manufacturers.

SHAREHOLDER PERKS   (no points)

Shaw Industries does not offer a dividend reinvestment plan for its shareholders, nor does it provide any other perks.

SUMMARY

Fiscal year ended: June 30*
(Revenue and net income in millions)

	1991**	1990	1989	1988	1987	1986	1985	5-year growth, %† (annual/total)
Revenue		1,475	1,176	958	694	550	519	23/184
Net income		65	48	34	29	24	26	20/150
Earnings/share		2.11	1.57	1.07	.85	.71	.76	23/178
Dividend/share		.45	.40	.33	.30	.19	.14	26/221
Dividend yield, %		1.6	2.6	3.2	2.3	2.3	2.8	—/—
Stock price	25.00	20.00	31.00	12.00	8.13	10.25	6.59	15/203
P/E ratio	17	13	8	9	13	10	6	—/—
Book value/share		7.89	6.15	5.11	4.61	4.14	3.51	17/124

 * Except stock price Dec. 31, 1985–90
** Stock price as of 5–1–91
† 1985–90
Source: Company sources

39

The newell group™

NEWELL CO.

29 Stephenson Street
Freeport, IL 61032
815-235-4171
Chairman: William R. Cuthbert
CEO: Daniel C. Ferguson
President: William P. Sovey

EARNINGS GROWTH	★ ★ ★
STOCK GROWTH	★ ★ ★ ★
DIVIDEND YIELD	★ ★
DIVIDEND GROWTH	★ ★ ★ ★
CONSISTENCY	★ ★ ★
SHAREHOLDER PERKS	(no points)
NYSE—NWL	**16 points**

Newell Co. has built its business on things around the house—cookware, hardware, houseware, glassware, faucets, blinds, drapes and door knobs. The company's success with the small things has turned Newell into one of America's biggest corporate success stories. Over the past 20 years, the Freeport, Illinois manufacturer's annual sales soared from $30 million to $1.1 billion.

Newell operates in two market segments: hardware and houseware products (72 percent of sales) and industrial products (28 percent of sales). Its industrial segment includes packaging, plastic and glass products. Anchor Hocking, the glassware, cookware and plastics manufacturer that Newell acquired in 1987, accounts for most of the sales in the company's industrial products segment.

Newell owns a range of consumer houseware brands sold in major retail stores such as Wal-Mart, K mart, Target and Sears. Among its product lines, in addition to Newell and Anchor Hocking, are Foley and Mirro cookware; Amerock cabinet, window and bath hardware; BernzOmatic and Surefire hand torches; Wear-Ever pots and pans; Bulldog hardware and EZ Paintr.

Within its hardware and houseware division, cabinet and window hardware accounts for about 24 percent of sales and cookware and bakeware account for 21 percent. The other 55 percent is divided among glassware, window furnishings, paints and other hardware and houseware products.

Newell has been a leader in developing a computerized link with its customers to monitor sales and inventory. When a store sells a Newell product, the transaction is automatically transmitted to Newell's sales center, enabling Newell to monitor inventory and automatically reorder products for its retail customers. The company reports that about 85 percent of the product sales handled by its top 20 customers are done through its electronic data interchange system.

Newell's industrial products division produces packaging materials primarily for the foods and consumer goods industry, glass containers, a line of disposable and reusable food service items, and metal, plastic and composite packaging closures.

EARNINGS GROWTH

Newell has enjoyed strong, sustained long-term growth. Over the past ten years, its earnings per share increased 394 percent (17 percent per year).

The company has about 11,000 employees and 3,000 shareholders.

STOCK GROWTH

The company has had exceptional stock price appreciation the past ten years, jumping 1,450 percent (31.5 percent per year) for the period.

Including reinvested dividends, a $10,000 investment in Newell stock at its closing stock price in 1980 would have grown to about $190,000 ten years later. Average annual compounded rate of return (including stock growth and reinvested dividends): about 34 percent.

DIVIDEND YIELD

Newell generally pays a good yield, averaging about 2.2 percent over the past five years. During the most recent two-year rating period (fiscal 1990 and 1991) the stock paid an average annual current return (dividend yield) of 2 percent.

DIVIDEND GROWTH

Newell has raised its dividend for five consecutive years. The dividend jumped 284 percent (31 percent per year) from 1985 to 1990.

CONSISTENCY

The company has had increased earnings and revenue nine of the past ten years, and increased book value 14 consecutive years. Its price-earnings ratio of around 16 to 19 is in line with other growing companies.

SHAREHOLDER PERKS   (no points)

Newell provides no dividend reinvestment plan, nor does it offer any other standard shareholder perks, although it sometimes gives shareholders a gift at its annual meeting. At its most recent meeting, the company gave shareholders a decorative glass vase produced by its Anchor Hocking glassware division.

SUMMARY

Fiscal year ended: Dec. 31
(Revenue and net income in millions)

	1991*	1990	1989	1988	1987	1986	1985	5-year growth, %† (annual/total)
Revenue		1,073	1,123	988	720	401	350	25/206
Net income		96	85	61	37	24	19	38/405
Earnings/share		1.58	1.41	1.09	.69	.54	.52	25/203
Dividend/share		.50	.43	.28	.21	.19	.13	31/284
Dividend yield, %	2.0	2.0	2.2	2.5	2.5	2.6	3.0	—/—
Stock price	30.63	24.75	22.13	15.50	7.75	7.88	6.88	29/259
P/E ratio	19	16	14	11	12	13	8	—/—
Book value/share		8.40	7.61	5.32	4.72	3.99	3.04	22/176

* Stock price as of 5–1–91
† 1985–90
Source: Company sources

40

RALSTON PURINA COMPANY
Checkerboard Square
St. Louis, MO 63164
314-982-1000
Chairman and CEO: William P. Stiritz

EARNINGS GROWTH	★ ★
STOCK GROWTH	★ ★ ★ ★
DIVIDEND YIELD	★ ★
DIVIDEND GROWTH	★ ★
CONSISTENCY	★ ★ ★
SHAREHOLDER PERKS	★ ★ ★
NYSE—RAL	**16 points**

More dogs and cats the world over dine on Ralston Purina than any other pet food. But not all of Ralston's foods are for the dogs.

Its breakfast cereals—lead by Chex—generate sales of nearly half a billion dollars a year, and its Wonder breads and Hostess snacks—Twinkies, Ding Dongs, Suzy Q's and the like—ring up sales of about $2 billion a year.

The St. Louis-based manufacturer is also the world's leading producer of dry cell batteries. In 1986, Ralston Purina purchased Union Carbide's Eveready battery division, which includes Energizer and Eveready batteries. The battery division accounts for about 20 percent of the company's operating profits.

With total annual sales of $7.1 billion, Ralston Purina is among the ten largest food products companies in the U.S. The company divides its operations into several key segments:

- Pet foods (25 percent of revenue). Among the company's more familiar brands are Purina Dog and Cat Chow, Kit 'N Kaboodle, Butcher's Blend, Chuck Wagon, Fit & Trim, Grrravy, Lucky Dog, Moist & Meaty, Hearty Chews, Cheesedawgs, Meow Mix, Thrive, Special Dinners, Tender Vittles, Smart Cat, Purina Biscuits, Hearty Chews, Happy Cat and Alley Cat.

- Bakery products (29 percent of revenue). The company's Hostess snack cakes include Twinkies, Fruit & Creme Twinkies, Cupcakes, Breakfast Bake Shop Donuts and Muffins, Suzy Q's, Pudding Cake, ChocoDiles, Choco-Bliss, Crumb Cakes, Ding Dongs, Ho Hos, Sno Balls and Fruit Pies.

    Ralston, which acquired its baked goods division with the 1984 acquisition of Continental Bakery, also produces Wonder breads and operates about 600 Thrift stores that serve as outlets for its surplus bakery goods.

    The most recognizable of Ralston's brand name foods are Wheat Chex, Rice Chex and Corn Chex. Some of its newer brands are Cookie Crisp, Ghostbusters, Nintendo, Teenage Mutant Ninja Turtles, Breakfast with Barbie, Batman, Muesli, Oat Bran Options, Sun Flakes and Almond Delight.

    Ralston also acquired Beech-Nut Baby Foods in late 1989, which added another $150 million in sales each year.
- Battery products (20 percent of revenue). In addition to its Eveready and Energizer batteries, the company manufactures flashlights; home, auto and personal safety devices; replacement bulbs and lanterns.
- Agricultural products (14 percent of revenue). Ralston sold its U.S. Purina Mills operation in 1986 but continues to maintain its foreign operations. It has 63 facilities in 14 countries that distribute the company's livestock and poultry feed and animal health products through about 3,500 independent dealers.
- Soy protein products (3 percent of revenue). The company's Protein Technologies International is the world's leading manufacturer of isolated soy proteins, soy fibre food ingredients and soy polymer products.

EARNINGS GROWTH

Ralston has enjoyed excellent long-term growth. Over the past ten years, its earnings per share increased 325 percent (16 percent per year).

The company has about 56,000 employees and 29,000 shareholders.

STOCK GROWTH

The company has had outstanding, sustained stock price appreciation the past ten years, climbing 1,020 percent (27 percent per year) during the period.

Including reinvested dividends, a $10,000 investment in Ralston stock at its closing stock price in 1980 would have grown to about $150,000 ten years later. Average annual compounded rate of return (including stock growth and reinvested dividends): about 31 percent.

DIVIDEND YIELD

Ralston generally pays a moderate yield, averaging almost 2 percent over the past five years. During the most recent two-year rating period (fiscal 1990 and 1991) the stock paid an average annual current return (dividend yield) of 2 percent.

DIVIDEND GROWTH

Ralston has raised its dividend for more than 18 consecutive years. The dividend increased 84 percent (13 percent per year) from 1985 to 1990.

CONSISTENCY

The company has had 11 consecutive years of increased earnings. Its price-earnings ratio of around 14 to 16 is well in line with other growing foods companies.

SHAREHOLDER PERKS

Ralston provides an excellent dividend reinvestment plan for its shareholders. There are no commissions or service fees, and shareholders may contribute any amount up to $25,000 a year to the voluntary cash stock purchase plan.

At Ralston annual meetings, shareholders can dine on Twinkies and other Hostess snacks, and then take home products such as cereal, batteries and coupons for pet food.

The company, which is part owner of Keystone ski resort in Colorado, sends a discount coupon for Keystone lodging, ski rental and lift tickets to shareholders in September along with their dividend checks.

CORPORATE RESPONSIBILITY

Ralston Purina has a moderate record on corporate social responsibility. The company does not have a single woman or minority in top management or on its board of directors. Through its Eveready subsidiary, Ralston had a $169,000 Strategic Defense Initiative (SDI) contract in 1989 according to Eagle Eye Publishers Inc.'s *Federal Contracts on CD-ROM.* (Source: Council on Economic Priorities)

SUMMARY

Fiscal year ended: Sept. 30*
(Revenue and net income in millions)

	1991**	1990	1989	1988	1987	1986	1985	5-year growth, %† (annual/total)
Revenue		7,101	6,658	5,875	5,868	5,514	5,864	4/21
Net income		396	351	363	274	288	256	9/55
Earnings/share		3.23	2.66	2.64	1.89	1.87	1.57	16/106
Dividend/share		.92	.83	.75	.62	.55	.50	13/84
Dividend yield, %	1.9	2.1	1.9	2.1	1.6	1.9	2.6	—/—
Stock price	55.50	51.50	41.50	41.00	31.80	35.38	23.50	14/94
P/E ratio	16.0	13.5	16.0	13.7	20.9	15.8	12.4	—/—
Book value/share		1.35	2.92	7.99	6.85	6.60	5.76	−27/−326

  * Except stock price Dec. 31, 1985–90
** Stock price as of 5–1–91
† 1985–90
Source: Company sources

41

HERSHEY FOODS CORPORATION

14 E. Chocolate Avenue
P.O. Box 814
Hershey, PA 17033-0814
717-534-4001
Chairman and CEO: Richard A. Zimmerman
President: Kenneth L. Wolfe

EARNINGS GROWTH	★
STOCK GROWTH	★ ★ ★ ★
DIVIDEND YIELD	★ ★
DIVIDEND GROWTH	★ ★ ★
CONSISTENCY	★ ★ ★
SHAREHOLDER PERKS	★ ★ ★
NYSE—HSY	**16 points**

For 98 years, Hershey Foods has been tapping a profitable vein in America's sweet tooth. The Hershey, Pennsylvania manufacturer, founded in 1893 by Milton Hershey, is the nation's leading producer of confectionery products, selling about $2 billion a year in chocolates and other candies.

Through a series of acquisitions, Hershey has assembled a long list of goodies guaranteed to stimulate the saliva glands of any confectionery aficionado. One of its more recent acquisitions was the Peter Paul/Cadbury operation (in 1988), which added Peter Paul Almond Joy, Mounds Bars, Caramello and Cadbury's Creme Eggs to Hershey's seductive slate of sweets.

Other Hershey candies include Hershey's Big Block, Special Dark, Golden Almond, Kit Kat, Krackel, Rolo caramels, Hershey's Kisses, Marabou Mint Crisp, Skor, Mr. Goodbar, Reese's Peanut Butter Cups, Reese's Pieces, 5th Avenue, Twizzlers, Bar None, Hershey's chocolate bar with almonds, York peppermint pattie, its new Symphony chocolate bar and, the perennial favorite, Hershey's milk chocolate bar.

The company also produces Hershey's cocoa, chocolate milk mix, baking chocolate, chocolate syrup, fudge topping, chocolate chips and premium chunks.

Other recent acquisitions include Luden's (Luden's cough drops, 5th Avenue and Luden's Mello Mints), Queen Anne (chocolate-covered cherries), and Nabisco's Canadian confectionery operations, which includes (for the Canadian market only) Life Savers, Oh Henry!, Planters Nuts, Bubble Yum bubble gum, Care*Free chewing gum and several other candies.

About two-thirds of Hershey's $2.7 billion in annual revenue comes from its candies operation. International sales account for about 7.5 percent of total revenue.

The company's other key group is its pasta division. With such brands as Ronzoni, American Beauty, San Giorgio, Skinner, Delmonico, P & R and Light 'n Fluffy, the pasta group accounts for more than 10 percent of Hershey's total annual revenue.

Hershey has improved its candy sales in recent years through a beefed up advertising budget. In 1970, advertising and promotional expenses amounted to about 4 percent of revenues. In contrast, by 1989, the company devoted 16 percent of revenues—$377 million—to its advertising and promotion program.

EARNINGS GROWTH ★

Hershey Foods has had consistent long-term growth. Over the past ten years, its earnings per share increased 197 percent (an average of 11.5 percent per year).

The company has about 12,000 employees and 30,000 shareholders.

STOCK GROWTH

The company has had exceptional stock growth the past ten years, increasing 860 percent (25.5 percent per year) for the period.

Including reinvested dividends, a $10,000 investment in Hershey Foods stock at its closing stock price in 1980 would have grown to about $127,000 ten years later. Average annual compounded rate of return (including stock growth and reinvested dividends): about 29 percent.

DIVIDEND YIELD

Hershey Foods generally pays a good yield, averaging just over 2 percent over the past five years. During the most recent two-year rating period (fiscal 1990 and 1991) the stock paid an average annual current return (dividend yield) of 2.2 percent.

DIVIDEND GROWTH

Hershey has raised its dividend for 16 consecutive years. The dividend increased 16 percent (106 percent per year) from 1985 to 1990.

CONSISTENCY

The company has had increased earnings per share nine of the past ten years, and increased book value and revenue ten consecutive years. Its price-earnings ratio of about 18 is normal for growing foods companies.

SHAREHOLDER PERKS

Hershey Foods provides several shareholder perks. The company makes Christmas shopping a lot easier for shareholders with chocolate-loving friends. Each year Hershey mails its Christmas gift catalog to all of its shareholders of record. Shareholders may purchase special gift packages from the catalog and have them wrapped and mailed directly to their friends.

Shareholders who attend the annual meeting are treated to a free packet of Hershey's candies and pasta. At the 1990 meeting, shareholders received Hershey's milk chocolate bar with almonds, Luden's throat drops, Peter Paul Mounds, Y&S, Nibs, Twizzlers, a box of pasta and a few other samples.

The company also offers a good dividend reinvestment and voluntary stock purchase plan. Shareholders may buy up to $20,000 in additional stock each year through the company plan with nominal fees.

CORPORATE RESPONSIBILITY

Hershey is well known as a company concerned with social responsibility, especially in its hometown of Hershey, Pennsylvania.

In 1909, three years after starting the corporation, Milton Hershey founded the Milton S. Hershey School for Orphan Boys, and in 1918, donated the entire business to the school trust, which still owns 50.1 percent of the corporation. More than 1,000 students (girls were admitted in 1976) currently attend the school, which provides free education as well as room and board to children from broken homes and low-income backgrounds. The school also provides the children with medical care, clothing and weekly allowances, and free college aid of up to $12,000 for those students seeking higher education.

Hershey encourages employees to become involved in their communities through policies allowing leaves of absence for civic, political and community volunteerism for up to a year. (Source: Council on Economic Priorities)

SUMMARY

Fiscal year ended: Dec. 31
(Revenue and net income in millions)

	1991*	1990	1989	1988	1987	1986	1985	5-year growth, %† (annual/total)
Revenue		2,716	2,421	2,168	1,864	1,635	1,527	12/77
Net income		216[1]	171	214	148	133	112	14/92
Earnings/share		2.39[1]	1.90	2.37	1.64	1.42	1.19	15/101
Dividend/share		.99[2]	.74	.66	.58	.52	.48	16/106
Dividend yield, %	2.2	2.6[3]	2.1	2.5	2.4	2.1	2.8	—/—
Stock price	41.25	37.50	35.875	26.00	24.50	24.63	17.13	17/119
P/E ratio[4]	17.0	17.9	19.8	15.1	15.3	17.8	13.6	—/—
Book value/share		13.79	12.39	11.15	9.23	8.07	7.74	12/78

* Stock price as of 5–1–91
† 1985–90
1 Includes $20.3 million, or $.22 per share, after-tax gain on business restructuring, net. If excluded, net income and EPS would have been $196 million and $2.17 per share.
2 Includes a special dividend of $.15 per share.
3 Includes a special dividend of $.15 per share. If excluded, dividend yield would be 2.2%.
4 P/E is calculated by dividing year-end stock price by EPS from continuing and discontinued operations for the trailing four quarters.
Source: Company sources

CROMPTON & KNOWLES CORP.

One Station Place, Metro Center
Stamford, CT 06902
203-353-5400
Chairman, President and CEO: Vincent A. Calarco

EARNINGS GROWTH	★ ★
STOCK GROWTH	★ ★ ★ ★
DIVIDEND YIELD	★ ★
DIVIDEND GROWTH	★ ★ ★ ★
CONSISTENCY	★ ★
SHAREHOLDER PERKS	★ ★
NYSE—CNK	**16 points**

They put the color in your clothing, the spice in your soup, the scent in your soap and the sweeteners in your soda. Bombarding the senses from every direction is Crompton & Knowles' unique specialty.

The Stamford, Connecticut manufacturer makes an international market in dyes, flavors, fragrances, food colorings, sweeteners, seasonings and coatings.

With annual revenues of $390 million, Crompton & Knowles is one of the smaller stocks among the *100 Best,* but it's certainly no fledgling start-up. Known originally as Crompton Loom Works, the company first opened for business in 1840.

When Crompton joined with Knowles in 1898, the merged company became the world's largest manufacturer of fancy looms.

The looms are long in the company's past, but Crompton & Knowles has continued to maintain a presence in the fabrics industry. The lion's share of its customers are involved in the manufacture of apparel, carpeting, leather and upholstery. Its dyes are also used for inks and paper products.

A newer area for Crompton & Knowles, but one that has grown quickly thanks to its 1988 acquisition of Ingredient Technology Corp., is the manufacture of food flavorings and colors. The company produces seasonings, flavors, food colors, sweeteners, malt extracts and syrups for the foods industry. It also produces fragrances for personal care and household products.

In all, the company derives about 80 percent of its revenues from its specialty chemicals segment.

The balance comes from the manufacture and sale of its plastics and rubber extrusion equipment used to produce such items as consumer goods packaging, medical tubing and insulation for wire and cable.

EARNINGS GROWTH

Crompton & Knowles has had strong growth, particularly over the past eight years. Over the ten-year period from 1980 through 1990, its earnings per share increased 336 percent (an average of 16 percent per year).

The company has about 1,800 employees and 2,500 shareholders.

STOCK GROWTH

The company has had exceptional stock growth the past ten years, increasing 750 percent (24 percent per year) during the period.

Including reinvested dividends, a $10,000 investment in Crompton & Knowles stock at its closing stock price in 1980 would have grown to about $130,000 ten years later. Average annual compounded rate of return (including stock growth and reinvested dividends): about 29 percent.

DIVIDEND YIELD

Crompton & Knowles generally pays a fairly good yield, averaging about 2.5 percent over the past five years. During the most recent two-year rating period (fiscal 1990 and 1991) the stock paid an average annual current return (dividend yield) of 2.2 percent.

DIVIDEND GROWTH

Crompton & Knowles normally raises its dividend every year. The dividend increased 160 percent (21 percent per year) from 1985 to 1990.

CONSISTENCY

The company has enjoyed consistent growth the past eight years in its earnings per share, although its revenue has gone up only six of the past ten years. Its book value per share has gone up nine of the past ten years. Its price-earnings ratio of around 15 to 20 is normal for growing U.S. companies.

SHAREHOLDER PERKS

The company offers a good dividend reinvestment and stock purchase plan. Shareholders may contribute $30 to $3,000 per quarter toward the purchase of additional shares.

SUMMARY

Fiscal year ended: Dec. 31
(Revenue and net income in millions)

	1991*	1990	1989	1988	1987	1986	1985	5-year growth, %† (annual/total)
Revenue		390	356	290	199	178	163	19/139
Net income		30	25	17	12	9	8	30/275
Earnings/share		1.22	1.00	0.71	0.50	0.35	0.30	32/306
Dividend/share		.39	.29	.21	.17	.16	.15	21/160
Dividend yield, %	2.1	2.3	1.9	2.7	3.3	3.5	4.5	—/—
Stock price	26.50	17.13	15.38	7.66	5.06	4.53	3.30	39/419
P/E ratio	21.0	14.0	15.4	10.8	10.1	12.9	11.0	—/—
Book value/share		4.94	4.16	3.50	3.18	2.85	2.68	13/84

* Stock price as of 5–1–91
† 1985–90
Source: Company sources

𝒲𝒶𝓁𝑔𝓇𝑒𝑒𝓃𝓈

WALGREEN COMPANY

200 Wilmot Road
Deerfield, IL 60015
708-940-2500
Chairman and CEO: Charles R. Walgreen III
President: L. Daniel Jorndt

EARNINGS GROWTH	★ ★
STOCK GROWTH	★ ★ ★ ★
DIVIDEND YIELD	★ ★
DIVIDEND GROWTH	★ ★
CONSISTENCY	★ ★ ★ ★
SHAREHOLDER PERKS	★ ★
NYSE—WAG	**16 points**

If you want to see the future of retail technology, take a walk through Walgreen's.

You've seen zebra bars and laser scanners, on-line inventory tracking systems and the latest in automatic order entry networks.

That's kid stuff to Walgreen.

Each Walgreen's store is fitted with its own satellite dish, with a direct feed to both the home office and each of the other 1,600 stores in the 29-state chain.

Walgreen's new Vernon, Illinois distribution center—with nearly half a million square feet of floor space—houses the world's largest state-of-the-art inventory replenishment system. The system can fill small quantity store orders up to seven times faster than traditional equipment.

The company's prescription drug customers have had the advantage of Walgreen's advanced technology for a couple of years with its "Intercom" on-line pharmacy network. Its systemwide satellite link-up enables Walgreen to give its customers easy transferability between stores. Each pharmacy in the chain has automatic computer access to health profiles, prescription histories and allergy information on every Walgreen's customer from Minnesota to Miami Beach.

Walgreen is the nation's largest drugstore retailer, filling more than 6 percent of all prescriptions purchased in the U.S. (Rite Aid, another *100 Best* stock, has more stores, but Walgreen generates higher revenue and profits.)

The greatest concentration of Walgreen stores is in and around its Chicago home base, where Charles R. Walgreen, Sr. opened his first store in 1901. (His grandson, 55-year-old Charles R. Walgreen III, is currently the company's chairman and chief executive officer.) The company is also well represented in Wisconsin (90 stores), Indiana (65 stores), Texas (about 180 stores), Arizona (nearly 100 stores) and Florida (nearly 300 stores).

Pharmaceutical sales account for 33 percent of the company's $6 billion a year in total revenue. Nonprescription drugs account for 14 percent, liquor and beverages, 12 percent; cosmetics and toiletries, 10 percent; general merchandise, 26 percent, and other, 5 percent.

The company has posted 16 consecutive years of record sales and earnings.

Walgreen stores are much larger than most drug retailers, averaging nearly 10,000 square feet per store. The stores carry a wide range of merchandise, including clocks, calculators, jewelry, artwork, lunch buckets, waste baskets, coffeemakers, mixers, telephones, tape decks and TV sets along with the usual line of cosmetics, toiletries and tobacco.

More than 500 Walgreen stores now carry dairy products, frozen foods and a large selection of other grocery items. Walgreen has also extended its store hours in recent years. In fact, a number of Walgreen outlets now offer 24-hour service.

The company has been expanding rapidly, adding about 100 new stores per year. More than half of Walgreen's stores have opened since 1984. But unlike many growing retail chains, most of Walgreen's growth has come internally by building its own stores, rather than through an aggressive acquisition policy.

Walgreen's drugstore operations account for 100 percent of its total revenue. It recently sold its chain of 90 Wag's 24-hour family restaurants.

EARNINGS GROWTH

Walgreen has enjoyed strong, sustained growth. Over the past ten years, its earnings per share increased 344 percent (16 percent per year).

The company has about 49,000 employees and 21,000 shareholders.

STOCK GROWTH

The company has had exceptional stock growth the past ten years, increasing 928 percent (26 percent per year) during the period.

Including reinvested dividends, a $10,000 investment in Walgreen stock at its closing stock price in 1980 would have grown to about $125,000 ten years later. Average annual compounded rate of return (including stock growth and reinvested dividends): about 28.5 percent.

DIVIDEND YIELD

Walgreen generally pays a modest yield, averaging about 1.7 percent over the past five years. During the most recent two-year rating period (fiscal 1990 and 1991) the stock paid an average annual current return (dividend yield) of 1.6 percent.

DIVIDEND GROWTH

Walgreen has raised its dividend for more than 15 years. The dividend rose 82 percent (13 percent per year) from 1985 to 1990.

CONSISTENCY

The company has had 17 consecutive years of record sales and earnings per share. Its price-earnings ratio of around 15 to 22 is a little higher than average, but not unusual for a growing company.

SHAREHOLDER PERKS

Shareholders who attend the Walgreen annual meeting usually receive vitamins or other types of health aids.

The company also offers its shareholders of record a good dividend reinvestment and voluntary stock purchase plan. There are no fees or commissions, and shareholders of record may contribute $10 to $1,000 to the voluntary stock purchase plan up to eight times per year.

SUMMARY

Fiscal year ended: Aug. 31*
(Revenue and net income in millions)

	1991**	1990	1989	1988	1987	1986	1985	5-year growth, %† (annual/total)
Revenue		6,047	5,380	4,883	4,281	3,660	3,161	14/91
Net income		175	154	129	104	103	94	13/86
Earnings/share		1.42	1.25	1.05	.84	.83	.76	13/85
Dividend/share		.40	.34	.30	.27	.25	.22	13/82
Dividend yield, %	1.4	1.8	1.8	1.8	1.5	1.6	1.8	—/—
Stock price	32.13	25.69	23.94	15.19	15.78	16.75	13.69	14/87
P/E ratio	22.0	15.8	14.6	15.5	21.5	18.5	15.8	—/—
Book value/share		7.70	6.69	5.79	5.06	4.50	3.91	15/97

  * Except stock price Dec. 31, 1985–90
** Stock price as of 5–1–91
  † 1985–90
Source: Company sources

44

SYSCO CORPORATION

1390 Enclave Parkway
Houston, TX 77077-2027
713-584-1390
Chairman and CEO: John F. Woodhouse
President: Bill M. Lindig

EARNINGS GROWTH	★ ★ ★
STOCK GROWTH	★ ★ ★ ★
DIVIDEND YIELD	★
DIVIDEND GROWTH	★ ★
CONSISTENCY	★ ★ ★ ★
SHAREHOLDER PERKS	★ ★
NYSE—SYY	**16 points**

With a food distribution network that spans the continent, Sysco has become the largest marketer and distributor of food service products in America.

The Houston-based operation has been one of the fastest-growing companies in the U.S. over the past two decades. When it was formed in 1969 through the merger of nine small companies, its total annual sales amounted to $115 million.

Since then, it has acquired 46 other food-related companies and grown in annual revenue by 6,500 percent to $7.6 billion in 1990. The company has posted 14 consecutive years of increased earnings per share.

Sysco has operations in the nation's 150 largest cities, and services about 230,000 restaurants, hotels, schools, health care facilities and other institutions.

Its principal products include frozen meats, fruits, vegetables, desserts and fully prepared frozen entrees. It also supplies a full line of canned and dry goods, fresh meat and produce and imported specialties. The company procures products from more than 30 countries.

Sysco's nonfood products include napkins, disposable plates and cups; silverware, china and other tableware; restaurant and kitchen equipment and cleaning supplies.

As a sideline, the company's 6,000 sales and service representatives help with menu planning and inventory control. They also install and service beverage dispensers and other kitchen equipment.

The bulk of Sysco's sales (57 percent) is to restaurants. Its other major markets include: hospitals and nursing homes (14 percent of sales), schools and colleges (9 percent of revenue), hotels and motels (7 percent). The other 13 percent of the company's revenue comes from various sources, including retail groceries.

EARNINGS GROWTH

Sysco has enjoyed excellent long-term growth. Over the past ten years, its earnings per share increased 437 percent (18 percent per year).

The company has about 20,000 employees and 12,000 shareholders.

STOCK GROWTH

The company has had outstanding, sustained stock price appreciation the past ten years, increasing 797 percent (24.5 percent per year) for the period.

Including reinvested dividends, a $10,000 investment in Sysco stock at its closing stock price in 1980 would have grown to about $97,000 ten years later. Average annual compounded rate of return (including stock growth and reinvested dividends): about 25.5 percent.

DIVIDEND YIELD

Sysco generally pays a very modest yield, averaging just under 1 percent over the past five years. During the most recent two-year rating period (fiscal 1990 and 1991) the stock paid an average annual current return (dividend yield) of 0.7 percent.

DIVIDEND GROWTH

Sysco has raised its dividend for 13 consecutive years. The dividend rose 90 percent (14 percent per year) from 1985 to 1990.

CONSISTENCY

The company has had 14 consecutive years of record earnings per share, 11 consecutive years of record revenue and more than 15 years of increased book value per share. Its price-earnings ratio of about 20 to 25 is higher than most food wholesalers, but it is not surprising considering the company's performance history.

SHAREHOLDER PERKS

The company offers its shareholders a good dividend reinvestment and voluntary stock purchase plan with no fees or commissions.

SUMMARY

Fiscal year ended: June 30*
(Revenue and net income in millions)

	1991**	1990	1989	1988	1987	1986	1985	5-year growth, %† (annual/total)
Revenue		7,591	6,851	4,385	3,656	3,172	2,641	23/187
Net income		133	108	85	62	58	50	21/166
Earnings/share		1.45	1.19	0.95	0.70	0.67	0.59	20/145
Dividend/share		.19	.17	.16	.13	.12	.10	14/90
Dividend yield, %	0.7	0.7	0.9	1.0	0.8	1.0	1.1	—/—
Stock price	39.75	33.63	31.63	20.00	15.50	16.00	12.00	27/231
P/E ratio	25.0	20.1	16.3	16.6	25.0	17.2	14.6	—/—
Book value/share		8.40	7.07	6.02	5.10	4.50	3.93	16/113

* Except stock price Dec. 31, 1985–90
** Stock price 5–1–91
† 1985–90
Source: Company sources

45

BANC ONE CORP.

100 E. Broad Street
Columbus, OH 43215
614-248-5944
Chairman and CEO: John B. McCoy

EARNINGS GROWTH	★ ★
STOCK GROWTH	★ ★
DIVIDEND YIELD	★ ★ ★ ★
DIVIDEND GROWTH	★ ★
CONSISTENCY	★ ★ ★ ★
SHAREHOLDER PERKS	★ ★
NYSE—ONE	**16 points**

In an industry marred the past few years by scandal, upheaval and insolvency, Banc One continues to amaze. The Columbus, Ohio banking institution recorded its 22nd consecutive year of record earnings per share in 1990—a feat unmatched by any other major U.S. banking organization.

Banc One also continues to lead the industry in some other key financial categories. The past three years it has recorded the highest return on average assets among the nation's 50 largest banks, and it has ranked number one in average common equity to assets for the past five consecutive years.

Part of Banc One's success is that its customer base is concentrated in mid-America—Ohio, Indiana, Michigan, Kentucky, Wisconsin—an area that has been less affected than the coasts by the recent housing slump and the recession.

But solid management and a knack for profitable acquisitions have also kept the company on track. Banc One has quickly nibbled its way through the Midwest. Originally established in Columbus, Banc One now has branches in more than 20 Ohio citics, four in Michigan, 11 in Indiana, one in Kentucky and 14 in Wisconsin. Its most recent acquisition was MBank Corp. in Texas, where the company now operates branches in 24 cities.

Among its biggest acquisitions (along with MBank) were American Fletcher National Bank in Indianapolis, Marine in Milwaukee, Spartan in East Lansing and KYNB Bancshares in Lexington. In 1991, the company added to its Ohio holdings by buying 67 bank offices from PNC Financial Corp.

The company's management has vowed to continue its aggressive program of acquisitions throughout the U.S.

Banc One's loan portfolio breaks down this way: commercial loans, 37 percent; real estate, 25 percent; consumer, 32 percent; other, 6 percent.

EARNINGS GROWTH

Banc One has had solid, consistent long-term growth. Over the past ten years, its earnings per share increased 247 percent (an average of 14 percent per year).

The company has about 20,000 employees and 45,000 shareholders.

STOCK GROWTH

The company has had strong stock growth the past ten years, increasing 362 percent (16.5 percent per year) during the period. The company has had three 3-for-2 stock splits and five extra 10 percent dividend bonuses in the past ten years.

Including reinvested dividends, a $10,000 investment in Banc One stock at its closing stock price in 1980 would have grown to about $97,000 ten years later. Average annual compounded rate of return (including stock growth and reinvested dividends): about 25.5 percent.

DIVIDEND YIELD

Banc One generally pays a very good yield, averaging about 4 percent over the past five years. During the most recent two-year rating period (fiscal 1990 and 1991) the stock paid an average annual current return (dividend yield) of 3.5 percent, plus a special 10 percent dividend bonus in 1990.

DIVIDEND GROWTH

Banc One has raised its dividend for more than 18 consecutive years. The dividend increased 82 percent (13 percent per year) from 1985 to 1990.

CONSISTENCY

The company has been the nation's most consistent banking organization, with 22 consecutive years of record earnings per share. Its book value growth has also been flawless over the past two decades. Its price-earnings ratio of about 10 to 11 is on par for successful banking organizations.

SHAREHOLDER PERKS

The company offers its shareholders a good dividend reinvestment and voluntary stock purchase plan. There are no fees or commissions, and shareholders of record may purchase up to $5,000 per quarter in additional shares through the voluntary stock purchase plan.

SUMMARY

Fiscal year ended: Dec. 31
(Revenue and net income in millions)

	1991*	1990	1989	1988	1987	1986	1985	5-year growth, %† (annual/total)
Revenue		3,460	3,163	2,735	2,385	2,261	2,097	11/65
Net income		423	363	340	232	237	205	16/106
Earnings/share		2.76	2.52	2.37	1.66	1.74	1.59	12/73
Dividend/share		1.04	0.94	0.84	0.75	0.68	0.57	13/82
Dividend yield, %[1]	3.1	3.7	3.2	4.2	3.8	3.6	2.9	—/—
Stock price	37.38	27.75	29.44	20.23	19.84	18.91	19.35	7/43
P/E ratio	13	10	12	9	11	11	12	—/—
Book value/share		18.11	15.65	14.18	12.65	11.71	10.52	12/72

* Stock price as of 5–1–91
† 1985–90
[1] Also paid special 10 percent dividends in 1986, 1988 and 1990.
Source: Company sources

46

Kimberly-Clark

KIMBERLY-CLARK CORP.

P.O. Box 619100
Dallas, TX 75261-9100
214-830-1200
Chairman and CEO: Darwin E. Smith

EARNINGS GROWTH	★
STOCK GROWTH	★ ★ ★
DIVIDEND YIELD	★ ★ ★
DIVIDEND GROWTH	★ ★ ★
CONSISTENCY	★ ★ ★
SHAREHOLDER PERKS	★ ★ ★
NYSE—KMB	**16 points**

There's a new baby boom afoot in America, and no one is happier to see it than Kimberly-Clark. With the birth rate at its highest level since 1964, the company's top-grossing product, Huggies disposable diapers, is draping more bottoms than ever before.

About 16 billion disposable diapers are sold in the U.S. each year—roughly $4 billion worth—and Huggies accounts for about one-third of them. U.S. diaper sales comprise about 20 percent of the company's $6.4 billion a year in total revenue.

The company's other leading brands include Kleenex, which Kimberly-Clark introduced in 1924, and Kotex, which it brought to market in 1920. The company controls about 45 percent of the $1 billion-a-year U.S. tissue market, and a 30 percent share of the $1.1 billion feminine pads market.

Other familiar Kimberly-Clark products include Hi-Dri paper towels, Delsey toilet paper, Depend adult shields and undergarments and New Freedom feminine pads. The company also makes napkins, baby wipes, tampons, bathroom tissue, surgical gowns, and commercial and industrial wipers and towels.

Kimberly-Clark's personal care and household paper products account for 77 percent of its annual revenue.

The company's other two segments include:

- Paper products (19 percent of revenue). Kimberly-Clark manufactures a range of papers, including newsprint, text papers, lightweight bible papers, cigarette papers, stationery, envelopes, labels, films and foils.
- Air transportation (4 percent of revenue). The company owns Midwest Express Airlines a Milwaukee, Wisconsin-based commercial airline and air transport service that serves 19 cities throughout the U.S. with a fleet of 13 aircraft.

Kimberly-Clark has a worldwide presence with production facilities in about 20 foreign countries. About 12 percent of its total revenues come from Canadian sales, and about 18 percent come from Europe and other foreign markets.

EARNINGS GROWTH

Kimberly-Clark has enjoyed outstanding earnings growth the past five years after very slow growth in the early 1980s. Over the ten-year rating period (through 1990), its earnings per share increased 204 percent (an average of 12 percent per year).

The company has about 40,000 employees and 20,000 shareholders.

STOCK GROWTH

The company has had excellent stock price appreciation the past ten years, increasing 532 percent (20 percent per year) during the period.

Including reinvested dividends, a $10,000 investment in Kimberly-Clark stock at its closing stock price in 1980 would have grown to about $90,000 ten years later. Average annual compounded rate of return (including stock growth and reinvested dividends): about 24.5 percent.

DIVIDEND YIELD

Kimberly-Clark traditionally pays a very good dividend yield, averaging just over 3 percent over the past five years. During the most recent two-year rating period (fiscal 1990 and 1991) the stock paid an average annual current return (dividend yield) of 3.2 percent.

DIVIDEND GROWTH

Kimberly-Clark has raised its dividend for more than 18 consecutive years. The dividend increased 134 percent (18 percent per year) from 1985 to 1990.

CONSISTENCY

Over the past ten years, the company has had eight years of increased book value per share, nine years of increased earnings per share and ten years of increased revenue. Its price-earnings ratio of around 17 is well in line with other growing manufacturers.

SHAREHOLDER PERKS

The company gives away a sample package of its products to shareholders who attend the annual meeting.

Kimberly-Clark offers a dividend reinvestment and voluntary stock purchase plan in which shareholders may purchase up to $3,000 per quarter in additional stock. Participants are subject to a small fee and commission.

CORPORATE RESPONSIBILITY

Disposable diapers, while a great convenience for new parents, have become one of the biggest problems for landfill operators. The diapers are not biodegradable. There is some speculation that disposable diaper manufacturers like Kimberly-Clark may be asked to either redesign their diapers or help defray the rising costs of their disposal.

Women and minorities are well represented on Kimberly-Clark's 16-member board of directors. A minority male and two women, one of whom is a minority, serve on the board.

The company has an affiliate in South Africa, Carlton Paper Corp. Ltd., in which it holds almost 13 percent of the equity directly and 26 percent indirectly. Carlton employs 1,721 people and manufactures and distributes paper and nonwoven products. In 1989, the affiliate had sales of $121.3 million and assets totaling $71.6 million. Kimberly-Clark is not a signatory of the Statement of Principles for U.S. companies operating in South Africa.

Kimberly-Clark tests on animals. (Source: Council on Economic Priorities)

SUMMARY

Fiscal year ended: Dec. 31
(Revenue and net income in millions)

	1991*	1990	1989	1988	1987	1986	1985	5-year growth, %† (annual/total)
Revenue		6,407	5,734	5,394	4,885	4,303	4,073	9/57
Net income		476**	424	379	325	269	267	12/78
Earnings/share		5.95**	5.26	4.71	3.73	2.93	2.92	15/103
Dividend/share		2.72	2.60	1.60	1.44	1.24	1.16	18/134
Dividend yield, %	3.1	3.2	3.5	2.7	2.9	3.1	3.5	—/—
Stock price	94.00	84.00	73.50	58.25	50.00	39.94	33.50	20/150
P/E ratio	17.0	14.2	14.5	12.9	14.5	14.2	11.53	—/—
Book value/share		28.28	25.85	23.18	19.60	20.89	19.04	8/49

 * Stock price as of 5–1–91
** Excluding $44 million charge ($.55 per share) for sale of Canadian newsprint mill.
 † 1985–90
Source: Company sources

47

THE QUAKER OATS COMPANY

321 N. Clark Street
P.O. Box 9001
Chicago, IL 60604-9001
312-222-7111
Chairman, President and CEO: William D. Smithburg

EARNINGS GROWTH	★
STOCK GROWTH	★ ★ ★
DIVIDEND YIELD	★ ★ ★
DIVIDEND GROWTH	★ ★ ★
CONSISTENCY	★ ★ ★
SHAREHOLDER PERKS	★ ★ ★
NYSE—OAT	**16 points**

Quaker Oats has struggled through some tough times in recent years. Major losses forced it to deal away its troubled Fisher-Price toys division and refocus its efforts on foods—reasoning, no doubt, that while it may know its oats, it doesn't know oats about toys. The result is a leaner, meaner, wiser Quaker that's feeling its oats again.

Fisher-Price, which is one of the nation's leading toy makers, had a dismal fiscal 1990 (ended June 30), going from an operating income of $97 million in 1989 to a net loss in 1990. Quaker spun off Fisher-Price to its shareholders as a separately traded stock in early 1991, enabling Quaker to concentrate entirely on its foods business.

The company posted total annual revenue of $5 billion in 1990. Its revenue, by product segment, is as follows:

- Hot cereals ($369 million) include Quaker Oats and Instant Quaker Oatmeal.
- Ready-to-eat cereals ($441 million) include Life, Cap'n Crunch, Quaker Oat Squares, Oh!s and Quaker 100% Natural.

- Wholesome snacks ($110 million) include Quaker Chewy Granola Bars, Granola Dipps, Rice Cakes, Butter Popped Corn Cakes and Rice and Grain Cakes.
- Aunt Jemima products ($236 million) include pancake syrups and mixes and frozen waffles, french toast, pancakes, batter and breakfast entrees.
- Celeste pizza, corn products and other products ($196 million).
- Canadian division ($232 million).
- Pet foods ($517 million) include Ken-L Ration, Gaines, Puss 'n Boots, Pounce and Kibbles 'n Bits.
- Food service ($460 million) supplies foods to 70 of the leading 100 food service operators in the U.S. The foods are distributed to fast-food restaurants, airlines, health facilities and schools.
- Golden Grain ($275 million) includes pastas, Rice-A-Roni and Noodle Roni.
- Grocery specialties ($765 million) includes Gatorade, Van Camp's beans and Wolf chili.

In all, Quaker produces about 400 products for the grocery and food services market.

Quaker's international division accounts for $1.4 billion in revenue per year (28 percent of total revenue), with most of it coming from the European market.

The company has production facilities in 17 states plus Canada, Latin America and Europe.

EARNINGS GROWTH

Quaker has experienced solid long-term growth. Over the past ten years, its earnings per share increased 157 percent (an average of 10 percent per year).

The company has about 28,000 employees and 34,000 shareholders.

STOCK GROWTH

The company has had excellent stock price appreciation the past ten years, increasing 567 percent (21 percent per year) during the period.

Including reinvested dividends, a $10,000 investment in Quaker stock at its closing stock price in 1980 would have grown to about $90,000 ten years later. Average annual compounded rate of return (including stock growth and reinvested dividends): about 24.5 percent.

DIVIDEND YIELD

Quaker generally pays a good yield, averaging about 2.3 percent over the past five years. During the most recent two-year rating period (fiscal 1990 and 1991) the stock paid an average annual current return (dividend yield) of 2.6 percent.

DIVIDEND GROWTH

Quaker has raised its dividend for 24 consecutive years. The dividend increased 126 percent (18 percent per year) from 1985 to 1990.

CONSISTENCY

The company has increased earnings per share nine of the past ten years, increased revenue eight of the past ten years and increased book value per share seven of the past ten years. Its price-earnings ratio of about 19 is in line with other growing foods companies.

SHAREHOLDER PERKS

Coupons for a percentage off some of Quaker's new products are often sent to shareholders along with their quarterly reports.

Shareholders who attend the annual meeting are given a sample packet that includes products such as Instant Oatmeal, Granola Bars and ready-to-eat cereals.

Quaker offers an excellent dividend reinvestment plan for its shareholders. There are no commissions or service fees, and shareholders may contribute as little as $10 or as much as $30,000 a year to the voluntary cash stock purchase plan.

CORPORATE RESPONSIBILITY

Quaker Oats gets high ratings in most social responsibility areas. Two of its top 25 employees are minorities, and one is a woman. Quaker Oats does not test its products on animals and has no involvement in South Africa.

The company has an active minority investment program. In 1989, Quaker purchased $29 million in goods and services from minority-owned businesses, an increase of nearly 60 percent over 1988. In the same year, the company purchased $14.5 million in goods and services from women-owned businesses. In addition, Quaker Oats maintains $150 million in tax accounts, $350,000 in demand accounts and $100,000 in time deposits with minority-owned banks.

Quaker is an investor in the Chicago Equity Fund, which was formed by Chicago's major corporations to finance housing rehabilitation in low-income neighborhoods. Quaker Oats has invested more than $750,000 in the Fund. The company also invests in the Minority Venture Capital Fund—a limited partnership of local corporations to provide venture capital for minority-owned and -operated businesses. (Source: Council on Economic Priorities)

SUMMARY

Fiscal year ended: June 30*
(Revenue and net income in millions)

	1991**	1990	1989	1988	1987	1986	1985	5-year growth, %† (annual/total)
Revenue		5,030	4,879	4,508	3,823	2,968	2,925	12/72
Net income		229	203	255	243	179	156	8/46
Earnings/share		2.93	2.56	3.20	3.10	2.24	1.88	9/56
Dividend/share	1.56	1.40	1.20	1.00	.80	.70	.62	18/126
Dividend yield, %	2.7	2.5	2.2	2.1	1.8	2.3	3.3	—/—
Stock price	57.88	50.15	59.25	50.00	44.70	36.15	24.00	16/108
P/E ratio	19.0	19.1	21.1	14.6	18.6	13.9	10.1	—/—
Book value/share		13.46	14.44	15.76	13.68	10.64	9.76	7/38

 * Except stock price based on average for calendar year
** Stock price as of 5–1–91
 † 1985–90
Source: Company sources

48

BANDAG, INC.

Bandag Center
Muscatine, IA 52761
319-262-1400
Chairman, President and CEO: Martin G. Carver

EARNINGS GROWTH	★ ★ ★
STOCK GROWTH	★ ★ ★ ★
DIVIDEND YIELD	★
DIVIDEND GROWTH	★ ★
CONSISTENCY	★ ★ ★ ★
SHAREHOLDER PERKS	★ ★
NYSE—BDG	**16 points**

While most of the American auto industry has been spinning in its tracks, retread giant Bandag has been riding on air. The company's patented process for giving old tires new life has helped Bandag roll to 13 consecutive years of record earnings.

Bandag is the world's largest producer of procured tread rubber and equipment. The Muscatine, Iowa operation has more than 1,000 franchised dealers worldwide that are licensed to use the special Bandag cold-bonding retread process.

Introduced in 1957, the two-step Bandag process starts at the factory where the rubber is molded under high pressure and high temperatures to make it denser, harder and more durable. Then the tread is sent to the franchise shops where it is bonded to tires using a lower-temperature, lower-pressure process. The company claims that its two-step process, while more expensive than the alternative "hot-capped" retreating processes, is more durable and ultimately costs less per mile.

Bandag manufactures more than 275 separate tread designs and sizes. While the company makes treads for automobile tires, more than 90 percent of its business involves truck and bus retreads.

Of the company's roughly 1,100 franchised dealers, about 60 percent are located outside the U.S. It has dealers in Canada, Western Europe, Central America, South America, the Far East and South Africa. The company also has licensees in Australia, Kenya, Mexico, India and Taiwan. Its foreign operations account for about 35 percent of its $586 million in annual revenue and 25 percent of operating profit.

In addition to its retreading process, Bandag custom-formulates rubber compounds to customer specifications for a variety of uses, including insulation for rocket motors and electrical cable, abrasion protection for mining machinery, liners for caustic and acid tanks and seals and gaskets for cars and trucks.

Retread materials and supplies account for 88 percent of Bandag's revenue, while its other products provide 12 percent of revenue.

EARNINGS GROWTH

Bandag has had consistent long-term growth. Over the past ten years, its earnings per share increased 382 percent (an average of 17 percent per year).

The company has about 2,500 employees and 2,100 shareholders. Bandag chairman, president and CEO Martin G. Carver (and his family) own about 70 percent of the voting stock.

STOCK GROWTH

The company has enjoyed excellent stock growth the past ten years, increasing 600 percent (21.5 percent per year) during the period.

Including reinvested dividends, a $10,000 investment in Bandag stock at its closing stock price in 1980 would have grown to about $83,000 ten years later. Average annual compounded rate of return (including stock growth and reinvested dividends): about 23.5 percent.

DIVIDEND YIELD

Bandag generally pays a modest yield, averaging about 1.3 percent over the past five years. During the most recent two-year rating period (fiscal 1990 and 1991) the stock paid an average annual current return (dividend yield) of 1.2 percent.

DIVIDEND GROWTH

Bandag has raised its dividend 14 consecutive years. The dividend was raised 71 percent (11 percent per year) from 1985 to 1990.

CONSISTENCY

The company has had a flawless run of growth in its earnings, revenue and book value per share over the past 13 years. Its price-earnings ratio of 15 to 18 is about average for growing manufacturers.

SHAREHOLDER PERKS

Bandag offers its shareholders an excellent dividend reinvestment and stock purchase plan. Shareholders may contribute $50 to $10,000 per quarter toward the purchase of additional shares.

SUMMARY

Fiscal year ended: Dec. 31
(Revenue and net income in millions)

	1991*	1990	1989	1988	1987	1986	1985	5-year growth, %† (annual/total)
Revenue		586	525	491	423	370	330	12/78
Net income		79	76	70	63	49	43	13/84
Earnings/share		5.50	5.22	4.68	3.90	2.85	2.51	17/119
Dividend/share		1.03	0.93	0.83	0.75	0.66	0.60	11/71
Dividend yield, %	1.2	1.3	1.2	1.3	1.3	1.7	2.1	—/—
Stock price	94.88	84.00	84.25	65.13	53.13	43.50	29.75	23/182
P/E ratio	18	15	14	13	15	13	11	—/—
Book value/share		16.00	14.70	10.80	8.84	11.38	9.49	11/69

* Stock price as of 5–1–91
† 1985–90
Source: Company sources

49

SYNTEX CORP.

3401 Hillview Avenue
Palo Alto, CA 94304
415-855-5050
Chairman and CEO: Paul E. Freiman
President and COO: James N. Wilson

EARNINGS GROWTH	★ ★ ★
STOCK GROWTH	★ ★ ★
DIVIDEND YIELD	★ ★ ★
DIVIDEND GROWTH	★ ★ ★ ★
CONSISTENCY	★ ★ ★
SHAREHOLDER PERKS	(no points)
NYSE—SYN	**16 points**

Syntex's quest for new medical remedies began in the jungles of Mexico in the 1940s. There its researchers extracted the roots of the Mexican yam plant to use in the development of topical cortico-steroids for the treatment of skin diseases, and later for the development of oral contraceptives.

Syntex moved from Mexico to Panama in 1957, and there, technically speaking, is where it stayed. The company still keeps a small office in Panama City, with a handful of people, and, more importantly, it still has its articles of incorporation on file with the Republic of Panama. But don't let the postmark fool you. This is an American company in every way but taxes.

Syntex trades on the New York Stock Exchange. The company's executive offices, and all of its key personnel from chairman and CEO Paul Freiman on down, are located in Palo Alto, California. So is its chief research center, where Naprosyn, the nation's leading arthritis medicine, was developed. In all, Syntex has about 5,000 U.S. employees.

But in spite of its Yankee leanings, the company prefers to hold onto its Panamanian citizenship for a number of reasons, not the least of which are far better corporate tax treatment and less likelihood of a takeover—

especially since Syntex's favorable tax status wouldn't apply to the acquiring firm.

Syntex's primary business is pharmaceuticals, which accounts for 88 percent of its $1.52 billion a year in revenue. Diagnostic equipment accounts for the other 12 percent.

More than half of Syntex's revenue (55 percent) is generated by Naprosyn and Anaprox, its nonsteroidal anti-inflammatories. Naprosyn is the leading seller of all prescription arthritis, pain and inflammation medications, with an 18 percent share of the U.S. market.

About 11 percent of Syntex's revenue comes from the sale of steroids for the treatment of skin diseases and allergies.

Oral contraceptives and related products account for 8 percent of revenue. Its leading lines include Norinyl, Brevicon and Genora.

Syva, Syntex's medical diagnostic subsidiary, is the world leader in the sale of drug abuse screening and monitoring systems.

EARNINGS GROWTH

Syntex has enjoyed outstanding sustained growth. Over the past ten years, its earnings per share climbed 465 percent (19 percent per year).

The company has about 10,000 employees and 17,000 shareholders.

STOCK GROWTH

The company has had exceptional stock price appreciation the past ten years, jumping 526 percent (20 percent per year) for the period.

Including reinvested dividends, a $10,000 investment in Syntex stock at its closing stock price in 1980 would have grown to about $80,000 ten years later. Average annual compounded rate of return (including stock growth and reinvested dividends): about 23 percent.

DIVIDEND YIELD

Syntex traditionally pays a good dividend yield, averaging about 3 percent over the past five years. During the most recent two-year rating period (fiscal 1990 and 1991) the stock paid an average annual current return (dividend yield) of 2.6 percent.

DIVIDEND GROWTH

Syntex has raised its dividend for more than 15 consecutive years. The dividend increased 247 percent (28 percent per year) from 1985 to 1990.

CONSISTENCY

The company has had increased earnings per share nine of the past ten years, increased book value eight of the past ten years and record revenue for the past 15 consecutive years. Its price-earnings ratio of about 18 is normal for growing U.S. companies.

SHAREHOLDER PERKS   (no points)

Syntex offers no dividend reinvestment plan and no other perks.

SUMMARY

Fiscal year ended: July 31*
(Revenue and net income in millions)

	1991**	1990	1989	1988	1987	1986	1985	5-year growth, %† (annual/total)
Revenue		1,521	1,349	1,272	1,129	980	850	13/79
Net income		342	303	297	249	199	150	18/128
Earnings/share		1.52	1.34	1.26	1.04	.80	.61	20/150
Dividend/share		.77	.68	.54	.43	.29	.22	28/247
Dividend yield, %	2.2	3.0	3.3	3.3	2.9	2.5	3.7	—/—
Stock price	42.13	29.13	25.25	20.32	16.44	14.56	11.41	21/155
P/E ratio	24	17	15	13	14	14	10	—/—
Book value/share		3.44	2.63	3.19	2.56	2.89	2.71	5/27

*Except stock price Dec. 31, 1985–90
** Stock price as of 5–1–91
† 1985–90
Source: Company sources

50

DELUXE CORP.
P.O. Box 64399
St. Paul, MN 55164-0399
612-483-7111
Chairman: Eugene R. Olson
President and CEO: Harold V. Haverty

EARNINGS GROWTH	★ ★
STOCK GROWTH	★ ★ ★
DIVIDEND YIELD	★ ★ ★
DIVIDEND GROWTH	★ ★ ★
CONSISTENCY	★ ★ ★ ★
SHAREHOLDER PERKS	★
NYSE—DLX	**16 points**

You'll find few companies in corporate America as dominant in their industry as Deluxe is in the business of moving money.

Americans write nearly a million checks a day, and Deluxe prints more than half of them. The 77-year-old St. Paul operation has printing plants in 60 cities throughout the country and does business with 22,000 financial institutions, including more than 90 percent of the nation's banks.

Deluxe is also the country's largest processor of regional network "automatic teller machine" transactions and is a leading producer of software for electronic funds transfer services.

The business of moving money (or "payment systems," as Deluxe terms it) is constantly evolving and expanding—a fact reflected in the 52 consecutive years of increased revenues Deluxe has posted.

It's not hard to see why Deluxe has become so dominant in its industry. Its corporate emphasis continues to be on quality and service. Despite its huge volume of business (more than 400,000 check orders received each working day and more than 100 million annually), Deluxe is able to print and ship 96 percent of its orders within two days of the time they're received. And 99 percent of those orders are shipped without error. To help keep the orders flowing out, the company's 60 printing plants around the country are electronically linked.

Of Deluxe's $1.4 billion in annual revenue, 75 percent comes from its payment systems division. Its business systems group, which is a major supplier of short-run computer forms, business forms and record-keeping systems, accounts for 11 percent of total revenue.

In late 1987, Deluxe acquired Current, Inc., the nation's largest direct mail marketer of greeting cards, stationery and related consumer products. Current's sales, along with other sales in the company's consumer specialty products group, account for about 14 percent of the company's total revenue.

EARNINGS GROWTH

Deluxe has enjoyed steady, solid growth for many years. Over the past ten years, the company's earnings per share increased 314 percent (15 percent per year).

The company has about 16,000 employees and 23,000 shareholders.

STOCK GROWTH

The company's stock price has been flat since 1986, but because of rapid growth early in the decade, the stock has grown 438 percent over the past ten years (18.5 percent per year).

Including reinvested dividends, a $10,000 investment in Deluxe stock at its closing stock price in 1980 would have grown to about $73,000 ten years later. Average annual compounded rate of return (including stock growth and reinvested dividends): about 22 percent.

DIVIDEND YIELD

Deluxe has traditionally paid a very good yield, averaging more than 3 percent over the past ten years. During the most recent two-year rating period (fiscal 1990 and 1991) the stock paid an average annual current return (dividend yield) of 3.1 percent.

DIVIDEND GROWTH

Deluxe has raised its dividend for 30 consecutive years. The dividend rose 124 percent (18 percent per year) from 1985 to 1990.

CONSISTENCY

With 52 consecutive years of record revenues, Deluxe has been one of America's most consistent performers. The company has had 38 consecutive years of increased operating earnings per share. (Its net earnings per share dropped in 1988 strictly as result of a nonrecurring gain the company took in 1987.) Its price-earnings ratio of around 17 to 19 is somewhat higher than most other printing industry stocks.

SHAREHOLDER PERKS

Deluxe offers no dividend reinvestment plan, but it does offer one perk. Shareholders who attend the annual meeting are invited to dinner—on the company—after the meeting. Meetings rotate around six locations: St. Paul, Chicago, Kansas City, Houston, Los Angeles and New Jersey, where the company has its largest concentration of shareholders.

CORPORATE RESPONSIBILITY

Deluxe is often included in ethically screened portfolios, as the company has a reputation for a commitment to social responsibility. Charitable gifts represented nearly 2.1 percent of average pretax income in 1989, totaling more than $4.9 million, and earning the company high marks from the Council on Economic Priorities. Grants are made directly through the Deluxe Corporation Foundation, a major Minnesota giver. Formed in 1952, the foundation focuses on human services (43 percent of 1989 foundation gifts), education (42 percent) and cultural activities (15 percent).

Deluxe offers employees participation in the Federal Dependent Care Assistance Plan, which enables employees to set aside, tax-free, up to $5,000 of pretax income for child care expenses. The company also offers financial assistance to employees pursuing higher education. (Source: Council on Economic Priorities)

SUMMARY

Fiscal year ended: Dec. 31
(Revenue and net income in millions)

	1991*	1990	1989	1988	1987	1986	1985	5-year growth, %† (annual/total)
Revenue		1,414	1,315	1,196	948	867	764	13/85
Net income		172	153	148	132	121	104	11/65
Earnings/share		2.03	1.79	1.68	1.74	1.42	1.22	11/66
Dividend/share		1.10	.98	.86	.76	.58	.49	18/124
Dividend yield, %	2.9	3.3	3.2	3.5	2.4	1.9	2.6	—/—
Stock price	40.13	35.00	34.38	25.00	24.38	35.25	23.38	9/50
P/E ratio	19	17	17	15	21	22	15	—/—
Book value/share		8.05	7.39	6.65	5.77	4.85	4.14	14/94

* Stock price as of 5–1–91
† 1985–90
Source: Company sources

51

PEPSICO, INC.

700 Anderson Hill Road
Purchase, NY 10577
914-253-2000
Chairman and CEO: Wayne Calloway

EARNINGS GROWTH	★ ★
STOCK GROWTH	★ ★ ★ ★
DIVIDEND YIELD	★ ★
DIVIDEND GROWTH	★ ★ ★
CONSISTENCY	★ ★ ★
SHAREHOLDER PERKS	★ ★
NYSE—PEP	**16 points**

PepsiCo does a lot more than quench thirsts. Its Taco Bell, Kentucky Fried Chicken and Pizza Hut restaurants—with more than 18,000 owned or franchised outlets worldwide—make PepsiCo the world's leading restaurant system.

But even more profitable for the Purchase, New York, producer is its snack foods business. Led by Doritos, Fritos, Chee-tos, Lay's and Ruffles, eight of the nation's ten top-selling snack chips are PepsiCo brands.

While snack foods account for just 28 percent of PepsiCo's $17.8 billion in annual revenue, the segment generates 42 percent of its operating profits.

The company is the leading snack food producer not only in the U.S., but in the European market as well. PepsiCo recently acquired two large British snack food producers, Smiths Crisps and Walkers Crisps.

Restaurants account for 34 percent of the company's revenue and about 22 percent of its operating profit. PepsiCo owns or franchises about 6,500 Pizza Hut restaurants and 1,800 Taco Bell restaurants in the U.S., plus 1,300 (combined) abroad. The company also owns or franchises about 5,000 Kentucky Fried Chicken restaurants in the U.S. and about 4,000 abroad, scattered through 57 other countries.

PepsiCo is the world's second largest soft drink producer (behind Coca-Cola). Its beverages are produced at 210 bottling plants in the U.S. and 725 plants outside the U.S. Pepsi is sold in 150 foreign countries and territories.

Soft drinks make up 38 percent of Pepsi's total revenue and 36 percent of its operating profit. In addition to its namesake cola, Pepsi also produces Diet Pepsi, Mountain Dew and Slice soft drinks, and recently acquired 7-Up International.

The soft drink business has been on a steady incline for many years. On average, each American consumer drinks about 43 gallons of soft drinks each year—about twice the per capita average of 20 years ago. Total soft drink sales in the U.S. have reached about $43 billion a year, of which Pepsi holds a 33 percent share.

EARNINGS GROWTH

PepsiCo has enjoyed strong long-term growth. Over the past ten years, its earnings per share increased 264 percent (14 percent per year).

The company has about 235,000 employees and 95,000 shareholders.

STOCK GROWTH

The company has had exceptional stock growth the past ten years, increasing 739 percent (24 percent per year) during the period.

Including reinvested dividends, a $10,000 investment in PepsiCo stock at its closing stock price in 1980 would have grown to about $110,000 ten years later. Average annual compounded rate of return (including stock growth and reinvested dividends): about 27 percent.

DIVIDEND YIELD

PepsiCo generally pays a fairly modest yield, averaging about 1.8 percent over the past five years. During the most recent two-year rating period (fiscal 1989 and 1990) the stock paid an average annual current return (dividend yield) of 1.7 percent.

DIVIDEND GROWTH

PepsiCo has raised its dividend for more than 18 consecutive years. The dividend increased 100 percent (15 percent per year) from 1985 to 1990.

CONSISTENCY

The company has had increased earnings per share eight of the past ten years (including the past seven consecutive years), increased book value per share nine of the past ten years and increased revenues for more than 15 consecutive years. Its price-earnings ratio of around 19 to 23 is a little higher than average for a growing foods company.

SHAREHOLDER PERKS

The company offers its shareholders of record a good dividend reinvestment and voluntary stock purchase plan. There are no fees or commissions, and shareholders of record may purchase $10 to $60,000 per year in additional shares through the voluntary stock purchase plan.

CORPORATE RESPONSIBILITY

PepsiCo has a reputation for reaching out to the minority community. The company is one of the largest corporate sponsors of LEAD—Leadership Education and Development program. PepsiCo brings in 30 minority high school students to spend the summer at the company headquarters to learn about business. In 1982, PepsiCo established its Minority Business Enterprise program. In the first year of this program, the company purchased $4 million worth of goods and services from minority-owned businesses. By 1989, this figure had reached $200 million.

Some of the company's initiatives, like Book-It! and Parque de la Amistad, sponsored by PepsiCo subsidiaries Pizza Hut and Frito-Lay, respectively, rely on cause-related marketing to promote social responsibility. Book It! is an illiteracy prevention program that encourages elementary school children to read by having a teacher set goals, which, if met, result in a Pizza Award Certificate, redeemable at a local Pizza Hut, for the student. The program operates in all 50 states and has more than 14 million participants. The Parque de la Amistad project helps build playgrounds in Hispanic communities where the company operates. Community residents turn in empty bags of Frito-Lay snacks, and PepsiCo puts up some of the money to build the playground.

The company has an excellent charitable giving record, was one of the first sponsors of an eldercare program and has women in its top levels of management. One woman serves on the 14-member board of directors, and three women are among the top 29 executives at the company. (Source: Council on Economic Priorities)

SUMMARY

Fiscal year ended: Dec. 31
(Revenue and net income in millions)

	1991*	1990	1989	1988	1987	1986	1985	5-year growth, %† (annual/total)
Revenue		17,803	15,242	13,007	11,485	9,290	8,056	17/121
Net income		800	886	762	586	457	420	14/90
Earnings/share		1.31	1.12	0.97	0.74	0.58	0.50	21/162
Dividend/share		.40	.32	.27	.22	.21	.20	15/100
Dividend yield, %		1.5	1.8	2.2	1.9	2.2	3.1	—/—
Stock price	32.88	26.00	21.00	13.00	11.13	8.67	8.13	26/219
P/E ratio	23	19	16	13	16	16	12	—/—
Book value/share		5.90	4.92	4.01	3.21	2.64	2.33	20/153

* Stock price as of 5–1–91
† 1985–90
Source: Company sources

52

HARLAND

JOHN H. HARLAND COMPANY

P.O. Box 105250
Atlanta, GA 30348
800-241-0140
Chairman: J. William Robinson
President and CEO: Robert R. Woodson

EARNINGS GROWTH	★ ★
STOCK GROWTH	★ ★
DIVIDEND YIELD	★ ★ ★ ★
DIVIDEND GROWTH	★ ★ ★ ★
CONSISTENCY	★ ★ ★ ★
SHAREHOLDER PERKS	(no points)
NYSE—JH	**16 points**

After 36 consecutive years of record earnings, Harland suffered its first earnings decline (two cents per share) in 1990. The Georgia-based check printer did, however, keep a couple of strings alive. Its revenues rose for the 40th consecutive year, and its dividends were raised for the 37th straight year.

While earnings at Harland have been flattening out in recent years, the company's balance sheet—as well as its management—remains strong. The firm has reportedly been considering acquisitions beyond the increasingly competitive check-printing business to bolster its bottom line.

Harland, in fact, did make one acquisition in 1990—the purchase of a 51 percent share of Courier Dispatch, the Atlanta-based ground courier.

One of the company's biggest growth areas has been its Scantron subsidiary, a manufacturer of optical mark readers and scannable forms.

But by far the largest share of Harland's $371 million in annual revenue continues to come from its check- and bank slip-printing business.

Harland does business with 70,000 banks, savings and loans and other financial institutions. It operates 42 printing plants throughout the U.S., with combined printing capacity of about 400,000 checks per week. In 1990, the company printed more than 12 billion checks, deposit tickets and other forms, with an accuracy rate of 99 percent. The company holds about a 22 percent share of the U.S. check-printing market.

While tighter margins, a maturing market and increasing competition have started to cut into Harland's bottom line, the check-printing industry still offers some potential. Checks continue to be the primary method of payment in this country with an estimated 55 billion checks written each year—up 10 billion checks over the past three years. And with more dual-income families and more new services such as cable TV, day care, mail order goods and credit card expenses, the number of checks written each year should continue to climb.

EARNINGS GROWTH

Harland has enjoyed solid long-term growth. Over the past ten years, its earnings per share increased 347 percent (16 percent per year).

The company has about 6,000 employees and 5,000 shareholders.

STOCK GROWTH

The company has had flat stock appreciation since 1986, but over the past ten-year period the stock increased 283 percent (14 percent per year).

Including reinvested dividends, a $10,000 investment in Harland stock at its closing stock price in 1980 would have grown to about $46,000 ten years later. Average annual compounded rate of return (including stock growth and reinvested dividends): about 16.5 percent.

DIVIDEND YIELD

Harland generally pays a good yield, averaging about 3 percent over the past five years. During the most recent two-year rating period (fiscal 1990 and 1991) the stock paid an average annual current return (dividend yield) of 4 percent.

DIVIDEND GROWTH

Harland has raised its dividend for 37 consecutive years. The dividend increased 178 percent (23 percent per year) from 1985 to 1990.

CONSISTENCY

The company had its first drop in earnings per share in 1990 after 36 consecutive years of increases. Its revenue, however, rose for the 40th consecutive year, and its book value per share continued its record of more than two decades of continuous growth. The company's price-earnings ratio of about 15 is well in line with other publishers.

SHAREHOLDER PERKS   (no points)

Harland offers no dividend reinvestment plan and no other perks.

SUMMARY

Fiscal year ended: Dec. 31
(Revenue and net income in millions)

	1991*	1990	1989	1988	1987	1986	1985	5-year growth, %† (annual/total)
Revenue		371	345	333	318	292	267	7/38
Net income		57	58	53	47	39	32	12/78
Earnings/share		1.52	1.54	1.41	1.26	1.04	.87	12/75
Dividend/share		.78	.68	.58	.42	.34	.28	23/178
Dividend yield, %	3.8	4.1	3.0	2.7	1.7	1.5	1.8	—/—
Stock price	22.75	19.13	22.13	22.00	21.00	24.63	17.44	2/10
P/E ratio	15.0	14.5	14.6	15.2	19.9	21.3	17.8	—/—
Book value/share		8.20	7.26	6.49	5.48	4.69	3.94	18/108

* Stock price as of 5–1–91
† 1985–90
Source: Company sources

53

DILLARD DEPARTMENT STORES, INC.

DILLARD DEPARTMENT STORES, INC.
1600 Cantrell Road
Little Rock, AR 72201
501-376-5200
Chairman and CEO: William Dillard
President and COO: William Dillard II

EARNINGS GROWTH	★ ★ ★ ★
STOCK GROWTH	★ ★ ★ ★
DIVIDEND YIELD	(no points)
DIVIDEND GROWTH	★ ★ ★
CONSISTENCY	★ ★ ★ ★
SHAREHOLDER PERKS	(no points)
NYSE—DDS "A"	**15 points**

The retail market has always been hostage to the twists and turns of the economy—a fate that Dillard has somehow managed to elude. Over the past decade, while the stock growth curves of most department store chains bounced along in a yo-yo-like fashion, Dillard posted ten consecutive years of increased earnings.

The Little Rock retailer's steady, persistent expansion helped boost its revenue from $470 million in 1980 to $3.7 billion in 1990.

Dillard operates about 190 stores located predominantly in the Southwest. Its biggest concentration is in Texas, where it operates about 60 stores. It also operates about 20 stores in both Louisiana and Missouri, 16 in Oklahoma, 13 in Arizona, and others in Kansas, Arkansas, Tennessee, New Mexico, Nebraska, Nevada, Florida and Mississippi.

The company plans to open 10 to 12 new stores a year for the next several years. While much of Dillard's growth has come from the construction of new stores, it has also grown by acquisition. It acquired Stix, Baer and Diamond department stores in 1984, 12 Macy stores in 1986, Joske's and Cain-Sloan's in 1987, D.H. Holmes in 1989 and J.B. Ivey & Co. in 1990.

Dillard specializes in mid- to high-priced merchandise, with emphasis on apparel and home furnishings. Its stores vary in size, but its newer stores have been in the range of 170,000 to 200,000 square feet.

Much of the company's recent success can be attributed to its ability to maintain high margins (around 36 percent), and to its Quick Response inventory control and reorder system. The computerized inventory network enables Dillard to keep inventories to a minimum while maintaining adequate supplies of its better-selling merchandise.

The first Dillard store was opened in 1938 by William Dillard. The 76-year-old founder continues to serve as chairman and CEO of the company. His son, William II, 46, serves as president and chief operating officer, and sons Alex, 41, and Mike, 39, serve as executive vice presidents.

EARNINGS GROWTH

Dillard has had tremendous long-term growth. Over the past ten years, its earnings per share increased 1,292 percent (30 percent per year).

The company has about 26,000 employees and 6,000 shareholders. Insiders own 99 percent of the class B voting stock.

STOCK GROWTH

The company has had spectacular stock growth the past ten years, jumping 4,893 percent (49 percent per year) during the period.

Including reinvested dividends, a $10,000 investment in Dillard stock at its closing stock price in 1980 would have grown to about $500,000 ten years later. Average annual compounded rate of return (including stock growth and reinvested dividends): about 49.5 percent.

DIVIDEND YIELD   (no points)

Dillard generally pays a very modest yield, averaging under 0.5 percent over the past five years. During the most recent two-year rating period (fiscal 1990 and 1991) the stock paid an average annual current return (dividend yield) of 0.3 percent.

DIVIDEND GROWTH

Dillard has raised its dividend for eight consecutive years. The dividend increased 100 percent (15 percent per year) from 1985 to 1990.

CONSISTENCY

The company has had ten consecutive years of record revenue, earnings per share and book value per share. Its price-earnings ratio of about 15 is fairly low for a fast-growing retailer.

SHAREHOLDER PERKS   (no points)

The company offers no dividend reinvestment plan and no other perks.

SUMMARY

Fiscal year ended: Jan. 31*
(Revenue and net income in millions)

	1991**	1990	1989	1988	1987	1986	1985	5-year growth, %† (annual/total)
Revenue	3,606	3,049	2,558	2,206	1,851	1,601	1,277	18/125
Net income	183	148	114	91	75	67	50	22/173
Earnings/share	5.01	4.36	3.53	2.83	2.35	2.29	1.82	17/119
Dividend/share	.20	.18	.16	.14	.12	.10	.09	15/100
Dividend yield, %	0.2	0.3	0.4	0.3	0.3	0.3	0.6	—/—
Stock price	115.75	87.38	71.00	46.00	30.00	45.00	39.00	18/124
P/E ratio	15.3	14.1	11.6	14.5	17.0	14.3	8.7	—/—
Book value/share	36.92	30.68	23.39	20.00	17.31	12.42	10.24	24/197

* Except stock price Dec. 31, 1985–90
** Stock price as of 5–1–91
† 1986–91; except stock price 5–90
Source: Company sources

TYSON FOODS, INC.

2020 West Oaklawn Drive
Springdale, AR 72764
501-756-4000
Chairman and CEO: Don Tyson
President: Leland Tollett

EARNINGS GROWTH	★ ★ ★ ★
STOCK GROWTH	★ ★ ★ ★
DIVIDEND YIELD	(no points)
DIVIDEND GROWTH	★ ★ ★
CONSISTENCY	★ ★ ★ ★
SHAREHOLDER PERKS	(no points)
OTC—TYSN "A"	**15 points**

Health-conscious Americans have been in a fowl mood lately, pounding down more pounds of poultry per person than ever before. The world's preeminent poultry producer, Tyson Foods, couldn't be more pleased with poultry's new appeal, nor with its rising position of prominence and profitability.

The Springdale, Arkansas meat packer processes 25 million chickens a week—more than a billion birds a year. It packages its fowl in many forms: fresh, frozen, mixed and marinated, plus more than 50 sizes, shapes and styles of boneless breasts and breaded patties.

Tyson runs a fully integrated operation, processing its poultry through every phase of the production process. It operates a nationwide network of hatcheries, feed mills and processing plants.

Tyson markets its poultry to the food services industry (51 percent of its $3.8 billion in annual revenue) and retail trade (49 percent of revenue). The company does business with more than 80 percent of the nation's fast-food chains.

In addition to its chicken, turkey, cornish hens and other poultry products, Tyson has been increasing its position in the pork and beef market.

The company has experienced tremendous growth over the past decade. Its revenues have risen nearly tenfold, from $390 million in 1980 to $3.8 billion in 1990. Acquisitions have had a lot to do with its growth. Of its 53 processing plants, 50 came through acquisitions. The company made its biggest catch in 1989, when it acquired Holly Farms, its largest competitor, after a ferocious takeover battle.

A couple of other factors have also helped Tyson's growth. The poultry market has exploded over the past ten years as consumers looked for healthier and less expensive meats. The market is expected to continue to rise by 10 to 15 percent per year through the next few years.

Another key to Tyson's success has been its emphasis on "value-enhanced" products. "Today nearly 85 percent of our poultry is what we call 'value-enhanced,' which is to say that we convert fresh chicken into products ranging from microwaveable chicken breast strips to premium frozen dinners to five flavors of chicken wings," says Tyson chairman Don Tyson. "It significantly reduces our exposure to fresh or iced chicken, which is the least profitable, most volatile side of the poultry business. By moving into value-enhanced products we have more stable profits."

Product line extension is another key. "Let the dog have pups," says Leland Tollett, Tyson's president. "Once we have a winner, we ask ourselves what else we can do with it." After watching sales of its precooked boneless chicken rise quickly among its food service customers, Tyson began marketing precooked boneless chicken to the retail trade, then followed the same strategy with chunks and patties. The company now produces 500 different meat products for the food service industry.

Tyson has been moving steadily into the foreign market. Its largest foreign customer by volume is now the Soviet Union. In dollars, Japan remains its most profitable foreign market.

EARNINGS GROWTH

Tyson has enjoyed excellent long-term growth. Over the past 11 years, the earnings have gone up 1,107 percent (24.5 percent per year). The company had split-adjusted earnings of just 2 cents per share in 1980, after a sharp drop, which is why the 11-year growth history beginning with its 15-cent per share 1979 earnings is a more representative indicator of the company's earnings growth.

Tyson, which was founded in 1935 and first incorporated in 1947, has 44,000 employees and 32,000 shareholders. Insiders (primarily the Tyson family) control about 60 percent of the company's stock.

STOCK GROWTH

The company has had phenomenal stock price appreciation the past ten years, increasing 3,300 percent (42 percent per year) for the period.

Including reinvested dividends, a $10,000 investment in Tyson stock at its closing stock price in 1980 would have grown to about $350,000 ten years later. Average annual compounded rate of return (including stock growth and reinvested dividends): about 42.5 percent.

DIVIDEND YIELD   (no points)

Tyson generally pays a very meager yield, which has averaged about 0.2 percent over the past five years. During the most recent two-year rating period (fiscal 1990 and 1991) the stock paid an average annual current return (dividend yield) of 0.15 percent.

DIVIDEND GROWTH

Tyson has not raised its dividend in four years, but in 1986 it doubled the dividend (from 2 cents to 4 cents; 100 percent total gain), which explains this misleading three-point rating.

CONSISTENCY

The company has had ten consecutive years of record revenue, earnings and book value per share. Its price-earnings ratio of about 15 is well in line with other growing foods companies.

SHAREHOLDER PERKS   (no points)

The company offers no dividend reinvestment plan, nor does it offer any other shareholder perks.

CORPORATE RESPONSIBILITY

Tyson owns Holly Farms, which is one of the companies listed on the AFL-CIO's national boycott list. In 1989, when Holly Farms stopped paying drivers for the time they had to wait while their trucks were unloaded, company drivers and yardmen voted to become Teamsters members. In September of that year, the union was informed that Tyson would now operate the transportation division and that the employees were no longer represented by the Teamsters. Drivers' pay scales were reduced to the Tyson Foods level, which resulted in earnings decreases of up to $6,000 a year. The next month, the drivers and yardmen went on strike. There are currently 72 charges of unfair labor practices against Tyson pending before the National Labor Relations Board. The charges include: threatening employees with loss of jobs if a union was selected, interrogating employees concerning union activities and discharging employees for their union activities. (Source: Council on Economic Priorities)

SUMMARY

Fiscal year ended: Sept. 30*
(Revenue and net income in millions)

	1991**	1990	1989	1988	1987	1986	1985	5-year growth, %† (annual/total)
Revenue		3,825	2,538	1,936	1,786	1,504	1,136	27/236
Net income		120	100	67	68	50	35	28/243
Earnings/share		.90	.77	.63	.53	.39	.29	25/210
Dividend/share		.02	.02	.02	.02	.01	.01	15/100
Dividend yield, %		0.1	0.2	0.3	0.2	0.2	0.3	—/—
Stock price	21.63	16.50	12.50	8.50	6.50	9.08	4.08	32/304
P/E ratio		15	12	15	18	18	10	—/—
Book value/share		4.85	3.33	2.67	2.10	1.59	1.21	32/300

* Except stock price Dec. 31, 1985–90
** Stock price as of 5–1–91
† 1985–90
Source: Company sources

The Coca-Cola Company

THE COCA-COLA COMPANY

One Coca-Cola Plaza NW
Atlanta, GA 30313
404-676-2121
Chairman and CEO: Roberto C. Goizueta

EARNINGS GROWTH	★ ★
STOCK GROWTH	★ ★ ★ ★
DIVIDEND YIELD	★ ★
DIVIDEND GROWTH	★ ★
CONSISTENCY	★ ★ ★
SHAREHOLDER PERKS	★ ★
NYSE—KO	**15 points**

Here in America, the cola wars seem to rage on endlessly. But elsewhere around the world, "the real thing" has no peer. The Atlanta-based beverage giant commands a 46 percent share of all soft drink sales outside the U.S., four times the volume of its nearest competitor.

Even in the U.S. market, where competition from Pepsi and other soft drink makers has kept Coke's market share at 41 percent, the company still sells an amazing 292 eight-ounce servings per year for every man, woman and child in America. In Coke's vast worldwide market, the consumption rate of its line of soft drinks is 59 servings per capita per year.

After a period of flat profit growth in the early 1980s, Coke has popped the top on its earnings per share, advancing 15 to 20 percent per year each of the past five years.

Coca-Cola is one of the world's best-known products. It is sold in 160 countries. Worldwide, the company sells 9.4 billion cases (226 billion servings) of soft drinks a year. Foreign sales account for about 67 percent of the company's $10.2 billion in annual revenue, and 75 percent of its total operating income.

With its sale of Columbia Pictures to Sony in 1989, Coke divested itself of its only significant holding outside the beverage market. About 96 percent of the company's operating income (and 82 percent of revenue) now comes from its soft drink sales.

While Coke is by far the company's leading brand, the firm also produces several other soft drinks, including Diet Coke, Sprite, Fanta, Mr. PiBB, Mello Yello, Ramblin' Root Beer, Hi-C, TAB and Fresca.

Its other business is its foods division, which markets packaged citrus juices such as Minute Maid, Five Alive, Bright & Early and Bacardi tropical fruit mixers.

Although Coca-Cola has been around since 1886, its total volume sales continue to grow briskly. Worldwide consumption of the company's soft drinks increased 76 percent over the past decade.

In the U.S., Coke's share of the soft drink market has edged over the 40 percent mark with its recent success in wresting the Burger King, Wendy's and Marriott soft drink accounts from PepsiCo.

Internationally, the company's hottest new growth area appears to be Eastern Europe, where the end of communism has ushered in a new thirst for American soft drinks.

EARNINGS GROWTH

Coca-Cola has enjoyed solid, steady long-term growth. Over the past ten years, its earnings per share increased 258 percent (an average of 13.5 percent per year).

The company has about 19,000 employees and 96,000 shareholders.

STOCK GROWTH

The company has had excellent stock price appreciation the past ten years, rising 786 percent (24 percent per year) during the period.

Including reinvested dividends, a $10,000 investment in Coca-Cola stock at its closing stock price in 1980 would have grown to about $125,000 ten years later. Average annual compounded rate of return (including stock growth and reinvested dividends): about 29 percent.

DIVIDEND YIELD

Coca-Cola generally pays a good yield, averaging about 2.2 percent over the past five years. During the most recent two-year rating period (fiscal 1990 and 1991) the stock paid an average annual current return (dividend yield) of 1.8 percent.

DIVIDEND GROWTH

Coca-Cola has raised its dividend for more than 15 consecutive years. The dividend increased 63 percent (10 percent per year) from 1985 to 1990.

CONSISTENCY

The company has had consistent growth in its earnings per share for the past 15 years. It has posted revenue gains nine of the past ten years and book value per share gains seven of the past ten years. Its price-earnings ratio of around 25 is rather high even for a growing company and, historically speaking, very high for Coca-Cola.

SHAREHOLDER PERKS

Coke offers an excellent commission-free dividend reinvestment and stock purchase plan. Shareholders may contribute up to $60,000 a year toward the purchase of additional Coke stock. The company offers no other perks.

CORPORATE RESPONSIBILITY

Coca-Cola stands out from the *Fortune* 500 with a minority chief executive, Cuban-born Robert Goizueta. In the early eighties, the company created the Coca-Cola National Hispanic Business Agenda to serve as a liaison between the company and Americans of Puerto Rican, Cuban and Mexican origins. The company holds deposits and lines of credit of more than $3 million in Hispanic-owned banks, and it makes direct purchases in goods and services worth $5 million from Hispanic vendors. Coke has investments of $100,000 each in Minority Enterprise Small Business Investment Companies (MESBICs) in Dallas, Atlanta and Newark.

Coca-Cola has long been embattled with environmentalists over its use of Latin American rain forests to create orange groves for its Minute Maid subsidiary. In 1986, a consortium headed by Minute Maid bought more than 685,000 acres of uncleared tropical forest in Belize, which probably represented the largest tract of land still unexploited for agriculture in Central America. The company's share represented 196,000 acres, part of which was to be used to plant orange groves and build infrastructure. The remainder was to be sold to the highest bidder.

After protests by environmental groups at the destruction of this rain forest, Coca-Cola agreed in 1987 to preserve up to 166,000 acres of forested lands in their pristine state. The company later stated it would donate 42,000 acres for use as a nature preserve and set aside another 10,000 acres for subsistence farming by small farmers. In 1988, Coca-Cola sold about

90,000 acres of the property to Belizian interests: one-third to Belizian Mennonites for a settlement and the remainder to an individual for "selective forestry projects." Coca-Cola also agreed to hire a company recommended by the conservation community to do an environmental impact report on its holding and to honor whatever recommendations the report made before planting its orange groves.

Despite all these promises to donate land, there still remain 93,000 acres of habitat area for endangered animal species, which will simply be sold off to the highest bidder. The Boulder, Colorado group of the Rain Forest Action Network has started a protest against Coca-Cola for its rain forest acquisitions in Brazil. (Source: Council on Economic Priorities)

SUMMARY

Fiscal year ended: Dec. 31
(Revenue and net income in millions)

	1991*	1990	1989	1988	1987	1986	1985	5-year growth, %† (annual/total)
Revenue		10,236	8,622	8,065	7,658	6,977	5,879	12/74
Net income		1,382	1,724	1,045	916	934	722	14/91
Earnings/share		2.04	2.46	1.42	1.21	1.21	0.92	17/121
Dividend/share		.80	.68	.60	.56	.52	.49	10/63
Dividend yield, %	1.8	1.7	1.8	2.7	2.9	2.8	3.5	—/—
Stock price	54.13	46.50	38.63	22.31	19.06	18.88	14.08	27/230
P/E ratio	26	21	18	14	18	17	14	—/—
Book value/share		4.80	4.75	4.30	4.35	4.55	3.85	5/24

* Stock price 5–1–91
† 1985–90
Source: Company sources

56 *Bruno's,* INC.

BRUNO'S, INC.
800 Lakeshore Parkway
Birmingham, AL 35211
205-940-9400
Chairman: Angelo Bruno
President and CEO: Ronald Bruno

EARNINGS GROWTH	★ ★ ★
STOCK GROWTH	★ ★ ★ ★
DIVIDEND YIELD	★
DIVIDEND GROWTH	★ ★ ★
CONSISTENCY	★ ★ ★ ★
SHAREHOLDER PERKS	(no points)
OTC—BRNO	**15 points**

Large volume, low prices. That's how the Bruno brothers, Joseph, Angelo and Lee, built their business into one of the most profitable grocery store chains in America. The Birmingham-based operation has posted record sales and earnings per share the past 15 years, and its stock has split 2 for 1 four times over the past ten years.

Bruno's operates about 240 grocery stores throughout Alabama, Florida, Georgia, Mississippi and Tennessee and opens about 30 new stores a year. The company was founded in 1959 by the three Bruno brothers. Joseph, 78, served as chairman from 1959 to 1985; Angelo, 67, currently serves as chairman; and Lee, 71, now serves as a senior vice president. Ronald Bruno, Angelo's 40-year-old son, is now company president and CEO. The Bruno family holds about a 50 percent share of the company stock.

With total annual revenue of $2.4 billion, Bruno's operates grocery store chains under five different names:

- **Food World.** The company's 75 Food World supermarkets range in size from 40,000 to 48,000 square feet, attracting their customer base through discount prices.

- **Food Fair.** Smaller in size, from 17,000 to 32,000 square feet, the 28 Food Fair stores are located in areas that will not support the volume necessary for the large supermarkets.
- **Food Max.** The company's 28 "superwarehouse" stores range in size from 48,000 to 65,000 square feet. The stores offer discount prices on a wide range of foods, brand name merchandise and private label and generic products. The no-frills stores do feature expanded meat, produce and delicatessen departments.
- **Bruno's Food and Pharmacy.** With 52,000 to 60,000 square feet of floor space, the ten Bruno's Food and Pharmacy stores offer "one-stop shopping," with expanded produce, bakery and delicatessen departments; full-service seafood and meat departments; a floral department; pharmacy; and a large selection of general merchandise. Many also have in-store banking services.
- **Piggly Wiggly Stores.** Bruno's acquired its chain of 76 Piggly Wiggly supermarkets in 1988. The stores range in size from 18,000 to 41,000 square feet and are generally located in medium-sized to small towns in central and southern Georgia.

Since 1987, the company has opened three American Fare hyperstores in a joint venture with K mart Corporation. The stores, ranging in size from 147,000 to 240,000 square feet, carry a range of groceries, clothing and other merchandise.

EARNINGS GROWTH

Bruno's has enjoyed outstanding long-term growth. Over the past ten years, its earnings per share increased 469 percent (an average of 19 percent per year).

The company has about 20,000 employees and 6,400 shareholders. The Bruno family controls about 50 percent of the stock.

STOCK GROWTH

The company has had exceptional stock growth the past ten years, increasing 925 percent (26 percent per year) during the period.

Including reinvested dividends, a $10,000 investment in Bruno's stock at its closing stock price in 1980 would have grown to about $115,000 ten years later. Average annual compounded rate of return (including stock growth and reinvested dividends): about 27 percent.

DIVIDEND YIELD

Bruno's generally pays a modest yield, averaging less than 1 percent over the past five years. During the most recent two-year rating period (fiscal 1990 and 1991) the stock paid an average annual current return (dividend yield) of 1 percent.

DIVIDEND GROWTH

Bruno's has raised its dividend most years. The dividend increased 100 percent (15 percent per year) from 1985 to 1990.

CONSISTENCY

The company has had 15 consecutive years of record earnings, revenue and book value per share. Its price-earnings ratio, which has been around 18 to 25, is a little higher than usual for a growing company.

SHAREHOLDER PERKS (no points)

Bruno's offers no perks; nor does it provide a dividend reinvestment plan for its shareholders.

CORPORATE RESPONSIBILITY

Little public information exists concerning Bruno's social initiatives. The company was not at all forthcoming when questioned by the Council on Economic Priorities. Bruno's does have a corporate officer who focuses on environmental affairs. The company has taken some positive steps in its stores, including making environmental brochures and reusable bags available to customers. But Bruno's falls short in other areas where supermarkets can make a positive impact. The company does not have recycling programs for the shrink wrap used in shipping or for its paper or plastic bags. Bruno's has not followed the lead of some of its competitors that offer rebates to customers using their own shopping bags and that highlight environmentally benign products. (Source: Council on Economic Priorities)

SUMMARY

Fiscal year ended: June 30*
(Revenue and net income in millions)

	1991**	1990	1989	1988	1987	1986	1985	5-year growth, %† (annual/total)
Revenue		2,395	2,134	1,982	1,415	1,018	886	22/170
Net income		58	50	41	33	30	25	18/132
Earnings/share		.71	.62	.50	.41	.38	.34	16/109
Dividend/share		.14	.12	.10	.09	.08	.07	15/100
Dividend yield, %	0.9	1.0	1.1	0.9	0.5	0.5	1.3	—/—
Stock price	20.13	15.38	15.00	10.50	11.00	8.38	9.25	11/66
P/E ratio	25	18	18	21	23	21	16	—/—
Book value/share		4.15	3.55	3.05	2.55	2.25	1.95	16/112

 * Except stock price Dec. 31, 1985–90
** Stock price as of 5–1–91
 † 1985–90
Source: Company sources

57 WARNER LAMBERT

WARNER-LAMBERT COMPANY

210 Tabor Road
Morris Plains, NJ 07950
201-540-2000
Chairman and CEO: Joseph D. Williams
President and COO: Melvin R. Goodes

EARNINGS GROWTH	★
STOCK GROWTH	★ ★ ★ ★
DIVIDEND YIELD	★ ★
DIVIDEND GROWTH	★ ★ ★
CONSISTENCY	★ ★
SHAREHOLDER PERKS	★ ★ ★
NYSE—WLA	**15 points**

Here's a trivia test to try on your friends: What company leads the world in the production of chewing gum? One hint: It starts with "W."

Most would guess Wrigley—and they would be close. Wrigley is the most recognizable name in gum. But it's Warner-Lambert, with its Trident, Dentyne, Freshen-Up, Chewels, Bubblicious, Chiclets, Clorets, Beeman's, Black Jack and Clove brands, that leads the world in the sale of gum.

Gums and mints account for about one-quarter of Warner-Lambert's $4.7 billion in annual revenue. The company also manufactures prescription drugs, brand name over-the-counter remedies and other consumer products.

Among its more recognizable brands are Schick razors, Rolaids, Listerine, Halls throat lozenges, Sinutab and Efferdent.

The New Jersey-based operation does business in 130 countries. Two-thirds of Warner's 33,000 employees work outside the U.S., and 46 percent of the company's revenue comes from foreign markets. Its major markets outside the U.S. are Japan, Canada, Germany, France, Britain and Mexico.

The company divides its operation into four key segments:

- Prescription drugs (33 percent of revenue). Warner-Lambert's most notable subsidiaries in the prescription drugs area are Parke-Davis and Goedecke. The company produces a line of analgesics, anesthetics, anticonvulsants, anti-infectives, antihistamines, antiviral agents, bronchodilators, cardiovascular products, dermatologics, hemorrhoidal preparations, influenza vaccines, oral contraceptives and other products. Its Warner Chilcott Laboratories produce more than 200 generic pharmaceutical products.
- Nonprescription drugs (32.5 percent of revenue). Name brand products include Benylin, Benadryl, Rolaids, Lubriderm, Corn Huskers, Paramet, Listerex, Sinutab, Anusol, Agoral, Halls, Listerine, Listermint, Sterisol, Efferdent and Promega.
- Gums and mints (23 percent of revenue). In addition to its chewing gums, Warner-Lambert makes Certs and Clorets breath mints, Junior Mints, Pom Poms, Sugar Daddy and Sugar Babies.
- Other products (12 percent of revenue). Its Schick razors include the Injector Plus Platinum, Super II, Slim Twin, Schick Disposable, Schick Plus, Ultrex Disposable and Slim Twin. The company is also the world's leading producer of empty hard gelatin capsules used by pharmaceutical companies for their production of encapsulated products.

EARNINGS GROWTH

Warner-Lambert has had excellent growth the past five years, although its earnings per share over the most recent ten-year period (through 1990) was only 198 percent (11.5 percent per year).

The company has about 33,000 employees and 48,000 shareholders.

STOCK GROWTH

The company has had outstanding stock price appreciation the past ten years, increasing 630 percent (22 percent per year) for the period.

Including reinvested dividends, a $10,000 investment in Warner-Lambert stock at its closing stock price in 1980 would have grown to about $102,000 ten years later. Average annual compounded rate of return (including stock growth and reinvested dividends): about 26 percent.

DIVIDEND YIELD

Warner-Lambert generally pays a good dividend yield, averaging about 2.5 percent over the past five years. During the most recent two-year rating period (fiscal 1990 and 1991) the stock paid an average annual current return (dividend yield) of 2.3 percent.

DIVIDEND GROWTH

Warner-Lambert has raised its dividend for more than 15 consecutive years. The dividend rose 102 percent (15 percent per year) from 1985 to 1990.

CONSISTENCY

The company has had nine consecutive years of increased earnings per share, but its book value and revenue have increased only six of the past ten years. Its price-earnings ratio of around 20 is consistent with other growing medical products companies.

SHAREHOLDER PERKS

The company offers a good dividend reinvestment and voluntary stock purchase plan. There are no fees or commissions, and shareholders of record may purchase $10 to $1,000 per month in additional shares through the voluntary stock purchase plan.

At its annual meeting, the company passes out a nice sample packet of Warner products such as Trident, Dentyne, Freshen-Up, Clove, Rolaids, Listerine, Halls, Sinutab, Benylin, Benadryl, Rolaids and Efferdent.

CORPORATE RESPONSIBILITY

Warner-Lambert rates moderately well on social responsibility issues, with two notable exceptions. The company has a subsidiary in South Africa that sells consumer health care products and pharmaceuticals. Warner-Lambert South Africa (Pty.) Ltd. employs 558 people and had sales of less than $39 million in 1988. In addition, the Investor Responsibility Research Center reports that Warner-Lambert is one of "the top 50 companies reporting the highest number of animals used in research and testing in fiscal year 1989." In that year, the company tested 6,368 animals (excluding rats and mice) at its in-house laboratories. (Source: Council on Economic Priorities)

SUMMARY

Fiscal year ended: Dec. 31
(Revenue and net income in millions)

	1991*	1990	1989	1988	1987	1986	1985	5-year growth, %† (annual/total)
Revenue		4,687	4,196	3,908	3,441	3,064	3,162	8/48
Net income		485	413	340	296	261	237	15/104
Earnings/share		3.61	3.05	2.50	2.08	1.77	1.53	19/136
Dividend/share		1.52	1.28	1.08	.89	.80	.75	15/102
Dividend yield, %	2.3	2.3	2.2	2.8	2.6	2.7	3.2	—/—
Stock price	75.00	67.50	57.75	39.19	33.75	29.31	23.75	23/184
P/E ratio	20.0	18.7	18.9	15.7	16.2	16.6	15.5	—/—
Book value/share		10.44	8.38	7.36	6.37	6.32	5.89	12/77

* Stock price as of 5–1–91
† 1985–90
Source: Company sources

58

GENERAL MILLS, INC.

P.O. Box 1113
Minneapolis, MN 55440
612-540-2311
Chairman: H. B. Atwater, Jr.
Vice Chairman and CFO: F. Caleb Blodgett
President: Mark H. Willes

EARNINGS GROWTH	★
STOCK GROWTH	★ ★ ★
DIVIDEND YIELD	★ ★ ★
DIVIDEND GROWTH	★ ★
CONSISTENCY	★ ★ ★
SHAREHOLDER PERKS	★ ★ ★
NYSE—GIS	**15 points**

What do Michael Jordan, Mary Lou Retton, Bob Richards, Bruce Jenner, Chris Evert-Lloyd, Walter Payton and the now-infamous Pete Rose all have in common—besides national renown as sports legends?

That select group of seven are the only superstars to have appeared as cover models on Wheaties boxes coast to coast since General Mills first began its sports star cover promotion 35 years ago. (A few other athletes and teams have been on Wheaties boxes in regional markets.)

But Wheaties' association with sports celebrities began long before Olympic pole vaulter Bob Richards first struck a pose for the cover of a Wheaties box in 1956. General Mills first began billing the cereal as the "Breakfast of Champions" in 1933. Some of the sports stars who have endorsed Wheaties through the years include Babe Ruth, Joe DiMaggio, Lou Gehrig, Bob Feller, Ted Williams, Stan Musial, Jackie Robinson, Yogi Berra, Mickey Mantle and Johnny Bench.

Wheaties had one other brush with greatness in 1937, when its award for "most popular Wheaties sports announcer" was presented to a Des Moines, Iowa sportscaster who made play-by-play re-creations of Chicago

Cubs games using telegraph reports. The announcer was flown to California, where he took a Warner Brothers screen test that led to a successful film career—and later an eight-year term in the White House. The announcer, of course, was one Ronald "Dutch" Reagan.

While Wheaties is General Mills' oldest cereal, Cheerios is its most popular. In fact, Cheerios is the nation's top-selling cereal, while Honey Nut Cheerios is the third leading seller. Together, the Cheerios brands hold nearly a 10 percent share of the total U.S. cereal market.

Among the company's other leading brands are Total, Kix, Trix, Lucky Charms, Cocoa Puffs, Fiber One and Golden Grahams.

With annual revenue of $6.5 billion, General Mills is among the nation's ten largest food producers. About 90 percent of its sales are within the U.S. The company divides its operations into two key segments:

- Consumer foods (70 percent of revenue). In addition to its cereals, the Minneapolis-based firm produces a line of Betty Crocker desserts and other foods including Hamburger Helper and Potato Buds. The company also makes a variety of fruit candies including Shark Bites and The Berry Bears. Other leading General Mills brands include Pop Secret microwave popcorn, Gold Medal flour, Bisquick, Yoplait yogurt and Gorton's seafoods.
- Restaurants (30 percent of revenue). General Mills owns 521 Red Lobster restaurants and 208 Olive Garden Italian restaurants. In all, the company has restaurants in 39 states. It also operates 69 restaurants in Canada and is engaged in a partnership that operates 42 Red Lobster restaurants in Japan.

EARNINGS GROWTH ★

General Mills has had solid long-term growth. Over the past ten years, its earnings per share increased 170 percent (an average of 10.5 percent per year).

The company has about 100,000 employees and 34,000 shareholders.

STOCK GROWTH ★ ★ ★

The company has had excellent stock price appreciation the past ten years, increasing 477 percent (19 percent per year) for the period.

Including reinvested dividends, a $10,000 investment in General Mills stock at its closing stock price in 1980 would have grown to about $80,000 ten years later. Average annual compounded rate of return (including stock growth and reinvested dividends): about 23 percent.

DIVIDEND YIELD

General Mills generally pays a good dividend yield, averaging about 3.3 percent over the past five years. During the most recent two-year rating period (fiscal 1990 and 1991) the stock paid an average annual current return (dividend yield) of 3 percent.

DIVIDEND GROWTH

General Mills has raised its dividend for 25 consecutive years. The dividend increased 96 percent (14 percent per year) from 1985 to 1990.

CONSISTENCY

The company has had fairly consistent growth in its earnings, revenue and book value per share, although the company had a steep nonrecurring loss in 1985. Its price-earnings ratio of about 15 to 20 is well in line with other growing U.S. foods manufacturers.

SHAREHOLDER PERKS

General Mills occasionally sends out coupons for some of its products along with its quarterly reports. It also offers holiday gift boxes in December at very attractive prices. In 1990, for example, the boxes included more than $40 worth of goods and coupons (including Betty Crocker's *Southwest Cooking* cookbook and packages of cake mix, muffin mix, Total corn flakes, Hamburger Helper, Homestyle Potatoes and other products, plus a coupon for $5 off dinner for two at Red Lobster) all for $15.95.

The company also offers its shareholders a good dividend reinvestment and voluntary stock purchase plan. There are no fees or commissions, and shareholders of record may purchase $10 to $3,000 per quarter in additional shares through the voluntary stock purchase plan.

CORPORATE RESPONSIBILITY

One of the top-rated companies in the Council on Economic Priorities' (CEP) 1991 edition of *Shopping for a Better World,* General Mills rates well across the board. The company gave $8.3 million, or a high 1.7 percent, of average pretax income to charity in 1989. General Mills has two women, one of whom is black, on its 16-member board of directors. It also has a minority male and three women, one of whom is a minority, among its top 24 corporate officers. General Mills does not test its products on animals and has no involvement in South Africa.

General Mills is known for taking strong initiatives regarding people with disabilities and has often been honored for these efforts. In 1988, it received an America's Corporate Conscience Award from CEP. In 1981, the company formed an in-house International Year of Disabled Persons committee to develop programs that sensitize employees to the concerns of disabled people. The committee also arranges annual coupon auditing and packing project contracts of $400,000 to $600,000 to workshops for disabled people. Disabled athletes have been featured on General Mills' Wheaties cereal boxes.

The company receives CEP's "neutral" rating on the environment, meaning that it appears to be in compliance with minimum legal standards but has no significant proactive programs. (Source: Council on Economic Priorities)

SUMMARY

Fiscal year ended: May 31
(Revenue and net income in millions)

	1991*	1990	1989	1988	1987	1986	1985	5-year growth, %† annual/total)
Revenue		6,448	5,621	4,980	4,510	3,946	3,757	12/72
**Net income		374	315	282	215	179	136	22/175
**Earnings/share		2.27	1.92	1.62	1.21	1.00	.76	24/198
Dividend/share		1.10	0.94	0.80	0.63	0.57	0.56	14/96
Dividend yield, %	2.9	3.1	3.5	3.1	2.8	3.6	4.2	—/—
Stock price	56.00	38.94	33.75	22.88	27.00	19.06	14.56	22/167
P/E ratio	20	16	14	17	18	16	15	—/—
Book value/share		4.96	4.54	3.88	4.14	3.81	5.76	-3/-14

 * Stock price as of 5–1–91
** Primary earnings. Excludes nonrecurring gains (losses) and accounting changes.
 † 1985–90
Source: Company sources

59 *JOSTENS*

JOSTENS, INC.

5501 Norman Center Drive
Minneapolis, MN 55437
612-830-3300
Chairman and CEO: H. William Lurton
President: Don Lein

EARNINGS GROWTH	★
STOCK GROWTH	★ ★ ★
DIVIDEND YIELD	★ ★ ★
DIVIDEND GROWTH	★ ★
CONSISTENCY	★ ★ ★ ★
SHAREHOLDER PERKS	★ ★
NYSE—JOS	**15 points**

Move over Bo Jackson. Jostens proved to be a four-sport champion in 1989–90, when it crafted the championship rings for the World Series champion Oakland A's, the Super Bowl champion San Francisco 49ers, the NBA champion Detroit Pistons and the NHL Stanley Cup champs Edmonton Oilers.

Jostens has long been a leader in the sports award market—from Olympic medals to college and professional championship rings to high school trophies.

But despite its reputation as the "jeweler of champions," Jostens is even more widely known as "America's class ring company." It produces the class rings for thousands of high schools and colleges throughout the country.

Its scholastic division is its biggest segment, accounting for 63 percent of the company's $787.5 million in annual revenue (1990). Jostens produces the graduation announcements, diplomas and related graphic products for more than 10,000 U.S. high schools and colleges. It is also a leader in the publishing of school yearbooks, plaques and custom-printed apparel and computer-based education products.

Jostens was founded in 1897 as a small jewelry and watch shop in Owatonna, Minnesota. The firm moved its headquarters to Minneapolis in 1969.

The company has compiled one of the most consistent records of growth of any corporation in America, with 34 consecutive years of increased sales and earnings.

The firm's fastest-growing segment is its computer-aided learning products division, which accounts for 15 percent of Jostens' annual revenue. It is the nation's leading producer of technology-based learning systems for the education market. The firm acquired Prescription Learning Corp. and Education Systems Corp. in 1989.

Jostens' custom recognition products division, which produces championship rings and other awards, generates about 23 percent of the company's annual revenue. Its Artex division is a leading producer of "imprinted garments."

The company operates 36 plants and offices throughout the U.S. and Canada.

EARNINGS GROWTH   ★

Jostens has had solid, consistent long-term growth. Over the past ten years, its earnings per share increased 160 percent (an average of 10 percent per year).

The company has about 8,000 employees and 8,000 shareholders.

STOCK GROWTH

The company has enjoyed outstanding stock price appreciation the past ten years, increasing 433 percent (18 percent per year) for the period.

Including reinvested dividends, a $10,000 investment in Jostens stock at its closing stock price in 1980 would have grown to about $73,000 ten years later. Average annual compounded rate of return (including stock growth and reinvested dividends): about 22 percent.

DIVIDEND YIELD

Jostens generally pays a very good yield, averaging almost 3 percent over the past five years. During the most recent two-year rating period (fiscal 1990 and 1991) the stock paid an average annual current return (dividend yield) of 2.7 percent.

DIVIDEND GROWTH

Jostens has raised its dividend for 24 consecutive years. The dividend increased 80 percent (13 percent per year) from 1985 to 1990.

CONSISTENCY

The company has had 34 consecutive years of record sales and earnings. Its recent price-earnings ratio of about 20 is its highest in recent history and slightly higher than normal for growing U.S. companies.

SHAREHOLDER PERKS

Jostens offers a good dividend reinvestment and voluntary stock purchase plan for its shareholders of record. There are no fees or commissions, and shareholders may contribute $25 to $1,000 per month toward the purchase of additional stock.

SUMMARY

Fiscal year ended: June 30*
(Revenue and net income in millions)

	1991**	1990	1989	1988	1987	1986	1985	5-year growth, %† (annual/total)
Revenue		787	696	576	507	449	402	14/95
Net income		60	54	82	39	37	38	9/57
Earnings/share		1.51	1.39	2.15	1.03	.87	.86	12/75
Dividend/share		.72	.64	.56	.48	.44	.40	13/80
Dividend yield, %	2.6	2.8	3.3	2.8	2.4	3.2	3.7	—/—
Stock price	31.00	32.00	28.13	18.63	18.50	19.25	14.25	18/124
P/E ratio	20.0	18.5	13.3	14.8	18.0	15.0	12.9	—/—
Book value/share		6.42	5.64	4.92	3.15	4.65	4.59	7/39

 * Except stock price Dec. 31, 1985–90
** Stock price as of 5-1-91
 † 1985–90
Source: Company sources

60

ELI LILLY AND COMPANY

Lilly Corporate Center
Indianapolis, IN 46285
317-276-2000
Chairman and CEO: Richard D. Wood

EARNINGS GROWTH	★ ★
STOCK GROWTH	★ ★
DIVIDEND YIELD	★ ★
DIVIDEND GROWTH	★ ★ ★
CONSISTENCY	★ ★ ★ ★
SHAREHOLDER PERKS	★ ★
NYSE—LLY	**15 points**

Of all the medications produced by Eli Lilly in its 114-year history, perhaps none is more celebrated than the antidepressant Prozac. Released in 1988, within two years it was selling nearly a million prescriptions a month worldwide. It is considered one of the greatest mood medicines in medical history, alleviating an array of mental maladies from anxiety and depression to bulimia, anorexia and obsessive-compulsive disorders.

But for all its good, Prozac has drawn even more attention for what a few users claim to be a dangerous side effect. The drug, they say, can cause suicidal and sometimes violent behavior. Some users have taken their cases to court. Despite the complaints, however, doctors continue to prescribe the miracle drug, and a growing number of users rely on it every day—most with exceptional results.

Prozac is one of a line of central nervous system treatments—including Darvon and Darvoncet-N 100—that produce about 14 percent of Eli Lilly's $5.1 billion in annual revenue.

The company's biggest segment is antibiotics, which accounts for 35 percent of its annual revenue. The Indianapolis-based manufacturer first entered the antibiotics market in the early 1950s. Now it is one of the premier antibiotics manufacturers in the world. Its star product, Ceclor, is the world's number one selling oral antibiotic, with sales in 70 countries.

Another of Lilly's leading medications is Humulin, a diabetes insulin that is considered the world's first human medication developed through recombinant DNA technology. Humulin is used by more diabetic patients in the U.S. than any other insulin.

In all, Lilly does business in about 120 countries. About 36 percent of its sales are generated overseas. The company has built an exceptional track record of profit growth, with 30 consecutive years of record earnings.

Along with its anti-infectives and central nervous system treatments, Lilly breaks its operations into four other key categories:

- Medical instruments (17 percent of revenue). Two of Lilly's strongest subsidiaries are Advanced Cardiovascular Systems, a leading developer of coronary angioplasty catheters used to open blood vessels, and Cardiac Pacemakers, a manufacturer of heart pacemakers and implantable heart defibrillators. Lilly (and its subsidiaries) also manufacture monitoring systems, intravenous fluid delivery and control systems and a number of diagnostic products.
- Diabetic care products (12 percent of revenue). In addition to Humulin, Lilly produces Iletin insulin and Dymelor, an oral antidiabetic.
- Animal health (8 percent of revenue). Through its Elanco Products subsidiary, the company manufactures livestock feed additives designed to help hogs and cattle bulk up more efficiently and herbicides (including Treflan) and pesticides to help farmers control weeds and bugs.
- All other products (15 percent of revenue). Lilly produces a wide range of other medications including Onovin, a treatment for acute leukemia, Velban, a cancer medication, and Axid, an ulcer medication, which was introduced with great fanfare in 1988 and has been selling briskly ever since.

EARNINGS GROWTH

Lilly has enjoyed strong, sustained long-term growth. Over the past ten years, its earnings per share increased 245 percent (an average of 13 percent per year).

The company has about 30,000 employees and 39,000 shareholders.

STOCK GROWTH

The company has had excellent stock growth the past ten years, increasing 387 percent (17 percent per year) during the period.

Including reinvested dividends, a $10,000 investment in Lilly stock at its closing stock price in 1980 would have grown to about $65,000 ten years later. Average annual compounded rate of return (including stock growth and reinvested dividends): about 21 percent.

DIVIDEND YIELD

Lilly generally pays a good dividend yield, averaging about 2.5 percent over the past five years. During the most recent two-year rating period (fiscal 1990 and 1991) the stock paid an average annual current return (dividend yield) of 2.4 percent.

DIVIDEND GROWTH

Lilly has raised its dividend for more than 20 consecutive years. The dividend increased 105 percent (15 percent per year) from 1985 to 1990.

CONSISTENCY

The company has had 30 consecutive years of record revenue and earnings per share. Its price-earnings ratio of around 19 is well in line with other growing pharmaceutical companies.

SHAREHOLDER PERKS

Lilly offers its shareholders an excellent dividend reinvestment and voluntary stock purchase plan. There are no fees or commissions, and shareholders of record may purchase $25 to $25,000 per year in additional shares through the voluntary stock purchase plan.

SUMMARY

Fiscal year ended: Dec. 31
(Revenue and net income in millions)

	1991*	1990	1989	1988	1987	1986	1985	5-year growth, %† (annual/total)
Revenue	-	5,192	4,176	4,070	3,644	3,720	3,270	9/59
Net income		1,127	940	761	627	558	518	17/117
Earnings/share		3.90	3.20	2.67	2.15	2.01	1.85	16/110
Dividend/share		1.64	1.35	1.15	1.00	.90	.80	15/105
Dividend yield, %	2.5	2.3	2.4	2.8	2.3	2.6	3.8	—/—
Stock price	78.63	73.00	63.00	43.00	39.00	37.13	27.88	21/153
P/E ratio	19.0	18.4	17.7	15.6	20.5	17.5	11.5	—/—
Book value/share		13.75	13.48	11.76	10.92	9.85	8.56	10/61

* Stock price as of 5–1–91
† 1985–90
Source: Company sources

61

Pitney Bowes

PITNEY BOWES, INC.

World Headquarters
Stamford, CT 06926-0700
203-356-5000
Chairman, President and CEO: George B. Harvey

EARNINGS GROWTH	★
STOCK GROWTH	★ ★
DIVIDEND YIELD	★ ★ ★
DIVIDEND GROWTH	★ ★ ★
CONSISTENCY	★ ★ ★ ★
SHAREHOLDER PERKS	★ ★
NYSE—PBI	**15 points**

Aside from the U.S. Postal Service, come rain, sleet, ice or snow, no one does more to get out the mail than Pitney Bowes. The Stamford, Connecticut manufacturer is the market leader worldwide for postage meters, mailing machines, scales, inserting systems, parcel registers, shipping systems and mailroom furniture.

Pitney has more than a million meters in service at businesses throughout the U.S., Canada and the United Kingdom.

Pitney Bowes manufactures or markcts a wide range of other business equipment, including fax machines, copying machines, dictating machines, telephone answering systems, voice recording loggers and other voice processing systems.

The company has sales and service offices in 18 countries and dealer networks in more than 100 other countries. International sales account for 23 percent of the company's total revenue.

Pitney divides its operations into four key segments:

- Mailing systems (accounts for 53 percent of the company's $3.2 billion in annual revenue). The company sells and leases a full line of mailing equipment and fax machines. The beauty of its business is that about 51

217

percent of its operating profit is generated by recurring sources such as rental, service and financing charges. The company has spent about $250 million in the past three years developing a new generation of mailing equipment. It should enjoy the fruits of its research efforts as the new equipment hits the market in the next year or two.

- Business supplies and services (10 percent of revenue). Pitney Bowes markets price-marking and merchandise identification equipment and electronic article surveillance systems through its Monarch Marking Systems subsidiary. Pitney Management Services provides facilities management of mail, mailrooms, reprographics and related areas.
- Copying machines (11 percent of revenue) and voice processing systems (10 percent of revenue). The company's Dictaphone Corp. subsidiary is the world leader in voice processing systems. Pitney also markets a full range of copiers to businesses throughout the U.S.
- Financial services (16 percent of revenue). The company provides lease financing to customers for Pitney products, and sales-aid leasing programs for vendors of noncompetitive equipment.

EARNINGS GROWTH

Pitney Bowes has experienced solid, sustained long-term growth. Over the past ten years, its earnings per share increased 200 percent (an average of 11.5 percent per year).

The company has about 30,000 employees and 31,000 shareholders.

STOCK GROWTH

The company has had excellent stock price appreciation the past ten years, climbing 370 percent (17 percent per year) for the period.

Including reinvested dividends, a $10,000 investment in Pitney Bowes stock at its closing stock price in 1980 would have grown to about $65,000 ten years later. Average annual compounded rate of return (including stock growth and reinvested dividends): about 20.5 percent.

DIVIDEND YIELD

Pitney traditionally pays a good yield, averaging almost 2.4 percent over the past five years. During the most recent two-year rating period (fiscal 1990 and 1991) the stock paid an average annual current return (dividend yield) of 2.5 percent.

DIVIDEND GROWTH

Pitney Bowes has raised its dividend for eight consecutive years. The dividend increased 100 percent (15 percent per year) from 1985 to 1990.

CONSISTENCY

The company has had nine consecutive years of increased earnings per share and more than ten consecutive years of record sales and book value per share. Its price-earnings ratio of around 15 to 20 is about in line with other growing companies.

SHAREHOLDER PERKS

Pitney offers its shareholders of record a good dividend reinvestment and voluntary stock purchase plan. There are no fees or commissions, and shareholders of record may purchase $100 to $3,000 per quarter in additional shares through the voluntary stock purchase plan.

CORPORATE RESPONSIBILITY

Pitney Bowes is a favorite of socially responsible financial advisors who admire not just its product and performance, but also its excellent social record. Pitney Bowes' chief executive officer, George B. Harvey, has gone out of his way to respond to employee concerns and to support advancement of women and minorities.

In the early 1980s, Harvey announced plans to build new world headquarters in a run-down section of Stamford, Connecticut. This decision occurred at a time when companies were more likely to relocate to fancier parts of town or suburban industrial parks. By remaining in the inner city, Pitney Bowes remained accessible to blue-collar workers who might not have found convenient or inexpensive transportation out of the city. Harvey used the announcement to celebrate the diversity of Pitney Bowes' workforce and Stamford's neighborhoods.

In 1985, the company introduced a new affirmative action program mandating that at least 35 percent of all administrative hires be women and 15 percent be persons from minority groups. By the late 1980s, not only had the percentage of female hires reached 40 percent, but women had also ascended to among the most powerful positions in the company. In 1988, Carole St. Mark was named president of the company's business supplies and services unit, which is responsible for about 20 percent of Pitney Bowes' total business. Three women sit on Pitney Bowes' 13-member board of directors. In 1990, the company won a Corporate Conscience Award from the

Council on Economic Priorities for its responsiveness to its employees. (Source: Council on Economic Priorities)

SUMMARY

Fiscal year ended: Dec. 31
(Revenue and net income in millions)

	1991*	1990	1989	1988	1987	1986	1985	5-year growth, %† (annual/total)
Revenue		3,200	2,876	2,575	2,269	1,989	1,786	12/74
Net income		259	253	237	200	166	145	12/78
Earnings/share		3.24	3.19	3.08	2.53	2.12	1.97	11/64
Dividend/share		1.20	1.04	0.92	0.76	0.66	.60	15/100
Dividend yield, %	2.2	2.8	2.2	2.1	1.8	2.2	2.9	—/—
Stock price	56.50	40.00	48.00	43.00	38.25	36.63	24.25	19/135
P/E ratio	21	13	15	14	16	14	11	—/—
Book value/share		20.15	18.15	16.15	13.47	11.70	10.35	14/94

* Stock price as of 5–1–91
† 1985–90
Source: Company sources

62

Schering-Plough

SCHERING-PLOUGH CORPORATION

One Giralda Farms
Madison, NJ 07940-1000
201-822-7000
Chairman and CEO: Robert P. Luciano
President: Richard J. Kogan

EARNINGS GROWTH	★
STOCK GROWTH	★ ★
DIVIDEND YIELD	★ ★ ★
DIVIDEND GROWTH	★ ★ ★
CONSISTENCY	★ ★ ★
SHAREHOLDER PERKS	★ ★ ★
NYSE—SGP	**15 points**

You may not know Schering-Plough by name, but you've probably reached for some of its products to ease your aches and pains. Dr. Scholl's foot pads and powders, Coppertone tanning lotion, Solarcaine sunburn medicine, Drixoral cold formula and Afrin nasal spray are all produced by Schering-Plough.

But most of the revenue generated by the New Jersey manufacturer comes from its prescription pharmaceuticals and vision care products. It has sales and operations around the world.

The company was formed in 1971 through the merger of Schering and Plough. With annual revenues of $3.3 billion, the company now ranks among the nation's ten largest medical manufacturers. The firm has had strong gains in earnings per share the past seven consecutive years.

Consumer products account for about 22 percent of the company's total revenue. Some of its other leading consumer name brands include Di-Gel antacid, Correctol and Feen-a-mint laxatives, St. Joseph analgesics and cold products, Mexsana medicated powder, Duration nasal decongestant, Tropical Blend suntan products and Muskol insect repellent.

Schering-Plough's pharmaceutical products account for the other 78 percent of revenue. The firm is well known for its vision care products, including its DuraSoft and Aquaflex contact lenses.

The company's leading revenue products are its asthma and allergy medications. Its largest single line is Proventil asthma therapies, with annual sales well in excess of $200 million.

The firm also does a strong business in the dermatological market. Lotrisone is among the nation's leading antifungal medications.

Schering-Plough also produces a number of anti-infectives and anticancer products, two brands of anti-inflammatory steroids, a line of psychotherapeutic drugs and several cardiovascular medications.

Animal health products, including antibiotics, analgesics and anthelmintics, account for more than $100 million in sales for Schering-Plough.

EARNINGS GROWTH

Schering-Plough has had strong growth the past five years, following several years of flat performance. Over the most recent ten-year period, the company's earnings per share increased 125 percent (an average of 8.5 percent per year).

The company has about 21,000 employees and 33,000 shareholders.

STOCK GROWTH

The company has had strong stock price appreciation the past ten years, increasing 338 percent (16 percent per year) for the period.

Including reinvested dividends, a $10,000 investment in Schering-Plough stock at its closing stock price in 1980 would have grown to about $62,000 ten years later. Average annual compounded rate of return (including stock growth and reinvested dividends): about 20 percent.

DIVIDEND YIELD

Schering-Plough generally pays a good yield, averaging about 2.5 percent over the past five years. During the most recent two-year rating period (fiscal 1990 and 1991) the stock paid an average annual current return (dividend yield) of 2.6 percent.

DIVIDEND GROWTH

Schering-Plough has raised its dividend for five consecutive years. The dividend increased 154 percent (20 percent per year) from 1985 to 1990.

CONSISTENCY

The company has had increased earnings eight of the past ten years and increased revenue and book value per share nine of the past ten years. Its price-earnings ratio of about 18 is in line with other growing health care companies.

SHAREHOLDER PERKS

The company offers its shareholders an excellent dividend reinvestment and voluntary stock purchase plan. There are no fees or commissions, and shareholders of record may purchase $25 to $36,000 per quarter in additional shares through the voluntary stock purchase plan.

The company also gives out a generous sample pack at its annual meetings. At its most recent meeting, the company gave each shareholder a soft-sided cooler along with samples of such products such as Solarcaine, Drixoral, Afrin and Dr. Scholl's foot care products.

CORPORATE RESPONSIBILITY

Schering-Plough is invested in South Africa through its Scherag Pty. Ltd. subsidiary, which sells pharmaceutical products. Scherag employs 166 people and had sales of $2.7 million in 1989. The company is also a major animal tester. The Investor Responsibility Research Center reports that Schering-Plough is one of "the top 50 companies reporting the highest number of animals used in research and testing in fiscal year 1989." The company used 21,192 animals in testing (excluding rats and mice) at its in-house laboratories that year.

Schering-Plough reports that women and minorities have progressed to the highest levels of management. Two of the 27 corporate officers at the vice presidential level or higher are women, and an impressive six are minorities. Three of the 25 highest-paid officers at Schering-Plough are minorities, and one is a woman. (Source: Council on Economic Priorities)

SUMMARY

Fiscal year ended: Dec. 31
(Revenue and net income in millions)

	1991*	1990	1989	1988	1987	1986	1985	5-year growth, %† (annual/total)
Revenue		3,323	3,158	2,969	2,699	2,399	2,079	10/60
Net income		565	471	390	316	266	192	24/193
Earnings/share		2.50	2.09	1.74	1.36	1.08	.79	26/216
Dividend/share		1.07	0.88	0.70	0.51	0.45	0.42	20/154
Dividend yield, %	2.7	2.5	2.5	2.6	2.2	2.4	3.6	—/—
Stock price	49.38	44.38	42.75	28.38	23.50	19.75	14.53	25/205
P/E ratio	19.0	17.6	16.7	15.3	17.5	17.2	12.3	—/—
Book value/share		9.37	8.64	7.46	6.45	6.24	6.26	8/49

* Stock price as of 5–1–91
† 1985–90
Source: Company sources

63

Luby's

Good food from good people.®

LUBY'S CAFETERIAS, INC.

2211 Northeast Loop 410
P.O. Box 33069
San Antonio, TX 78265-3069
512-654-9000
Chairman: John B. Lahourcade
President and CEO: Ralph Erben

EARNINGS GROWTH	★ ★
STOCK GROWTH	★ ★
DIVIDEND YIELD	★ ★ ★
DIVIDEND GROWTH	★ ★
CONSISTENCY	★ ★ ★ ★
SHAREHOLDER PERKS	★ ★
NYSE—LUB	**15 points**

"Good food from good people." That's the Luby's promise. And apparently the company delivers. Its customers have been singing its praises—and savoring its fare—for 44 years.

A 1990 survey by Restaurants & Institutions rated Luby's "America's first choice in cafeterias." It should be Wall Street's first choice, as well. The San Antonio restauranteur has posted 22 consecutive years of record earnings per share.

Not all of America has had the chance to sample Luby's offerings. The company's 140 cafeterias are located primarily in the Southwest. By state, Luby's has 10 restaurants in Arizona, nine in Oklahoma, four in New Mexico, two in Arkansas and 111 in its home state of Texas. The company adds about 13 new restaurants a year.

Luby's cafeterias are large, carpeted facilities—10,000 to 11,000 square feet on average—that can handle up to 300 diners at a time. Customers can choose from a wide selection of foods that, on a typical night, would include 22 to 25 salads, 12 to 14 entrees, 12 to 14 vegetables and 22 to 25 desserts.

In addition to its sit-down service, Luby's has offered food-to-go for a number of years. It recently began market testing separate to-go facilities. To-go sales account for about 6 percent of the company's total sales.

The restaurants are all company-owned—with incentives for restaurant managers. The management team—the manager, associate manager and two or three assistants—is allotted 40 percent of the restaurant's operating profits.

Managers are carefully selected and meticulously trained the Luby's way. That means three months of boot camp—mopping floors, taking orders, brewing coffee—learning the Luby's system. At the same time, they receive training in buying, hiring, accounting, labor laws, regulatory compliance, employee motivation and the whole realm of functions involved in offering "good food from good people."

EARNINGS GROWTH

Luby's has enjoyed steady long-term growth. Over the past ten years, its earnings per share increased 266 percent (an average of 14 percent per year).

The company has about 8,600 employees and 3,600 shareholders.

STOCK GROWTH

The company has had solid stock price appreciation the past ten years, increasing 275 percent (14 percent per year) for the period.

Including reinvested dividends, a $10,000 investment in Luby's stock at its closing stock price in 1980 would have grown to about $44,000 ten years later. Average annual compounded rate of return (including stock growth and reinvested dividends): about 16 percent.

DIVIDEND YIELD

Luby's generally pays a fairly good yield, averaging just over 2 percent over the past five years. During the most recent two-year rating period (fiscal 1990 and 1991) the stock paid an average annual current return (dividend yield) of 2.5 percent.

DIVIDEND GROWTH

Luby's has raised its dividend for more than 15 consecutive years. The dividend increased 76 percent (12 percent per year) from 1985 to 1990.

CONSISTENCY

The company has had 22 consecutive years of increased revenue and earnings per share. Its price-earnings ratio of around 16 is well in line with other growing companies.

SHAREHOLDER PERKS

Luby's offers its shareholders a good dividend reinvestment and voluntary stock purchase plan. There are no fees or commissions, and shareholders of record may purchase $20 to $5,000 per quarter in additional shares through the voluntary stock purchase plan.

SUMMARY

Fiscal year ended: Aug. 31*
(Revenue and net income in millions)

	1991**	1990	1989	1988	1987	1986	1985	5-year growth, %† (annual/total)
Revenue		311	283	254	233	215	196	10/58
Net income		32	30	28	24	22	20	10/60
Earnings/share		1.17	1.08	1.01	0.87	0.80	0.72	10/62
Dividend/share	.46	.44	.39	.34	.30	.27	.25	12/76
Dividend yield, %	2.4	2.5	2.2	2.2	1.6	1.6	1.9	—/—
Stock price	19.50	18.00	17.93	15.83	16.25	17.50	18.22	–0.2/–1
P/E ratio	16.0	15.0	15.9	15.8	22.2	21.0	18.6	—/—
Book value/share		6.69	5.94	5.25	4.59	4.02	3.50	14/91

  * Except stock price Dec. 31, 1985–90
** Stock price as of 5–1–91
  † 1985–90
Source: Company sources

64  A. Schulman Inc.

A. SCHULMAN, INC.
3550 W. Market Street
Akron, OH 44333
216-666-3751
Chairman: Robert A. Stefanko
President and CEO: Terry L. Haines

EARNINGS GROWTH	★ ★ ★
STOCK GROWTH	★ ★ ★ ★
DIVIDEND YIELD	★
DIVIDEND GROWTH	★ ★ ★
CONSISTENCY	★ ★ ★
SHAREHOLDER PERKS	(no points)
OTC—SHLM	**14 points**

You won't see its name on the label, but Schulman's plastics provide the soul and substance of myriads of consumer and industrial products.

The Akron, Ohio manufacturer supplies the plastics for toys, pens, outdoor furniture, disposable diapers, shelving, videotape cassettes, batteries, lawn sprinklers, artificial turf, skateboards, toys and plastic parts for various household appliances.

In many cases, Schulman also supplies the chemical concentrates that give the plastic products their color.

The company's operations are worldwide. About 70 percent of its $679 million in annual revenue comes from foreign sales. Schulman operates seven production plants in North America and Europe.

The company has enjoyed tremendous success over the past decade, with nine consecutive years of increased earnings and an average annual return to shareholders (including stock growth and reinvested dividends) of about 38 percent over the past ten years.

In addition to consumer products, Schulman's plastics are used in a range of products for the electronics industry, including telephone parts, wire insulation, transformers, outdoor lighting and wire and cable insulation. Other markets include the packaging industry (packaging for foods, soap, flowers and other household items), office equipment (computer cases and housings, folders and binders, stack trays), automotive (protective bumper strips and bumper guards, window seals, air ducts, steering wheels, fan shrouds, grills, body and body side moldings) and agriculture (greenhouse coverings and protective film for animal feed and agricultural mulch).

Schulman also manufactures flame retardants used in such applications as telephone system terminal blocks, color television tube covers, appliance housings and electrical components.

One of its more innovative new plastics is Polytrope-R, which has both high resiliency and good impact resistance. It is used for automotive body parts, side panels, moldings, grills and bumper rub strips. Polytrope-R parts weigh less than metal parts, yet are impact resistant and may be painted to match adjoining body parts.

EARNINGS GROWTH

Schulman has had strong, sustained long-term growth. Over the past ten years, its earnings per share increased 397 percent (17.5 percent per year).

The company has about 1,400 employees and 1,200 shareholders.

STOCK GROWTH

The company has enjoyed tremendous stock price appreciation the past ten years, increasing 1,724 percent (33 percent per year) for the period.

Including reinvested dividends, a $10,000 investment in Schulman stock at its closing stock price in 1980 would have grown to about $200,000 ten years later. Average annual compounded rate of return (including stock growth and reinvested dividends): about 35 percent.

DIVIDEND YIELD

Schulman generally pays a modest yield, averaging about 1.3 percent over the past five years. During the most recent two-year rating period (fiscal 1990 and 1991) the stock paid an average annual current return (dividend yield) of 1.1 percent.

DIVIDEND GROWTH

Schulman traditionally raises its dividend each year. The dividend rose 141 percent (19 percent per year) from 1985 to 1990.

CONSISTENCY

The company has increased revenue and earnings per share nine of the past ten years and increased book value per share for more than 15 consecutive years. Its price-earnings ratio of around 13 to 17 is well in line with other growing manufacturing companies.

SHAREHOLDER PERKS   (no points)

The company has no dividend reinvestment plan, nor does it offer any other shareholder perks.

SUMMARY

Fiscal year ended: Aug. 31*
(Revenue and net income in millions)

	1991**	1990	1989	1988	1987	1986	1985	5-year growth, %† (annual/total)
Revenue		679	624	598	464	388	319	16/112
Net income		36	31	28	20	15	12	25/200
Earnings/share		1.79	1.53	1.37	0.98	0.76	0.59	25/203
Dividend/share		.29	.25	.25	.16	.13	.12	19/141
Dividend yield, %	1.0	1.2	1.3	1.5	1.3	1.6	2.4	—/—
Stock price	34.50	31.00	24.00	19.00	16.00	12.00	8.00	31/288
P/E ratio	17.0	13.4	12.4	11.7	12.2	10.5	8.5	—/—
Book value/share		11.08	8.24	7.17	6.21	5.02	3.77	24/193

  * Except stock price Dec. 31, 1985–90
 ** Stock price as of 5–1–91
  † 1985–90
Source: Company sources

65 The Gillette Company

THE GILLETTE COMPANY
Prudential Tower Building
Boston, MA 02199
617-421-7000
Chairman and CEO: Alfred M. Zeien

EARNINGS GROWTH	★
STOCK GROWTH	★ ★ ★ ★
DIVIDEND YIELD	★ ★
DIVIDEND GROWTH	★ ★
CONSISTENCY	★ ★
SHAREHOLDER PERKS	★ ★ ★
NYSE—GS	**14 points**

Gillette has been on the razor's edge of shaving technology since 1903, when King C. Gillette introduced his first safety razor. The razor had a compact brass shaving head and a sleek wooden handle, and it came with 20 steel blades. It sold for $5.

Today, Gillette sells its razors by the millions. It has 54 manufacturing facilities in 26 countries. It markets its products in more than 200 countries and territories. The Boston-based manufacturer posts total revenue of more than $4 billion a year, about one-third of which is generated by razor blade sales. A *very* high margin product, razor sales account for about 62 percent of the company's $370 million in annual net profit.

Gillette's latest shaving innovation is the twin-blade Sensor shaver. The shaving head is mounted on springs, enabling the Sensor to move more smoothly across the contour of the face. Introduced in 1990, the Sensor sold 20 million units in its first year.

Gillette also makes a number of other razors, including the Trac II (the first of the twin-blade razors), the Atra and the Good News disposable.

Gillette has operations in four other consumer segments:

- Toiletries and cosmetics (27 percent of revenue, 20 percent of earnings). Gillette manufactures Right Guard and Soft & Dri deodorants, White Rain shampoo, Epic Wave home permanents, Jafra skin care products and Gillette shaving creams and gels.
- Stationery products (11 percent of revenue, 10 percent of earnings). Gillette is the world's leading manufacturer of writing instruments. It makes Paper Mate, Flair and Flexigrip pens. Through its LeMan subsidiary in France, it makes Waterman fountain and ballpoint pens. It also sells Liquid Paper correction fluid.
- Braun products (24 percent of revenue, 15 percent of sales). Gillette's German subsidiary is the market leader of electric shavers in Germany and among the leaders throughout Europe and North America. The company also makes toasters, clocks, coffeemakers, food processors and other household appliances.
- Oral-B products (6 percent of revenue, 3 percent of earnings). Oral-B is the leading seller of toothbrushes in the U.S. and several international markets. It also makes dental floss and other dental care products.

EARNINGS GROWTH ★

Gillette has had solid long-term growth. Over the past ten years, its earnings per share rose 214 percent (an average of 12 percent per year).

The company has about 30,000 employees and 25,000 shareholders.

STOCK GROWTH ★ ★ ★ ★

The company has enjoyed exceptional stock price appreciation the past ten years, jumping 957 percent (26.5 percent per year) for the period.

Including reinvested dividends, a $10,000 investment in Gillette stock at its closing stock price in 1980 would have grown to about $150,000 ten years later. Average annual compounded rate of return (including stock growth and reinvested dividends): about 31 percent.

DIVIDEND YIELD ★ ★

Gillette generally pays a good dividend yield, averaging just over 2 percent over the past five years. During the most recent two-year rating period (fiscal 1990 and 1991) the stock paid an average annual current return (dividend yield) of 1.6 percent.

DIVIDEND GROWTH

Gillette has raised its dividend for 13 consecutive years. The dividend increased 66 percent (11 percent per year) from 1985 to 1990.

CONSISTENCY

The company has had seven consecutive years of record revenues, but has posted increased earnings per share only seven of the past ten years, and record book value per share only three of the past ten years. Its price-earnings ratio of about 20 is in line with other fast-growing manufacturers.

SHAREHOLDER PERKS

Shareholders who attend the annual meeting receive an excellent selection of products. In 1991, they received a durable canvas tote bag (with Gillette's logo on the front) filled with a Sensor razor, a Liquid Paper pen, a bottle of White Rain Plus shampoo/conditioner, Foamy shaving cream, Right Guard Sports Stick, an Oral-B toothbrush and a jar of Jafra facial treatment.

The company occasionally sends out new products or coupons for new products to all of its shareholders of record.

The company also offers a good commission-free dividend reinvestment and stock purchase plan. Shareholders may contribute $10 to $1,000 per month toward the purchase of additional shares.

CORPORATE RESPONSIBILITY

For the past few years, Gillette has been the target of shareholder resolutions concerning the company's involvement in South Africa and its role as an animal tester. Gillette has two fully owned subsidiaries in South Africa employing a total of 118 persons. The subsidiaries sell toothbrushes, razors, shaving cream and razor blades. In 1988, Gillette's South African sales were less than $36 million.

Gillette became the target of a boycott by animal rights activists in 1986, when a company employee went public with her observations of what went on at the company's testing lab. Since that time, Gillette has moved all of its animal testing to outside laboratories. Shareholders at the company filed proposals in 1988, 1989 and 1990, asking Gillette to report on and reduce its animal testing. In 1988, the proposal received its highest percentage of the vote—16 percent. Gillette finally reached an agreement with the activists and released an animal testing report which indicated that the company used 2,342 animals in 1990, down from 4,953 in 1986; a reduction of 53 percent. In addition, the company reported spending more than $600,000 on developing nonanimal tests. (Source: Council on Economic Priorities)

SUMMARY

Fiscal year ended: Dec. 31
(Revenue and net income in millions)

	1991*	1990	1989	1988	1987	1986**	1985	5-year growth, %† (annual/total)
Revenue		4,345	3,819	3,581	3,167	2,818	2,400	13/81
Net income		368	285	269	230	16	160	18/130
Earnings/share		1.60	1.35	1.23	1.00	0.06	0.65	20/146
Dividend/share		.54	.96	.43	.39	.34	.33	11/66
Dividend yield, %	1.5	1.7	2.0	2.6	2.8	2.8	3.7	—/—
Stock price	36.00	31.38	24.56	16.63	14.19	12.32	8.69	29/261
P/E ratio	21	20	18	14	14	205	14	—/—
Book value/share[1]		1.36	.36	-.44	2.60	2.00	3.63	-19/-138

 * Stock price as of 5-1-91
** 1986 earnings included a one-time restructuring expense of 65 cents per share.
 † 1985-90
 1 From 12-31-85 to 12-31-88 Gillette Company repurchased 40.9 million shares of its common stock at a cost of $1.5 billion.
Source: Company sources

66

The
WALT DISNEY
Company©

THE WALT DISNEY COMPANY

500 S. Buena Vista Street
Burbank, CA 91521
818-560-5151
Chairman and CEO: Michael D. Eisner
President: Frank G. Wells

EARNINGS GROWTH	★ ★ ★
STOCK GROWTH	★ ★ ★ ★
DIVIDEND YIELD	★
DIVIDEND GROWTH	★ ★
CONSISTENCY	★ ★ ★
SHAREHOLDER PERKS	★
NYSE—DIS	**14 points**

The Magic Kingdom could pave its streets in gold with the soaring stream of income Disney has been reaping in recent years. The Burbank, California entertainment enterprise has watched its earnings—from its theme park and resort business, its motion picture division, its TV and cable programming—soar, on average, 38 percent per year over the past six years.

The largest portion of the Disney kingdom is its theme parks and resorts, accounting for 52 percent of the company's $5.8 billion in annual revenue and 62 percent of operating income. In addition to Disneyland in California, and Disney World and the Epcot Center in Orlando, Florida, Disney opened a new $500 million Disney-MGM Studios theme park in its Orlando complex in 1989. The company is also involved with a Disney park in Japan and holds a 49 percent stake of Euro Disney in France.

Disney plans to spend several billion dollars over the next decade expanding its existing theme parks in Florida and California, and adding a new park in Southern California, a second theme park in Tokyo and a second one in Europe.

Disney's other major segment, "filmed entertainment" (39 percent of revenue and 22 percent of operating earnings), has also been thriving lately.

Walt Disney Studios—with its Touchstone Pictures, Disney and Hollywood Pictures divisions—jumped from last in box office success among the major studios in 1985 to first in 1988, 1989 and 1990. The firm's top films have included *Honey, I Shrunk the Kids, Little Mermaid, Pretty Woman, Dick Tracy, Three Men and a Little Lady, The Jungle Book, Green Card* and *Scenes from a Mall.*

Disney's other filmed entertainment divisions have also done well. Its television programs "Golden Girls" and "Empty Nest" were among the top ten-rated programs in 1989, and "Duck Tales" and "Chip 'n Dale's Rescue Rangers" ranked one and two in the afternoon children's programming niche.

The Disney Channel (cable) has grown to about 5 million subscribers.

Disney's Buena Vista Home Video division has been the industry leader in video sales the past three or four years. Among its biggest sellers have been *Little Mermaid, Dick Tracy, Peter Pan, Pretty Woman, Honey, I Shrunk the Kids, Bambi* and *Who Framed Roger Rabbit?* Disney accounts for seven of the top ten video releases of all time.

The smallest of Disney's divisions—but the fastest growing—is its consumer products group (10 percent of revenue; 16 percent of operating income). The division, which is responsible for the sale of Disney apparel, dolls, software games, books and assorted merchandise, has doubled its sales and earnings the past two years. Mickey Mouse, now a spry 61 years old, remains the market favorite among Disney memorabilia buffs.

EARNINGS GROWTH

Disney has had extraordinary growth the past five years, following some shaky years early in the 1980s. Over the most recent ten-year period (through 1990), its earnings per share increased 477 percent (an average of 19 percent per year).

The company has about 52,000 employees and 175,000 shareholders.

STOCK GROWTH

The company has enjoyed outstanding stock growth the past ten years, jumping 885 percent (26 percent per year) during the period.

Including reinvested dividends, a $10,000 investment in Disney stock at its closing stock price in 1980 would have grown to about $112,000 ten years later. Average annual compounded rate of return (including stock growth and reinvested dividends): about 27.5 percent.

DIVIDEND YIELD

Disney generally pays a very modest yield, which has averaged well under 1 percent over the past five years. During the most recent two-year rating period (fiscal 1990 and 1991) the stock paid an average annual current return (dividend yield) of 0.6 percent.

DIVIDEND GROWTH

Disney has raised its dividend only four times in the past eight years. The dividend rose 86 percent (13 percent per year) from 1985 to 1990.

CONSISTENCY

The company has had eight consecutive years of increased earnings per share, following some down years in the early 1980s—which indicates that the business may be vulnerable to recession. Its revenue and book value per share have increased 14 of the past 15 years. Its price-earnings ratio of about 19 to 20 is well in line with other fast-growing U.S. companies.

SHAREHOLDER PERKS

If you plan to visit one of the Disney amusement parks in the near future, it would pay to pick up a few shares of Disney stock. Shareholders are eligible for membership in the Magic Kingdom Club, which entitles them to 10 percent off admission to the amusement parks, 5 to 20 percent off the price of accommodations, 10 percent off purchases at Disney Village, access to special cruise and travel packages exclusively for Magic Kingdom members and discounts on Delta flights to Disney areas.

The company recently discontinued its shareholder dividend reinvestment and stock purchase plan.

CORPORATE RESPONSIBILITY

It's hard to find fault with Disney's "product." Its theme parks are well designed and make excellent provisions for the disabled, and its children's programming is high quality and nonexploitative. However, Disney's image was tarnished in 1989 when it attracted the wrath of animal rights activists for a "bird-bashing" incident. Following a two-month investigation, the U.S. Fish & Wildlife Service and the Florida Game and Fresh Water Fish Commission sued Disney World and its head gamekeeper for illegally trapping, confining and killing protected hawks, falcons, vultures, egrets and ibises. The company stated that the birds were noisy, bothered customers and left droppings. Florida dropped 13 cruelty counts against Disney World at the end of January, when Disney pleaded guilty to one misdemeanor and paid $95,000. The company also set up an advisory commission of zoologists and hired a wildlife consultant.

In 1988, it was discovered that a system of artificial wetlands at Disney World, which was intended to cleanse sewage, had instead doubled or tripled the levels of phosphorus and nitrogen. Later that year, Florida's environmental agency fined the company $150,000 for seven major violations involving spilled or leaked hazardous waste. At the time, the penalty was the largest ever imposed in central Florida. In 1990, Disney paid a $550,000 fine to the U.S. EPA as part of a settlement concerning allegations that the company illegally dumped hazardous paint thinner and other toxic solvents for two years in Utah and Wyoming.

The company has two women on its 14-member board of directors and one woman among its top ten officers. (Source: Council on Economic Priorities)

SUMMARY

Fiscal year ended: Sept. 30*
(Revenue and net income in millions)

	1991**	1990	1989	1988	1987	1986	1985	5-year growth, %† (annual/total)
Revenue		5,844	4,594	3,438	2,877	2,166	1,700	28/243
Net income		824	703	522	445	247	174	37/373
Earnings/share		6.00	5.10	3.80	2.85	1.57	.98	44/512
Dividend/share		.56	.46	.38	.32	.32	.30	13/86
Dividend yield, %	0.6	0.6	0.4	0.4	0.4	0.8	1.4	—/—
Stock price	117.63	102.00	112.00	66.00	59.25	43.15	28.00	29/264
P/E ratio	21	19	17	16	21	20	15	—/—
Book value/share		26.45	22.50	17.70	14.00	10.85	9.16	24/188

 * Except stock price Dec. 31, 1985–90
** Stock price as of 5–1–91
 † 1985–90
Source: Company sources

67

KELLY SERVICES, INC.

999 W. Big Beaver Road
Troy, MI 48084
313-362-4444
Chairman: William Russell Kelly
President: Terence E. Adderley

EARNINGS GROWTH	★ ★ ★
STOCK GROWTH	★ ★ ★
DIVIDEND YIELD	★ ★
DIVIDEND GROWTH	★ ★ ★
CONSISTENCY	★ ★ ★
SHAREHOLDER PERKS	(no points)
OTC—KELY "A"	**14 points**

Temporary help services are supposed to be immune to recession, or so the theory goes. When dollars are tight, and companies are laying off workers, they typically turn to temp-help services to pick up the slack. But that's one theory that Kelly Services would be hard pressed to quantify.

The Troy, Michigan operation saw its earnings drop considerably during the recession of the early 1980s. More recently, with the economy slipping and unemployment on the rise in 1990–91, Kelly again found itself scrambling to keep its bottom line growing.

Just the same, Kelly is one company that will be around, making money, for a long time to come. With annual revenue of $1.5 billion, it is the world's largest temporary help service.

One of the keys to Kelly's success has been its ability to adapt to changes in the work environment. There was a time not long ago when a Kelly worker needed to know little more than how to work a typewriter and answer a phone. But technology has changed—and Kelly has tried to change with it.

Nowadays, Kelly workers may be expected to walk into an office and type out their work on any of 20 or 30 different software programs—and handle a complex office telephone system. The increasingly sophisticated corporate office has created both a challenge and a growing niche for Kelly Services.

Kelly is responding by providing advanced training for many of its 580,000 temporary workers. About 6,000 workers a week go through the Kelly PC-Pro hands-on training program that provides tutoring in nearly 30 different computer software programs, including Display Write, Lotus 1-2-3, Microsoft, PCWriter, Professional Write, WordPerfect and most other commonly used programs.

If workers find that they're still stumped after arriving at their temporary assignment, they can call the Kelly Office Automation Hotline, where a helpful voice will talk them through their troubles.

Kelly has 950 offices worldwide and serves 180,000 corporate customers, primarily in the U.S., Canada, the United Kingdom and France.

The company has expanded beyond secretarial work. It now also offers temporary marketing, technical, light industrial and home care services.

Kelly counts on the unpredictable—as well as the predictable—for its steady flow of assignments. Its workers step in for ailing full-time employees, help out at businesses during peak times or supplement the regular staff during special projects or new promotions.

Kelly Services was founded in 1946 by William Kelly, the 85-year-old chairman of the Detroit temp-help firm. When he opened his first service bureau in 1946, Kelly sold his customers on the concept of sending their work to his office. But the concept didn't really blossom until he altered the original plan and began sending workers into his clients' offices to handle the work. That change in strategy has kept Kelly's coffers growing for more than 40 years.

EARNINGS GROWTH

Kelly has had strong, steady long-term growth. Over the past ten years, its earnings per share increased 384 percent (17 percent per year).

The company has about 4,000 permanent employees, 580,000 temporary employees and 1,500 Class A shareholders.

STOCK GROWTH

The company has had exceptional stock growth the past ten years, increasing 560 percent (21 percent per year) during the period.

Including reinvested dividends, a $10,000 investment in Kelly stock at its closing stock price in 1980 would have grown to about $80,000 ten years later. Average annual compounded rate of return (including stock growth and reinvested dividends): about 23 percent.

DIVIDEND YIELD

Kelly generally pays a modest yield, averaging about 1.7 percent over the past five years. During the most recent two-year rating period (fiscal 1990 and 1991) the stock paid an average annual current return (dividend yield) of 2 percent.

DIVIDEND GROWTH

Kelly has raised its dividend for 19 consecutive years. The dividend increased 120 percent (17 percent per year) from 1985 to 1990.

CONSISTENCY

The company has had increased revenue and earnings per share nine of the past ten years and increased book value per share for more than 15 consecutive years. Its price-earnings ratio of about 18 is well in line with other growing U.S. companies.

SHAREHOLDER PERKS (no points)

The company offers no dividend reinvestment plan and no other perks.

SUMMARY

Fiscal year ended: Dec. 31
(Revenue and net income in millions)

	1991*	1990	1989	1988	1987	1986	1985	5-year growth, %† (annual/total)
Revenue		1,471	1,378	1,269	1,161	1,034	876	11/68
Net income		71	71	60	51	36	33	16/115
Earnings/share		2.37	2.36	2.01	1.68	1.21	1.07	17/121
Dividend/share		.66	.58	.48	.41	.35	.30	17/120
Dividend yield, %	1.9	2.0	1.6	1.5	1.3	1.2	1.7	—/—
Stock price	38.00	33.00	39.00	30.00	31.25	27.00	24.75	6/33
P/E ratio	18.0	13.9	16.6	14.7	18.6	22.3	23.1	—/—
Book value/share		11.23	9.45	7.65	6.15	4.90	4.25	21/163

* Stock price as of 5–1–91
† 1985–90
Source: Company sources

MAY

THE MAY DEPARTMENT STORES COMPANY

611 Olive Street
St. Louis, MO 63101
314-342-6300
Chairman and CEO: David C. Farrell
President: Thomas A. Hays

EARNINGS GROWTH	★
STOCK GROWTH	★ ★ ★
DIVIDEND YIELD	★ ★ ★
DIVIDEND GROWTH	★ ★ ★
CONSISTENCY	★ ★ ★ ★
SHAREHOLDER PERKS	(no points)
NYSE—MA	**14 points**

The retail trade has always been prone to the twists and turns of the economy. But May Department Stores has managed to keep profits on a steady climb. The St. Louis-based retailer, with annual sales of about $10 billion, has posted record earnings per share for the past 11 consecutive years.

The company's consistent performance may be due in part to its geographic diversity. May operates some 14 department store chains throughout the U.S. The company also owns Payless ShoeSource, the nation's largest chain of self-service shoe stores. With 2,800 stores in 44 states, Payless accounts for about 13 percent of May's total annual revenue.

May's family of department stores includes:

- **Lord & Taylor,** New York, 47 stores (accounts for 11 percent of May's total sales)
- **Foley's,** Houston, 35 stores (12 percent of sales)
- **May Company,** California, 35 stores (10 percent of sales)
- **Hecht's,** Washington, D.C., 22 stores (9 percent of sales)
- **Robinson's,** Los Angeles, 29 stores (8 percent of sales)
- **Kaufmann's,** Pittsburgh, 23 stores (8 percent of sales)

- **Famous-Barr,** St. Louis, 17 stores (5 percent of sales)
- **Filene's,** Boston, 18 stores (5 percent of sales)
- **May Company,** Ohio, 16 stores (5 percent of sales)
- **G. Fox,** Hartford, 11 stores (4.5 percent of sales)
- **L.S. Ayres,** Indianapolis, 14 stores (3.5 percent of sales)
- **May D&F,** Denver, 13 stores (3 percent of sales)
- **Meier & Frank,** Portland, 8 stores (3 percent of sales)

In all, the company operates nearly 300 department stores in 29 states and the District of Columbia. May plans to open about 100 new department stores and 1,250 shoe stores by 1994 as part of a four-year, $4 billion expansion plan. The company also pursues ongoing remodeling and expansion of its existing stores.

EARNINGS GROWTH

May has had solid long-term growth. Over the past ten years, its earnings per share increased 212 percent (an average of 12 percent per year).

The company has about 115,000 employees and 43,000 shareholders.

STOCK GROWTH

The company has enjoyed strong, sustained stock price appreciation the past ten years, increasing 408 percent (18 percent per year) for the period.

Including reinvested dividends, a $10,000 investment in May stock at its closing stock price in 1980 would have grown to about $73,000 ten years later. Average annual compounded rate of return (including stock growth and reinvested dividends): about 22 percent.

DIVIDEND YIELD

May generally pays a very good yield, averaging about 3.5 percent over the past five years. During the most recent two-year rating period (fiscal 1990 and 1991) the stock paid an average annual current return (dividend yield) of 3.4 percent.

DIVIDEND GROWTH

May has raised its dividend for 16 consecutive years. The dividend increased 97 percent (14 percent per year) from 1985 to 1990.

CONSISTENCY

The company has been one of the nation's most consistent retailers, with 11 consecutive years of increased revenue and earnings per share. Its price-earnings ratio of about 12 to 14 is well in line with other retail chains.

SHAREHOLDER PERKS   (no points)

May provides no dividend reinvestment plan, nor does it offer any other standard shareholder perks (although the company did give each of its shareholders a box of candy at its last annual meeting).

SUMMARY

Fiscal year ended: Jan. 31*
(Revenue and net income in millions)

	1991**	1990	1989	1988	1987	1986	1985	5-year growth, %† (annual/total)
Revenue	10,007	9,602	8,874	7,480	7,437	6,825	6,361	8/46
Net income	500	515	448	393	333	286	277	12/74
Earnings/share	3.74	3.64	3.04	2.56	2.10	1.82	1.79	15/105
Dividend/share	1.54	1.39	1.25	1.12	1.02	1.92	0.78	14/97
Dividend yield, %	3.4	3.3	3.5	2.7	2.8	3.5	4.2	—/—
Stock price	53.25	40.63	48.50	35.88	30.50	35.75	30.88	6/31
P/E ratio	14.0	11.6	10.3	14.1	15.2	9.9	7.5	—/—
Book value/share	20.08	18.65	21.50	18.26	17.01	15.73	14.50	5/27

  * Except stock price Dec. 31, 1985–90
 ** Stock price as of 5–1–91
  † 1986–91: Except stock price 1985–90
Source: Company sources

69  Loctite Corporation

LOCTITE CORP.

Hartford Square North
Ten Columbus Boulevard
Hartford, CT 06106
203-520-5000
Chairman and CEO: Kenneth W. Butterworth

EARNINGS GROWTH	★
STOCK GROWTH	★ ★ ★
DIVIDEND YIELD	★ ★
DIVIDEND GROWTH	★ ★ ★ ★
CONSISTENCY	★ ★
SHAREHOLDER PERKS	★ ★
NYSE—LOC	**14 points**

Like the name says, Loctite locks tight. The multinational manufacturer produces sealants, adhesives and related products for industrial, hobby and household uses.

The Hartford, Connecticut corporation has operations throughout the world. Its products are distributed in some 80 countries. In fact, its U.S. operations account for only about 43 percent of Loctite's $510 million in annual revenue. European sales generate 38 percent of revenue, while sales elsewhere around the world make up the final 19 percent.

The company's primary source of business has been the automotive industry, but in recent years Loctite has attempted to broaden its customer base to reduce its reliance on the cyclical auto sector. Even within the automotive business, Loctite has sought a wider customer base and now sells its sealants and adhesives to automakers in Europe and Japan.

Other customers include manufacturers of machine tools, light bulbs, cameras, pumps and compressors, toys, watches, farm machinery, lampshades, ballpoint pens, fighter aircraft and industrial gear boxes.

Loctite has also pushed hard to cultivate a market among general consumers. Its Loctite and Duro glues and caulking compounds and Super

Glue are geared to homeowners and hobbyists. It also markets a line of cleaning solutions for tile, porcelain, wood, metal and fiberglass.

For the industrial market, Loctite produces several types of sealants and adhesives. Its anaerobic adhesives are used for bonding parts in automobiles, household appliances, electronic equipment and other mechanical assemblies.

Its cyanoacrylates adhesives are used to glue metal, plastics, rubber, glass, ceramics and wood together or in combination. Typical uses include the assembly of rubber and vinyl products, glass containers, auto accessories, electronic components and office equipment.

EARNINGS GROWTH

Loctite has had strong long-term growth. Over the past ten years, its earnings per share increased 182 percent (an average of 11 percent per year)—which is somewhat deceiving. The earnings dropped off dramatically in 1981 and increased steadily through 1990, for a nine-year increase of 615 percent.

The company has about 3,300 employees and 2,300 shareholders.

STOCK GROWTH

The company has had excellent stock price appreciation the past ten years, rising 503 percent (20 percent per year) during the period.

Including reinvested dividends, a $10,000 investment in Loctite stock at its closing stock price in 1980 would have grown to about $73,000 ten years later. Average annual compounded rate of return (including stock growth and reinvested dividends): about 22 percent.

DIVIDEND YIELD

Loctite generally pays a moderate yield, averaging just over 2 percent over the past five years. During the most recent two-year rating period (fiscal 1990 and 1991) the stock paid an average annual current return (dividend yield) of 2.3 percent.

DIVIDEND GROWTH

Loctite has raised its dividend for seven consecutive years. The dividend increased 195 percent (24 percent per year) from 1985 to 1990.

CONSISTENCY

The company has had increased revenue and earnings per share eight of the past ten years and increased book value nine of the past ten years. Its price-earnings ratio of about 14 to 18 is well in line with other growing manufacturers.

SHAREHOLDER PERKS

Loctite offers its shareholders a good dividend reinvestment plan and voluntary stock purchase plan. There are no fees or commissions, and shareholders of record may purchase $25 to $1,000 per month in additional shares through the voluntary stock purchase plan.

The company occasionally hands out tubes of Super Glue to shareholders at its annual meeting.

SUMMARY

Fiscal year ended: Dec. 31
(Revenue and net income in millions)

	1991*	1990	1989	1988	1987	1986	1985	5-year growth, %† (annual/total)
Revenue		555	474	439	383	292	240	18/131
Net income		67	58	48	37	25	19	28/252
Earnings/share		1.86	1.62	1.33	1.01	.70	.53	28/250
Dividend/share		.59	.53	.37	.27	.22	.20	24/195
Dividend yield, %	2.1	2.4	2.6	2.0	1.8	2.3	2.4	—/—
Stock price	32.88	29.69	23.38	16.38	14.56	11.88	8.50	28/249
P/E ratio	18	14	12	13	15	14	15	—/—
Book value/share		7.86	6.38	5.72	5.00	4.23	3.47	18/126

* Stock price as of 5–1–91
† 1985–90
Source: Company sources

National Service Industries

NATIONAL SERVICE INDUSTRIES

1420 Peachtree Street, NE
Atlanta, GA 30309
404-853-1000
Chairman: Erwin Zaban
President and CEO: Sidney Kirschner

EARNINGS GROWTH	★
STOCK GROWTH	★ ★
DIVIDEND YIELD	★ ★ ★
DIVIDEND GROWTH	★ ★
CONSISTENCY	★ ★ ★ ★
SHAREHOLDER PERKS	★ ★
NYSE—NSI	**14 points**

National Service Industries got its start 72 years ago as the National Linen Service, renting out towels, tablecloths, bed sheets and other linen products. And while textile rental remains a key component of NSI's operation, the Atlanta-based business has also moved into six other key industrial segments.

The diversification has helped keep NSI's earnings growing at a steady pace. The company has posted record earnings per share for 15 consecutive years and 28 of the past 29 years. Growth the past couple of years, however, has been at a snail's pace as the company battles to overcome the effects of the slowing economy. Earnings rose only 10 percent in 1989 and 5 percent in 1990.

NSI's largest subsidiary is Lithonia Lighting, which accounts for 41 percent of the company's $1.65 billion in annual revenue. Lithonia is the nation's largest lighting fixture manufacturer. The company makes fluorescent and high-intensity discharge fixtures and architectural downlighting fixtures, outdoor lighting, track lighting, vandal-resistant fixtures, emergency lighting, wiring systems and lighting and dimming controls.

The company's other key divisions include:

- Textile rental (23 percent of revenue). Through its National Linen Service, National Uniform Service, National Healthcare Linen Service and National Dust Control Service, NSI rents uniforms, table linen, bed linens, towels, operating room packs and dust control materials.
- Chemical manufacturing (14 percent of revenue). The company manufactures chemical products primarily for the maintenance, sanitation and water treatment industries, including soaps, detergents, waxes and disinfectants. NSI's chemical-related subsidiaries include Zep Manufacturing, Selig Chemical, National Chemical and Canadian Industrial Chemical.
- Envelopes (6 percent of revenue). NSI produces business and specialty envelopes through its Atlantic Envelope Company, and record-filling systems through its ATENCO subsidiary.
- Marketing services (3 percent of revenue). The firm provides sales aids for the carpet, upholstery, tile and wallpaper industries, including binders, booklets, sales kits and display racks.
- Insulation (8 percent of revenue). Through ten subsidiaries, NSI fabricates, installs, maintains and sells commercial, industrial and institutional insulation products.
- Men's apparel (3 percent of revenue). Through its Block Sportswear and PM Company of New York, NSI sells men's dress and sports shirts, jackets, sweaters and other sportswear.

EARNINGS GROWTH

NSI has had steady long-term growth. Over the past ten years, its earnings per share increased 127 percent (an average of 8.5 percent per year).

The company has about 22,000 employees and 8,000 shareholders.

STOCK GROWTH

The company has had flat stock price appreciation for the past five years. Over the ten-year rating period (through 1990), the stock rose 373 percent (17 percent per year) for the period.

Including reinvested dividends, a $10,000 investment in NSI stock at its closing stock price in 1980 would have grown to about $67,000 ten years later. Average annual compounded rate of return (including stock growth and reinvested dividends): about 21 percent.

DIVIDEND YIELD

NSI generally pays an excellent yield, averaging about 3.3 percent over the past five years. During the most recent two-year rating period (fiscal 1990

and 1991) the stock paid an average annual current return (dividend yield) of 3.6 percent.

DIVIDEND GROWTH

NSI has raised its dividend for 28 consecutive years. The dividend increased 84 percent (13 percent per year) from 1985 to 1990.

CONSISTENCY

The company has posted record earnings per share, revenue and book value per share for 15 consecutive years and 28 of the past 29 years. Its price-earnings ratio of about 13 is a little lower than average for a growing company.

SHAREHOLDER PERKS

NSI company offers its shareholders an excellent dividend reinvestment plan and voluntary stock purchase plan. For a nominal fee, shareholders of record may purchase $10 to $4,000 per month in additional shares through the voluntary stock purchase plan.

SUMMARY

Fiscal year ended: Aug. 31
(Revenue and net income in millions)

	1991*	1990	1989	1988	1987	1986	1985	5-year growth, %† (annual/total)
Revenue		1,648	1,540	1,414	1,327	1,283	1,191	7/38
Net income		100	95	86	76	71	68	8/47
Earnings/share		2.02	1.92	1.75	1.54	1.45	1.37	8/46
Dividend/share		.90	.82	.73	.62	.54	.49	13/84
Dividend yield, %	3.9	3.3	3.4	3.3	2.6	2.5	3.4	—/—
Stock price	24.63	25.13	27.63	21.25	25.63	24.25	16.13	9/55
P/E ratio	13	14	12	13	16	15	11	—/—
Book value/share		13.63	12.44	11.33	10.31	9.39	8.48	10/60

* Stock price as of 5–1–91
† 1985–90
Source: Company sources

71

MCDONALD'S CORPORATION

McDonald's Plaza
Oak Brook, IL 60521
708-575-3000
Senior Chairman: Fred L. Turner
Chairman and CEO: Michael R. Quinlan

EARNINGS GROWTH	★ ★
STOCK GROWTH	★ ★ ★
DIVIDEND YIELD	★
DIVIDEND GROWTH	★ ★
CONSISTENCY	★ ★ ★ ★
SHAREHOLDER PERKS	★ ★
NYSE—MCD	**14 points**

"McLean" is the word at the new McDonald's. Sure, you can still get the Big Mac, the McDLT, the Quarter Pounder, the Egg McMuffin. But now, cholesterol-conscious consumers can also find some comfort in the revised McDonald's menu. Even its hot golden fries—long the industry favorite because of their crisp, tasty animal-fried flavor—have gone upscale. They are now prepared strictly in vegetable oil.

The new "91 percent fat-free" McLean burger is one of the most innovative new products the Chicago-based fast-food franchiser has introduced in recent years. Early reviews on the new leaner burger—hailed for its low fat and low cholesterol level—have been very favorable. Credit the researchers at McDonald's hamburger laboratories. They found a way to keep the flavor without the fat—which just might help put a little more fat in the company's bottom line.

It needs it. Profit growth at McDonald's has been lagging in recent years as the franchiser has evolved to a more mature stage in its corporate development. The competition is stiffer, its U.S. market is becoming increasingly saturated and, while the company continues its growth overseas, increased profits have become harder than ever to come by.

By offering salads, reduced-fat fries and the new McLean burger, McDonald's hopes to attract the very segment of health-conscious consumers that its Big Macs and fatty fries had been scaring off before.

In spite of slowing sales, McDonald's has continued its string of consecutive years of record earnings. Last year, 1990, marked its 25th straight year—and 100th straight quarter—of record earnings per share, dating back to the year the company was taken public.

McDonald's is the most advertised single brand name in the world. More than 3,000 of McDonald's 12,000 restaurants are located outside the U.S. There are about 1,000 in Europe, 1,200 in Asia and Australia and more than 600 in Canada. Japan has more than 700 McD's.

And every 16 hours, somewhere in the world, a new McDonald's opens. The company opens more than 600 new restaurants each year. Each day, 22 million people dine at McDonald's. Since the late Ray Kroc opened his first McDonald's in 1955, more than 70 billion burgers have been served beneath the Golden Arches.

Most McDonald's restaurants are owned by independent businesspeople who operate them through a franchise agreement. Typically, the company tries to recruit investors who will be active, on-premises owners rather than outside investors. The conventional franchise arrangement is for a term of 20 years and requires an investment of about half a million dollars, 60 percent of which may be financed. Each outlet is also subject to franchise fees based on a percentage of sales.

EARNINGS GROWTH

McDonald's has enjoyed strong, steady long-term growth. Over the past ten years, its earnings per share increased 307 percent (an average of 15 percent per year).

The company has about 170,000 employees and 90,000 shareholders.

STOCK GROWTH

The company has had exceptional stock growth the past ten years, increasing 483 percent (19 percent per year) during the period.

Including reinvested dividends, a $10,000 investment in McDonald's stock at its closing stock price in 1980 would have grown to about $65,000 ten years later. Average annual compounded rate of return (including stock growth and reinvested dividends): about 20.5 percent.

DIVIDEND YIELD

McDonald's generally pays a fairly modest yield, averaging about 1 percent over the past five years. During the most recent two-year rating period (fiscal 1990 and 1991) the stock paid an average annual current return (dividend yield) of 1.1 percent.

DIVIDEND GROWTH

McDonald's has raised its dividend every year since 1966, when the company went public. The dividend increased 65 percent (11 percent per year) from 1985 to 1990.

CONSISTENCY

The company has had 25 straight years of record earnings per share and revenue—dating back to the year the company was taken public. Its price-earnings ratio of around 15 is well in line with other growing U.S. companies.

SHAREHOLDER PERKS

McDonald's offers no coupons or special gifts for new shareholders, but it does have an investor hotline (although it is not a toll-free number) that gives the latest company news. A wealth of material on McDonald's, including a directory of McDonald's locations and a listing of ingredients in each McDonald's product, is available to shareholders (and to anyone else who requests it).

The company offers an outstanding dividend reinvestment and voluntary stock purchase plan. There are no fees or service charges, and shareholders may contribute $50 to $75,000 a year toward the purchase of additional stock. About 45 percent of the company's 90,000 shareholders participate in the program.

CORPORATE RESPONSIBILITY

In 1990, after consulting with the Environmental Defense Fund on waste reduction strategies, McDonald's announced its decision to phase out all polystyrene packaging from its U.S. restaurants. The new containers will be cellophane-coated paper wrappers. Although these wrappers are currently considered unrecyclable, the move was applauded by some environmental groups. McDonald's recently elected one woman to serve on its 17-member board of directors. One minority member has served on the board since 1984. (Source: Council on Economic Priorities)

SUMMARY

Fiscal year ended: Dec. 31
(Revenue and net income in millions)

	1991*	1990	1989	1988	1987	1986	1985	5-year growth, %† (annual/total)
Revenue		6,640	6,066	5,521	4,583	4,143	3,694	12/80
Net income		802	727	646	549	480	433	13/85
Earnings/share		2.20	1.95	1.71	1.45	1.24	1.11	15/98
Dividend/share		.33	.30	.27	.24	.21	.20	11/65
Dividend yield, %	1.0	1.1	0.9	1.1	1.1	1.0	1.1	—/—
Stock price	34.00	29.13	34.50	24.06	22.00	20.38	17.92	11/63
P/E ratio	15.0	13.2	17.7	14.1	15.2	16.4	16.1	—/—
Book value/share		11.64	9.81	9.09	7.72	6.45	5.67	16/105

* Stock price as of 5–1–91
† 1985–90
Source: Company sources

AMERICAN HOME PRODUCTS CORP.

685 Third Avenue
New York, NY 10017
212-878-5000
Chairman and CEO: John R. Stafford
President: Dr. Bernard Canavan

EARNINGS GROWTH	★
STOCK GROWTH	★ ★
DIVIDEND YIELD	★ ★ ★ ★
DIVIDEND GROWTH	★
CONSISTENCY	★ ★ ★ ★
SHAREHOLDER PERKS	★ ★
NYSE—AMP	**14 points**

So many ills; so many cures. By addressing the most pressing problems of the American consumer—from foul odors to flaking scalps—American Home Products has managed to string together 39 consecutive years of record earnings and revenue.

The New York conglomerate produces a host of home care items, over-the-counter drugs and prescription medications. American Home, which began operations in 1926, posts annual revenue of $6.8 billion.

The company sells a long list of popular nonprescription medications including Advil (the nation's second largest selling analgesic), Robitussin and Dimetapp cold and cough formulas, Anacin pain reliever, Dristan decongestant, Primatene Mist. It also produces Denorex dandruff shampoo, Anbesol oral pain reliever, Preparation H hemorrhoidal medication, Clearblue Easy pregnancy tests and Chap Stick lip balm.

Consumer health care products account for about 19 percent of American Home's annual revenue.

American Home does business in several other industry segments:

- Household products (11 percent of revenue). Among the company's leading products are Black Flag insect killer, Easy-Off glass and oven cleaners, Woolite detergent, Sani-Flush toilet cleaner, Pam cooking sprays, Wizard air fresheners, GulfLite and KwikLite charcoal lighters, 3-in-One oils, Easy-On starch, Old English furniture polish and Antrol insect killer.
- Foods (11 percent of revenue). The company produces a small line of foods, including Chef Boyardee pizzas and Italian foods, Gulden's mustard, Jiffy Pop popcorn and Dennison's chili.
- Pharmaceuticals (49 percent of revenue). The company's Wyeth-Ayerst subsidiary manufactures a number of prescription medicines, including antibiotics, infant nutritionals, psychotherapeutics, an antiarthritic medicine, an antileukemia drug, an influenza vaccine, an antihistamine and several types of medications to treat hormonal and cardiovascular ailments.

    Its A.H. Robins subsidiary produces a wide range of prescription drugs, including Reglan, the leading antinausea medication, and Micro-K, the leading prescription potassium supplement.
- Medical supplies and diagnostic products (10 percent of revenue). American Home's Sherwood Medical subsidiary manufactures products for patient care, nursing care, operating room procedures, dental care and diagnostic procedures. Its Corometrics Medical Systems division makes medical monitors and data storage systems. Fort Dodge Laboratories specializes in veterinary medicines.

The company sells its products worldwide. Foreign sales account for about 30 percent of its total revenue. It has subsidiary operations in 19 foreign countries around the world.

EARNINGS GROWTH ★

American Home's growth has been extraordinarily consistent but far from spectacular. Over the past ten years, its earnings per share increased 160 percent (an average of 10 percent per year).

The company has about 51,000 employees and 74,000 shareholders.

STOCK GROWTH ★ ★

The company has had solid stock growth the past ten years, increasing 279 percent (14 percent per year) during the period.

Including reinvested dividends, a $10,000 investment in American Home's stock at its closing stock price in 1980 would have grown to about

$57,000 ten years later. Average annual compounded rate of return (including stock growth and reinvested dividends): about 19 percent.

DIVIDEND YIELD

American Home pays an excellent yield, averaging about 1.8 percent over the past five years. During the most recent two-year rating period (fiscal 1990 and 1991) the stock paid an average annual current return (dividend yield) of 4.2 percent.

DIVIDEND GROWTH

The company has raised its dividend for 38 consecutive years. The dividend increased 48 percent (8 percent per year) from 1985 to 1990.

CONSISTENCY

Though its growth has been modest, American Home has been one of the country's most consistent performers, with 39 consecutive years of increased sales and earnings. Its price-earnings ratio of about 12 to 14 is lower than average for a health and consumer goods manufacturer.

SHAREHOLDER PERKS

Occasionally the company sends out coupons for some of its food and health care products along with its dividend mailings.

The company also offers an excellent dividend reinvestment and voluntary stock purchase plan. Shareholders may contribute $50 to $10,000 per month to the voluntary stock purchase plan.

CORPORATE RESPONSIBILITY

In December 1989, American Home Products acquired A.H. Robins, which made and marketed the Dalkon Shield contraceptive device in the early seventies despite growing evidence that it caused pelvic infections, spontaneous abortions and sterility. Thousands of product liability cases forced Robins to file for bankruptcy. When American Home took over A.H. Robins, it set up a $2.23 billion trust for victims seeking settlements.

In October 1988, the Minneapolis-based Action for Corporate Accountability (Action) began boycotting both American Home Products and Nestle for their infant formula marketing practices. Action felt that the companies' practice of providing free or subsidized samples of formula to mothers in third world countries discouraged them from breastfeeding, which led to misuse of the formula and sometimes disease and death for the children. Action contended that the companies were in violation of the World Health Organization's 1981 Code of Marketing for Breastmilk Substitutes. In January of 1991, American Home Products, in a move praised by church groups and others, announced that it would stop providing free samples of its formula to hospitals in developing countries.

American Home Products is also one of the companies under investigation by the Federal Trade Commission (FTC) for alleged price fixing. Infant formula price increases resulting from the alleged collusion are of particular concern because the formula is an important element of the federal food program for poor women and children.

The Oil, Chemical and Atomic Workers Union (OCAW), has filed a $100 million lawsuit against American Home Products, alleging that the company committed criminal fraud in relocating an Indiana plant to Puerto Rico. As a result, the Federation for Industrial Retention and Renewal (FIRR), a national coalition of antishutdown organizations, named the company one of the plant closing "Dirty Dozen." According to FIRR, when American Home Products closed the 755-worker plant in Indiana, "It possibly [set] the record for the most laws broken in a shutdown." The company's contends that its decision to build the Puerto Rico plant was unrelated to its plan to close the Indiana plant.

AHP's Wyeth-Ayerst unit, maker of the controversial $350 contraceptive, Norplant, said it had funded a foundation with $2.8 million to disburse the device to women who can't afford it. Critics are unappeased as the company is still not providing the product to public health agencies at a discount, though it is selling it overseas through a Finnish company for as low as $23. (Source: Council on Economic Priorities)

SUMMARY

Fiscal year ended: Dec. 31
(Revenue and net income in millions)

	1991*	1990	1989	1988	1987	1986	1985	5-year growth, %† (annual/total)
Revenue		6,775	6,747	5,500	5,028	4,926	4,684	8/45
Net income		1,175	1,102	932	845	763	717	10/64
Earnings/share		3.69	3.54	3.19	2.87	2.54	2.35	9/57
Dividend/share		2.15	1.95	1.80	1.67	1.55	1.45	8/48
Dividend yield, %	3.9	4.3	4.1	4.6	4.0	3.9	4.9	—/—
Stock price	59.38	53.00	54.00	41.00	37.00	40.13	33.13	10/60
P/E ratio	15	14	14	12	15	16	13	—/—
Book value/share		8.10	6.30	10.18	8.71	8.03	7.59	1/7

* Stock price as of 5-1-91
† 1985-90
Source: Company sources

73

GENERAL ELECTRIC COMPANY

3135 Easton Turnpike
Fairfield, CT 06431
203-373-2459
Chairman and CEO: John F. Welch, Jr.

EARNINGS GROWTH	★
STOCK GROWTH	★ ★
DIVIDEND YIELD	★ ★ ★
DIVIDEND GROWTH	★ ★
CONSISTENCY	★ ★ ★ ★
SHAREHOLDER PERKS	★ ★
NYSE—GE	**14 points**

Here are the top 10 reasons NBC "Late Night" host David Letterman might give to explain why he enjoys working for General Electric:

10. Still has fond memories of 1986 takeover party—the night GE acquired NBC (as part of RCA).
 9. Likes to think he has a common bond with immortal inventor and GE founder Thomas A. Edison (founded as Edison Electric, 1878).
 8. Gives him an excuse to do "stupid light bulb jokes."
 7. Enjoys trying his hand at GE's newest "combat simulation systems."
 6. Enjoys break times more now that NBC commissary has new, improved GE touch control coffeemaker.
 5. Gets free stock tips from brokers at GE subsidiary Kidder, Peabody.
 4. Likes the freedom of being lost in the shuffle of $58 billion-a-year conglomerate.
 3. Gets free fuel rod refills for the GE nuclear reactor he uses to keep the lights burning at his 18-room Connecticut getaway.
 2. Likes heating up leftovers in his Uncle Earl's dependable GE Hotpoint microwave.

And the number-one reason David Letterman likes working for General Electric . . .
1. Still gets all choked up when he hums old GE jingle, "We bring good things to life."

There is one other thing Letterman might like about GE: its ever-rising stock price. Despite its enormous size—with revenues of $58 billion a year— the Fairfield, Connecticut conglomerate continues to keep its profits growing at a sprightly pace. The company has posted 15 consecutive years of record earnings per share.

General Electric, which does business in nearly every country on the globe, divides its operations into nine key segments:

- Broadcasting (6 percent of total revenue). GE owns the National Broadcasting Company (NBC), which serves more than 200 affiliated stations throughout the U.S. NBC also owns television stations in Chicago, Cleveland, Denver, Los Angeles, Miami, New York and Washington, D.C.
- Major appliances (10 percent of revenue). The company is known for its GE, Hotpoint and Monogram appliances, including refrigerators, ranges, microwaves, freezers, dishwashers, clothes washers and dryers and room air conditioners.
- Industrial (13 percent of revenue). The company manufactures factory automation products, motors, electrical equipment, transportation systems (including locomotives and transit propulsion equipment), light bulbs and other types of lighting products.
- Aircraft engines (12.5 percent of revenue). The company builds engines for both military and commercial aircraft.
- Aerospace (10 percent of revenue). GE manufactures avionic systems, spacecraft, military vehicle equipment, armament systems, missile system components, combat simulation systems, communications systems, radar, sonar and computer software.
- Materials (9 percent of revenue). The company makes high-performance plastics for such uses as automobile bumpers, computer casings and other office equipment. It also produces silicones, superabrasives and laminates.
- Power systems (9 percent of revenue). GE builds power generators (primarily steam-turbine generators) and transmitters for worldwide utility, industrial and government customers. While it has not sold a nuclear power plant in the U.S. since the mid-1970s, the company continues to develop new technology and service existing boiling-water nuclear reactors.
- Technical products and services (8 percent of revenue). The company manufactures scanners, x-rays, nuclear imaging, ultrasound and other

medical diagnostic equipment. The company also manufactures communications systems.

- GE Financial Services (24 percent of revenue). GE owns the Wall Street securities firm of Kidder Peabody. It also operates GE Capital, a financing institution that specializes in revolving credit and inventory financing for retail merchants. And it owns ERC, a multiple-line property and casualty reinsurer.

EARNINGS GROWTH

GE has had solid, steady long-term growth. Over the past ten years, its earnings per share increased 192 percent (11 percent per year).

The company has about 300,000 employees and 500,000 shareholders.

STOCK GROWTH

The company has enjoyed strong stock appreciation the past ten years, increasing 270 percent (14 percent per year) for the period.

Including reinvested dividends, a $10,000 investment in GE stock at its closing stock price in 1980 would have grown to about $53,000 ten years later. Average annual compounded rate of return (including stock growth and reinvested dividends): about 18 percent.

DIVIDEND YIELD

GE generally pays a good dividend yield, averaging about 3 percent over the past five years. During the most recent two-year rating period (fiscal 1990 and 1991) the stock paid an average annual current return (dividend yield) of 3 percent.

DIVIDEND GROWTH

GE has raised its dividend for more than 15 consecutive years. The dividend increased 73 percent (12 percent per year) from 1985 to 1990.

CONSISTENCY

The company has had more than 15 consecutive years of increased earnings and book value per share, including 44 consistent quarters of record earnings per share through 1990. Its price-earnings ratio of 12 to 15 is in line with other large growing manufacturers.

SHAREHOLDER PERKS

GE offers its shareholders an excellent dividend reinvestment and voluntary stock purchase plan. Shareholders may purchase up to $10,000 per month in additional shares through the voluntary stock purchase plan.

CORPORATE RESPONSIBILITY

General Electric was the first company to match employees' charitable gifts and is a leader in instituting national programs to help minority youths get into engineering. However, the company has been the target of a boycott by the grassroots action organization INFACT since 1986.

INFACT cites GE's role in promoting and producing nuclear weapons and creating numerous Superfund sites as the reasons for the boycott. In 1990, General Electric received $2.7 billion in contracts from the Departments of Energy and Defense for nuclear weapons systems. In addition, according to INFACT, GE is responsible for 47 superfund toxic waste sites, more than any other company in the United States.

The company has also faced a good deal of litigation relating to its design, building and/or operation of nuclear reactors. A federal judge ruled in 1990 that General Electric hid serious doubts about its design of a giant nuclear-containment vessel for a Washington Public Power Supply System (WPPSS) electric plant. In a *Wall Street Journal* article, he called the cover-up an "unconscionable" breach of GE's "duty of good faith and fair dealing," adding that "key personnel with [GE] were aware of the existence of a number of serious, unresolved questions" about the system, but that the tests required to resolve those questions were never done before the contract with the Washington utility was signed. General Electric disagreed with the judge's ruling.

GE has two women, one of whom is a minority, on its 19-member board. (Source: Council on Economic Priorities)

SUMMARY

Fiscal year ended: Dec. 31
(Revenue and net income in millions)

	1991*	1990	1989	1988	1987	1986	1985	5-year growth, %† (annual/total)
Revenue[1]		44,879	42,650	40,292	40,516	36,725	29,252	9/53
Net income		4,303	3,939	3,386	2,915	2,492	2,277	13/88
Earnings/share		4.85	4.36	3.75	3.20	2.73	2.50	14/94
Dividend/share		1.94	1.70	1.46	1.33	1.19	1.12	12/73
Dividend yield, %	2.8	3.1	3.2	3.4	2.5	3.1	3.6	—/—
Stock price	72.50	57.38	64.50	44.75	44.13	43.00	36.38	10/58
P/E ratio	15	13	12	11	17	14	12	—/—
Book value/share		24.83	23.09	20.47	18.25	16.57	15.25	10/62

* Stock price as of 5–1–91
† 1985–90
1 Including GE Financial Services income, total revenue came to $58.4 billion in 1990, $54.6 billion in 1989, $50.1 billion in 1988 and $48.2 billion in 1987.
Source: Company sources

74 Johnson & Johnson

JOHNSON & JOHNSON

One Johnson & Johnson Plaza
New Brunswick, NJ 08933
201-524-0400
Chairman and CEO: Ralph S. Larsen

EARNINGS GROWTH	★ ★
STOCK GROWTH	★ ★
DIVIDEND YIELD	★ ★
DIVIDEND GROWTH	★ ★ ★
CONSISTENCY	★ ★ ★
SHAREHOLDER PERKS	★ ★
NYSE—JNJ	**14 points**

For decades, Johnson & Johnson has been the most recognized name in infant toiletries. But the New Brunswick, New Jersey manufacturer's reach goes well beyond the crib. It has something for everybody—Tylenol for dad, Stayfrees for mom, plus hundreds of prescription and consumer medications, surgical instruments, implants and hospital aids. With revenues of $11 billion a year, Johnson & Johnson is America's largest medical products company.

The firm employs 83,000 people, owns dozens of subsidiaries and has manufacturing operations in 54 countries.

Aside from its Tylenol, Stayfree and baby products (powder, soap, cream, oil, shampoo and lotion), Johnson & Johnson's better-known consumer products include Sine-Aid, Band-Aid, Sure & Natural panty shields and Imodium A-D. Consumer product sales account for 40 percent of the company's total revenue.

Johnson & Johnson sells its products in well over 100 countries. About 50 percent of the company's total revenue comes from foreign sales.

Along with consumer products, Johnson & Johnson divides its operations into two other segments:

265

- Pharmaceutical. While this segment accounts for only 27 percent of total sales, it provides 50 percent of operating profit. Products include a range of prescription medications including Ortho-Novum oral contraceptives, Tolectin nonsteroidal anti-inflammatory, Imodium antidiarrheal, Nizoral antifungal and its recently approved PROCRIT erythropoietin for AIDS patients.
- Professional (33 percent of revenue, 25 percent of operating profit). Johnson & Johnson's professional products include ligatures and sutures, mechanical wound closure products, diagnostic products, dental products, medical equipment, surgical instruments, surgical dressings, bandages, caps, gowns, gloves and other accessories.

EARNINGS GROWTH

Johnson & Johnson has enjoyed steady long-term growth. Over the past ten years, its earnings per share increased 253 percent (an average of 13 percent per year).

The company has about 83,000 employees and 60,000 shareholders.

STOCK GROWTH

The company has had excellent stock price appreciation the past ten years, increasing 324 percent (15.5 percent per year) for the period.

Including reinvested dividends, a $10,000 investment in Johnson & Johnson stock at its closing stock price in 1980 would have grown to about $52,000 ten years later. Average annual compounded rate of return (including stock growth and reinvested dividends): about 18 percent.

DIVIDEND YIELD

Johnson & Johnson generally pays a good dividend yield, averaging about 2.2 percent over the past five years. During the most recent two-year rating period (fiscal 1990 and 1991) the stock paid an average annual current return (dividend yield) of 1.9 percent.

DIVIDEND GROWTH

Johnson & Johnson has raised its dividend for more than 15 consecutive years. The dividend rose 104 percent (15 percent per year) from 1985 to 1990.

CONSISTENCY

The company's book value and earnings per share have increased 14 of the past 15 years, and its revenue has gone up 15 consecutive years. Its price-earnings ratio of about 19 to 24 is a bit higher than that of most large medical products manufacturers.

SHAREHOLDER PERKS

Johnson & Johnson offers its shareholders an excellent dividend reinvestment and voluntary stock purchase plan. There are no fees or commissions, and shareholders of record may purchase up to $3,000 per month in additional shares through the voluntary stock purchase plan.

CORPORATE RESPONSIBILITY

Johnson & Johnson has come under fire for its continued presence in South Africa, where it is one of the top ten U.S. investors and employs nearly 1,400 workers. In other areas, however, the company's record is more positive.

In 1989, Johnson & Johnson launched its Balancing Work & Family initiative, a comprehensive program of policies, benefits and services developed to help employees meet family needs. The first Johnson & Johnson on-site child care center opened in May 1990 at the company headquarters in New Brunswick, New Jersey.

Since 1978, Johnson & Johnson's acclaimed Live for Life program has provided 33,000 employees in the U.S., Puerto Rico, the United Kingdom and the Netherlands with an all-encompassing, free, primarily on-site health promotion program. (Source: Council on Economic Priorities)

SUMMARY

Fiscal year ended: Dec. 31
(Revenue and net income in millions)

	1991*	1990	1989	1988	1987	1986	1985	5-year growth, %† (annual/total)
Revenue		11,232	9,757	9,000	8,012	7,003	6,421	12/75
Net income		1,143	1,082	974	833	330	614	13/86
Earnings/share		3.43	3.25	2.86	2.41	.92	1.68	15/104
Dividend/share		1.31	1.12	.96	.81	.69	.64	15/104
Dividend yield, %	1.7	2.0	2.2	2.4	2.3	2.3	2.9	—/—
Stock price	96.25	71.00	59.38	42.50	37.38	33.88	26.25	22/170
P/E ratio	24.0	19.0	15.7	14.0	14.8	32.7	13.2	—/—
Book value/share		14.71	12.45	10.52	10.13	8.17	9.16	10/60

* Stock price as of 5–1–91
† 1985–90
Source: Company sources

RPM, INC.
2628 Pearl Road
P.O. Box 777
Medina, Ohio 44258
Tel: 216-273-5090
Chairman and CEO: Thomas C. Sullivan
President: James A. Karman

EARNINGS GROWTH	★
STOCK GROWTH	★ ★
DIVIDEND YIELD	★ ★ ★
DIVIDEND GROWTH	★ ★
CONSISTENCY	★ ★ ★ ★
SHAREHOLDER PERKS	★ ★
OTC—RPOW	**14 points**

Already a world leader in the development of paints and coatings, RPM has recently established a new niche in the business that promises still greater growth in the future. Its new "environmentally sound" line of products—including water-based paints and primers, concrete additives, an ozone-safe airbrush propellant and an inorganic zinc corrosion control coating—should keep RPM at the leading edge of the paints and coatings technology for years to come.

RPM's original product was Alumanation, a coating process for outdoor metal structures that RPM founder Frank C. Sullivan brought to market in 1947. Alumanation today remains the world's leading liquid aluminum coating solution.

The success of Alumanation and RPM's other broad line of paints and coatings has helped the company post 44 consecutive years of record sales and earnings. The Ohio-based manufacturer, which has built its business through internal growth and a series of acquisitions, has become one of the world's leading paints and coatings manufacturers. Its coatings cover the Statue of Liberty, the Eiffel Tower and hundreds of bridges, ships, highways, factories, office towers, warehouses and other structures in more than 70 countries.

Most of RPM's 30 subsidiaries are involved in the manufacture of corrosion protection, waterproofing and maintenance products. Among its key products are paints, sealants, roofing materials and touch-up products for autos and furniture. It also makes fabrics and wall coverings.

About 60 percent of the company's sales comes from the industrial market, and the other 40 percent comes from its line of consumer products.

RPM divides its business into five market segments:

- Corrosion control. RPM produces coatings and chemicals for power plants, oil rigs, railcars, tankers, smokestacks and other structures that are subject to harsh environments. Leading brands include Carboline, Plasite and Bitumastic.
- Specialty chemicals. The company makes concrete additives that provide corrosion resistance and add strength to cement used in construction; it makes additives for coatings and dyes, and coatings and cleaners for the textile trade. It produces furniture stains, fillers and polishes, auto refinishing products and auto corrosion control additives. Its leading lines include Euco, Chemspec and Mohawk.
- Waterproofing and general maintenance. The company makes coatings for metal structures such as buildings, bridges and industrial facilities; it also produces sheet roofing, sealants and deck coatings. Its leading lines include Geoflex single sheet roofing, Alumanation coating and Mameco sealants.
- Consumer hobby and leisure. RPM's Testor subsidiary is America's leading producer of models, paints and accessory items for the model and hobby market. RPM's Craft House subsidiary makes Sesame Street and Magic Rocks toys and Paint-by-Numbers art kits.
- Consumer do-it-yourself. This has been among the company's fastest-growing segments, now accounting for more than 25 percent of RPM's revenue. The company's Bondex subsidiary makes patch, repair and waterproofing products. Its Zinsser subsidiary makes shellacs, sealants and primers.

EARNINGS GROWTH   ★

RPM has enjoyed solid, consistent long-term growth. Over the past ten years, its earnings per share increased 188 percent (an average of 11 percent per year).

The company has about 2,500 employees and 12,000 shareholders.

STOCK GROWTH

The company has had strong, steady stock price appreciation the past ten years, increasing 300 percent (15 percent per year) during the period.

Including reinvested dividends, a $10,000 investment in RPM stock at its closing stock price in 1980 would have grown to about $53,000 ten years later. Average annual compounded rate of return (including stock growth and reinvested dividends): about 18 percent.

DIVIDEND YIELD

RPM generally pays a very good dividend yield, averaging about 3.4 percent over the past five years. During the most recent two-year rating period (fiscal 1990 and 1991) the stock paid an average annual current return (dividend yield) of 3.3 percent.

DIVIDEND GROWTH

RPM has raised its dividend for 17 consecutive years. The dividend increased 86 percent (13 percent per year) from 1985 to 1990.

CONSISTENCY

The company has had 44 consecutive years of record sales and earnings. Its price-earnings ratio of around 15 is well in line with other growing U.S. manufacturers.

SHAREHOLDER PERKS

The company offers a good dividend reinvestment plan that allows shareholders to buy up to $2,000 a month in additional RPM stock with no fees or service charges.

SUMMARY

Fiscal year ended: May 31*
(Revenue and net income in millions)

	1991**	1990	1989	1988	1987	1986	1985	5-year growth, %† (annual/total)
Revenue		445	376	342	306	269	223	15/99
Net income		28	24	21	17	13	11	20/154
Earnings/share		.98	.86	.76	.62	.56	.55	12/78
Dividend/share		.54	.49	.43	.37	.32	.29	13/86
Dividend yield, %	3.0	3.5	3.8	3.6	3.1	3.3	3.6	—/—
Stock price	20.75	18.00	15.00	13.00	12.50	12.00	10.54	11/70
P/E ratio	16.0	13.8	14.8	15.7	18.6	17.0	13.5	—/—
Book value/share		5.71	5.23	4.87	4.59	4.39	3.29	12/73

 * Except stock price Dec. 31, 1985–90
** Stock price as of 5–1–91
 † 1985–90
Source: Company sources

76

THE PROCTER & GAMBLE COMPANY

One Procter & Gamble Plaza
Cincinnati, OH 45202
513-983-1100
Chairman and CEO: Edwin L. Artzt
President: John Pepper

EARNINGS GROWTH	★
STOCK GROWTH	★ ★ ★
DIVIDEND YIELD	★ ★ ★
DIVIDEND GROWTH	(no points)
CONSISTENCY	★ ★ ★
SHAREHOLDER PERKS	★ ★ ★
NYSE—PG	**13 points**

Almost single-handedly, Procter & Gamble has taken on the enormous task of keeping dishes cleaner, blouses brighter, teeth whiter and daytime television on the air.

Turn on any TV network any weekday afternoon, and whatever you're watching is probably sponsored in part by Procter & Gamble. P&G for many years has been TV's biggest advertiser.

Here's a quick test of your P&G IQ. What P&G products go with the following slogans:

1. "Raise your hand."
2. "Please don't squeeze..."
3. "Mountain grown."
4. "The one that coats."
5. "April fresh."
6. "The quicker picker-upper."
7. "You're not really clean unless you're _____ fully clean."
8. "99 44/100 percent pure."
9. "Wash and go."

10. "Old baldy."
11. "More dentists recommend..."
12. "For cake so moist..."
13. "All tempa-..."
14. "If you don't look good, we don't look good."
15. "Choosy mothers choose..."

Answers: 1. Sure; 2. Charmin; 3. Folger's; 4. Pepto-Bismol; 5. Downy fabric softener; 6. Bounty; 7. Zest soap; 8. Ivory; 9. Pert shampoo; 10. Mr. Clean; 11. Crest; 12. Duncan Hines; 13. Cheer; 14. Vidal Sassoon; 15. Jif.

If you answered correctly on most slogans, congratulations! Consider yourself a member of the human race. P&G products are household names the world over. If ever there was living proof that "it pays to advertise," Procter & Gamble is it.

P&G is the largest manufacturer of soaps and cosmetics in America and among the biggest in the world. Its foreign sales account for 40 percent ($10 billion) of its $24.5 billion in total annual revenue. Procter & Gamble has manufacturing plants in 33 foreign countries.

The company's three primary stock segments include:

- Laundry and cleaning (32 percent of revenue). In addition to brands already listed, the company makes Tide laundry detergent, Bounce softener, Dawn and Cascade dish soaps, Comet, White Cloud and one of the oldest brands in the cleaning business, Spic and Span.
- Personal care (48 percent of revenue). Some of P&G's other leading personal care brands include Pampers disposable diapers, Scope mouthwash, Secret deodorant, Clearasil, Cover Girl, Oil of Olay, Vicks, Always, Attends, Bain de Soleil and Chloraseptic. The company recently acquired Noxell and Old Spice.
- Food and beverages (14 percent of revenue). P&G's other leading food brands include Citrus Hill, Crisco and Pringles. It recently purchased Hawaiian Punch.

EARNINGS GROWTH

Procter & Gamble has had solid, steady long-term growth. Over the past ten years, its earnings per share increased 131 percent (9 percent per year).

The company has about 77,000 employees and 110,000 shareholders.

STOCK GROWTH

P&G has enjoyed excellent stock price appreciation the past ten years, rising 431 percent (18 percent per year) for the period.

Including reinvested dividends, a $10,000 investment in Procter & Gamble stock at its closing stock price in 1980 would have grown to about $75,000 ten years later. Average annual compounded rate of return (including stock growth and reinvested dividends): about 22.5 percent.

DIVIDEND YIELD

Procter & Gamble generally pays a good dividend yield, averaging about 3 percent over the past five years. During the most recent two-year rating period (fiscal 1990 and 1991) the stock paid an average annual current return (dividend yield) of 2.5 percent.

DIVIDEND GROWTH (no points)

Procter & Gamble has raised its dividend for 34 consecutive years—but not always by much. The dividend rose only 34 percent (6 percent per year) from 1985 to 1990.

CONSISTENCY

The company has had increased revenue for 15 consecutive years and increased earnings per share 13 of the past 15 years. Its price-earnings ratio of around 15 to 17 is well in line with other growing manufacturers.

SHAREHOLDER PERKS

The company offers an excellent dividend reinvestment and stock purchase plan. Shareholders may contribute as little as $20 or as much as $120,000 a year to purchase additional shares of P&G stock.

Procter & Gamble also provides a couple of perks for its shareholders. The company occasionally sends out coupons for some of its products in its quarterly reports. It also sponsors three "dividend days" a year in which shareholders are invited to participate in special company-sponsored events. Recently, for example, P&G treated it shareholders to a concert by Kenny Rogers. It also recently sponsored an afternoon at Cincinnati's King's Island amusement park for its shareholders.

CORPORATE RESPONSIBILITY

Procter & Gamble rates well in most social responsibility areas. The company gives to charity through both its U.S. foundation, the P&G Fund, and through direct corporate giving. In 1989, Procter & Gamble's combined charitable contributions were just over $21 million or an impressive 1.5

percent of average pretax income. The company has three minorities among its top 57 corporate officers.

One area of controversy for Procter & Gamble has been its continued use of animal testing both in-house and through outside contractors. In mid-1989, animal protectionists were appalled to learn through a leaked internal Procter & Gamble memo that the company was promoting an industry group to educate and legislate against the cessation of animal testing. People for the Ethical Treatment of Animals (PETA) and others launched a nationwide boycott of P&G. The company contends that it wants to educate the public as to the corporate side of the animal-testing debate and that the memo was a trial balloon, not a concrete policy. P&G has made some positive efforts to reduce its animal testing and spent more than $3.9 million in 1989 to research nonanimal alternative tests. The company has decreased the number of animals used in testing by 43 percent over the last five years.

Procter & Gamble has also been criticized by environmentalists for its involvement in the disposable diaper market. Disposable diapers make up 2 percent of our municipal solid waste and have become a symbol of our penchant for using disposable products that are expensive and harmful to the environment. Procter & Gamble has attempted to address its critics by researching the possibilities of recycling and/or composting its diapers. (Source: Council on Economic Priorities)

SUMMARY

Fiscal year ended: June 30*
(Revenue and net income in millions)

	1991**	1990	1989	1988	1987	1986	1985	5-year growth, %† (annual/total)
Revenue		24,081	21,398	19,336	17,000	15,439	13,552	12/77
Net income		1,602	1,206	1,020	327	709	635	20/152
Earnings/share		4.49	3.56	2.98	.94	2.10	1.90	19/136
Dividend/share		1.75	1.50	1.38	1.35	1.31	1.30	6/34
Dividend yield, %	2.4	2.6	3.4	3.2	3.3	4.0	4.7	—/—
Stock price	83.63	86.63	70.25	43.50	42.69	38.19	34.00	20/154
P/E ratio	17	15	12	14	18	16	15	—/—
Book value/share		18.82	16.10	18.71	16.98	16.95	15.74	4/20

* Except stock price Dec. 31, 1985–90
** Stock price as of 5–1–91
† 1985–90
Source: Company sources

77 SIGMA-ALDRICH

CORPORATION

SIGMA-ALDRICH CORP.
3050 Spruce Street
St. Louis, MO 63103
314-771-5765
Chairman: Dr. Alfred Bader
President and CEO: Dr. Tom Cori

EARNINGS GROWTH	★ ★ ★
STOCK GROWTH	★ ★ ★
DIVIDEND YIELD	★
DIVIDEND GROWTH	★ ★
CONSISTENCY	★ ★ ★ ★
SHAREHOLDER PERKS	(no points)
OTC—SIAL	**13 points**

In scientific laboratories the world over, researchers probe for the next medical breakthrough largely through a process of trial and error. They try one compound, then another, testing and retesting 50 to 100 solutions—and often many more—in their search for the next miracle drug.

Sigma-Aldrich supplies the chemicals used by laboratory researchers worldwide. The St. Louis-based company distributes about 51,000 chemical products for use in research and development, in the diagnosis of disease and as components in chemical specialties.

Since Sigma merged with Aldrich in 1975, the company has posted 16 consecutive years of increased earnings per share—with increases of 15 to 20 percent most years.

Sigma-Aldrich's chemical products are used in the fields of biochemistry, synthetic chemistry, quality control and testing, immunology, hematology, pharmacology, microbiology, neurology, endocrinology and agriculture.

Its diagnostic products are used in the detection of liver and kidney diseases, heart ailments and a variety of metabolic disorders. The company sells to about 100,000 customers, including scientists and technicians in hospitals, universities, clinical laboratories and private and governmental research laboratories.

The company offers a diagnostic kit for some of its customers that includes about 350 combinations of its most common diagnostic products for testing for a variety of conditions and diseases.

Sigma has clients in nearly every country. In 1989, the company acquired Switzerland-based Fluka Chemie AG, strengthening its position in the European market. About 47 percent of all its sales are made to foreign customers.

Chemical products account for 81 percent of the company's $529 million in annual revenue.

The company's other business segment is its B-Line Systems manufacturing unit (19 percent of revenue), which manufactures metal components for strut, cable tray and pipe support systems used in routing electrical, heating, air-conditioning and piping services in power plants, refineries and manufacturing facilities.

EARNINGS GROWTH

Sigma-Aldrich has enjoyed outstanding long-term growth. Over the past ten years, its earnings per share increased 476 percent (19 percent per year).

The company has about 4,000 employees and 2,000 shareholders.

STOCK GROWTH

The company has had excellent, sustained stock price appreciation the past ten years, climbing 591 percent (21 percent per year) for the period.

Including reinvested dividends, a $10,000 investment in Sigma-Aldrich stock at its closing stock price in 1980 would have grown to about $73,000 ten years later. Average annual compounded rate of return (including stock growth and reinvested dividends): about 22 percent.

DIVIDEND YIELD

Sigma-Aldrich generally pays a very modest yield, averaging under 1 percent over the past five years. During the most recent two-year rating period (fiscal 1989 and 1990) the stock paid an average annual current return (dividend yield) of 0.7 percent.

DIVIDEND GROWTH

Sigma-Aldrich generally raises its dividend each year. The dividend rose 91 percent (14 percent per year) from 1985 to 1990.

CONSISTENCY

★ ★ ★ ★

The company has had 16 consecutive years of increased revenue, book value and earnings per share. Its price-earnings ratio of around 20 to 25 is higher than most chemical specialty manufacturers, but it is in line with its own P/E levels of past years.

SHAREHOLDER PERKS

(no points)

Sigma-Aldrich offers no dividend reinvestment plan and no other perks.

SUMMARY

Fiscal year ended: Dec. 31
(Revenue and net income in millions)

	1991*	1990	1989	1988	1987	1986	1985	5-year growth, %† (annual/total)
Revenue		529	441	375	305	253	215	20/146
Net income		71	64	57	42	34	29	20/144
Earnings/share		1.44	1.30	1.15	0.85	0.69	0.57	20/152
Dividend/share		.21	.19	.17	.15	.13	.11	14/91
Dividend yield		0.7	0.7	0.7	0.7	0.7	0.8	—/—
Stock price	36.25	29.38	28.88	25.13	23.88	20.13	14.25	16/106
P/E ratio	25	21	20	20	26	24	19	—/—
Book value/share		7.25	6.03	4.94	3.98	3.17	2.57	23/182

* Stock price as of 5–1–91
† 1985–90
Source: Company sources

78

R.R. DONNELLEY & SONS COMPANY

2223 Martin Luther King Drive
Chicago, IL 60616
312-326-8000
Chairman and CEO: John R. Walter
President: Carl Doty

EARNINGS GROWTH	★
STOCK GROWTH	★ ★
DIVIDEND YIELD	★ ★
DIVIDEND GROWTH	★ ★
CONSISTENCY	★ ★ ★ ★
SHAREHOLDER PERKS	★ ★
NYSE—DNY	**13 points**

No one since Gutenberg has done more for the printed word than R.R. Donnelley & Sons. With more than 40 printing plants throughout the U.S. and the United Kingdom, Donnelley turns out more printed pages than any other company in the world.

The Chicago printer does business with more than 3,000 customers, publishing thousands of books, magazines, catalogs and directories every year. The firm has been in business 127 years.

Donnelley prints many of the nation's leading periodicals, including *Time, Business Week, Newsweek, TV Guide, People, Sports Illustrated, Family Circle, Ladies Home Journal, Modern Maturity, Scientific American, Advertising Age, Glamour, Redbook* and scores of others. It also prints Sunday magazines for such newspapers as the *Chicago Tribune* and the *Los Angeles Times*. Magazine printing accounts for about 20 percent of Donnelley's $3.5 billion a year in total revenue.

Along with its magazine publishing business, Donnelley breaks its operation into five other key segments:

- Catalogs (33 percent of revenue). This is the largest segment of Donnelley's operation. The company prints catalogs and newspaper inserts, and provides specialized service for retail advertisers. It prints catalogs for such major retailers as Sears and J.C. Penney, as well as for smaller specialty merchants. It also handles preprinted newspaper inserts for such retailers as K mart, Wal-Mart, Dayton-Hudson, Macy's, Zayre and Radio Shack.
- Books (13 percent of revenue). Donnelley is the nation's leading book producer in nearly every category, including textbooks, trade books (soft and hard cover), bibles, college and professional books, subscription and mail order books, encyclopedias and other reference books. The company prints books for more than 900 publishers.
- Directories (18 percent of revenue). The firm publishes phone directories for more than 3,000 U.S. communities, as well as for cities and towns in the U.K.
- Documentation services (6 percent of revenue). Donnelley prints computer and software manuals, documentation, binders and packaging.
- Other (10 percent of revenue). The company is involved in several other business areas, including financial document publishing, graphic design and custom cartography. Its Metromail subsidiary, which Donnelley acquired in 1987, provides mailing lists, list enhancement and mail production services to direct mail merchandisers.

EARNINGS GROWTH

Donnelley has enjoyed steady growth the past decade, with earnings per share rising 212 percent (12 percent per year).

The company has about 26,000 employees and 10,000 shareholders.

STOCK GROWTH

The company has had strong stock growth the past ten years, increasing 342 percent (16 percent per year) during the period.

Including reinvested dividends, a $10,000 investment in Donnelley stock at its closing stock price in 1980 would have grown to about $55,000 ten years later. Average annual compounded rate of return (including stock growth and reinvested dividends): about 18.5 percent.

DIVIDEND YIELD

Donnelley generally pays a fairly good yield, averaging just over 2 percent the past five years. During the most recent two-year rating period (fiscal

1990 and 1991) the stock paid an average annual current return (dividend yield) of 2.2 percent.

DIVIDEND GROWTH

Donnelley has raised its dividend for more than 15 consecutive years. The dividend rose 65 percent (11 percent per year) from 1985 to 1990.

CONSISTENCY

The company has had very consistent growth in its earnings, revenue and book value per share, including more than 16 consecutive years of record sales and earnings. Its price-earnings ratio of around 14 to 17 is in line with other large printing and publishing companies.

SHAREHOLDER PERKS

Donnelley offers a good dividend reinvestment and voluntary stock purchase plan that is free to shareholders of record. Shareholders may contribute as little as $10 a month or as much as $60,000 a year to the stock purchase plan.

SUMMARY

Fiscal year ended: Dec. 31
(Revenue and net income in millions)

	1991*	1990	1989	1988	1987	1986	1985	5-year growth, %† (annual/total)
Revenue		3,498	3,122	2,878	2,483	2,234	2,038	12/72
Net income		226	222	205	218	158	148	9/52
Earnings/share		2.91	2.85	2.64	2.80	2.03	1.94	9/50
Dividend/share		.96	.88	.78	.70	.64	.58	11/65
Dividend yield, %	2.1	2.3	2.1	2.2	1.9	1.9	2.1	—/—
Stock price	47.50	39.75	51.25	35.00	32.13	32.00	32.13	5/24
P/E ratio	17	14	15	13	16	17	14	—/—
Book value/share		20.60	18.56	16.69	14.91	12.67	11.73	12/75

* Stock price as of 5–1–91
† 1985–90
Source: Company sources

AUTOMATIC DATA PROCESSING, INC.

One ADP Boulevard
Roseland, NJ 07068
201-994-5000
Chairman and CEO: Josh S. Weston

EARNINGS GROWTH	★ ★ ★
STOCK GROWTH	★ ★
DIVIDEND YIELD	★
DIVIDEND GROWTH	★ ★ ★
CONSISTENCY	★ ★ ★ ★
SHAREHOLDER PERKS	(no points)
NYSE—AUD	**13 points**

Automatic Data Processing (ADP) first began operations in 1949, long before most Americans had even heard the term "data processing." But for ADP—and the more than 200,000 corporate customers who now benefit from its services—the timing could not have been better.

Since its first year of operations, ADP has rolled to 41 consecutive years of record earnings and revenue. Even more impressive: Since 1961, when the company went public, it has compiled an extraordinary string of 116 consecutive quarters (29 years) of *double-digit* earnings-per-share growth.

ADP provides a broad range of computer processing services, billing itself as "the largest independent company in the U.S. dedicated exclusively to providing computerized transaction processing, record-keeping, data communication and information services."

The Roseland, New Jersey firm is the market leader in payroll processing. It handles the payroll checks for 200,000 businesses in the U.S. and abroad, doling out pay checks to nearly 11 million workers.

ADP's oldest and largest sector is "employer services," which accounts for 55 percent the company's $1.7 billion in total annual revenue. In addition to its payroll processing, the division handles payroll tax filing, management reports, labor distribution, job costing, personnel, benefits and human resource information and unemployment compensation management. The company serves employers throughout the U.S. and Canada, as well as in a handful of other countries around the world.

About 50,000 of the company's payroll customers have now joined ADP's new PC-Payroll network, using their own PCs to input their payroll data to ADP.

For the brokerage industry, ADP provides record-keeping, stock quotations, order entry, proxy services and other trading services for about 350 financial institutions. The company has about 70,000 stock quote terminals presently in service at brokerage firms throughout the country. ADP's brokerage services account for about 25 percent of its revenue.

ADP's dealer services division offers a variety of specialized information services for 6,000 automobile, truck, farm and heavy equipment dealers in the U.S. and Canada. This division accounts for about 10 percent of ADP's revenue.

The company's automotive claims services provide computerized repair and replacement estimating services for 18 of the nation's 20 largest auto insurance companies, as well as for thousands of claims adjusters and repair shops.

EARNINGS GROWTH

ADP has had very steady long-term earnings growth. Its earnings per share increased 364 percent (16.5 percent per year) over the past ten years.

ADP has about 19,000 employees and 16,000 shareholders.

STOCK GROWTH

The company's stock has posted strong gains the past ten years, increasing 360 percent (16.5 percent per year) during the period.

Including reinvested dividends, a $10,000 investment in ADP stock at its closing stock price in 1980 would have grown to about $52,000 ten years later. Average annual compounded rate of return (including stock growth and reinvested dividends): about 18 percent.

DIVIDEND YIELD

The company generally pays a modest yield, averaging about 1.2 percent over the past five years. During the most recent two-year rating period (1990 and 1991) the stock paid an average annual current return (dividend yield) of 1.2 percent.

DIVIDEND GROWTH

ADP has raised its dividend for 17 consecutive years. The dividend increased 100 percent (15 percent per year) from 1985 to 1990.

CONSISTENCY

ADP has been one of the most consistent companies in America, with 41 consecutive years of record sales and earnings. Its price-earnings ratio of about 15 to 20 over the past three years is typical for growing U.S. companies.

SHAREHOLDER PERKS   (no points)

The company provides no dividend reinvestment plan, nor does it offer any other perks for its shareholders.

SUMMARY

Fiscal year ended: June 30*
(Revenue and net income in millions)

	1991**	1990	1989	1988	1987	1986	1985	5-year growth, %† (annual/total)
Revenue		1,714	1,677	1,549	1,384	1,204	1,030	11/66
Net income		211	187	170	132	106	87	19/142
Earnings/share		1.44	1.26	1.10	0.88	0.73	0.62	18/132
Dividend/share		.32	.28	.24	.20	.18	.16	15/100
Dividend yield, %	1.1	1.3	1.5	1.0	1.0	1.2	1.6	—/—
Stock price	34.13	27.00	24.50	19.50	22.44	17.63	14.75	13/83
P/E ratio	27	17	15	20	23	21	17	—/—
Book value/share		7.63	6.50	6.35	5.65	4.52	3.88	15/96

* Except stock price Dec. 31, 1985–90
** Stock price as of 5–1–91
† 1985–90
Source: Company sources

80 PREMIER INDUSTRIAL CORPORATION

PREMIER INDUSTRIAL CORP.

4500 Euclid Avenue
Cleveland, OH 44103
216-391-8300
Chairman: Morton L. Mandel
President: William M. Hamilton

EARNINGS GROWTH	★
STOCK GROWTH	★ ★
DIVIDEND YIELD	★ ★
DIVIDEND GROWTH	★ ★ ★
CONSISTENCY	★ ★ ★
SHAREHOLDER PERKS	★ ★
NYSE—PRE	**13 points**

Premier Industrial was founded half a century ago by three brothers, Joseph, Jack and Morton Mandel. The company, which first opened shop in 1940 as an auto parts distributor, has gone through a lot of changes, but the three Mandels still man the helm of the burgeoning Cleveland-based concern. Morton Mandel is chairman of the board, Jack is finance committee chairman and Joseph is executive committee chairman.

The Mandels have steered Premier through five decades of steady growth and diversification. The company is now a distributor of more than 100,000 electronic components for the industrial, maintenance and repair markets.

Premier, which reported revenues of $626 million in its fiscal 1990, has been a very steady performer since going public in 1960. Over the past 31 years, the company has posted 29 years of record earnings.

The company now has operations in more than 300 locations worldwide. Its biggest division is Newark Electronics, with 242 sales offices. According to company figures, Newark is the nation's leading broadline electronics distributor. It takes a 1,250-page catalog to list all the parts, components, instruments and equipment the company stocks. The catalog goes out to about a million customers and prospects.

Premier divides its operations into two segments:

- Electronics (65 percent of sales). Through Newark and its other distribution channels, the company sells motor controls, lamps, fuses, wire, cable, hardware, connectors and other electronic components and products.
- General products (35 percent of sales). Through some 13 subsidiaries, Premier distributes and manufactures lubricants, hardware, machinery parts, welding products, cleaners, degreasers, disinfectants, coatings, adhesives, sealers, fastners, cord, cable and other maintenance-related products for industrial, commercial and institutional markets.

Through its Akron Brass and Western Fire Equipment subsidiaries, Premier also manufactures a line of fire-fighting hoses, nozzles, valves and related equipment.

EARNINGS GROWTH

Premier has had solid, steady long-term growth. Over the past ten years, its earnings per share increased 193 percent (an average of 11 percent per year).

The company has about 4,800 employees and 5,700 shareholders.

STOCK GROWTH

The company has enjoyed strong stock price appreciation the past ten years, increasing 294 percent (15 percent per year) for the period.

Including reinvested dividends, a $10,000 investment in Premier stock at its closing stock price in 1980 would have grown to about $46,000 ten years later. Average annual compounded rate of return (including stock growth and reinvested dividends): about 16.5 percent.

DIVIDEND YIELD

Premier generally pays a modest yield, averaging about 1.5 percent over the past ten years. During the most recent two-year rating period (fiscal 1990 and 1991) the stock paid an average annual current return (dividend yield) of 1.6 percent.

DIVIDEND GROWTH ★ ★ ★

Premier has raised its dividend for 15 consecutive years. The dividend increased 140 percent (19 percent per year) from 1985 to 1990.

CONSISTENCY

The company has had increased revenue, book value and earnings per share nine of the past ten years—although some analysts projected a slight recession-induced earnings decline in fiscal 1991. Its price-earnings ratio of around 20 is slightly higher than average for growing U.S. companies.

SHAREHOLDER PERKS

The company offers its shareholders an excellent dividend reinvestment and voluntary stock purchase plan. There are no fees or commissions, and shareholders of record may purchase $10 to $5,000 per quarter in additional shares through the voluntary stock purchase plan.

SUMMARY

Fiscal year ended: May 31*
(Revenue and net income in millions)

	1991**	1990	1989	1988	1987	1986	1985	5-year growth, %† (annual/total)
Revenue		626	596	528	459	435	432	8/45
Net income		75	70	64	48	41	39	14/92
Earnings/share		1.29	1.13	0.98	0.72	0.62	0.58	17/122
Dividend/share		.36	.29	.23	.19	.17	.15	19/140
Dividend yield, %	1.6	1.5	1.5	1.3	1.3	1.4	1.6	—/—
Stock price	28.37	24.63	25.17	18.63	18.63	12.88	12.88	14/91
P/E ratio	22.0	18.2	16.6	18.4	19.4	18.4	15.7	—/—
Book value/share		4.35	3.65	4.47	4.04	3.60	3.10	7/40

  * Except stock price Dec. 31, 1985–90
** Stock price as of 5–1–91
  † 1985–90
Source: Company sources

81

GENUINE PARTS COMPANY

2999 Circle 75 Parkway
Atlanta, GA 30339
404-953-1700
Chairman and CEO: Larry L. Prince
President: Thomas C. Gallagher

EARNINGS GROWTH	★
STOCK GROWTH	★
DIVIDEND YIELD	★ ★ ★
DIVIDEND GROWTH	★ ★
CONSISTENCY	★ ★ ★ ★
SHAREHOLDER PERKS	★ ★
NYSE—GPC	**13 points**

Genuine Parts has established itself as a market leader in one of the few niches of the auto industry that seems immune to recession. Even when a faltering economy sends new car sales plummeting, the automotive after-market does a thriving business supplying replacement parts to consumers who are driving their older cars longer. That's one good reason why Genuine Parts has managed to increase its sales for 41 consecutive years, its profits for 30 years and its dividend for 34 years.

The Atlanta-based parts distributor owns about 475 automotive parts stores in 34 states and another 20 stores in Canada (most under the NAPA Auto Parts name). In all, Genuine serves about 6,100 jobbing stores (most of which are independently owned) through its 65 distribution centers. Each center carries about 100,000 different parts for domestic and foreign automobiles.

Genuine does no manufacturing itself. The firm, which was founded in 1928, is strictly a wholesale distributor. It buys parts from more than 170 domestic suppliers. The company does, however, operate six plants that rebuild small automotive parts.

Genuine's automotive parts group accounts for about 64 percent of its $3.3 billion in annual revenue.

The company also owns Motion Industries, a distributor of industrial parts, including bearings and fluid transmission equipment, and agricultural and irrigation equipment. Motion operates 176 outlets in 21 states and sells more than 100,000 different items to some 80,000 customers. Genuine's Canadian subsidiary, Oliver Industrial Supply, operates five industrial parts and agricultural supply distribution centers and three irrigation sales centers.

The industrial parts segment accounts for about 20 percent of the company's revenue.

Genuine's other business is its S.P. Richards office products group (16 percent of revenue), which distributes a broad line of computer supplies, office furniture, office machines and general office supplies. The company distributes more than 17,000 items to 8,000 office supply dealers in 21 states.

EARNINGS GROWTH

Genuine has had steady, consistent long-term growth. Over the past ten years, its earnings per share increased 147 percent (9.5 percent per year).

The company has about 16,000 employees and 7,000 shareholders.

STOCK GROWTH ★

The company has had solid stock price appreciation the past ten years, increasing 225 percent (12.5 percent per year) for the period.

Including reinvested dividends, a $10,000 investment in Genuine stock at its closing stock price in 1980 would have grown to about $40,000 ten years later. Average annual compounded rate of return (including stock growth and reinvested dividends): about 15 percent.

DIVIDEND YIELD

Genuine generally pays a very good dividend yield, averaging about 3.5 percent over the past ten years. During the most recent two-year rating period (fiscal 1990 and 1991) the stock paid an average annual current return (dividend yield) of 3.7 percent.

DIVIDEND GROWTH

Genuine has raised its dividend for 34 consecutive years. The dividend increased 75 percent (12 percent per year) from 1985 to 1990.

CONSISTENCY

The company has had very consistent growth in its earnings, revenue and book value per share, including 41 consecutive years of increased revenue and 30 years of increased earnings. Its price-earnings ratio of about 15 is normal for growing U.S. companies.

SHAREHOLDER PERKS

The company offers a good dividend reinvestment and voluntary stock purchase plan. There are no fees or commissions, and shareholders of record may buy $10 to $3,000 per quarter in additional shares.

SUMMARY

Fiscal year ended: Dec. 31
(Revenue and net income in millions)

	1991*	1990	1989	1988	1987	1986	1985	5-year growth, %† (annual/total)
Revenue		3,319	3,161	2,942	2,606	2,394	2,279	8/45
Net income		207	199	181	148	121	126	10/64
Earnings/share		2.69	2.58	2.35	1.88	1.52	1.49	13/81
Dividend/share		1.38	1.20	1.04	.92	1.01	.79	12/75
Dividend yield, %	3.7	3.6	3.1	2.8	2.6	3.5	3.6	—/—
Stock price	39.50	38.00	42.00	35.50	35.12	28.75	25.41	8/49
P/E ratio	15	14	15	15	19	19	14	—/—
Book value/share		13.40	12.54	11.16	9.84	9.55	9.14	8/46

* Stock price as of 5–1–91
† 1985–90
Source: Company sources

Microsoft ®

MICROSOFT CORP.

One Microsoft Way
Redmond, WA 98052-6399
206-882-8080
Chairman and CEO: William H. Gates
President and COO: Michael R. Hallman

EARNINGS GROWTH	★ ★ ★ ★
STOCK GROWTH	★ ★ ★ ★
DIVIDEND YIELD	(no points)
DIVIDEND GROWTH	(no points)
CONSISTENCY	★ ★ ★ ★
SHAREHOLDER PERKS	(no points)
OTC—MSFT	**12 points**

There aren't many chief executive officers in corporate America as young as Microsoft's chairman and CEO, Bill Gates. In fact, his lean features and thick shock of hair give the bespectacled Gates a boyish appearance even more youthful than his 35 years. But by computer industry standards, Gates is a wily veteran. He cofounded the Redmond, Washington computer software giant in 1975 at the age of 19 and has been presiding over its phenomenal growth ever since.

Over the past five years, the company's stock price has soared from a split-adjusted $5.30 a share in 1986 to more than $100 a share in 1991. Gates still owns 40.3 *million* shares (35.5 percent of all shares outstanding).

Microsoft's success has made Gates somewhat of a legend in the computer industry. As the *Financial Times of London* recently wrote, "Microsoft has become the company that competitors love to hate. . . . Intensely competitive, Gates 'always plays to win and to leave the other guy knowing that he has lost,' says a long-time business associate."

In terms of sustained outstanding growth, the company has been megabytes ahead of the rest of the American computer industry. Even IBM, despite its enormous size, has paled in comparison to the extraordinarily rapid ascent of Microsoft.

The company's sales have exploded from $24.5 million in 1981 when it was first incorporated (after six years as a partnership) to about $1.75 billion in fiscal 1991 (ended June 30). Microsoft, which has become one of the world's leading computer software manufacturers, has piggybacked on the meteoric growth of the personal computer industry. About one million Americans used personal computers in 1980; by 1990, that figure had grown to an estimated 50 million users.

The company's well-known Windows software series includes word processing, graphics, communications, spreadsheet and project management programs. Since introducing the MS-DOS program on IBM PCs in 1981, the company has created MS-DOS versions for 300 other computers.

Microsoft spends vast amounts of money on research and development to stay ahead of the ever-evolving computer business. The company spent $360 million on new product development between 1988 and 1990.

Microsoft has manufacturing plants in the U.S., Puerto Rico and the Republic of Ireland, and sales offices in 22 countries. About 55 percent of its revenue is generated by sales outside the U.S.

The company breaks its business into three key areas:

- Systems software (39 percent of revenue). Systems software includes operating systems to control the hardware, allocate computer memory, schedule the execution of applications software and manage the flow of information among the components of the microcomputer system. It also includes microcomputer language programs that enable users to write programs in a particular computer language and translate programs into a set of commands that activate and instruct the hardware.
- Applications software (48 percent of revenue). Applications software provides the microcomputer with instructions for the performance of end-user tasks such as word processing, spreadsheet, graphics and database programs.
- Hardware, books and other products (13 percent). Microsoft produces a line of computer peripherals and accessories. Its leading hardware product is the Microsoft Mouse, a hand-held pointing device that facilitates editing text on the screen.

    The company also publishes instructional books about Microsoft products and other software. It also operates Microsoft University, which offers 18 classes on various subjects related to Microsoft products.

EARNINGS GROWTH

Microsoft has had tremendous growth in its short history. Since 1982, the first year for which its records are available, its earnings per share have increased 5,700 percent (through 1990), an average annual increase of 65 percent.

The company has about 6,000 employees and 9,000 shareholders.

STOCK GROWTH

The company has had phenomenal stock price appreciation since 1986, when the stock became publicly traded. Over the past five years, the stock has grown 1,268 percent (65 percent per year) for the period. A $10,000 investment in Microsoft stock when it was issued in 1986 would have grown to about $127,000 by the end of 1990.

DIVIDEND YIELD   (no points)

Microsoft pays no dividend.

DIVIDEND GROWTH   (no points)

CONSISTENCY

In its short history, the company has had very consistent growth, with increased earnings, revenue and book value each of the eight years for which its records are available. Its price-earnings ratio of about 30 is very high, but not unusual for a company with Microsoft's growth record.

SHAREHOLDER PERKS   (no points)

Microsoft offers no shareholder perks.

SUMMARY

Fiscal year ended: June 30*
(Revenue and net income in millions)

	1991**	1990	1989	1988	1987	1986	1985	5-year growth, %† (annual/total)
Revenue		1,183	804	591	346	198	140	53/745
Net income		279	171	124	78	39	24	63/1,062
Earnings/share		2.34	1.52	1.11	0.70	0.39	0.26	55/800
Dividend/share¹								NA
Dividend yield, %								—/—
Stock price	100.75	75.25	46.00	28.00	28.00	12.00	—	58/527
P/E ratio	31	20	18	25	20	20	18	—/—
Book value/share		8.08	5.15	3.50	2.27	1.37	.63	65/1,182

 * Except stock price Dec. 31, 1985–90 (not traded publicly till 3–86)
** Stock price as of 5–1–91
 † 1985–90; except stock price 1986–90
 1 No cash dividends being paid
Source: Company sources

INTERNATIONAL DAIRY QUEEN, INC.

5701 Green Valley Drive
Minneapolis, MN 55439
612-830-0200
Chairman: John W. Mooty
President: Michael P. Sullivan

EARNINGS GROWTH	★ ★ ★ ★
STOCK GROWTH	★ ★ ★ ★
DIVIDEND YIELD	(no points)
DIVIDEND GROWTH	(no points)
CONSISTENCY	★ ★ ★ ★
SHAREHOLDER PERKS	(no points)
OTC—INDQ "A"	**12 points**

Double-digit stock price increases have become as commonplace at Dairy Queen as its patented DQ cone with the curl on top. The international queen of soft-serve ice cream has scooped out a remarkable record of profit growth, with earnings increases of at least 18 percent each year for more than 15 consecutive years.

Dairy Queen is one of the nation's oldest restaurant franchisers. Its first store opened in 1940 in Joliet, Illinois, selling cones, sundaes and take-home pints. Since then, the Minneapolis-based firm has expanded to more than 6,100 franchised stores in 19 countries. Its leading markets outside the U.S. are Canada with 540 stores and Japan with 125.

Dairy Queen's sensational record of increased earnings underscores the recession-resistant nature of its ice cream business. No matter what shape the economy is in, if the sun is shining and the temperature is rising, you can bet your last investment dollar that the lines will be forming at your neighborhood DQ.

International Dairy Queen is one of the smaller companies on the *100 Best* list, with annual sales of $290 million.

While it's not entirely a one-product company, DQ's ice cream store sales do account for the vast share of its revenue. Many of the stores sell Brazier foods, including hamburgers, hot dogs, fish, french fries and onion rings.

Most of the company's restaurants are owned by private investors who typically pay a $30,000 initial franchise fee plus an ongoing fee of 4 percent of gross sales revenue. The company generally adds at least 100 new franchises each year.

Dairy Queen's other corporate holdings include:

- **Golden Skillet Restaurants** (acquired in 1981), with 76 franchised stores, including 24 outside the U.S.
- **KarmelKorn Shoppes** (acquired in 1986), 164 franchised shops in 39 states.
- **Orange Julius** (acquired in 1987), 660 franchises, including 131 in Canada and 23 others outside the U.S.

EARNINGS GROWTH

DQ has enjoyed exceptional, sustained growth. Over the past ten years, its earnings per share increased 978 percent (27 percent per year).

The company has about 600 employees.

STOCK GROWTH

Dairy Queen has had tremendous stock price appreciation the past ten years, soaring 2,662 percent (39.5 percent per year) for the period.

A $10,000 investment in DQ stock at its closing price in 1980 would have grown to about $276,000 ten years later.

DIVIDEND YIELD (no points)

Dairy Queen pays no dividend.

DIVIDEND GROWTH (no points)

CONSISTENCY

The company has posted more than 15 consecutive years of record sales, earnings and book value per share. Its price-earnings ratio of about 18 to 24 is well above average, but not unusual for a company that has had this kind of accelerated growth.

SHAREHOLDER PERKS   (no points)

At its annual meeting, the company serves some of its Brazier foods and newer ice cream products to shareholders.

SUMMARY

Fiscal year ended: Nov. 30*
(Revenue and net income in millions)

	1991**	1990	1989	1988	1987	1986	1985	5-year growth, %† (annual/total)
Revenue		283	255	243	211	184	159	12/78
Net income		26	23	20	15	12	10	21/160
Earnings/share[1]		.97	.83	.70	.51	.42	.33	24/194
Dividend/share								NA
Dividend yield, %								—/—
Stock price[1]	24.00	16.57	14.75	11.50	8.00	7.74	5.20	26/219
P/E ratio	24.0	18.0	15.8	14.0	18.9	18.3	11.4	—/—
Book value/share[1]		3.08	2.70	2.03	1.50	1.00	.49	44/528

  * Except stock price Dec. 31, 1985–90
 ** Stock price as of 5–1–91
  1 Adjusted for stock split 3–12–91
Source: Company sources

stryker

STRYKER CORP.

2725 Fairfield Road
P.O. Box 4085
Kalamazoo, MI 49003-4085
616-385-2600
Chairman, President and CEO: John W. Brown

EARNINGS GROWTH	★ ★ ★ ★
STOCK GROWTH	★ ★ ★ ★
DIVIDEND YIELD	(no points)
DIVIDEND GROWTH	(no points)
CONSISTENCY	★ ★ ★ ★
SHAREHOLDER PERKS	(no points)
OTC—STRY	**12 points**

Orthopedic arthroscopics has revolutionized medical surgery. Operations that once required weeks or months of recovery now take just days. The difference is the new arthroscopic technology that enables doctors to see inside a patient's body. In this new age of orthopedic arthroscopics, Stryker serves as the eyes of the surgeon.

One of Stryker's biggest breakthroughs in recent years has been the development of a high definition medical video system that, for the first time, gives surgeons a broadcast quality image of the interior of a joint.

Stryker's ability to stay at the top of its markets has kept the company's profit growth on a steady spiral. The Kalamazoo manufacturer, founded in 1940 by Dr. Homer H. Stryker, has posted earnings gains of 20 percent or more for 13 consecutive years.

The company manufactures a line of arthroscopic equipment geared primarily to the orthopedic profession. Its equipment includes arthroscopes, a light source, powered instruments and miniature television cameras. These instruments require only small punctures to enter the joint compared with the long incisions and major surgery required by conventional instruments.

With annual revenues of $281 million, Stryker is among the smallest of the *100 Best*. Foreign sales account for about 30 percent of the company's total revenue.

Stryker divides its operations into two segments:

- Surgical products (79 percent of revenue). The company develops and manufactures a range of specialized surgical equipment, including arthroscopic systems and powered surgical equipment (drills, saws, fixation and reaming equipment and other instruments used for drilling, burring, rasping or cutting bones, wiring or pinning bone fractures, preparing hip or knee joint, performing cranial operations or treating skin defects by surgical abrasion). The company has been a leader in the development of battery-powered surgical equipment.

  The company also produces a line of total and partial hip and knee replacements.

  Stryker also manufactures surgical irrigation systems, the most innovative of which is its new CBC-ConstaVac, which collects a patient's blood after surgery, filters it and prepares it for reinfusion into the patient after surgery—reducing or eliminating the need for blood bank transfusions.

- Medical products (21 percent of revenue). The company manufactures patient handling equipment, including stretchers, stretcher beds, "infant warmers" and critical care beds that enable physicians to weigh patients, take X-rays and perform other functions without removing the patient from the bed.

EARNINGS GROWTH

Stryker has enjoyed exceptional growth since going public in 1979. Over the past ten years, its earnings per share increased 567 percent (21 percent per year).

The company has about 2,000 employees and 2,400 shareholders.

STOCK GROWTH

Stryker has had outstanding stock price appreciation the past ten years, increasing 793 percent (24.5 percent per year).

A $10,000 investment in Stryker stock at its closing price in 1980 would have grown to about $90,000 ten years later.

DIVIDEND YIELD   (no points)

Stryker pays no dividend.

DIVIDEND GROWTH   (no points)

CONSISTENCY

The company has had double-digit increases in revenue, book value and earnings per share each of the 12 years since it became publicly traded.

Its recent price-earnings ratio of 42 was the highest ever for Stryker and much higher than that of most medical products manufacturers. Traditionally, the company has been in the 15 to 25 price-earnings range.

SHAREHOLDER PERKS   (no points)

Stryker offers no shareholder perks.

SUMMARY

Fiscal year ended: Dec. 31
(Revenue and net income in millions)

	1991*	1990	1989	1988	1987	1986	1985	5-year growth, %† (annual/total)
Revenue		281	226	179	148	129	108	21/160
Net income		24	19	16	13	10	9	21/166
Earnings/share		1.00	0.82	0.68	0.55	0.45	0.37	22/170
Dividend/share[1]								—/—
Dividend yield, %								—/—
Stock price	44.00	31.25	24.75	13.50	11.67	10.67	8.00	31/290
P/E ratio	42.0	31.3	30.2	19.9	21.2	24.4	21.1	—/—
Book value/share		6.23	4.75	3.88	3.21	2.60	2.13	24/192

* Stock price as of 5–1–91
† 1985–90
1 No cash dividends; no dividend reinvestment
Source: Company sources

85

PPG INDUSTRIES, INC.
One PPG Place
Pittsburgh, PA 15272
412-434-3131
Chairman and CEO: Vincent A. Sarni

EARNINGS GROWTH	★
STOCK GROWTH	★ ★
DIVIDEND YIELD	★ ★ ★
DIVIDEND GROWTH	★ ★ ★
CONSISTENCY	★
SHAREHOLDER PERKS	★ ★
NYSE—PPG	**12 points**

PPG opened the first successful plate glass factory in America more than 100 years ago. Formerly the Pittsburgh Plate Glass Company, PPG opened shop in 1883 in Creighton, Pennsylvania.

The company makes glass for automobiles, homes, commercial buildings, aircraft, furniture and the electronics industry. It manufactures about one-third of the total North American industry output of flat glass. It is also the world's second largest manufacturer of continuous strand fiberglass. PPG's glass segment accounts for 40 percent of its $6 billion a year in total revenue.

PPG is worldwide in scope. Its foreign sales account for 34 percent of total revenue. The company has 78 manufacturing plants and 13 research facilities around the world, including plants in Canada, France, Germany, Italy, Mexico, the Netherlands, Spain, Taiwan and the United Kingdom.

In addition to its glass operations, the company operates in two other key business segments:

• Coatings and resins (38 percent of revenue). PPG is the world's leading supplier of auto and industrial coatings. It makes primers, finishes, adhesives and sealants for automobiles, and protective coatings for appli-

ances, buildings, containers and other consumer, maintenance and industrial products. It is also a major supplier of architectural finishes.
- Chemicals (19 percent of revenue). PPG is the world's third largest supplier of chlorine and caustic soda, and the largest producer of optical resins. Its products are used in the manufacture of soaps, detergents, pulp, paper, ophthalmic lenses and a variety of personal care products.

    It also produces chemicals for waste treatment, food additives, pharmaceuticals and other industrial markets.

The company has made several recent acquisitions to broaden its product base. Through its subsidiaries, PPG manufactures medical electronics units and systems for operating rooms, intensive care units and cardiac catheterization laboratories.

EARNINGS GROWTH

PPG has had steady long-term growth. Over the past ten years, its earnings per share increased 179 percent (an average of 11 percent per year).

The company has about 35,000 employees and 42,000 shareholders.

STOCK GROWTH

The company has had flat stock price appreciation the past four years, but over the ten-year rating period through 1990, its stock price rose 370 percent (17 percent per year).

Including reinvested dividends, a $10,000 investment in PPG stock at its closing stock price in 1980 would have grown to about $70,000 ten years later. Average annual compounded rate of return (including stock growth and reinvested dividends): about 21.5 percent.

DIVIDEND YIELD

PPG generally pays a very good yield, averaging almost 3.5 percent over the past five years. During the most recent two-year rating period (fiscal 1990 and 1991) the stock paid an average annual current return (dividend yield) of 3.6 percent.

DIVIDEND GROWTH

PPG has raised its dividend for 19 consecutive years. The dividend increased 100 percent (15 percent per year) from 1985 to 1990.

CONSISTENCY   ★

The company has had increased earnings per share only seven of the past ten years and was projected to have an earnings drop in 1991. Its revenues and book value per share have gone up nine of the past ten years. Its price-earnings ratio of about 11 is about right for a company that has faced some stagnant earnings growth.

SHAREHOLDER PERKS

PPG offers a good dividend reinvestment plan with all fees absorbed by the company. Shareholders may make voluntary cash payments of $10 to $3,000 per quarter.

SUMMARY

Fiscal year ended: Dec. 31
(Revenue and net income in millions)

	1991*	1990	1989	1988	1987	1986	1985	5-year growth, %† (annual/total)
Revenue		6,021	5,734	5,617	5,183	4,687	4,346	7/38
Net income		475	465	468	377	316	303	9/56
Earnings/share		4.43	4.18	4.26	3.19	2.66	2.27	14/95
Dividend/share		1.64	1.48	1.28	1.11	0.94	0.82	15/100
Dividend yield, %	3.5	3.7	3.4	3.2	2.6	2.9	3.9	—/—
Stock price	48.13	47.00	39.75	40.38	33.13	36.38	25.50	13/84
P/E ratio	11.0	9.9	10.3	9.5	13.2	12.1	9.2	—/—
Book value/share		24.00	20.98	20.48	18.43	16.56	14.39	11/66

* Stock price as of 5–1–91
† 1985–90
Source: Company sources

86

Melville

MELVILLE CORP.

One Theall Road
Rye, NY 10580
914-925-4000
Chairman, President and CEO: Stanley P. Goldstein

EARNINGS GROWTH	★
STOCK GROWTH	★ ★
DIVIDEND YIELD	★ ★ ★
DIVIDEND GROWTH	★ ★
CONSISTENCY	★ ★ ★ ★
SHAREHOLDER PERKS	(no points)
NYSE—MES	**12 points**

Melville has long been recognized as one of America's largest fashion and footwear retailers. It owns Thom McAn and Meldisco shoes, plus a long list of apparel retailers, including discount giant Marshalls. In recent years, the New York retailer has stretched its dominance to other areas as well. It is now one of the nation's leading drug retailers and one of the largest toy store chains.

In all, Melville operates nearly 8,000 stores across all 50 states, plus Canada, Puerto Rico and the Virgin Islands.

The company acquired the 326-store Circus World chain in 1990 and merged it into its Kay-Bee Toys subsidiary. With more than 1,100 stores, Kay-Bee now has outlets in more malls than any other toy retailer.

The company's other major acquisition in 1990 was the 490-store Peoples Drug chain, which was merged into Melville's CVS stores operation. The Peoples acquisition brings to more than 1,200 the number of drugstores under the Melville corporate banner.

Melville's broad diversification strategy has helped it maintain steady earnings growth. The company has had increased sales for 26 consecutive years and increased earnings per share for 17 consecutive years.

While acquisitions play a key role in the company's growth, Melville has also been expanding rapidly from within. The company opened about 300 new stores in 1990 (in addition to its acquisitions) and anticipates opening 400 more in 1991. On the other hand, the company also knows when to pull the plug. It closed 294 of its less-profitable outlets in 1990 and anticipates closing another 224 stores in 1991.

The company breaks its operations into four divisions:

- Apparel (35 percent of sales). Marshalls, with 386 stores and $2.2 billion in 1990 net sales, continues to be Melville's largest clothing retailer. Its other clothing chains include Chess King (541 apparel stores), Wilsons (524 leather fashion stores) and Accessory Lady (94 stores).
- Footwear (20 percent of sales). The company operates 2,464 Meldisco shoe shops in K mart stores throughout the U.S. It also operates Thom McAn (835 stores) and Fan Club (88 athletic shoes stores).
- Drug, health and beauty aids (31 percent of sales). Melville operates 1,196 CVS drugstores and 29 Freddy's deep-discount drugstores.
- Toys and household furnishings (14 percent of sales). The company owns 1,116 Kay-Bee toy stores, 141 Linens 'n Things stores, 247 This End Up furniture stores and 86 Prints Plus prints and posters stores.

EARNINGS GROWTH

Melville has had consistent long-term growth. Over the past ten years, its earnings per share increased 215 percent (an average of 12 percent per year).

The company has about 100,000 employees and 8,500 shareholders.

STOCK GROWTH

The company has had strong, sustained stock price appreciation the past ten years, increasing 377 percent (17 percent per year) for the period.

Including reinvested dividends, a $10,000 investment in Melville stock at its closing price in 1980 would have grown to about $65,000 ten years later. Average annual compounded rate of return (including stock growth and reinvested dividends): about 20.5 percent.

DIVIDEND YIELD

Melville traditionally pays a good dividend yield, averaging about 3 percent over the past five years. During the most recent two-year rating period (fiscal 1990 and 1991) the stock paid an average annual current return (dividend yield) of 3.1 percent.

DIVIDEND GROWTH

Melville has raised its dividend for 27 consecutive years. The dividend increased 97 percent (15 percent per year) from 1985 to 1990.

CONSISTENCY

The company has had 26 consecutive years of increased revenues, and increased earnings per share 26 of the past 27 years. Its price-earnings ratio of about 12 to 14 is quite low for a growing retail company.

SHAREHOLDER PERKS   (no points)

Melville provides no dividend reinvestment plan, nor does it offer any shareholder perks.

SUMMARY

Fiscal year ended: Dec. 31
(Revenue and net income in millions)

	1991*	1990	1989	1988	1987	1986	1985	5-year growth, %† (annual/total)
Revenue		8,687	7,554	6,780	5,930	5,262	4,775	13/82
Net income		385	398	355	285	238	211	13/82
Earnings/share		3.59	3.56	3.26	2.63	2.20	2.03	12/77
Dividend/share		1.42	1.30	1.05	0.88	0.78	0.72	15/97
Dividend yield, %	2.9	3.2	2.9	3.1	2.6	2.5	3.3	—/—
Stock price	49.00	42.00	45.00	37.00	26.50	27.00	25.25	9/53
P/E ratio	14.0	12.5	12.5	10.4	12.7	13.9	11.0	—/—
Book value/share		17.99	15.75	15.65	13.41	11.64	10.20	12/76

* Stock price as of 5–1–91
† 1985–90
Source: Company sources

87

Westinghouse

WESTINGHOUSE ELECTRIC CORP.
Westinghouse Building
Gateway Center
Stanwix Street
Pittsburgh, PA 15222
412-244-2000
Chairman and CEO: Paul E. Lego

EARNINGS GROWTH	★
STOCK GROWTH	★ ★
DIVIDEND YIELD	★ ★ ★ ★
DIVIDEND GROWTH	★ ★ ★
CONSISTENCY	★ ★
SHAREHOLDER PERKS	(no points)
NYSE—WX	**12 points**

Westinghouse Electric is plugged into a wide range of corporate pursuits, most of which deal in some way with the power of electricity. From massive nuclear reactors to tiny electronic components, the Pittsburgh conglomerate manufactures products that generate electricity, conduct it, transmit it, control it and utilize it for surveillance, sanitation, transportation, refrigeration and communication.

With annual revenues of $12.9 billion, Westinghouse is the nation's second largest electronics concern (behind General Electric). It has operations and subsidiaries worldwide, with foreign sales that account for about 21 percent of total revenue.

Among the company's key areas are: electrical generating equipment, Group W radio and TV stations, waste treatment services, Thermo King transport refrigeration units, defense radar and surveillance systems.

The company divides its operations into six market areas:

- Broadcasting (5 percent of total revenue). Westinghouse Broadcasting Company (Group W) owns TV stations in Boston, Baltimore, Philadelphia, Pittsburgh and San Francisco, plus 22 radio stations. It also produces syndicated TV programming and provides satellite access for cable networks.

- Electronic systems (22 percent of revenue). Westinghouse installed the radar systems for all of the U.S. Air Force's F-16 fighter planes and is currently at work on the newest generation of fighter planes, the Advanced Tactical Fighter (ATF). Westinghouse is providing the radar systems, electrical generators and other integrated electronic systems for the ATFs. It is also involved in space electronics, control communications systems, intelligence systems, antisubmarine and marine systems, aircraft electrical systems and air control systems. It manufactures infrared detection systems, torpedoes, missile launching systems and airborne surveillance equipment.

- Energy and utility systems (17 percent of revenue). Westinghouse manufactures nuclear reactor systems and components, steam turbine generators, combustion turbine generators and combined cycle plants. It sells nuclear fuel to plants, transports radioactive wastes, and makes fuel assemblies and zirconium tubing for nuclear fuel rods used in nuclear reactors. The company also constructs waste-to-energy plants that generate electricity through the burning of solid wastes.

- Industries (24.5 percent of revenue). Westinghouse's Thermo King subsidiary manufactures transport refrigeration systems for trucks, ships and railway cars. Westinghouse also provides toxic and hazardous wastes services; produces electronic components and systems such as motor starters, circuit devices, transformers, safety switches, panelboards, switchboards and wiring systems; and manufactures large industrial motors and emission-control products.

- Commercial (19 percent of revenue). Westinghouse owns Longines-Wittnauer Watch Company (the official timekeeper of the 1988 Summer and Winter Olympics), sells office furnishings and modular furniture systems, markets business communications systems and software and is the largest 7-Up bottler in the U.S. (It also bottles A&W, Hawaiian Punch, Schweppes and others.)

    The company sold its elevator installation business in 1989.

- Financial services (9 percent of revenue). The Westinghouse financial services arm provides corporate financing, commercial and residential real estate financing, community land development, leasing and project financing, and merchant banking services.

Westinghouse was founded in 1886 by George Westinghouse, one of America's most prolific inventors. Before his death in 1914, Mr. Westinghouse was credited with nearly 400 inventions ranging from railroad car airbrakes to electric turbines, and from air compressors to distribution systems for natural gas.

EARNINGS GROWTH

Westinghouse has had solid long-term growth. Over the past ten years, its earnings per share increased 189 percent (an average of 11 percent per year).

The company has about 115,000 employees and 120,000 shareholders.

STOCK GROWTH

The company has had strong stock growth the past ten years, increasing 287 percent (14.5 percent per year) during the period.

Including reinvested dividends, a $10,000 investment in Westinghouse stock at its closing stock price in 1980 would have grown to about $55,000 ten years later. Average annual compounded rate of return (including stock growth and reinvested dividends): about 19 percent.

DIVIDEND YIELD ★ ★ ★ ★

Westinghouse generally pays an excellent yield, averaging about 4 percent over the past five years. During the most recent two-year rating period (fiscal 1990 and 1991) the stock paid an average annual current return (dividend yield) of 5 percent.

DIVIDEND GROWTH

Westinghouse has raised its dividend for seven consecutive years. The dividend rose 132 percent (18 percent per year) from 1985 to 1990.

CONSISTENCY

Westinghouse has had earnings increases 14 of the past 15 years through 1990, although earnings for 1991 were expected to drop sharply due primarily to some shaky loans and holdings by its finance division. But if history is any indicator, whatever financial weakness Westinghouse may have experienced in 1991 will only be temporary.

SHAREHOLDER PERKS   (no points)

Westinghouse does not offer a dividend reinvestment plan for its shareholders, nor does it offer any shareholder perks.

CORPORATE RESPONSIBILITY

The company's involvement with nuclear power and nuclear weapons, as well as its poor environmental record, has made it unpopular with ethical investors. Westinghouse Electric operates some of the most troubled and controversial U.S. military nuclear plants. These plants manufacture plutonium and other weapons-grade materials and have been the target of citizens' lawsuits and allegations of mismanagement related to poor maintenance or toxic leaks. Westinghouse inherited many of the problems at these plants from prior management. However, recently, Energy Department investigators inspecting Westinghouse's Savannah River Site (formerly managed by Du Pont as the Savannah River Plant and home to five nuclear reactors) found extensive problems in waste management, handling of tritium, and deficiencies in "training, quality assurance, radiation protection and emergency preparedness programs," including 250 violations of workplace safety and hygiene regulations.

Westinghouse was further criticized for failing to seek out problems and for minimizing them when they came to light. The problems included: serious radiological pollution in the Savannah River Swamp and Creek Plantation Swamp, contamination of several inactive disposal sites and improper decontamination of decommissioned facilities. (Source: Council on Economic Priorities)

SUMMARY

Fiscal year ended: Dec. 31
(Revenue and net income in millions)

	1991*	1990	1989	1988	1987	1986	1985	5-year growth, %† (annual/total)
Revenue		12,915	12,844	12,500	10,679	10,731	10,700	4/21
Net income		1,001	922	823	739	671	605	11/65
Earnings/share		3.41	3.16	2.83	2.56	2.21	1.76	14/94
Dividend/share		1.35	1.15	0.97	0.82	0.68	0.58	18/132
Dividend yield, %	5.1	4.9	3.7	3.7	2.7	2.5	3.3	—/—
Stock price	27.25	29.00	37.00	26.31	24.88	27.88	22.25	5/30
P/E ratio		10	10	9	12	12	10	—/—
Book value/share		16.00	15.10	13.18	12.46	10.56	10.52	9/52

* Stock price as of 5–1–91
† 1985–90
Source: Company source

GANNETT

GANNETT CO., INC.

1100 Wilson Boulevard
Arlington, VA 22234
703-284-6000
Chairman, President and CEO: John J. Curley

EARNINGS GROWTH	★
STOCK GROWTH	★
DIVIDEND YIELD	★ ★ ★
DIVIDEND GROWTH	★ ★
CONSISTENCY	★ ★ ★
SHAREHOLDER PERKS	★ ★
NYSE—GCI	**12 points**

You could say it was inevitable, that the law of averages would have to catch up with Gannett Co. and its extraordinary streak of financial proficiency.

After 22 years and 88 consecutive quarters of record earnings—dating back to the very quarter the company went public—the USA's largest newspaper publisher finally posted its first dip in earnings in 1990.

The Arlington, Virginia media group owns 83 daily newspapers—including *USA Today,* "The Nation's Newspaper"—51 nondailies and a string of television and radio stations. Its total circulation is 6.3 million.

Gannett's recent drop in earnings mirrors an industry trend that has squeezed such other media bellwethers as The New York Times Company, Dow Jones Corporation and The Times Mirror Company to their lowest earnings levels in years.

Reasons for the slump:

- Lower newspaper readership as consumers turn increasingly to TV for information.
- Recession-fueled drop in ad revenues as weakened U.S. retailers and consumer goods marketers trim budgets.

- Further drop in ad space orders in late 1990 as Persian Gulf crisis trans-fixed nation.

Analysts predict that the news industry could make a quick rebound as the economy improves. Gannett, with daily newspapers in Detroit, Louisville, Cincinnati, Des Moines and 32 other states, is poised to benefit from a media turnaround.

The company's newspaper operations account for 83 percent of its $3.4 billion in annual revenue.

Gannett's other corporate interests include:

- Broadcasting (12 percent of revenue). Owns 16 radio and 10 television stations, including network affiliates in Phoenix, Denver, Washington, D.C., Jacksonville, Atlanta, Minneapolis-St. Paul, Greensboro, Oklahoma City and Austin.
- Billboards for lease (7 percent of total revenue). Gannett Outdoor is North America's largest outdoor advertising group, with 47,000 advertising displays for lease, including large outdoor billboards and smaller panels on buses and in public transit shelters.

The crown jewel of the Gannett group continues to be *USA Today,* the nine-year-old nationwide newspaper known for its:

- Nation-leading readership of nearly 6 million (circulation: 1.75 million)
- National perspective
- Color and graphics
- Short, easily digestible articles
- Lists and bullets
- Long history of red ink

After nearly a decade of losses, *USA Today* appeared to be on the verge of profitability when the recent media slump set in. As it stands now, the paper will probably not post its first profitable year until the advertising slump abates.

Although its critics sometimes poke fun at its punchy, upbeat style, *USA Today* has been one of the most imitated newspapers in USA history. The paper—published mornings, five days a week—has ushered in a new renaissance of colors, graphics and capsulized articles among newspapers across the country.

EARNINGS GROWTH

Gannett has had solid, steady long-term growth. Over the past ten years, its earnings per share increased 151 percent (an average of 10 percent per year).

The company has about 37,000 employees and 15,000 shareholders.

STOCK GROWTH

The company had very flat stock price appreciation from 1985 to 1990. Over the most recent ten-year period, the stock price rose 220 percent (12 percent per year).

Including reinvested dividends, a $10,000 investment in Gannett stock at its closing stock price in 1980 would have grown to about $40,000 ten years later. Average annual compounded rate of return (including stock growth and reinvested dividends): about 15 percent.

DIVIDEND YIELD

Gannett has traditionally paid a very good dividend yield, averaging about 2.8 percent over the past five years. During the most recent two-year rating period (fiscal 1990 and 1991) the stock paid an average annual current return (dividend yield) of 3.2 percent.

DIVIDEND GROWTH

Gannett has raised its dividend for 23 consecutive years. The dividend rose 62 percent (10 percent per year) from 1985 to 1990.

CONSISTENCY

The company had very consistent growth until 1990, when it posted its first drop in revenue and earnings per share in its 23-year history. Its recent price-earnings ratio of about 19 is a little higher than normal for a company with relatively flat earnings growth. But, when the news industry breaks out of its slump, this stock could take off.

SHAREHOLDER PERKS

Gannett offers an excellent dividend reinvestment and voluntary stock purchase plan for its shareholders of record. There are no fees or service charges, and shareholders may contribute $10 to $5,000 per month to the stock purchase plan.

CORPORATE RESPONSIBILITY

One of Gannett's most notable social investments, and one for which it received the 1988 Corporate Conscience Award from the Council on Economic Priorities, is in the area of equal opportunity. In 1989, 29 women were the top or managing editors of Gannett's 82 daily newspapers, 17 of

Gannett's 77 publishers were women, and 33 percent of managers and 43 percent of professionals were women. Until her recent resignation, Cathleen Black was the publisher of Gannett's flagship *USA Today* and one of four women on the company's 17-member board of directors. Pam Johnson became the first black woman to publish a general circulation daily in the United States when she was promoted to the post at the *Ithaca Daily Journal* in 1981. Three of Gannett's directors are minorities, as are 11 percent of managers and 15 percent of professionals. Blacks are managing or executive editors at three Gannett papers and publishers at four others.

The company's aggressive policy of affirmative action, called Partners in Progress, is also evident in reportage. Reporters covering local or national issues are required to seek out the opinions of women, blacks and other minorities, a policy called "mainstreaming." (Source: Council on Economic Priorities)

SUMMARY

Fiscal year ended: Dec. 31
(Revenue and net income in millions)

	1991*	1990	1989	1988	1987	1986	1985	5-year growth, %† (annual/total)
Revenue		3,441	3,518	3,314	3,079	2,801	2,209	9/56
Net income		377	397	364	319	276	253	8/49
Earnings/share		2.36	2.47	2.26	1.98	1.71	1.58	8/49
Dividend/share		1.20	1.08	1.00	.92	.84	.74	10/62
Dividend yield, %	2.9	3.4	2.7	3.0	2.1	2.3	2.6	—/—
Stock price	42.30	36.00	44.00	36.00	36.50	36.06	30.62	3/18
P/E ratio	19	15	17	15	23	21	18	—/—
Book value/share		12.97	12.40	11.09	9.94	8.87	7.94	10/63

* Stock price as of 5–1–91
† 1985–90
Source: Company sources

SUPER VALU STORES, INC.

P.O. Box 990
Minneapolis, MN 55440
612-828-4000
Chairman, President and CEO: Michael W. Wright

EARNINGS GROWTH	★
STOCK GROWTH	★
DIVIDEND YIELD	★ ★ ★
DIVIDEND GROWTH	★ ★
CONSISTENCY	★ ★ ★
SHAREHOLDER PERKS	★ ★
NYSE—SVU	**12 points**

Super Valu is ranked as the nation's second largest food wholesaler, but the company does a lot more for its 2,800 customers than stock shelves. It offers marketing, management, accounting, payroll and a plethora of other services designed to help its broad clientele of independent supermarkets survive in the cutthroat business of grocery retailing.

Super Valu likes to refer to its services not as wholesaling but as "retail support." Sometimes that "support" begins long before the first case of groceries is wheeled into the store. The company helps its customers with building design and construction, subleasing, consumer research and financial assistance. It also offers trading stamp programs, insurance, personnel management assistance, advertising and inventory control.

About 84 percent of the company's $11.6 billion in annual revenue is generated by its wholesaling and retail support program.

Now if Super Valu can gets its *own* retail division up to speed, its long drought in the stock market might finally come to an end. While the company's revenue and earnings per share have crept up year after year (14 of the past 15 years), its stock price has been hanging around the $20 to $30 range since 1985.

Part of the problem has been the poor performance of the company's retail groceries division—which reported a slight loss in fiscal 1990, despite sales of $1.5 billion. Undaunted, the company continues to add new Cub Foods stores (up to 86 in 1991) and has reported growing success in the retail foods area.

Super Valu also owns a chain of 104 ShopKo department stores. The stores sell housewares, hardware, appliances, paint, toys, sporting goods, photo supplies, clothing, cosmetics, drugs, health aids and other general merchandise. ShopKo stores range in size from 30,000 square feet to 106,000 square feet and are located in medium-size cities throughout the Upper Midwest and Northwest.

ShopKo has been very profitable, accounting for about 15 percent of Super Valu's total revenues and about 30 percent of its earnings.

EARNINGS GROWTH

Super Valu has had solid, steady long-term growth. Over the past ten years, its earnings per share increased 171 percent (an average of 10.5 percent per year).

The company has about 19,000 employees and 9,000 shareholders.

STOCK GROWTH

The company had flat stock price appreciation from 1986 through 1990, following five years of strong growth. Over the ten-year period through 1990, the stock price increased 238 percent (13 percent per year).

Including reinvested dividends, a $10,000 investment in Super Valu stock at its closing stock price in 1980 would have grown to about $40,000 ten years later. Average annual compounded rate of return (including stock growth and reinvested dividends): about 15 percent.

DIVIDEND YIELD

Super Valu generally pays a good yield, averaging just over 2 percent over the past five years. During the most recent two-year rating period (fiscal 1990 and 1991) the stock paid an average annual current return (dividend yield) of 2.5 percent.

DIVIDEND GROWTH

Super Valu has raised its dividend for 18 consecutive years. The dividend climbed 70 percent (11 percent per year) from 1985 to 1990.

CONSISTENCY

The company has had increased earnings per share nine of the past ten years, and increased revenue and book value per share the past 15 consecutive years. Its price-earnings ratio of about 12 to 14 is slightly below average among U.S. foods companies.

SHAREHOLDER PERKS

Super Valu provides a couple of perks for its shareholders. Shareholders who attend the annual meeting receive a complimentary box of the company's private label groceries and general merchandise including candy, cookies, crackers, toothbrushes and soap dishes.

The company offers a dividend reinvestment plan, but a company spokesperson reported that the voluntary stock purchase plan has been discontinued.

SUMMARY

Fiscal year ended: Feb. 27*
(Revenue and net income in millions)

| | 1991** | 1990 | 1989 | 1988 | 1987 | 1986 | 1985 | 5-year growth, %†
(annual/total) |
|---|---|---|---|---|---|---|---|---|
| Revenue | 11,612 | 11,136 | 10,296 | 9,372 | 9,066 | 7,905 | 6,547 | 8/46 |
| Net income | 155 | 148 | 137 | 113 | 87 | 91 | 83 | 11/70 |
| Earnings/share | 2.08 | 1.97 | 1.84 | 1.51 | 1.16 | 1.23 | 1.13 | 11/67 |
| Dividend/share | .63 | .59 | .49 | .44 | .41 | .37 | .33 | 11/70 |
| Dividend yield, % | 2.4 | 2.5 | 2.3 | 1.7 | 1.8 | 2.3 | 2.6 | —/— |
| Stock price | 27.88 | 24.00 | 26.25 | 23.00 | 21.38 | 25.88 | 23.00 | 1/4 |
| P/E ratio | 14.0 | 13.3 | 12.5 | 14.1 | 22.3 | 18.7 | 14.1 | —/— |
| Book value/share | 12.85 | 11.59 | 10.20 | 8.84 | 7.76 | 7.20 | 6.33 | 12/78 |

  * Except stock price Dec. 31, 1985–90
 ** Stock price as of 5-1-91
  † 1985–90
Source: Company sources

WALLACE COMPUTER SERVICES, INC.

4600 W. Roosevelt Road
Hillside, IL 60162
708-626-2000
Chairman and CEO: Ted Dimitriou
President: John W. Turner

EARNINGS GROWTH	★
STOCK GROWTH	★
DIVIDEND YIELD	★ ★
DIVIDEND GROWTH	★ ★ ★
CONSISTENCY	★ ★ ★ ★
SHAREHOLDER PERKS	★
NYSE—WCS	**12 points**

Wallace Computer Services. The name conjures up images of chip boards, baud rates, megabytes and mainframes. Could it be another Microsoft? Big Blue II? The next NeXT?

The reality is, Wallace has carved its niche far from the cutting edge of chip technology. For years, the firm has hung out on the fringe of the computer revolution, primarily selling business forms, labels and printing services.

Although Wallace does market some computer goods—a computerized labeling systems (Printware), business software, computer hardware, cables and various accessories—the vast share of its $449 million a year in revenue comes from the sale of business forms. Nearly 90 percent of its revenue is derived from the sale of printed material.

The forms business has been good for Wallace, which has compiled an unblemished string of 29 years of record revenues and earnings per share.

The brokerage firm Legg Mason calls Wallace "just the sort of high-quality company we want to own." The stock is also popular with analyst Judith G. Scott of the brokerage firm Robert W. Baird, who writes, "Wallace is in an enviable financial position with no short-term debt, long-term debt equal to less than 7 percent of debt and equity, and cash of $43 million.''

In addition to forms, labels and computerware, Wallace's product list includes industrial and consumer catalogs, price lists, one-time carbon paper, carbon inks, computer and business machine ribbons, tax and utility billing forms, and a standard line of office products and forms. In all, Wallace markets more than 14,000 products.

The Chicago operation also offers a broad range of commercial printing services through its Wallace Press division. Wallace Press is the oldest division of the company, dating back to 1908, when Walter Wallace founded the company. The name was changed to Wallace Computer Services in 1981.

EARNINGS GROWTH

Wallace has enjoyed strong, steady long-term growth. Over the past ten years, its earnings per share increased 205 percent (an average of 11.5 percent per year).

The company has about 3,000 employees and 4,500 shareholders.

STOCK GROWTH ★

The company has had very flat stock price appreciation the past five years. Over the most recent ten-year period (through 1990), the stock rose 236 percent (13 percent per year).

Including reinvested dividends, a $10,000 investment in Wallace stock at its closing stock price in 1980 would have grown to about $39,000 ten years later. Average annual compounded rate of return (including stock growth and reinvested dividends): about 14.5 percent.

DIVIDEND YIELD

Wallace generally pays a fairly modest yield, averaging about 1.7 percent over the past five years. During the most recent two-year rating period (fiscal 1990 and 1991) the stock paid an average annual current return (dividend yield) of 1.9 percent.

DIVIDEND GROWTH

Wallace has raised its dividend for 18 consecutive years. The dividend increased 100 percent (15 percent per year) from 1985 to 1990.

CONSISTENCY

The company has had 29 consecutive years of record revenue and earnings per share. Its price-earnings ratio of about 14 is very reasonable for a growing company.

SHAREHOLDER PERKS

Wallace has no dividend reinvestment and stock purchase program but plans to begin one by 1992.

SUMMARY

Fiscal year ended: July 31*
(Revenue and net income in millions)

	1991**	1990	1989	1988	1987	1986	1985	5-year growth, %† (annual/total)
Revenue		449	429	383	341	305	275	10/63
Net income		40	37	32	26	24	22	13/81
Earnings/share		1.86	1.76	1.53	1.27	1.20	1.10	11/69
Dividend/share		.46	.40	.33	.30	.25	.23	15/100
Dividend yield, %	1.9	1.8	1.8	1.6	1.4	1.2	1.4	—/—
Stock price	26.63	20.13	31.13	21.31	19.31	21.75	19.63	1/3
P/E ratio	14.0	14.1	13.0	13.3	17.2	17.3	15.0	—/—
Book value/share		13.04	11.53	10.09	8.83	7.76	6.74	14/93

* Except stock price Dec. 31, 1985–90
** Stock price as of 5–1–91
† 1985–90
Source: Company sources

91

NATIONAL MEDICAL ENTERPRISES, INC.

2700 Colorado Avenue
Santa Monica, CA 90404
213-315-8000
Chairman and CEO: Richard K. Eamer

EARNINGS GROWTH	★ ★
STOCK GROWTH	★
DIVIDEND YIELD	★ ★ ★
DIVIDEND GROWTH	★
CONSISTENCY	★ ★ ★
SHAREHOLDER PERKS	★ ★
NYSE—NME	**12 points**

As civilization races forward, lives change, pressures mount, spirits fray and sometimes crack. National Medical Enterprises (NME) has spread a network of psychic safety nets across America to catch and mend the fallen souls.

As NME has learned, what's good for the soul is also good for the balance sheet. With its growing chain of medical, psychiatric and substance abuse rehabilitation centers, the company has been raising profits as it lifts spirits.

The Santa Monica, California health care concern operates psychiatric centers and drug and alcohol recovery centers in 26 states and general hospitals in nine states. In all, NME operates 67 psychiatric centers (under its subsidiary Psychiatric Institutes of America), 13 substance abuse recovery centers (under its Recovery Centers of America subsidiary), 27 acute care rehabilitation centers (under its Rehab Hospital Services Corp.) and 36 general hospitals (half of which are in California). It also manages 27 substance abuse centers and 26 psychiatric units within other hospitals.

The company recently spun off its less profitable nursing home chain and pharmacy operation.

NME's general hospital segment accounts for 53 percent of the company's $3.9 billion in annual revenue, and its specialty centers account for 46 percent. But while the general hospitals generate more revenue, the specialty centers have been far more profitable, providing about 60 percent of the company's operating earnings.

Because of the higher profit margins and increasing demand, NME has been placing greater emphasis on expanding its substance abuse and psychiatric treatment operations. The company has more than doubled its facilities and total capacity over the past five years—and yet still maintains an excellent occupancy rate of about 80 percent in its specialty centers.

Its general hospitals, on the other hand, have been running at about 50 percent capacity. In fact, the company has been scaling back its general hospitals, dropping from 48 hospitals with 7,856 beds in 1985 to 36 facilities with 6,800 beds in 1990.

NME's fastest-growing segment has been its physical rehabilitation centers, climbing from nine facilities with 989 beds in 1985 to 27 centers with 2,296 beds in 1990.

EARNINGS GROWTH

NME has had solid, steady long-term growth. Over the past ten years, its earnings per share increased 266 percent (14 percent per year).

The company has about 45,000 employees and 11,000 shareholders.

STOCK GROWTH ★

The company has had bumpy stock price performance the past ten years, increasing 153 percent (10 percent per year) during the period.

Including reinvested dividends, a $10,000 investment in NME stock at its closing stock price in 1980 would have grown to about $31,000 ten years later. Average annual compounded rate of return (including stock growth and reinvested dividends): about 12 percent.

DIVIDEND YIELD

NME generally pays a good yield, averaging about 2.5 percent over the past five years. During the most recent two-year rating period (1989 and 1990), the stock paid an average annual current return (dividend yield) of 2.5 percent.

DIVIDEND GROWTH

NME has raised its dividend for more than 16 consecutive years. The dividend increased 44 percent (7 percent per year) from 1985 to 1990.

CONSISTENCY

The company has had increased earnings and book value per share nine of the past ten years. Its price-earnings ratio of around 11 to 14 is lower than average for a growing company.

SHAREHOLDER PERKS

The company offers a good dividend reinvestment and voluntary stock purchase plan. There are no fees or commissions, and shareholders of record may buy $10 to $1,000 per month in additional shares.

SUMMARY

Fiscal year ended: May 31*
(Revenue and net income in millions)

	1991**	1990	1989	1988	1987	1986	1985	5-year growth, %† (annual/total)
Revenue		3,935	3,676	3,202	2,881	2,577	2,191	12/79
Net income		242	192	170	140	116	144	11/68
Earnings/share		2.67	2.32	2.09	1.68	1.45	1.85	7/44
Dividend/share		.72	.68	.63	.59	.55	.50	7/44
Dividend yield, %		2.1	2.8	2.8	2.4	2.3	2.1	—/—
Stock price	48.25	38.00	39.00	22.00	18.88	22.50	22.38	10/58
P/E ratio	14	11	9	10	14	16	12	—/—
Book value/share		15.93	14.80	13.11	12.47	12.63	12.36	5/28

 * Except stock price Dec. 31, 1985–90
** Stock price as of 5–1–91
 † 1985–90
Source: Company sources

92

PALL CORPORATION

2200 Northern Boulevard
East Hills, NY 11548
516-484-5400
Founder Chairman: Dr. David B. Pall
Chairman: Abraham Krasnoff
President & CEO: Maurice G. Hardy

EARNINGS GROWTH	★
STOCK GROWTH	(no points)
DIVIDEND YIELD	★ ★
DIVIDEND GROWTH	★ ★ ★
CONSISTENCY	★ ★ ★ ★
SHAREHOLDER PERKS	★ ★
NYSE—PLL	**12 points**

They are everywhere: germs, dust, particles, microscopic debris of one sort or another—in the air we breathe, the water we drink, the food we eat.

Dr. David B. Pall, the 76-year-old founder of Pall Corporation, has spent most of his life fighting these microscopic intruders. Pall, the company he founded in the mid-1940s, has become one of the world's leading manufacturers of filtering systems for a range of applications, including the purification of medical and pharmaceutical products, foods, beverages, fluids, chemicals, gas, oil, steel and aerospace and industrial equipment.

Outside the U.S., Pall has manufacturing operations in England, Japan, Canada, Puerto Rico and Germany, with sales in many other countries. Of its $564 million a year in total revenue (1990), 42 percent came from Europe, the Middle East and Africa; 11 percent from Asia; and 47 percent in the Western hemisphere (primarily the U.S., Canada and Mexico).

With its diverse customer base, Pall has enjoyed consistent growth for many years, including 19 consecutive years of record earnings per share. Earnings were up only 1 cent per share in 1989 but jumped 21 cents (14 percent) in 1990.

The company divides its business into three principal segments:

- Health care (38 percent of revenue). Pall makes prefilters, sterilizing filters and final filters to cleanse blood (for transfusions), tissue culture, vaccines, intravenous fluids, breathing gases and other health care-related products. Pall also supplies filters for the beverage industry that remove bacteria, yeast and other contaminants from wine, beer, water and other products.
- Aeropower (34 percent of revenue). The company makes hydraulic, fuel and lube filters for both commercial and military aircraft, as well as military tanks, helicopters and ships. It also makes filters for industrial customers who use or manufacture steel, paper, plastics, automobiles and other machinery.
- Fluid processing (28 percent of revenue). Pall sells filtration and sterilizing systems to advanced technology manufacturers to filter particles from water, chemicals and gases in the manufacture of microelectronic components. Its filters are also used to remove contaminants in the manufacture of film, synthetic fibres, magnetic computer tape, videotape, audiotape, hard discs, floppy discs and optical discs—as well as for a variety of other processes.

EARNINGS GROWTH

Pall has had steady long-term growth. Over the past ten years, its earnings per share increased 217 percent (12 percent per year).

The company has about 6,000 employees and 3,400 shareholders.

STOCK GROWTH   (no points)

The company has experienced solid stock price appreciation the past ten years, increasing 134 percent (9 percent per year) during the period.

Including reinvested dividends, a $10,000 investment in Pall stock at its closing price in 1980 would have grown to about $26,000 ten years later. Average annual compounded rate of return (including stock growth and reinvested dividends): about 10 percent.

DIVIDEND YIELD

Pall generally pays a moderate yield, averaging almost 1.5 percent over the past five years. During the most recent two-year rating period (fiscal 1990 and 1991) the stock paid an average annual current return (dividend yield) of 1.5 percent.

DIVIDEND GROWTH

Pall has raised its dividend for 16 consecutive years. The dividend increased 140 percent (19 percent per year) from 1985 to 1990.

CONSISTENCY

The company has had more than 17 consecutive years of record revenues, book value and earnings per share. Its price-earnings ratio of about 20 to 25 is higher than most growing U.S. companies.

SHAREHOLDER PERKS

Pall has an excellent dividend reinvestment and voluntary stock purchase plan for its shareholders. There are no commissions or service charges, and shareholders may contribute up to $60,000 per year to the stock purchase plan. The company also provides a free direct deposit service to shareholders who wish to have dividends automatically deposited in savings accounts at any financial institution that participates in the Automated Clearing House system.

SUMMARY

Fiscal year ended: July 31*
(Revenue and net income in millions)

	1991**	1990	1989	1988	1987	1986	1985	5-year growth, %† (annual/total)
Revenue		564	497	434	390	332	276	15/104
Net income		66	58	57	48	41	34	14/94
Earnings/share		1.14	1.00	1.00	0.85	0.75	0.63	13/81
Dividend/share		.36	.31	.26	.22	.18	.15	19/140
Dividend yield, %	1.4	1.6	1.6	1.4	1.1	1.0	1.3	—/—
Stock price	30.75	23.00	19.00	17.00	18.00	15.00	11.00	16/109
P/E ratio	25	20	20	18	23	23	19	—/—
Book value/share		7.61	6.46	5.77	4.87	4.02	3.17	19/140

* Except stock price Dec. 31, 1985–90
** Stock price as of 5–1–91
† 1985–90
Source: Company sources

93 *American Brands, Inc.*

AMERICAN BRANDS, INC.

1700 E. Putnam Avenue
P.O. Box 811
Old Greenwich, CT 06870
203-698-5000
Chairman and CEO: William J. Alley
President: Thomas C. Hays

EARNINGS GROWTH	(no points)
STOCK GROWTH	★ ★
DIVIDEND YIELD	★ ★ ★
DIVIDEND GROWTH	★
CONSISTENCY	★ ★ ★
SHAREHOLDER PERKS	★ ★
NYSE—AMB	**11 points**

The name is *American* Brands, but the biggest share of the cigarette maker's market is in Great Britain. Gallaher Ltd., American Brand's British subsidiary, dominates the country's tobacco trade. Its Silk Cut, Berkeley and Benson & Hedges brands account for 44 percent of all smokes sold in the United Kingdom.

American Brands sells 86 billion cigarettes a year worldwide. In the U.S., its Lucky Strike, Pall Mall, Tareyton, Carlton, Malibu and American brands account for about 7 percent of all domestic cigarette sales—fifth among U.S. tobacco companies. Its U.S. operations account for about one-fourth of all the company's cigarette sales.

Tobacco products (foreign and domestic) account for 59 percent of the company's $13.8 billion a year in total revenue. The balance of revenue comes from an array of subsidiaries the company has acquired with profits from its tobacco trade. Key segments include:

- Distilled spirits (6 percent of sales). The company acquired the distilled spirits operations of National Distillers and Chemical Corp. in 1987.

328

National owns Jim Beam whiskey, Old Grand-Dad bourbon, DeKuyper cordials, Gilbey's gin and vodka and Windsor Canadian Supreme whiskey. Jim Beam is the best-selling bourbon in the world and, along with its 20 related brands, the third largest liquor company in the U.S. It sells 17 million cases of liquor per year.

- Hardware and home improvement products (4 percent of sales). American Brands owns Master Lock, maker of padlocks, door locks, cable locks and built-in locker locks. Other products include Waterloo tool storage products, Aristokraft kitchen cabinets and bathroom vanities, and 20th Century plumbing.
- Office products (9 percent of sales). The company makes staplers, paper clips, folders, notebooks, pens, pencils, desk trays and other office products through ACCO World, Swingline and Wilson Jones subsidiaries.
- Financial services (7 percent of revenue). Franklin Life Insurance Company, a wholly owned subsidiary of American Brands, sells life insurance, annuities and accident and health insurance. The company has about $27.5 billion of insurance in force.
- Specialty businesses (16 percent of revenue). American Brands has several specialty divisions, including Titleist (golf balls, clubs and accessories), Foot-Joy (golf shoes and golf gloves), Dollond & Aitchison Group of England (the largest manufacturer of eye glasses and optical gear in Europe), TM Group (operates 55,000 vending machines in England) and Forbuoys (800 retail newspaper, tobacco, confectionery and stationery outlets in the U.K.). Other subsidiaries include Acushnet Rubber, Regal China, Golden Belt packaging and Prestige housewares.

EARNINGS GROWTH   (no points)

American Brands has had consistent but modest long-term growth. Over the past ten years, its earnings per share increased 115 percent (an average of 8.5 percent per year).

The company has about 43,000 employees and 70,000 shareholders.

STOCK GROWTH

American Brand's stock has reached new highs 17 consecutive years (through 1991)—one of the longest growth strings in corporate America. Over the past ten years, the stock had three 2-for-1 splits and increased 320 percent (15.5 percent per year).

Including reinvested dividends, a $10,000 investment in American Brands stock at its closing stock price in 1980 would have grown to about

$73,000 ten years later. Average annual compounded rate of return (including stock growth and reinvested dividends): about 22 percent.

DIVIDEND YIELD

The company generally pays an excellent yield, averaging about 6 percent over the past decade. During the most recent two-year rating period (fiscal 1990 and 1991) the stock paid an average annual current return (dividend yield) of 3.7 percent.

DIVIDEND GROWTH

American Brands has raised its dividend for 23 consecutive years, but not by much. The dividend was raised 43 percent (8 percent per year) from 1986 to 1991.

CONSISTENCY

The company has had fairly consistent growth in its earnings, revenue and book value per share over the past ten years, with eight consecutive years of increased earnings per share, and revenue growth four of the past five years. Its price-earnings ratio in the 9 to 12 range is about average for tobacco companies.

SHAREHOLDER PERKS

The company offers its shareholders of record an excellent dividend reinvestment and voluntary stock purchase plan. There are no fees or commissions, and shareholders of record may purchase $10 to $10,000 per quarter in additional shares through the voluntary stock purchase plan.

The company also hands out a small packet of product samples at its annual meeting.

CORPORATE RESPONSIBILITY

The most significant issue pertaining to American Brands as far as social investors are concerned is its sale of tobacco products. In addition to the fact that cigarette smoking has been determined to be a cause of cancer, respiratory illnesses and cardiovascular disease; that the World Health Organization (WHO) blames tobacco use for about 2.5 million deaths worldwide each year; that the surgeon general and WHO have concluded that smoking is the major cause of serious health problems in the U.S. and other industrialized countries; and that WHO and the U.S. National Institutes of Health consider smoking to be addictive, tobacco growing has environmental implications. Tobacco curing in third world countries is fueled predominantly by wood and is a major cause of deforestation. WHO estimates that fuel-wood curing consumes one tree per 300 cigarettes. The World Bank estimates the hypothetical cost of reforesting the areas depleted by tobacco growing to be $15 billion annually, and a report by Earthscan states that the tobacco industry could not survive if it had to pay for planting the trees that it uses.

American Brands' Swingline, Inc. facility was cited by the Consumer Policy Institute as one of the eight worst industrial polluters (in terms of toxic chemical air emissions) in New York City in 1988. (Source: Council on Economic Priorities)

SUMMARY

Fiscal year ended: Dec. 31
(Revenue and net income in millions)

	1991*	1990	1989	1988	1987	1986	1985	5-year growth, %† (annual/total)
Revenue		13,781	11,921	11,980	9,153	8,470	7,308	14/88
Net income		745	631	541	503	474	421	12/76
Earnings/share		3.76	3.26	2.72	2.21	2.09	1.84	15/104
Dividend/share		1.40	1.26	1.13	1.06	1.02	0.98	8/43
Dividend yield, %	3.7	4.1	3.6	4.6	4.4	4.8	6.2	—/—
Stock price	42.00	42.00	35.00	33.00	22.50	21.25	16.50	19/143
P/E ratio	14	9	11	9	11	10	9	—/—
Book value/share		18.15	15.35	13.30	13.30	11.50	11.00	11/67

* Stock price as of 5–1–91
† 1985–90
Source: Company sources

94

RITE AID CORP.
P.O. Box 3165
Harrisburg, PA 17105
717-761-2633
Chairman and CEO: Alex Grass
President: Martin L. Grass

EARNINGS GROWTH	★
STOCK GROWTH	★ ★
DIVIDEND YIELD	★ ★
DIVIDEND GROWTH	★ ★
CONSISTENCY	★ ★
SHAREHOLDER PERKS	★ ★
NYSE—RAD	**11 points**

Cut-rate prices and Rite Aid's insatiable appetite for acquisitions have kept the retailer's store count spiraling the past few years. More than 60 percent of Rite Aid's 2,400 pharmacies were added in the past four years, making the Harrisburg, Pennsylvania operation the largest chain of drugstores.

More than 700 of its newest stores have come through acquisition, including the 113-store SupeRx chain (from the Kroger Company) in 1987, the 356-store Gray Drug Fair chain (from Sherwin-Williams) in 1988, the 99-store Peoples Drug and the 18-unit Lane Drug chains, both in 1990.

Rite Aid has also opened 276 new stores during the same period, and closed 103. In an era of drug superstores, probably the most glaring statistic that emerges from Rite Aid's balance sheet is that a full 43 percent of its revenue comes directly from prescription drug sales.

The company sticks to a basic formula for nearly all of its stores. The stores encompass approximately 6,700 square feet of floor space—large enough for a fair offering of health and beauty aids, proprietary drugs, housewares, tobacco products, beverages and sundries—but still about a third smaller than many of its competitors. (By comparison, the average store size for Walgreens, another *100 Best* company, is about 10,000 square fcct.)

Much of Rite Aid's draw is its cut-rate prices. About 1,000 of its standard products are discount Rite Aid private label brands. Low-priced generic drugs account for about 30 percent of the more than 60 million prescriptions Rite Aid stores fill each year.

The company was founded in 1962, when Alex Grass opened a Thrif D Discount Center in Scranton, Pennsylvania. Grass continues to serve as chairman and CEO of Rite Aid, while son Martin has recently stepped up to company president.

The company's 2,400 stores are spread through 22 eastern, midwestern and southern states.

Drugstore operations account for about 95 percent of its $3.5 billion in annual revenues. The company also owns a chain of 78 ADAP auto parts stores, 63 Encore bookstores and 170 Concord Custom Cleaners. It also owns Sera-Tec Biologicals, which has 26 centers in 14 states that provide plasma for use in therapeutic and diagnostic products.

EARNINGS GROWTH ★

Rite Aid has had solid long-term growth. Over the past ten years, its earnings per share increased 205 percent (12 percent per year).

The company has about 30,000 employees and 9,000 shareholders.

STOCK GROWTH

The company has had very good stock price appreciation the past ten years, increasing 375 percent (17 percent per year) for the period.

Including reinvested dividends, a $10,000 investment in Rite Aid stock at its closing stock price in 1980 would have grown to about $57,000 ten years later. Average annual compounded rate of return (including stock growth and reinvested dividends): about 19 percent.

DIVIDEND YIELD

Rite Aid generally pays a moderate yield, averaging about 2.1 percent over the past five years. During the most recent two-year rating period (fiscal 1990 and 1991) the stock paid an average annual current return (dividend yield) of 2.3 percent.

DIVIDEND GROWTH

Rite Aid has raised its dividend for 18 consecutive years. The dividend increased 79 percent (12.5 percent per year) from 1985 to 1990.

CONSISTENCY

The company has had increased earnings per share seven of the past ten years, and increased revenue and book value per share for more than 15 consecutive years. Its price-earnings ratio of about 17 is in line with other growing retailers.

SHAREHOLDER PERKS

Rite Aid offers its shareholders a good dividend reinvestment and voluntary stock purchase plan. There are no fees or service charges, and shareholders may contribute up to $25,000 per year to the stock purchase plan.

SUMMARY

Fiscal year ended: Feb. 28*
(Revenue and net income in millions)

	1991**	1990	1989	1988	1987	1986	1985	5-year growth, %† (annual/total)
Revenue	3,447	3,173	2,868	2,486	1,757	1,564	1,360	17/120
Net income	107	102	95	145	78	63	70	11/70
Earnings/share	2.59	2.46	2.30	3.50	1.89	1.52	1.69	11/70
Dividend/share	.93	.84	.76	.68	.60	.52	.43	12.5/79
Dividend yield, %	2.3	2.3	2.1	1.9	1.9	2.0	1.9	—/—
Stock price	44.00	37.00	33.00	32.63	36.00	29.50	25.63	6/35
P/E ratio	17.0	15.8	15.5	16.0	16.8	15.9	13.7	—/—
Book value/share	18.65	17.80	15.35	13.80	10.96	9.66	8.58	14/93

  * Except stock price Dec. 31, 1985–90
** Stock price as of 5–1–91
 † 1986–91
Source: Company sources

95 Medtronic

MEDTRONIC, INC.

7000 Central Avenue, N.E.
Minneapolis, MN 55432
612-574-4000
Chairman and CEO: Winston R. Wallin
President and COO: William W. George

EARNINGS GROWTH	★ ★
STOCK GROWTH	★ ★
DIVIDEND YIELD	★
DIVIDEND GROWTH	★ ★ ★
CONSISTENCY	★ ★ ★
SHAREHOLDER PERKS	(no points)
NYSE—MDT	**11 points**

The faint of heart have a friend in Medtronic. For the past 30 years, the Minneapolis-based manufacturer has been responsible for keeping more hearts ticking than any other company in the world.

Medtronic supplies more than 45 percent of all heart pacemakers sold worldwide. Sales of its pacemaker products and services account for 69 percent of the company's $1 billion in annual revenue (fiscal 1991). The company has had record earnings nine of the past ten years.

The company makes pacemakers for a wide range of needs. Its smallest is the Micro-Minix, which weighs under an ounce and is about the size of a quarter. Its Legend pacemaker is programmed to collect and store data about the patient's natural heartbeats and those it stimulates itself, enabling the physician to evaluate the data and fine-tune the therapy. The Activitrax pacemaker senses the patient's activity and responds appropriately, speeding up the heartbeat when the patient is active, slowing it down when he or she is at rest.

Medtronic also manufactures a line of related products:

- Its CardioCare monitoring system is capable of monitoring the patient's pacemaker activity by telephone.

335

- It is one of the world's leading heart valve manufacturers, supplying about 20 percent of all heart valves sold worldwide. Valve sales account for about 7 percent of its revenue.
- Medtronic holds about a 15 percent share of the cardiopulmonary market. It makes oxygenators, tubing packs and other devices used by perfusionists during open heart surgery. It also makes accessories for use in open heart surgery, including heart wires, aortic punces, annuloplasty rings and other disposable cardiovascular products.
- It is the world leader in the production of neurological implants. Its products stimulate the spinal cord or deep brain through electrical pulses to nerve fibres, primarily for treatment of chronic pain.

Medtronic sells its products worldwide. Foreign sales account for about 40 percent of its total revenue. The company was founded in 1949 and incorporated in 1957.

EARNINGS GROWTH

Medtronic has had steady long-term growth. Over the past ten years, its earnings per share increased 241 percent (13 percent per year).

The company has about 6,000 employees and 6,000 shareholders.

STOCK GROWTH

The company has had exceptional stock growth the past five years after some rocky times in the early 1980s. Over the full ten-year rating period (through 1990), the stock increased 342 percent (16 percent per year).

Including reinvested dividends, a $10,000 investment in Medtronic stock at its closing stock price in 1980 would have grown to about $50,000 ten years later. Average annual compounded rate of return (including stock growth and reinvested dividends): about 17.5 percent.

DIVIDEND YIELD

Medtronic generally pays a fairly modest yield, averaging about 1 percent over the past five years. During the most recent two-year rating period (fiscal 1990 and 1991) the stock paid an average annual current return (dividend yield) of 0.9 percent.

DIVIDEND GROWTH　

Medtronic has raised its dividend for 13 consecutive years (through fiscal 1991). The dividend increased 105 percent (15 percent per year) from fiscal 1986 to 1991.

CONSISTENCY　

The company has had increased revenue, book value and earnings per share nine of the past ten years. Its recent price-earnings ratio of about 27 is quite high even for a growing medical products company.

SHAREHOLDER PERKS　(no points)

Medtronic offers no dividend reinvestment plan, although the company reports that it plans to begin a program in the near future.

SUMMARY

Fiscal year ended: Apr. 30
(Revenue and net income in millions)

	1991*	1990	1989	1988	1987	1986	1985	5-year growth, %† (annual/total)
Revenue	1,000	837	742	653	502	403	364	18/129
Net income	135	109	97	87	74	53	38	23/187
Earnings/share	4.60	4.03	3.65	3.16	2.63	1.83	1.24	27/225
Dividend/share	.82	.70	.60	.52	.44	.40	.38	15/105
Dividend yield, %	0.7	1.0	1.2	1.3	0.9	1.2	2.7	—/—
Stock price	111.75	63.75	47.38	38.13	44.63	32.25	13.88	28/247
P/E ratio	27	22	15	12	15	15	10	—/—
Book value/share	27.50	23.00	19.96	17.69	14.86	13.76	12.14	14/89

* 1991 estimated revenue, net income, earnings per share and book value
† 1985–90; except stock price and dividend growth (1986–91)
Source: Company sources

EMERSON

EMERSON ELECTRIC CO.

8000 W. Florissant
P.O. Box 4100
St. Louis, MO 63136-8506
314-553-2000
Chairman and CEO: Charles F. Knight
President: A. E. Suter

EARNINGS GROWTH	(no points)
STOCK GROWTH	★
DIVIDEND YIELD	★ ★ ★
DIVIDEND GROWTH	★
CONSISTENCY	★ ★ ★ ★
SHAREHOLDER PERKS	★ ★
NYSE—EMR	**11 points**

Shortly after Thomas A. Edison installed his first electrical generators, John Wesley Emerson opened up an electronics manufacturing shop in St. Louis, Missouri. Room fans, ceiling fans and electrical motors were its earliest products.

That was in 1890. A century later, Emerson Electric produces a long list of electrical equipment—including motors for industrial and heavy commercial applications, industrial automation equipment, gear drives, power distribution equipment, and temperature and environmental control systems.

The company, which had sales of $7.6 billion in 1990, has been one of America's steadiest corporate performers. It has had 33 consecutive years of increased earnings and 34 consecutive years of increased dividends.

Emerson has expanded its reach well beyond the U.S. About 30 percent of its revenue comes from foreign sales, including about $500 million in exports and nearly $2 billion generated by its overseas subsidiaries.

The company divides its business into three primary segments:

- Commercial and industrial (72 percent of revenue). By far the company's largest segment, commercial and industrial product sales account for more than $5 billion in annual revenue. The company manufactures motors, variable speed motor drives, regulators, measuring instruments, temperature and pressure controls, compressors, transmission products, aviation instrumentation, heating products and specialized valves.
- Consumer products (18 percent of revenue). Emerson produces portable and stationary power tools, hobby tools, hand tools, garbage disposers, hot water dispensers, dishwashers, ladders and shop vacuums.
- Government and defense products and systems (9.5 percent of revenue). The company manufactures airborne radar systems, electronic warfare systems, missile launching systems, simulator systems for training, satellite communication systems, shipborne defense systems, guidance and control systems, test equipment and other defense-related systems.

Among Emerson's more recognizable brand name products are Skil power saws and tools, Dremel handheld power tools and Louisville ladders.

EARNINGS GROWTH (no points)

Emerson has had steady, consistent long-term growth. Over the past ten years, its earnings per share increased 122 percent (an average of 8.5 percent per year).

The company has about 73,000 employees and 35,000 shareholders.

STOCK GROWTH

As with its earnings growth, Emerson has enjoyed steady, solid stock price appreciation the past ten years, increasing 215 percent (12 percent per year) during the period.

Including reinvested dividends, a $10,000 investment in Emerson stock at its closing price in 1980 would have grown to about $43,000 ten years later. Average annual compounded rate of return (including stock growth and reinvested dividends): about 16 percent.

DIVIDEND YIELD

Emerson generally pays a very good yield, averaging about 3.4 percent over the past five years. During the most recent two-year rating period (fiscal 1990 and 1991) the stock paid an average annual current return (dividend yield) of 3.2 percent.

DIVIDEND GROWTH

Emerson has raised its dividend for 34 consecutive years. The dividend edged up 45 percent (8 percent per year) from 1985 to 1990.

CONSISTENCY

The company has had 33 consecutive years of increased earnings per share. Its book value per share and revenues have gone up 14 of the past 15 years. Its price-earnings ratio of about 14 to 16 is in line with other steadily growing manufacturers.

SHAREHOLDER PERKS

Emerson offers its shareholders a good dividend reinvestment and voluntary stock purchase plan. There are minimal commissions, and shareholders of record may purchase $25 to $2,500 per quarter in additional shares through the voluntary stock purchase plan.

SUMMARY

Fiscal year ended: Sept. 30*
(Revenue and net income in millions)

	1991**	1990	1989	1988	1987	1986	1985	5-year growth, %† (annual/total)
Revenue		7,573	7,071	6,652	6,170	4,953	4,649	10/63
Net income		613	588	529	467	409	401	9/53
Earnings/share		2.75	2.63	2.31	2.00	1.87	1.81	9/52
Dividend/share		1.26	1.12	1.00	0.96	0.92	0.87	8/45
Dividend yield, %	3.0	3.3	3.4	3.2	2.8	3.4	3.7	—/—
Stock price	44.63	37.75	39.00	30.38	34.63	27.92	27.08	7/39
P/E ratio	16.0	13.9	12.4	13.6	16.9	14.6	13.1	—/—
Book value/share		13.39	13.79	12.51	11.68	10.90	10.03	6/33

 * Except stock price Dec. 31, 1985–90
** Stock price as of 5–1–91
 † 1985–90
Source: Company sources

97 *BECTON DICKINSON*

BECTON DICKINSON AND CO.

One Becton Drive
Franklin Lakes, NJ 07417-1880
201-848-6800
Chairman: Wesley J. Howe
President and CEO: Raymond V. Gilmartin

EARNINGS GROWTH	★
STOCK GROWTH	★
DIVIDEND YIELD	★ ★
DIVIDEND GROWTH	★ ★
CONSISTENCY	★ ★ ★
SHAREHOLDER PERKS	★ ★
NYSE—BDX	**11 points**

In the much-maligned "throw-away society," Becton Dickinson has proven that disposability can have its good points. The company leads the world in the production of disposable syringes, hypodermic needles and other single-use medical devices designed to reduce the spread of infection.

The Franklin Lakes, New Jersey manufacturer has operations around the world. Foreign demand for the company's disposable products has been growing steadily and already accounts for 42 percent of its $2 billion a year in total revenue.

The growing fear of AIDS and other infections has spurred rapid growth of the company's disposable product sales. Becton Dickinson has posted seven consecutive years of record earnings per share.

In addition to syringes and needles, Becton Dickinson manufactures a line of cardiovascular products, including intravenous catheters, operating room products, surgical gloves and presurgery patient prep kits. The company also manufactures suction products, elastic support products, surgical blades, thermometers and examination gloves. Becton Dickinson's medical products segment accounts for 57 percent of its annual revenue.

The company's other major division is diagnostic products (43 percent of revenue). The company makes blood collection products, laboratory ware and supplies, manual and instrumented microbiology products, hematology instruments and other diagnostic systems. It makes immunodiagnostic test kits and instrumentation. Its diagnostic disposables include petri dishes, pipettes and tuges, and plastic labware used in cultures.

Becton Dickinson's Fluorescence Activated Cell Sorter (FACS) is used in research laboratories worldwide to study and measure individual cells and to uncover basic information about cell populations.

Becton Dickinson was founded in 1897 and incorporated in 1906.

EARNINGS GROWTH

Becton Dickinson has had solid long-term growth. Over the past ten years, its earnings per share increased 197 percent (an average of 11.5 percent per year).

The company has about 43,000 employees and 70,000 shareholders.

STOCK GROWTH

The company has enjoyed strong stock growth the past ten years, increasing 187 percent (11 percent per year) during the period.

Including reinvested dividends, a $10,000 investment in Becton Dickinson stock at its closing price in 1980 would have grown to about $167,000 ten years later. Average annual compounded rate of return (including stock growth and reinvested dividends): about 13 percent.

DIVIDEND YIELD

Becton Dickinson pays a modest yield, averaging about 1.6 percent over the past five years. During the most recent two-year rating period (fiscal 1990 and 1991) the stock paid an average annual current return (dividend yield) of about 1.7 percent.

DIVIDEND GROWTH

The company has raised its dividend for 14 of the past 15 years. The dividend increased 80 percent (13 percent per year) from 1985 to 1990.

CONSISTENCY

The company has had seven consecutive years of increased earnings per share, plus revenue increases 14 of the past 15 years. Its price-earnings ratio of about 14 is fairly low compared to many other growing medical products producers.

SHAREHOLDER PERKS

Becton offers its shareholders an excellent dividend reinvestment and voluntary stock purchase plan. There are no fees or commissions, and shareholders of record may purchase $25 to $3,000 per month in additional shares through the voluntary stock purchase plan.

SUMMARY

Fiscal year ended: Sept. 30*
(Revenue and net income in millions)

	1991**	1990	1989	1988	1987	1986	1985	5-year growth, %† (annual/total)
Revenue		2,013	1,811	1,709	1,462	1,203	1,044	14/93
Net income		182	158	148	126	111	88	16/107
Earnings/share		4.67	4.00	3.69	3.04	2.62	2.10	18/123
Dividend/share		1.08	1.00	0.86	0.74	0.66	0.60	13/80
Dividend yield, %	1.5	1.7	1.8	1.6	1.3	1.6	2.5	—/—
Stock price	76.50	74.50	61.88	52.00	51.00	50.00	31.00	18/124
P/E ratio	16	13	14	15	19	16	11	—/—
Book value/share		32.77	27.99	24.33	21.62	19.62	16.82	14/95

 * Except stock price Dec. 31, 1985–90
** Stock price as of 5–1–91
 † 1985–90
Source: Company sources

GTE CORP.

One Stamford Forum
Stamford, CT 06904
203-965-2000
Chairman and CEO: James L. Johnson
President: Charles R. Lee

EARNINGS GROWTH	**(no points)**
STOCK GROWTH	★
DIVIDEND YIELD	★ ★ ★ ★
DIVIDEND GROWTH	★
CONSISTENCY	★ ★
SHAREHOLDER PERKS	★ ★
NYSE—GTE	**10 points**

GTE has carved its niche out of the Bell system's leftovers, slipping into the smaller towns, cities and rural areas in 31 states. In all, GTE serves about 18 million telephone customers, making it the nation's largest non-Bell phone company, and the fourth largest phone service of all.

GTE, which acquired Contel Corp. in early 1991, is also the nation's second largest player in the fast-growing cellular phone service market. Its GTE Mobile Communications division provides cellular mobile telephone service in markets throughout the U.S., sells cellular products and provides air-to-ground telephone service for airline passengers.

GTE, with revenues of about $21 billion a year (including the Contel operations), has been a slow, steady stock market performer for many years. While the Stamford, Connecticut, company's earnings per share and stock price have inched up slowly through the years, GTE has consistently paid an excellent annual dividend yield of 5 to 7 percent.

GTE's telephone operation accounts for about 72 percent of its total revenue (prior to the Contel merger).

Its mobile phone service is part of its telecommunications products and services division, which accounts for 16 percent of total revenue. In addition to the cellular service, the company manufactures command control communications, intelligence systems and electronic defense systems for the U.S. military.

It also sells telecommunications systems and services for businesses, news organizations and government agencies worldwide.

GTE's third largest segment, electrical products, accounts for 13 percent of revenue. The company makes more than 6,000 types of Sylvania lamps, plus automotive lighting products, lamp fixtures and lighting components.

It also produces metal, plastic, ceramic and other precision-engineered materials, and components for the aerospace, automotive, computer, communications and electrical industries.

In all, GTE has operations in 46 states and 40 foreign countries.

EARNINGS GROWTH (no points)

GTE has had slow, sustained long-term growth. Over the past ten years, its earnings per share increased 105 percent (an average of 7.5 percent per year).

The company has about 175,000 employees and 475,000 shareholders.

STOCK GROWTH ★

The company has experienced solid, steady stock growth the past ten years, increasing 225 percent (12.5 percent per year) during the period.

Including reinvested dividends, a $10,000 investment in GTE stock at its closing stock price in 1980 would have grown to about $62,000 ten years later. Average annual compounded rate of return (including stock growth and reinvested dividends): about 20 percent.

DIVIDEND YIELD ★ ★ ★ ★

GTE pays an excellent yield (the best of the *100 Best* stocks), averaging about 7 percent over the past ten years. During the most recent two-year rating period (fiscal 1990 and 1991) the stock paid an average annual current return (dividend yield) of 5.1 percent.

DIVIDEND GROWTH ★

GTE has raised its dividend for more than 36 of the past 37 years—although the increases are generally quite small. The dividend increased 46 percent (8 percent per year) from 1985 to 1990.

CONSISTENCY

The company has not been particularly consistent in its growth over the past few years, with earnings per share increases only six of the past ten years and revenue increases nine of the past ten years. Its recent price-earnings ratio of about 16 is much higher than normal for GTE.

SHAREHOLDER PERKS

GTE offers its shareholders an excellent dividend reinvestment and stock purchase plan. Shareholders may contribute $25 to $5,000 per quarter for the purchase of additional stock.

CORPORATE RESPONSIBILITY

GTE ranks 17th on the Department of Defense's listing of the 100 companies receiving the largest dollar volume of prime defense contract awards in fiscal year 1990. The company received contracts totaling almost $1.3 billion for weapons systems, including the MX and Minuteman missiles and the Strategic Defense Initiative (SDI). GTE also manufactures nuclear weapons and had prime contracts totaling $37 million in fiscal year 1989. Women and minorities are not well represented in top management or on GTE's board, and the company maintains licensing agreements with a former subsidiary in South Africa. (Source: Council on Economic Priorities)

SUMMARY

Fiscal year ended: Dec. 31
(Revenue and net income in millions)

	1991*	1990	1989	1988	1987	1986	1985	5-year growth, %† (annual/total)
Revenue		21,393	17,424	16,460	15,421	15,112	15,732	6/36
Net income		1,715	1,417	1,225	1,134	1,092	487	28/252
Earnings/share		1.93	2.08	1.77	1.62	1.69	1.72	2/12
Dividend/share		1.52	1.40	1.30	1.24	1.11	1.04	8/46
Dividend yield, %	5.0	5.1	5.1	6.6	6.3	6.1	7.5	—/—
Stock price	31.63	29.25	35.00	21.75	17.69	23.00	14.60	15/103
P/E ratio	16	13	13	11	12	11	8	—/—
Book value/share		12.00	12.00	12.45	11.90	11.60	10.75	2/12

* Stock price as of 5–1–91
† 1985–90
Source: Company sources

99

MARTIN MARIETTA

MARTIN MARIETTA CORP.
6801 Rockledge Drive
Bethesda, MD 20817
301-897-6000
Chairman and CEO: Norman R. Augustine
President: A. Thomas Young

EARNINGS GROWTH	★
STOCK GROWTH	(no points)
DIVIDEND YIELD	★ ★ ★
DIVIDEND GROWTH	★
CONSISTENCY	★ ★ ★
SHAREHOLDER PERKS	★ ★
NYSE—ML	**10 points**

In early 1990, with the Iron Curtain crumbling, U.S.–Soviet relations thawing and the prospects for lasting world peace becoming ever-more promising, Wall Street turned a cold shoulder to defense contractors such as Martin Marietta.

And then came Saddam Hussein.

Suddenly America's war machines were chic, sending defense company stocks up like a Patriot missile.

When the war ended, however, Wall Street's fascination with weapons manufacturers ended with it. But the battle in the Persian Gulf sent a grim message to the world powers that they had better either (a) stop selling implements of mass destruction to third world countries or (b) continue developing the kind of advanced weaponry the Allies used to defeat Iraq. Chances are the powers that be will probably choose the latter.

For one thing, the U.S. exports more than $50 billion a year in armaments. That's not a market it's going to give up without a battle. For another, U.S. weaponry made such an extraordinary showing in the Gulf that, by war's end, other governments were lining up to put in their orders for advanced weapons like the Patriot missile.

While the weapons business is certainly not on the verge of becoming a boom industry, the better companies should continue to do a fair business. Martin Marietta, which supplies 40 percent of the Patriot air defense system, should be among the defense industry leaders. In addition to the Patriot missile, the company is known most for its Pershing II, Peacekeeper and Titan missiles.

Of the company's $6.1 billion in annual revenue, 47 percent comes from its astronautics segment, 36 percent from its electronics and missiles division, 9 percent from information systems and 7 percent from materials.

The Titan missiles are the largest and oldest of the country's surviving strategic missiles. Many of the older Titan missiles are now being converted into space launch vehicles to propel commercial and military payloads and satellites into space. The company also manufactures the new Titan IV missiles for that purpose.

The Titan IVs are perhaps the company's most profitable area. They are expected to generate revenue of $1 billion a year through most of the 1990s, and perhaps into the 21st century.

The company has a contract with NASA for launch of the Mars Observer space vehicle in 1992.

Martin Marietta Space Systems produces planetary spacecraft, instruments and experiments and other space systems for NASA, as well as military space systems.

The Pershing and Pershing II missiles are strictly military. The strength of the Pershing II, known as a "surface-to-surface ballistic missile," is its mid-range speed and accuracy. Within six minutes of launch, a European-based Pershing could strike targeted cities inside the Soviet Union.

The Peacekeeper intercontinental ballistic missiles are larger and more powerful than the Pershing IIs and have a much greater range (7,000 miles), but they are being deployed far from their presumed targets in silos at F.E. Warren Air Force Base in Wyoming. The missiles are 70 feet long and weigh 195,000 pounds. They carry MIRV warheads (multiple independently targeted reentry vehicle), which include a cluster of bombs that split up when the missile nears its destination and head to separate targets. One MIRV warhead is capable of leveling an entire city. A single explosion can create a giant fireball with temperatures of about 100 million degrees Kelvin—roughly five times hotter than the center of the sun—and winds of 500 to 550 miles an hour.

Martin Marietta is also at work on other sophisticated military projects. Since 1981, the company has produced more than 27,000 Copperheads, a cannon-launched, guided projectile, and is currently involved in the manufacture of the Hellfire Laser Seeker, a component of the Hellfire air-to-ground missiles (being built by Rockwell), which seek out their targets by laser. The U.S. Army has ordered more than 17,000 Hellfire missiles, of which about 13,000 have been delivered.

Among the other ventures Martin Marietta is involved in are information and communication systems, data systems, energy systems and materials (the company is the second largest producer of crushed stone in the U.S.; it also supplies refractory materials for steel making).

EARNINGS GROWTH   ★

Martin Marietta has had consistent long-term growth. Over the past ten years, its earnings per share increased 180 percent (an average of 11 percent per year).

The company has about 62,000 employees and 37,000 shareholders.

STOCK GROWTH   (no points)

The company has had flat stock price appreciation the past ten years, increasing 105 percent (7.5 percent per year) for the period.

Including reinvested dividends, a $10,000 investment in Martin Marietta stock at its closing stock price in 1980 would have grown to about $30,000 ten years later. Average annual compounded rate of return (including stock growth and reinvested dividends): about 11.5 percent.

DIVIDEND YIELD

Martin Marietta generally pays a good dividend yield, averaging almost 3 percent over the past five years. During the most recent two-year rating period (fiscal 1990 and 1991) the stock paid an average annual current return (dividend yield) of 3.2 percent.

DIVIDEND GROWTH

Martin Marietta has raised its dividend for more than 18 consecutive years. The dividend rose 43 percent (8 percent per year) from 1985 to 1990.

CONSISTENCY

The company has increased earnings per share nine of the past ten years, increased book value eight of the past ten years and increased revenue for more than 15 consecutive years. Its price-earnings ratio of about 8 is normal for defense contractors.

SHAREHOLDER PERKS

The company offers an excellent dividend reinvestment and voluntary stock purchase plan. There are no fees or commissions, and shareholders of record may buy $50 to $100,000 per year in additional shares through the voluntary stock purchase plan.

SUMMARY

Fiscal year ended: Dec. 31
(Revenue and net income in millions)

	1991*	1990	1989	1988	1987	1986	1985	5-year growth, %† (annual/total)
Revenue		6,125	5,796	5,728	5,165	4,752	4,410	7/39
Net income		328	307	359	234	185	175	14/87
Earnings/share		6.52	5.82	5.25	4.30	3.36	3.05	16/113
Dividend/share		1.39	1.23	1.10	1.05	1.00	0.97	8/43
Dividend yield	2.8	3.5	2.7	2.6	2.3	2.4	2.8	—/—
Stock price	54.50	44.00	44.38	40.50	42.00	38.63	35.50	5/23
P/E ratio	8	7	8	10	11	12	12	—/—
Book value/share		31.53	26.67	22.73	17.16	14.98	12.52	20/151

* Stock price as of 5–1–91
† 1985–90
Source: Company sources

MCGRAW-HILL, INC.
1221 Avenue of the Americas
New York, NY 10020
212-512-2000
Chairman, President and CEO: Joseph L. Dionne

EARNINGS GROWTH	(no points)
STOCK GROWTH	(no points)
DIVIDEND YIELD	★ ★ ★
DIVIDEND GROWTH	★
CONSISTENCY	★ ★ ★
SHAREHOLDER PERKS	★ ★
NYSE—MHP	**9 points**

For many years, McGraw-Hill has had a reputation as one of the nation's leading book publishers. But books represent just a fraction of the company's total publishing empire. With more than 50 subsidiaries in 26 countries, McGraw-Hill has crossed over into an expanding range of magazines, technical journals, newsletters, computer software, database information systems and TV broadcasting.

Its best-known publication is *Business Week,* which has ranked first in ad pages among all U.S. magazines for 16 consecutive years. In addition to its U.S. edition, the company puts out an international edition in Europe and has recently launched a *Business Week/Hungary,* a *Business Week/ USSR* and a *Business Week/China.*

McGraw-Hill divides its business into four primary segments:

- Information and publication services (39 percent of the company's $1.9 billion in annual revenue). In addition to *Business Week,* the company publishes *Aviation Week Space Technology* and several other aviation-related publications. For the computer market, it publishes *BYTE* magazine, *LAN Tim* and *Unix World.* It also publishes journals for architects, engineers, contractors and building product manufacturers.

- Educational and professional publishing (28 percent of revenue). McGraw-Hill publishes a range of books for colleges and universities, as well as specialty publications for the engineering, science, medicine, health care, computer technology and legal professions.
- Financial services (28 percent of revenue). The company's Standard & Poor's division provides a debt rating service on more than 15,000 corporations, state and municipal governments and international entities. It also publishes a variety of information sources such as *CreditWeek* and *Platt's Global Alert,* and provides software and information services for financial institutions, government agencies and businesses.
- Broadcasting (5 percent of revenue). McGraw-Hill owns television stations in Indianapolis (WRTV), Denver (KMGH), San Diego (KGTV) and Bakersfield, California (KERO).

While the New York-based publisher traces its history back to 1888, the name McGraw-Hill was established in 1909 when James H. McGraw and John A. Hill merged their fledgling technical publications operations. As the story goes, when the two decided to merge, they flipped a coin to see whose name would go first on the company door. Eighty-two years later, that same name arches across the entranceway of the company's 50-story glass and granite office tower in New York's Rockefeller Center.

EARNINGS GROWTH   (no points)

McGraw-Hill has had solid, steady long-term growth. Over the past ten years, its earnings per share increased 103 percent (an average of 7.5 percent per year).

The company has about 15,000 employees and 7,000 shareholders.

STOCK GROWTH   (no points)

The company has had flat stock price appreciation through most of the past ten years, increasing 130 percent (9 percent per year) for the period.

Including reinvested dividends, a $10,000 investment in McGraw-Hill stock at its closing stock price in 1980 would have grown to about $31,000 ten years later. Average annual compounded rate of return (including stock growth and reinvested dividends): about 12 percent.

DIVIDEND YIELD

McGraw-Hill generally pays an excellent dividend yield, averaging almost 3.5 percent over the past five years. During the most recent two-year rating period (fiscal 1990 and 1991) the stock paid an average annual current return (dividend yield) of 3.9 percent.

DIVIDEND GROWTH

McGraw-Hill has raised its dividend each year since 1974. The dividend rose 54 percent (9 percent per year) from 1985 to 1990.

CONSISTENCY ★ ★ ★

After more than 15 years of increased earnings, the company had its first earnings dip in 1989. The company has had revenue and book value per share gains nine of the past ten years. Its price-earnings ratio of around 15 to 18 is well in line with other publishing companies.

SHAREHOLDER PERKS

The company offers a dividend reinvestment and voluntary stock purchase plan. There are no fees or commissions, and shareholders of record may buy $10 to $1,000 per quarter in additional shares through the voluntary stock purchase plan.

SUMMARY

Fiscal year ended: Dec. 31
(Revenue and net income in millions)

	1991*	1990	1989	1988	1987	1986	1985	5-year growth, %† (annual/total)
Revenue		1,939	1,789	1,673	1,600	1,427	1,360	7/43
Net income		172	48	186	165	154	147	4/17
Earnings/share		3.53	3.98	3.83	3.27	3.04	2.92	5/20
Dividend/share		2.16	2.00	1.84	1.68	1.52	1.40	9/54
Dividend yield	3.6	4.1	3.5	3.0	2.6	2.7	3.1	—/—
Stock price	60.50	53.00	57.00	62.00	49.75	52.00	49.00	2/8
P/E ratio	18.0	14.8	20.4	17.4	21.1	18.5	15.7	—/—
Book value/share		19.35	18.08	19.00	17.11	17.05	15.40	5/25

* Stock price as of 5–1–91
† 1985–90
Source: Company sources

THE 100 BEST BY STATE

Alabama   **Ranking**

Bruno's, Inc. (Birmingham)   56
Torchmark Corp. (Birmingham)   9

Arkansas

Dillard Department Stores, Inc. (Little Rock)   53
Tyson Foods, Inc. (Springdale)   54
Wal-Mart Stores, Inc. (Bentonville)   20

California

National Medical Enterprises, Inc. (Santa Monica)   91
Syntex Corp. (Palo Alto)   49
The Walt Disney Company (Burbank)   66

Connecticut

American Brands, Inc. (Old Greenwich)   93
Crompton & Knowles Corp. (Stamford)   42
GTE Corp. (Stamford)   98
General Electric Company (Fairfield)   73
Hubbell Incorporated (Orange)   36
Loctite Corp. (Hartford)   69
Pitney Bowes Inc. (Stamford)   61
UST, Inc. (Greenwich)   2

Georgia

The Coca-Cola Company (Atlanta)   55
Genuine Parts Company (Atlanta)   81
John H. Harland Company (Atlanta)   52
National Service Industries (Atlanta)   70
Shaw Industries, Inc. (Dalton)   38

Idaho	Ranking
Albertson's, Inc. (Boise)	22

Illinois	
Abbott Laboratories (Abbott Park)	19
Alberto-Culver Company (Melrose Park)	24
Dean Foods Company (Franklin Park)	31
R.R. Donnelley & Sons Company (Chicago)	78
McDonald's Corporation (Oak Brook)	71
Newell Co. (Freeport)	39
The Quaker Oats Company (Chicago)	47
Safety Kleen Corp. (Elgin)	34
Sara Lee Corporation (Chicago)	8
Walgreen Company (Deerfield)	43
Wallace Computer Services, Inc. (Hillside)	90
Waste Management, Inc. (Oak Brook)	13
Wm. Wrigley Jr. Company (Chicago)	4

Indiana	
Eli Lilly and Company (Indianapolis)	60

Iowa	
Bandag, Inc. (Muscatine)	48

Maryland	
Giant Food Inc. (Landover)	7
Martin Marietta Corp. (Bethesda)	99

Massachusetts	
The Gillette Company (Boston)	65
Stanhome, Inc. (Westfield)	15

Michigan	Ranking
Kellogg Company (Battle Creek)	29
Kelly Services, Inc. (Troy)	67
Stryker Corp. (Kalamazoo)	84

Minnesota

Bemis Company, Inc. (Minneapolis)	26
Deluxe Corp. (St. Paul)	50
General Mills, Inc. (Minneapolis)	58
International Dairy Queen, Inc. (Minneapolis)	83
Jostens Inc. (Minneapolis)	59
Medtronic, Inc. (Minneapolis)	95
SuperValu Stores, Inc. (Minneapolis)	89
Valspar Corp. (Minneapolis)	23

Missouri

Anheuser-Busch Companies Inc. (St. Louis)	5
H&R Block, Inc. (Kansas City)	33
Emerson Electric Co. (St. Louis)	96
The May Department Stores Company (St. Louis)	68
Ralston Purina Company (St. Louis)	40
Sigma-Aldrich Corp. (St. Louis)	77

Nebraska

ConAgra, Inc. (Omaha)	12

New Jersey

Automatic Data Processing, Inc. (Roseland)	79
Becton Dickinson and Co. (Franklin Lakes)	97
Johnson & Johnson (New Brunswick)	74
Merck & Company (Rahway)	17
Schering-Plough (Madison)	62
Warner-Lambert (Morris Plains)	57

New York	Ranking
American Home Products Corp. (New York)	72
Borden, Inc. (New York)	30
Bristol-Myers Squibb Company (New York)	18
Carter-Wallace, Inc. (New York)	27
The Interpublic Group of Companies, Inc. (New York)	32
Liz Claiborne, Inc. (New York)	14
McGraw-Hill, Inc. (New York)	100
Melville Corp. (Rye)	86
Pall Corporation (East Hills)	92
PepsiCo, Inc. (Purchase)	51
Philip Morris Companies, Inc. (New York)	1

North Carolina

Food Lion Inc. (Salisbury)	21

Ohio

BANC ONE CORP. (Columbus)	45
Fifth Third Bancorp (Cincinnati)	16
The Limited, Inc. (Columbus)	6
Premier Industrial Corp. (Cleveland)	80
The Proctor & Gamble Company (Cincinnati)	76
RPM, Inc. (Medina)	75
Rubbermaid Incorporated (Wooster)	3
A. Schulman, Inc. (Akron)	64
Sherwin-Williams Company (Cleveland)	28
The J.M. Smucker Company (Orville)	11

Pennsylvania

H.J. Heinz Company (Pittsburgh)	10
Hershey Foods Corp. (Hershey)	41
PPG Industries, Inc. (Pittsburgh)	85
Rite Aid Corp. (Harrisburg)	94
Westinghouse Electric Corp. (Pittsburgh)	87

South Carolina   **Ranking**

Sonoco Products Company (Hartsville)   35

Texas

Browning-Ferris Industries (Houston)   37
Kimberly-Clark Corp. (Dallas)   46
Luby's Cafeterias, Inc. (San Antonio)   63
Sysco Corporation (Houston)   44

Virginia

Gannett Co., Inc. (Arlington)   88

Washington

Microsoft Corp. (Redmond)   82

Wisconsin

Universal Foods Corp. (Milwaukee)   25

THE 100 BEST BY INDUSTRY

Aerospace and Defense

Martin Marietta Corp. (99)

Alcoholic Beverages

Anheuser-Busch Companies Inc. (5)

Apparel

The Limited, Inc. (6)
Liz Claiborne, Inc. (14)
Melville Corp. (86)

Automotive

Bandag, Inc. (48)
Genuine Parts Company (81)

Chemicals, Coatings and Plastics

Valspar Corp. (23)
Sherwin-Williams Company (28)
Crompton & Knowles Corp. (42)
A. Schulman, Inc. (64)
RPM, Inc. (75)
PPG Industries, Inc. (85)

Computers and Office Equipment

Pitney Bowes Inc. (61)
Microsoft Corp. (82)

Corporate Services

The Interpublic Group of Companies, Inc. (32)
H&R Block, Inc. (33)
Kelly Services, Inc. (67)
Automatic Data Processing, Inc. (79)

Wallace Computer Services, Inc. (90)
GTE Corp. (98)

Electronics

Hubbell Incorporated (36)
National Service Industries (70)
Premier Industrial Corp. (80)
Westinghouse Electric Corp. (87)

Entertainment

The Walt Disney Company (66)

Financial

Torchmark Corp. (9)
Fifth Third Bancorp (16)
Banc One Corp. (45)

Food and Beverage Production

Wm. Wrigley Jr. Company (4)
Sara Lee Corporation (8)
H.J. Heinz Company (10)
The J.M. Smucker Company (11)
ConAgra, Inc. (12)
Universal Foods Corp. (25)
Kellogg Company (29)
Borden, Inc. (30)
Dean Foods Company (31)
Ralston Purina Company (40)
Hershey Foods Corp. (41)
Sysco Corporation (44)
The Quaker Oats Company (47)
PepsiCo, Inc. (51)
Tyson Foods, Inc. (54)
The Coca-Cola Company (55)
General Mills, Inc. (58)

Food and Drug Retail

Giant Food Inc. (7)
Food Lion, Inc. (21)
Albertson's Inc. (22)
Walgreen Company (43)
Bruno's Inc. (56)
Luby's Cafeterias, Inc. (63)
McDonald's Corporation (71)
International Dairy Queen, Inc. (83)
SuperValu Stores, Inc. (89)
Rite Aid Corp. (94)

Health Care and Medical

Merck & Company (17)
Bristol-Myers Squibb Company (18)
Abbott Laboratories (19)
Alberto-Culver Company (24)
Carter-Wallace, Inc. (27)
Syntex Corp. (49)
Warner-Lambert (57)
Eli Lilly and Company (60)
Schering-Plough (62)
The Gillette Company (65)
American Home Products Corp. (72)
Johnson & Johnson (74)
The Procter & Gamble Company (76)
Sigma-Aldrich Corp. (77)
Stryker Corp. (84)
National Medical Enterprises, Inc. (91)
Medtronics, Inc. (95)
Becton Dickinson and Co. (97)

Household and Commercial Furnishings

Rubbermaid Incorporated (3)
Stanhome, Inc. (15)
Shaw Industries, Inc. (38)
Newell Co. (39)
Loctite Corp. (69)
General Electric Company (73)
Emerson Electric Co. (96)

Industrial Equipment

Pall Corporation (92)

Jewelry

Jostens Inc. (59)

Paper Products and Packaging

Bemis Company, Inc. (26)
Sonoco Products Company (35)
Kimberly-Clark Corp. (46)

Printers

Deluxe Corp. (50)
John H. Harland Company (52)
R.R. Donnelley & Sons Company (78)

Publishers

Gannett Co., Inc. (88)
McGraw-Hill, Inc. (100)

Retail Department Stores

Wal-Mart Stores, Inc. (20)
Dillard Department Stores (53)
The May Department Stores (68)

Tobacco

Philip Morris Companies Inc. (1)
UST, Inc. (2)
American Brands, Inc. (93)

Waste Handling

Waste Management, Inc. (13)
Safety-Kleen Corp. (34)
Browning Ferris Industries (37)

INDEX

A

A.H. Robins prescription drugs, 256, 257
A. Schulman, Inc., 228–30
Abbott, Wallace C., 69
Abbott Laboratories, 66, 68–71
Abercrombe & Fitch, 22
Accent artist and craft paint, 108
Accessories, 51, 306
Accessory Lady stores, 306
ACCO World office supplies, 329
Action for Corporate Accountability, 257
Activitrax heart pacemaker, 335
ADAP auto parts stores, 333
Adderley, Terence E., 239
Advanced Cardiovascular Systems, 214
Advanced Technical Fighter (ATF), 309
Adventure Island theme park, 16
Advertising agencies, 115–17
Advil analgesic, 255
Aeropower, 326
Aerosol products, 89, 101
Affirmative action programs, 62, 220, 315
AFL-CIO national boycott list, 192
Afrin nasal spray, 221
Agricultural commodities trading, 43
Agricultural products, 69, 142, 229
Agri-products, 43
AIDS
    antibody test for, 68
    medication for, 266
    testing market for, 69
Aircraft engines, 261
Air Products and Chemicals, Inc., 133
Air transportation, 163
Ajax scouring powder, 126
Akron Brass, 287
Alberto-Culver Company, 87–90
Alberto VO5 shampoos and conditioners, 88
Albertson, Kathryn, 82
Albertson's, Inc., 77, 80–83

Alcoholic beverages, 2, 6, 16–20, 328–29
Alka-Seltzer, 115
All-Bran cereal, 103, 104
Alley, William J., 328
Alley Cat pet food, 141
Almond Delight cereal, 142
Almond Joy candy bar, 145
Alsbo pipe tobacco, 6
Alumanation coating process, 269, 270
America's Corporate Conscience Award, 209, 219–20, 314
American Association of Pediatrics, 66
American Beauty pasta, 146
American Brands, Inc., 328–31
American Fare hyperstores, 199
American Fletcher National Bank, 160
American Home Products Corporation, 255–58
American Ref-Fuel Company, 133
American Store, 112
Amerock cabinet, window and bath hardware, 138
Amphora pipe tobacco, 5
Amurol Products, 14
Anacin, 255
Anbesol pain reliever, 255
Anchor Hocking housewares, 138
Anheuser-Busch Companies, Inc., 16–20
Animal health products, 214, 222
Animal medications, 61
Animal rights activists, 233–34, 237
Animal testing, 62, 66–67, 99, 164, 223, 233–34, 276
Antibiotics, 61, 213–14
Anticancer agents, 65
Antismoking campaigns, 330–31
Antitrust law violations, 48, 113
Antrol insect killer, 256
Apparel, 50–53, 249, 305, 306
Apple Jacks, 103
Appliances, 153, 232, 261
Applications software, 293
Aquaflex contact lens, 222

Aristokraft kitchen cabinets and
    bathroom vanities, 329
Armour Food Company, 45
Arrid Extra Dry deodorant, 97
Artificial wetlands, 238
Artzt, Edwin L., 273
Aspiro aspirin, 98
Atasol analgesics, 98
ATENCO record filing, 249
Atkins pickles, 112
Atlantic Envelope Company, 249
Atra razor, 231
Atwater, H.B., Jr., 206
Augustine, Norman R., 348
Aunt Jemima products, 167
Auto finishes and refinishes, 101
Automatic Data Processing, Inc., 283–85
Automotive claims service, 284
Automotive parts distribution, 289–91
Aviation Week Space Technology, 352
Axid ulcer medication, 214

B

Baby food, 66, 142
Bader, Alfred, 277
Baer department store, 187
Baker, Confectionery and Tobacco
    Workers Union, 30–31
Bakeries, 81, 142
Baker's Joy, 88
Balance cereal, 103
Balancing Work & Family Initiative, 267
Balsam, 64
Ban, 64
Banc One Corporation, 159–61
Bandag, Inc., 170–72
Band-Aid, 265
Bandits smokeless tobacco, 5
Banking, 32–34, 57–59, 159–61
Bank slip printing, 184–85
Bantle, Louis F., 5
Bacardi tropical fruit mixers, 195
Bar Flies mosquito repellent, 97–98
Bar None candy bar, 145
Baseball cards, 14
Baskin-Robbins ice cream, 112
Batman cereal, 142
Battery products, 142
Battle Creek Toasted Corn Flake
    Company, 104
Beatrice group, 42
Beauty aids, 64
Becton Dickinson and Co., 341–43
Beech-Nut baby foods, 142
Beeman's gum, 202
Beer industry, 2, 16–20

Behold, 64
Bell dairy products, 111
Bemis Company, Inc., 94–96
Bench, Johnny, 206
Ben Franklin variety stores, 73
Benson & Hedges cigarettes, 2, 328
Bentasil throat lozenges, 98
Berger and Company, 43
Berkeley cigarettes, 328
Bernick, Howard B., 87
BernzOmatic hand torches, 138
Berra, Yogi, 206
Berry Bears fruit candy, 207
Betty Crocker desserts, 207
Beverage and dairy flavors, 91
Beverage dispensers, 157
Bid-rigging, 113
Big Block candy bar, 145
Big League Chew, 14
Big Red gum, 13
Big Stone, Inc., 111
Billboard leasing, 313
Biological pesticides, 69
Birds Eye frozen foods, 116
Bird trapping, confinement and
    destruction, 237–38
Bisquick, 207
Bitumastic corrosion control, 270
Black, Cathleen, 315
Black, Daniel J., 97
Black employees, 60
Black Enterprise, 60
Black Flag insect killer, 256
Blackjack gum, 202
B-Line Systems, 278
Bloch, Henry W., 118
Bloch, Thomas M., 118
Block Sportswear, 249
Blodgett, F. Caleb, 206
Bluhill-American, 111
Body on Tap, 64
Bold Hold, 88
Bondex patch and repair products, 270
Bond pickles, 112
Book-It!, 182
Book printing, 281
Book publishers, 352–53
Borden, Inc., 107–10
Borden dairy products, 108
Borkum Riff chewing tobacco, 5
Bottle baby disease, 70
Bottling companies, 309
Bounce fabric softener, 274
Boundary mosquito repellent, 98
Bounty paper towels, 274
Bowman dairy products, 111
Bran Flakes cereal, 103

Breakfast Bake Shop Donuts and Muffins, 142
Breakfast with Barbie cereal, 142
Breen, John G., 100
Breyers ice cream, 2
Bright & Early fruit juice, 195
Brinckman, Donald W., 122
Bristol-Myers Squibb Company, 64–67
Broadcasting, 308–9, 313, 353
Brown, John W., 299
Browning-Ferris Industries, 132–34
Bruno, Angelo, 198
Bruno, Lee, 198
Bruno, Ronald, 198
Bruno's Food and Pharmacy, 199
Bruno's Inc., 198–201
Bruton smokeless tobacco, 5
Bryan, John H., Jr., 28
Brylane, 22
Bubble Tape gum, 14
Bubble Yum gum, 146
Bubblicious gum, 202
Bud Light beer, 16, 18
Budweiser beer, 16, 17, 18
Buena Vista Home Video, 236
Buenger, Clement L., 57
Bufferin, 64, 66
Bulldog hardware, 138
Bumble Bee tuna, 37
Buntrock, Dean L., 46
Burger King, 195
Burnham, Duane L., 68
Bus and van transportation services, 133
Busch, Adolphus, 17
Busch, August A., 18
Busch, August A. III, 16, 18
Busch beer, 16, 18
Busch Entertainment, 16
Business education services, 119
Business forms, 177, 319–21
Business supplies and services, 218
Business Week, 60, 352
Butcher's Blend pet food, 141
Butisol sedative-hypnotic drugs, 98
Butter Popped Corn Cakes and Rice, 167
Butterworth, Kenneth W., 245
BYTE magazine, 352

C

Cabin Craft carpets, 136
Cafeterias, 225–27
Cain-Sloan department stores, 187
Calarco, Vincent A., 149
California Air Resources Board, 90
California Department of Health Services, 124

Cambell-Ewald advertising agency, 115
Cambridge cigarettes, 2
Camel cigarettes, 116
Camerican International, 43
Canadian National Chemical, 249
Candies, 145–46, 207
Canned and dried foods, 156
Cap 'n Crunch cereal, 166
Caramello candy bar, 145
Caravan, Bernard, 255
Carboline corrosion control, 270
Cardiac Pacemakers, 214
CardioCare pacemaker monitoring system, 335
Cardiopulmonary products, 336
Cardiovascular medications, 60, 65, 69
Cardiovascular products, 214, 335, 336, 341
Care*Free chewing gum, 146
Carley, John B., 80
Carlsberg beer, 16
Carlton cigarettes, 328
Carlton Paper Corporation Ltd., 164
Carnival dairy products, 111
Carpeting industry, 135–37
Carter's Little Pills, 97
Carter-Wallace, Inc., 97–99
Carver, Martin G., 170
Cascade soap, 274
Catalog printing, 281
CBC-ConstaVac blood collection, 300
CC smokeless tobacco, 5
Celeste products, 167
Cellular phone service, 344–45
Cenex paint, 84
Cereal industry, 103–6, 142, 166–69, 206–9
Chap Stick lip balm, 255
Charitable giving, 41, 70, 178, 182, 208, 263, 275–76
Charmin toilet paper, 274
Chase Manhattan Bank, 57
Chateau Ste. Michelle wines, 6
Chazen, Jerome A., 50
Check printing, 176–79, 184–85
Cheer detergent, 274
Cheerios, 207
Cheesedawgs pet food, 141
Chee-tos, 180
Cheez Doodles, 108
Chef Boyardee pizzas and Italian food, 256
Chemical coatings, 101
Chemical manufacturing, 249
Chemical products, 277, 278, 302
Chemicals, 302
Chemical Waste Management, 47

Chem-Nuclear Systems, 47
Chess King apparel stores, 306
Chewels gum, 202
Chewing gum industry, 13–15, 202–3
Chewing gums and mints, 203
Chewing tobacco, 7
Chicago Equity Fund, 30, 169
Chicago Rawhide, 122
Chicken of the Sea tuna, 37
Chiclets gum, 202
Child-care centers, 267
Children's television, 236
Chirp bird vitamins, 97
Chlorofluorocarbons (CFC), 89
Choco-Bliss, 142
ChocoDiles, 142
Chuck Wagon pet food, 141
Cigarettes, 1, 2–3, 4, 6, 328
Cigars, 6, 7
Circus World toys, 305
CIRRUS, 59
Citrus Hill juices, 274
Citrus juices, 195
Claiborne sportswear, 50
Classic Dark beer, 18
Classico pasta sauce, 109
Classrings and school awards, 210–12
Clean 'n Gentle hair care products, 88
Clearblue Easy pregnancy test, 255
Clorets and Certs breath mints, 202, 203
Clothing industry, 21–23, 50–53, 249,
    305, 306
Clove gum, 202
Coach Leatherware, 29
Coalition for Food Irradiation, 37
Coated and graphics products, 95
Coca-Cola Company, 116, 194–97
Coca-Cola National Hispanic Business
    Agenda, 196
Cocoa Puffs cereal, 207
Code of Marketing for Breastmilk
    Substitutes, WHO, 258
Coffee, 29
Cohen, Israel, 24
Coker, Charles W., 126
Collectibles, 54–56
Colony paint, 84
Color and Paint paint shop, 85
Color Guard flea and tick collars, 97
Columbia Crest wines, 6
Columbia Pictures, 195
Comet cleanser, 274
Commercial electrical equipment, 339
Commercial printing, 320
Commercial products, 10
Commes, Thomas A., 100
Community involvement, 65, 147

CompuServe computer information
    service, 119
Computer and software manuals
    printing, 281
Computer-based education products,
    210, 211
Computer hardware and books, 293
Computer services, 119
Computer software, 292–95
ConAgra, Inc., 42–45
ConAgra Turkey Company, 44–45
Concord Custom Cleaners, 333
Condoms, 97
Conn Creek wines, 6
Consort men's hair spray, 88
Contel Corporation, 344
Continental Bakeries, 142
Converted products, 126
Cookie Crisp cereal, 142
Cool Whip, 2
Copenhagen smokeless tobacco, 5, 6
Copperhead guided projectile, 349
Coppertone tanning lotion, 221
Copying machines, 217, 218
Cori, Tom, 277
Corn Chex cereal, 142
Corn Flakes, 103
Corometrics Medical Systems, 256
Corporate Conscience Award, 314
Corporate responsibility
    Abbott Laboratories, 70
    Alberto-Culver Company, 89
    Albertson's Inc., 82
    American Brands, Inc., 330–31
    American Home Products
        Corporation, 257–58
    Anheuser-Busch Companies, Inc.,
        19
    Borden, Inc., 109–10
    Bristol-Myers Squibb Company,
        66–67
    Bruno's, Inc., 200
    Carter-Wallace, Inc., 99
    Coca-Cola Company, 196–97
    ConAgra, Inc., 44–45
    Dean Foods Company, 113
    Deluxe Corporation, 178
    Food Lion, Inc., 78
    Gannett Company, Inc., 314–15
    General Electric Company, 263
    General Mills, 208–9
    Giant Food, Inc., 256
    Gillette Company, 233–34
    GTE Corporation, 346
    H.J. Heinz Company, 37–38
    Hershey Foods Corporation, 147
    J.M. Smucker Company, 41

Johnson & Johnson, 267
Kellogg Company, 105–6
Kimberly-Clark Corporation, 164
Liz Claiborne, Inc., 52–53
McDonald's Corporation, 253
Merck & Company, 62
PepsiCo, Inc., 182
Philip Morris Companies, Inc., 4
Pitney Bowes, Inc., 219–20
Procter & Gamble Company, 275–76
Quaker Oats Company, 168–69
Ralston-Purina Company, 143
Rubbermaid, Inc., 11–12
Safety-Kleen Corporation, 124
Sara Lee Corporation, 30–31
Schering-Plough Corporation, 223
Tyson Foods, Inc., 192–93
Universal Foods Corporation, 93
UST, Inc., 7
Walt Disney Company, 237–38
Warner-Lambert Company, 204
Waste Management, Inc., 48
Westinghouse Electric Corporation, 311
Wal-Mart Stores, Inc., 74
Correctol laxative, 221
Corrosion control products, 270
Cosmetics, 51, 153, 232
Cough and cold formulas, 69
Country Colors artist and craft paint, 108
Country General Stores, 43
Courier Dispatch ground courier, 184
Courtesy paint, 84
Cracker Jack, 108
Cracklin' Oat Bran cereal, 103
Craft House leisure products, 270
Creamette pasta, 108
Creamland dairy products, 111
CreditWeek, 353
Creme Eggs candy bar, 145
Cremora Lite nondairy creamer, 109
Crest toothpaste, 274
Crisco, 274
Crispy Q frozen fries, 91
Crompton & Knowles Corp., 149–51
Crompton Loom Works, 149
Crumb Cakes, 142
Cumulative trauma disorders (CTD), 30
Cupcakes, 142
Curly Q frozen fries, 91
Custom-formulated rubber compounds, 171
Cuthbert, William R., 138
CVS drugstores, 305, 306

D

D.H. Holmes department store, 187
Daily & Associates advertising agency, 115
Dairy products, 107–8, 111–13, 153
Dalkon Shield contraceptive device, 257
Daly, Sister Patricia, 37–38
Dana Buchman sportswear, 50
Dark Continent theme park, 16
Darvon and Darvoncet-N 100 central nervous system drugs, 213
Data processing, 283–85
D'Amato, Anthony S., 107
Dawn soap, 274
Dayton-Hudson, 281
Dean, Howard M., 111
Dean Foods Company, 111–13
Defense Department, 346
Defense products and systems, 339
Dehydrated products, 92
DeKuyper cordials, 329
Delicatessens, 81
Delmonico pasta, 146
Del Monte fruits, 116
Delsey toilet paper, 162
Deluxe Corp., 176–79
Deluxe Corporation Foundation, 178
Dennison's chili, 256
Denorex shampoo, 255
Dental care products, 232
Dentyne gum, 202
Deodorants, 97
Deoped foot care products, 97
Department of Agriculture, 44
Department store chains, 187–89, 242–44, 317
Depend adult shields, 162
DeSoto paint, 101
Devoe smokeless tobacco, 5
Diabetic care products, 214
Diagnostic products, 69, 174, 256, 261, 277–78, 342
Diagnostic testing, 68
Diamond department store, 187
Dictaphone Corporation, 218
Diet Coke, 195
Diet foods, 35
Diet Pepsi, 181
Di-Gel antacid, 221
Dillard, Alex, 188
Dillard, Mike, 188
Dillard, William, 187
Dillard, William II, 187, 188
Dillard Department Stores, Inc., 187–89
Dill pipe cleaners, 6
DiMaggio, Joe, 206

Dimetapp cold and cough formula, 255
Dimitriou, Ted, 319
Ding Dongs, 141, 142
Dionne, Joseph L., 352
Diovol antacid products, 98
Directories printing, 281
Direct response, 55
Direct selling, 54–55
Disabled employees, 65, 209, 276
Discount department stores, 72–75
Disneyland, 235
Disney-MGM theme park, 235
Disney Village, 237
Disney World, 235, 237
Disposable diapers, 162, 276
Disposable dinnerware, 156
Disposable medical products, 341
Disposable razors, 203
Documentation services, 281
Dog and Cat Chow pet food, 141
Do-it-yourself products, 270
Dollon & Aichison Group eye-care
   products, 329
Dolphins, and tuna catch, 37
Don Tomas cigars, 6
Doritos, 180
dot Discount Drug stores, 73
Doty, Carl, 280
Doublemint gum, 13
Douwe Egberts tea and coffee, 29
Dovacas, Kenneth J., 111
Dow Jones Corporation, 312
Downy fabric softener, 274
Dr. Grabow presmoked pipes, 6
Dr. Scholl's foot pads and powders, 221
Drano, 64
Dremel handheld power tools, 339
Dresses, 51
Dristan decongestant, 115, 255
Drixoral cold formula, 221
Drug retailers, 152–54, 305, 306, 332–33
Drug testing market, 69
Dry cell batteries, 141, 142
Dry cleaning, 123
Duncan Hines cake mix, 274
Duplicolor paint, 100
Durasoft contact lens, 222
Duration nasal decongestant, 221
Duro glues and caulking compounds,
   245
Dutch Boy paint, 100, 101
Duyvis nuts, 29
Dyes, 149
Dymelor oral antidiabetic, 214
Dyson, Don, 190, 191

E

Eamer, Richard K., 322
Ear Rite miticide, 98
Earthscan, 331
Easy-Off cleaners, 256
Easy-On starch, 256
"Eco-pornography," 89
Edison, Thomas A., 260, 338
Edmonton Oilers, 210
Educational and professional publishing,
   353
Education Systems Corporation, 211
Efferdent, 202
Eggo frozen waffles, 104
Eisner, Michael D., 235
Elanco Products feed additives and
   herbicides, 214
Eldon Industries, 10
Electrical equipment, 338–40
Electrical products, 129–30, 345
Electric shavers, 232
Electronic funds transfer services, 176
Electronic parts distribution, 286–87
Electronics products, 130
Electronic systems, 308, 309
Elephant Malt Liquor, 16
Eli Lilly and Company, 213–16
Elisabeth sportswear, 50
Elmer's glue, 108, 109
Emerson, John Wesley, 338
Emerson Electric Company, 338–40
Encore bookstores, 333
Endangered animal species, 197
Endust, 64
Energizer and Eveready batteries, 141,
   142
Energy and utility systems, 309
Energy Department, 311
Enesco collectibles, 54
Enterprise paint, 84
Entertainment, 16, 235–38
Envelopes, 249
Environmental awareness, 19, 26, 41, 48,
   74, 82, 89, 106, 124, 196, 200, 253,
   276, 311
Environmental Defense Fund, 253
Environmental Protection Agency
   (EPA), 4, 124, 238
Epcot Center, 235
Epic Wave home permanents, 232
Erben, Ralph, 225
ERC reinsurer, 262
Erickson, A.W., 116
Ernst & Young, 74
Establissements Delhaize Freres et Cie,
   S.A., 77

Ethnic restaurants, 207
Euro Disney, 235
Evert Lloyd, Chris, 206
Evict liquid wormers, 97
Excedrin, 64, 66
Extra gum, 13
Exxon, 115
EZ Paintr, 138

F

F-16 fighter plane, 309
Fahlgren & Swink advertising agency, 115
Fairmont Products, 111
Family entertainment, 16, 235–38
Family-related benefits, 52, 93, 99, 178, 267
Famous-Barr department stores, 243
Famous Stanley Hostess Party Plan, 54–55
Fanta soft drink, 195
Farrell, David C., 242
Fast-food restaurants, 180, 182, 195, 251–54
Federal Dependent Care Assistance Plan, 178
Federal Trade Commission (FTC), 66, 70, 258
Federation for Industrial Retention and Renewal, 258
Feed additives, 214
Feen-a-mint laxatives, 221
Feller, Bob, 206
Femalt hairball remover, 98
Fiber One cereal, 207
Fieldcrest dairy products, 111
5th Avenue candy bar, 145, 146
Fifth National Bank, 59
Fifth Third Bancorp, 57–59
Filene department stores, 243
Filtering systems, 325–27
Final Net, 64
Financial services, 32–34, 218, 262, 309, 329, 353
Financial Times of London, 292
Fire-fighting equipment, 287
First Issue specialty stores, 51
Fischer, William D., 111
Fish and meat departments, 81
Fisher-Price toys, 166
Fit & Trim pet food, 141
Fitzgerald dairy products, 111
Five Alive fruit juice, 195
Flair pens, 232
Flavors, 149, 150
Fletcher, Philip B., 42

Flexigrip pens, 232
Florida environmental agency, 238
Florida Game and Fresh Water Fish Commission, 237
Fluid processing, 326
Fluka Chemie AG, 278
Fluorescence Activated Cell Sorter (FACS), 342
Foley cookware, 138
Foley's department stores, 242
Folger's coffee, 274
Food colors, 92
Food Fair, 199
Food flavors, 91
Food industry, 1–2, 17, 24–26, 28–31, 35–38, 39–41, 42–45, 76–79, 80–83, 88, 91–93, 103–6, 107–10, 111–13, 141–44, 166–67, 190–93, 198–201, 206–9
Food irradiation, 37
Food Lion, Inc., 76–79
Food Max, 199
Food processing, 43, 61
Food safety, 44
Food service, 29, 167
Food service products, 156–57
Food wholesaling, 316–18
Food World, 198
Foot-Joy golf shoes and gloves, 329
Forbe's, 60
Forbuoys sundries outlets, 329
Fort Dodge Laboratories, 256
Fortune's 1,000, 52
Fortune's most-admired rankings, 9, 60
Fortune's products of the year, 61
40% Bran Flakes, 104
Fragrances, 149, 150
Franklin Life Insurance Company, 329
Freddy's discount drugstores, 306
Freedent gum, 13
Freiman, Paul E., 173
Fresca soft drink, 195
Fresh 'n Clean grooming products, 98
Freshen-Up gum, 202
Freshlike vegetables, 112
Friskies cat food, 116
Frito-Lay, 182
Frito-Lay potato chips, 180
Fritos, 180
Fruit Loops, 103
Frosted Flakes, 103
Frosted Mini-Wheats, 103
Frozen desserts, 30
Frozen foods, 36, 91, 104, 111, 112, 116, 153, 156
Frozen french fries, 91
Fruit & Creme Twinkies, 142

Fruit juices, 40, 195, 274
Fruit Pies, 142
Fruity Marshmallow Krispies, 103
Frujen Gladjen ice cream, 2
Fuller Brush, 29
Fulton, Paul, 28
Fund for the Replacement of Animals in
    Medical Experiments (FRAME), 67
Furniture and automobile padding, 95

G

G. Fox department stores, 243
Gaines pet food, 167
Gallagher, Thomas C., 289
Gallaher Ltd., 328
Gandy's dairy products, 111
Gannett Company, Inc., 312–15
Gates, William H., 292
Gatorade, 167
Gehrig, Lou, 206
Geier, Philip, Jr., 115
Gelb, Richard L., 64
General Electric Company, 260–63
General hospitals, 323
General maintenance products, 270
General merchandise, 153
General Mills, Inc., 206–9
General Motors, 116
General Motors Acceptance
    Corporation, 116
Genuine Parts Company, 289–91
Geoflex roofing material, 270
George, William W., 335
Gerber Products, 66
Ghostbusters cereal, 142
Giant Food, Inc., 24–26
Gilbey's gin and vodka, 329
Gillette Company, 231–34
Gillette razors, 231
Gillette shaving creams and gels, 232
Gilmartin, Raymond V., 341
Gilt Edge dairy products, 111
Glass, David D., 72
Glass manufacturing, 302
Glerer, Vincent A., Jr., 5
Globe Life and Accident Insurance, 33
Goedecke pharmaceuticals, 203
Goizueta, Roberto O., 194
Golden Almond candy bar, 145
Golden Belt packaging, 329
Golden Grahams, 207
Golden Grain products, 167
Golden Skillet Restaurants, 297
Gold Medal flour, 207
Goldstein, Stanley P., 305
Golf equipment, 329

Good Bye Dry shampoo, 98
Goodes, Melvin R., 202
Good News Gillette disposable razor, 231
Gorton seafoods, 207
Goot leisure products, 10
Government Accountability Project
    (GAP), 44
Grain Cakes, 167
Granola Dipps, 167
Grass, Alex, 332, 333
Grass, Martin L., 332, 333
Grocery products, 29, 108
Grocery specialties, 167
Grocery store chains, 198–201
Grocery stores, 24–26, 76–79, 80–83, 112
Grrravy pet food, 141
GTE Corporation, 344–46
Gulden's mustard, 256
GulfLite charcoal lighter, 256

H

H.J. Heinz Company, 35–38
H.J. Heinz Company Foundation, 38
Haines, Terry L., 228
Hair care industry, 87–90
Hair care products, 64
Hallman, Michael R., 292
Halls throat lozenges, 202
Hamburger Helper, 207, 208
Hamilton, William M., 286
Hamilton Group direct response, 55
Hanes hosiery, 28, 29, 30
Happy Cat pet food, 141
Hardware, 138–40, 329
Hardy, Maurice G., 325
Harper, Charles M., 42
Hart's Dairy, 111
Harvey, George B., 217, 219
Haverty, Harold V., 176
Hawaiian Punch, 274
Hays, Thomas A., 242
Hays, Thomas C., 328
Hazardous Waste Control Law,
    California, 124
Hazardous wastes, 238
Head to Tail flea and tick products, 98
Health and beauty aids, 306
Health-care products, 97, 98, 326
Heart pacemakers, 335
Heart valves manufacturing, 336
Hearty Chews pet food, 141
Hecht department stores, 242
Heifetz pickles, 112
Hellfire Laser Seeker, 349
Herbicides, 69, 214
Hershey, Milton, 145, 147

Hershey chocolate bar with almonds, 145
Hershey Foods Corporation, 145–48
Hershey Kisses, 145
Hershey milk chocolate bar, 145
Hi-C soft drink, 195
Hi-Dri paper towels, 162
High-voltage products, 130
Hill, John A., 353
Hillshire Farm meats, 28, 30
Hobby and leisure products, 270
Hodgson, Thomas R., 68
Ho Hos, 142
Holly Farms, 191, 192
Home improvement products, 329
Homestyle Potatoes, 208
Honey Nut Cheerios, 207
Hospital equipment, 69
Hostess snacks, 141, 142
Hot cereals, 166
Hotpoint appliances, 261
Household paper products, 163
Household products, 64, 88, 256
Housewares, 9, 10, 29, 55, 138–40
Housing rehabilitation, 169
Howe, Wesley J., 341
Hoyt, Henry H., Jr., 97
H&R Block, Inc., 118–21
H-R lubricating jelly, 97
Hubba Bubba gum, 13
Hubbell Inc., 129–31
Huggies disposable diapers, 162
Huggin' Clean shampoo, 98
Humulin diabetes insulin, 214
Hussein, Saddam, 348
Hydrocarbon propellants, 89–90
Hypermart*USA stores, 73
Hyperstores, 199

I

Iammartino, Nicholas, 107
IBM, 115
Ice cream products, 2, 112, 296–98
Idaho Frozen Foods, 91
Iletin insulin, 214
Ilivine Industries, Inc., 38
Illiteracy prevention program, 182
Imodium A-D antidiarrheal, 265, 266
Industrial electrical and transportation
   equipment, 261
Industrial electrical equipment, 339
Industrial energy and equipment, 309
Industrial metal coatings, 85
INFACT, 263
Infant-care products, 265

Infant formula, 66, 68, 70
   marketing of, Third World
      countries, 257–58
Information and publication services, 352
Ingredient Technology Corporation,
   149–50
In-house career development programs,
   65
Injector Plus Platinum Schick razor, 203
Instant Quaker Oatmeal, 166
Insulation, 249
Insurance, 32–34
Inter-Continental Hotels, 116
Interfaith Center for Corporate
   Responsibility and Food & Water, 38
International Dairy Queen, Inc., 296–98
International Year of Disabled Persons,
   209
Interpublic Group of Companies, Inc.,
   115–17
Investigative toxicology unit,
   Bristol-Myers Squibb, 67
Investor Responsibility Research Center,
   62, 66–67
Isomil infant formula, 68
Isotones hosiery, 28, 29
Ithaca Daily Journal, 315
Ivermectin, 62
Ivory soap, 274

J

J.B. Ivey & Company department store,
   187
J.C. Penney, 281
J.M. Smucker Company, 39–41
Jackson, Bo, 210
Jacob Suchard, 2
Jafra skin care products, 232
Jams, jellies and preserves, 39–40
Japan
   Disney theme park in, 235
   Red Lobster restaurants in, 207
Jay's chips, 108
Jeanie ATM system, 59
Jell-O, 2
Jenner, Bruce, 206
Jewel stores, 112
Jiffy Pop popcorn, 256
Jif peanut butter, 274
Jim Beam whiskey, 329
Jimmy Dean meats, 28, 30
John H. Harland Company, 184–86
Johns Hopkins Center for Alternatives
   to Animal Testing, 67
Johnson, James L., 344
Johnson, Pam, 315

Johnson & Johnson, 115, 265–68
Jordan, Michael, 206
Jorndt, L. Daniel, 152
Joske department store, 187
Jostens, Inc., 210–12
Juicy Fruit gum, 13
Junior Mints, 203

K

Karman, James A., 269
Karmelcorn Shoppes, 297
Kaufmann department stores, 242
Kay-Bee toy stores, 305, 306
Kellogg, W.K., 104
Kellogg Company, 103–6
Kelly, William Russell, 239, 240
Kelly Office Automation Hotline, 240
Kelly PC-Pro training program, 240
Kelly Services, Inc., 239–41
Kem-Tone paint, 100
Ken-L Ration, 167
Kentucky Fried Chicken restaurants, 180
Keri Lotion, 64
Ketchup, 36
Ketner, Ralph W., 76
Kgalagadi Soap Industries, 38
Kibbles 'n Bits pet food, 167
Kidder, Peabody securities firm, 260, 262
Killark, 130
Kimberly-Clark Corporation, 163–65
King, Russell C., Jr., 126
Kirschner, Sidney, 248
Kitchen equipment, 157
Kit 'N Kaboodle pet food, 141
Kit Kat candy bar, 145
Kix, 207
Kleenex, 162
Kleen Guard, 88
K mart, 72, 138, 281, 306
Knight, Charles F., 338
Knott, Joseph F., 122
Knudson & Sons, 39
Kogan, Richard J., 221
Kool-Aid, 2
Kotex, 162
Krackel candy bar, 145
Kraft, 2
Krasnoff, Abraham, 325
Krazy glue, 108
Kroger, 332
Krunchers! potato chips, 108, 109
Krylon paint, 100, 108
KwikLite charcoal lighter, 256
KYNB Bancshares, 160

L

L.S. Ayers department stores, 243
LA beer, 18
Laboratory equipment, 69
Labor Management Award, 105
Ladies Home Journal, 104
Lahourcade, John B., 225
LaMothe, William E., 103
Lane Bryant, 22
Lane Drugs, 332
Langbo, Arnold G., 103
LAN Tim, 352
Larsen, Ralph S., 265
Larsen Company, 111, 112
"Lassie" pet products, 98
Laundry and cleaning products, 274
Lavin, Leonard H., 87
Leadership Education and Development
    program (LEAD), 182
L'Oreal cosmetics, 116
Lean Cuisine, 35
Lee, Charles R., 344
Legend heart pacemaker, 335
Legg Mason brokerage firm, 319
Lego, Paul E., 308
Lein, Don, 210
Lerner, 22
Letterman, David, 261, 262
Levi Strauss, 116
L'eggs hosiery, 28, 29, 30
Liberty National Fire, 32
Liberty National Insurance, 32–33
Life cereal, 166
Life Savers, 146
Light 'n Fluffy pasta, 146
Lighting fixtures, 248
Limited, Inc., The, 21–23
Limited Express, 22
Lindig, Bill M., 156
Linens 'n Things stores, 306
Lintas advertising agency, 115
Lipton tea, 116
Liquid Paper, 232
Listerine, 202
Lithonia Lighting, 248
Little Tikes toys, 10
Liz Claiborne, Inc., 50–53
Liz Claiborne Foundation, 52
Liz & Co. sportswear, 50
Lizsport sportswear, 50
Lizwear sportswear, 50
Loctite Corporation, 245–47
Longines-Wittnauer Watch Company,
    309
Lord & Taylor, 242
Lotrisone antifungal medication, 222

Louisville ladders, 339
Lowe Group advertising agency, 115
Lowe's paint, 84
Low-voltage products, 129
Luby's Cafeterias, Inc., 225–27
Luciano, Robert P., 221
Lucky Charms cereal, 207
Lucky Dog pet food, 141
Lucky Strike cigarettes, 328
Luden's cough drops and Mello Mints,
    146
Lurton, H. William, 210

M

McArthur dairy products, 111
McCadam cheese, 112
McCann, Harrison, 116
McCann-Erickson advertising agency,
    115
McCloskey paint, 84
McCoy, John B., 159
McDonald's Corporation, 251–54
McGraw, James H., 353
McGraw-Hill, Inc., 352–54
Macy department stores, 187, 201
Magee carpets, 136
Magic Kingdom Club, 237
Magicolor paint, 84
Magic Rock toys, 270
Mailing equipment and supplies, 217–18
Maintenance-related products, 287
Malibu cigarettes, 328
Malt extracts, 150
Mameco sealant, 270
Mandel, Jack, 286
Mandel, Joseph, 286
Mandel, Morton L., 286
Mantle, Mickey, 206
Marabou Mint Crisp, 145
Marine Bank, 160
Marketing services, 249
Marlboro cigarettes, 2–3
Marlboro Light cigarettes, 2
Marriott, 195
Marshalls discount stores, 305, 306
Mars Observer space vehicle, 349
Martin Marietta Corporation, 348–51
Martin Marietta Space Systems, 349
Martin-Senour paint, 100
MasterCard, 58
Mastercraft imported pipes, 6
Master Lock, 329
Masury paint, 84
Maxwell, Hamish, 1
Maxwell House coffee, 2

May Department Stores Company,
    242–44
May D&F department stores, 243
MBank Corporation, 159–60
Meadow Gold dairy products, 108
Medical, psychiatric and substance abuse
    rehabilitation centers, 322–24
Medical equipment, 266, 300
Medical instruments, 214
Medical products, 65, 341–42
Medical supplies, 256
Medical Waste Systems, 133
Medicare supplement insurance, 33
Medi-Clean shampoo, 98
Medtronic, Inc., 335–37
Meier & Frank department stores, 243
Meldisco shoes, 305, 306
Mello Yello soft drink, 195
Melville Corporation, 305–7
Men's apparel, 249
Men's sportswear, 51
Mentor and Magnum brand condoms,
    97
Mentor Corporation, 97
Meow Mix pet food, 141
Merck & Company, 60–64
Merit cigarettes, 2
Metromail list services, 281
Mevacor anticholesterol medication, 61
Mexsana medicated powder, 221
Michael, Gary G., 80
Michelob beer, 16, 17, 18
Michelob Classic beer, 18
Michelob Light beer, 18
MicroComputer Accessories, 10
Micro-K potassium supplement, 256
Micro-Minix heart pacemaker, 335
Microsoft Corporation, 292–95
Microsoft Mouse, 293
Midwest Express Airlines, 163
Midwest Payment Systems (MPS), 59
Miller beer, 2
Milton S. Hershey School for Orphan
    Boys, 147
Minnesota paint, 84
Minorities
    on boards of directors, 4, 109, 164,
        208, 253, 263, 346
    as chief executives, 196
    as corporate officers, 78, 168, 208,
        223, 315, 346
    as employees, 65, 93, 219
Minority Business Enterprise program,
    182
Minority Enterprise Small Business
    Investment Companies, 196
Minority investment programs, 168–69

Minority-owned businesses, 78
Minority programs, 182
Minority purchasing, 65
Minority Venture Capital Fund, 169
Minute Maid citrus juices, 195, 196
Minuteman missile, 346
Miracle Whip, 2
Mirro cookware, 138
Mobile Communications, 344
Mobile phones service, 344–45
Model-building products, 270
Modern Dairy, 111
Moist & Hearty pet food, 141
Molly McButter, 88
Monarch Marketing Systems, 218
Money Station, 59
Monofilm packaging, 94–95
Monogram appliances, 261
Montfort, Inc., 44
Montgomery County Opportunities
    Commission, 26
Mooty, John W., 296
Motion Industries industrial parts, 290
Mounds candy bars, 145
Mountain Dew, 181
Movie industry, 235–36
Mr. Clean, 274
Mr. Goodbar, 145
Mr. PiBB soft drink, 195
Mrs. Dash, 88
Mrs. Grass soup mix, 109
Mrs. Smith's frozen foods, 103
Muesli cereal, 142
Multinational Monitor, 48
Murine eye drops, 68, 70
Murphy, John A., 1
Musial, Stan, 206
Muskol insect repellent, 221
MX missile, 346

N

Nabisco, 115
Nabisco Canada, 146
Nair hair remover, 97
NAPA Auto Parts, 289
Naprosyn arthritis medicine, 173, 174
National Association for the
    Advancement of Colored People
    (NAACP), 78
National Basketball Association, 210
National Broadcasting Company, 260,
    261
National Chemical, 249
National Distillers and Chemical
    Corporation, 328
National Hockey League, 210

National Labor Relations Board
    (NLRB), 45, 78, 195
National Medical Enterprises, Inc.,
    322–24
National Pen and Pencil Company, 6
National Polystyrene Recycling Company
    (NPRC), 12
National Recycling Awards, 38
National Rental Service, 248
National Service Industries, 248–50
Natural Light beer, 18
Neurological implants, 336
Newark Electronics, 286–87
Newell Company, 138–40
New Freedom feminine pads, 162
Newspaper publishers, 312–15
New Woman, 60
New York Times Company, 312
Nibbs candy, 147
Nine-Lives cat food, 35
Nintendo cereal, 142
Nonprescription drugs, 153, 203, 255
Nonprescription health aids, 64
Noodle Roni, 167
Norplant contraceptive, 258
Nuclear power, 311
Nuclear reactors, 263, 308, 309
Nuclear weapons, 263, 311
Nuprin, 64, 66
Nut & Honey Crunch, 103
Nutri-Grain cereal, 103
Nutri-Grain frozen waffles, 104
Nutritional products, 68, 70

O

Oakland A's, 210
Oat Bran Options cereal, 142
Occupational Safety and Health
    Administration (OSHA), 44
Office products, 10, 329
Oh Henry! candy bar, 146
Oh!s cereal, 166
Oil, Chemical and Atomic Workers
    Union, 258
O'Reilly, Anthony J.F., 35
Oil recovery service, 123
Old Country theme park, 16
Old English furniture polish, 256
Old Grand-Dad bourbon, 329
Olive Garden Italian restaurants, 207
Oliver Industrial Supply, 290
Olson, Eugene R., 176
Olympics, 1988, 309
Onovin leukemia medication, 214
Optical mark readers, 184
Oral contraceptives, 173, 174, 266

Oral leukoplakia, 7
Orange Julius, 297
Ore-Ida frozen potatoes, 36
Orleans canned shrimp, 109
Ortho-Novum oral contraceptive, 266
Orthopedic arthroscopics, 299–300
Osborn, Guy A., 91
Oscar Mayer, 2
Ostenberg, Elisabeth Claiborne, 50
"Ozone friendly," 89

P

Packaged consumer products, 29
Packaged foods, 28
Packaging, 85, 94–96, 108, 126–27, 139
Packaging machinery, 94
Paint-by-Numbers art kits, 270
Paint refinishing service, 123
Paints and coatings, 84–86, 100–102,
   108, 269–72, 302–3
Pajor, Robert E., 84
Pall, David B., 325
Pall Corporation, 325–27
Pall Mall cigarettes, 328
Pam cooking spray, 256
Paper Mate pens, 232
Paper products, 127, 163
Parkay margarine, 2
Parke-Davis, 203
Parliament cigarettes, 2
Parque de la Amistad, 182
Partners in Progress, 315
Parts cleaner service, 122–23
Pasta, 146, 167, 256
Path Management Industries, 119
Patriot missile, 348, 349
Payless ShoeSource, 242
Payroll processing service, 283, 284
Payton, Walter, 206
PCBs, 48
PC-Payroll network, 284
Peacekeeper missile, 349
Pearl Drops dental polish, 97
Peavey Grain Company, 43
People for Community Recovery (PCR),
   48
People for the Ethical Treatment of
   Animals (PETA), 276
Peoples Drug, 305, 306, 332
Pepper, John, 273
PepsiCo, Inc., 180–82, 195
Pepto-Bismol, 274
Peptol antiulcer medication, 98
Perfumes, 51
Periodicals printing, 280
Periodontal disease, 7

Pershing II missile, 349
Persian Gulf War, 348
Personal care products, 55, 97, 162, 163,
   274
Pert shampoo, 274
Pesta pickles, 112
Pet care products, 97–98
Peter Paul/Cadbury, 145
Peter Piper pickles, 112
Pet foods, 35, 141, 167
Pharmaceuticals, 60–65, 68–69, 81, 97,
   98, 152–53, 173–74, 203, 213–16,
   221–23, 256, 265, 266, 332–34
Philadelphia carpets, 136
Philip Morris cigarettes, 2
Philip Morris Companies, Inc., 1–4
Piggly Wiggly Stores, 199
Pillsbury, 43
Pipes, 6
Pipe tobacco, 5–6
Pitney Bowes, Inc., 217–20
Pitney Management Services, 218
Pizza Award Certificate reading
   program, 182
Pizza Hut restaurants, 180, 182
Planters Nuts, 146
Plant growth regulators, 69
Plant relocation, 258
Plasite corrosion control, 270
Plastic housewares, 9
Plastics, 94–95, 108, 126, 138, 228–29,
   261
Platt's Global Alert, 353
Plus System, 59
PM Company men's apparel, 249
PNC Financial Corporation, 160
Political Action Committees, 70
Pollution, 89, 311, 331
Polyethylene terephthalate (PET) bottles,
   38
Polytrope-R plastics, 229
Pom Poms, 203
Pop Secret popcorn, 207
Portable restrooms, 47, 133
Port-O-Let portable lavatories, 47
Post cereals, 2
Potato Buds, 207
Potato chips, 108, 180, 274
Poultry industry, 190–93
Pounce cat food, 167
Power systems, 261
PPG Industries, Inc., 302–4
Precious Moments collectibles, 54
Pregnancy tests, 97
Premier Industrial Corporation, 286–88
Preparation H hemorrhoidal medication,
   255

Prepared foods, 43
Preprinted inserts, 281
Prescription drugs, 203, 266
Prescription Learning Corporation, 211
Prescription medications, 69
Prestige housewares, 329
Price fixing, 70
Primatene Mist, 255
Prince, Larry L., 289
Princess cruises, 116
Pringles potato chips, 274
Printing industry, 176–79, 280–82, 319–21
Print Plus prints and poster stores, 306
Printware computerized labeling
  systems, 319
PROCRIT erythropoietin, 266
Procter & Gamble Company, 273–76
Profit sharing plans, 78
Protein Technologies International, 142
Proventil asthma therapies, 222
Prozac antidepressant drug, 213
P&R pasta, 146
Psychiatric Institutes of America, 322
Publishing, 312–15, 352–53
Pudding Cake, 142
Pulse Communications, 130
Purina Biscuits pet food, 141
Purina Mills, 142
Puss 'n Boots cat food, 167
PYA/Monarch food service, 29

Q

Quaker 100% Natural cereal, 166
Quaker Chewy Granola Bars, 167
Quaker Oats Company, 166–69
Quaker Oats oatmeal, 166
Quaker Oat Squares cereal, 166
Quick Response inventory control
  system, 187
Quinlan, Michael R., 251

R

R.R. Donnelley & Sons Company,
  280–82
Racism, 62
Raco, Inc., 130
Radar and surveillance systems, 308
Radio and television stations, 308–9, 313,
  353
Radiological pollution, 311
Radio Shack, 281
Rain Dance Glass Cleaner, 108
Rainforest Action Network, 197
Rain forest destruction, 196–97
Rally Car Wash, 108
Ralston Purina Company, 141–44

Ramblin' Root Beer, 195
"Rapid refund" tax refunds, 119
Rasheed, Fred, 78
Ratcliffe, G.J., 129
Rauh, Thomas, 74
Razors, 202, 203, 231
Ready-to-eat cereals, 103–4, 142, 166,
  207–8
Reagan, Ronald, 207
ReaLemon lemon juice, 108
Recipe dog food, 35
Recombinant DNA technology, 214
Record-keeping systems, 177
Recovery Centers of America, 322
Recycle America program, 46
Recycling, 12, 38, 106, 122–23, 127,
  132–33, 276
Red Lobster restaurants, 207, 208
Red Seal smokeless tobacco, 5
Reese's Peanut Butter Cups, 145
Reese's Pieces candy, 145
"Refund anticipation loan service" tax
  refunds, 119
Regal China, 329
Regident denture adhesives, 97
Rehab Hospital Services Corporation,
  322
Reiter Dairy, 111
Resource Conservation and Recovery
  Act, 124
Restaurants, 180, 182, 195, 207, 208,
  225–27, 296–98
Retail specialty stores, 51
Retail technology, 152–53
Retreaded tires, 170–72
Retton, Mary Lou, 206
Rice-A-Roni, 167
Rice Cakes, 167
Rice Chex cereal, 142
Rice Krispies, 103
Richards, Bob, 206
Richard Shaw, Inc., 111
Richey, R.K., 32
Right Guard deodorant, 232
Rite Aid Corporation, 332–34
River blindness disease, 62
Robert W. Baird brokerage firm, 319
Robinson, J. William, 184
Robinson, Jackie, 206
Robinson department stores, 242
Robitussin cold and cough formula, 255
Rockwell International, 349
Rolaids, 202
Rolo caramels, 145
Ronzoni pasta, 146
Rooney, Phillip B., 46
Rooster smokeless tobacco, 5

Rose, Pete, 206
Rotenstreich, Jon W., 32
RPM, Inc., 269–72
Rubbermaid Inc., 9–12
Ruckelshaus, William D., 132
Ruffles potato chips, 180
Ruth, Babe, 206
Ryan Milk, 111
Rynatan and Ryantuss cough and cold
    products, 98

S

Safety-Kleen Corporation, 122–25
St. John, Carole, 219
St. Joseph analgesics, 221
St. Louis Cardinals baseball team, 16
Sally Beauty Company, 87–88
Sami, Vincent A., 302
Sam's Wholesale Club stores, 73
San Francisco 49ers, 210
San Giorgio pasta, 146
Sani-Flush toilet cleaner, 256
Sanka coffee, 2
Santa Cruz Natural organic juices, 39
Sara Lee Corporation, 28–31
Savannah River nuclear installation, 311
Scannable forms, 184
Schaefer, George A., 57
Scherag Pty. Ltd., 223
Schering-Plough Corporation, 221–23
Schick Disposable razor, 203
Schick Plus razor, 203
Schmitt, Wolfgang, 9
Scott, Judith G., 319–20
Seafoods, 109, 207
Sealants, adhesives and related products,
    245–47
Sears, 72, 100, 138, 281
Sea World parks, 16
SECO Industries, 10
Selig Chemical, 249
Selsun Blue shampoo, 68, 70
Sensor shaver, 231
Sera-Tec Biologicals, 333
Sesame Street toys, 270
Seven-Up International, 181
Sexism, 62
Seyfert's chips, 108
Shark Bites fruit candy, 207
Shaw, J.C., 135
Shaw, Robert E., 135
Shaw Industries, Inc., 135–37
Sherwin-Williams Company, 100–102,
    332
Sherwood Medical medical supplies, 256
Shield flea and tick products, 98

ShopKo department stores, 317
Short-run computer forms, 177
Sigma-Aldrich Corporation, 277–79
Silk Cut cigarettes, 328
Similac infant formula, 68
Simply Fruit spreads, 39
Sine-Aid, 265
Sinutab, 202
Skil power saws and tools, 339
Skin care products, 232
Skinner pasta, 146
Skippy Premium dog food, 35
Skoal smokeless tobacco, 5
Skor candy bar, 145
Slice soft drinks, 181
Slim Twin Schick razor, 203
Smart Cat pet food, 141
Smith, Tom E., 76
Smithburg, William D., 166
Smith Crisps snack food, 180
Smokeless tobacco, 5–6, 7
Smucker, Paul H., 39
Smucker, Richard K., 39
Smucker, Tim, 39
Snack foods, 108, 167, 180
Sno Balls, 142
Snowy Coat shampoo, 98
Snuggle fabric softener, 116
Socks Galore & More, 29
Soft & Dri deodorant, 232
Soft-drink industry, 180–82, 194–97
Solarcaine sunburn medicine, 221
Sonoco Products Company, 126–28
Sony, 195
Source computer information services,
    119
South Africa, U.S. companies in, 62, 66,
    70, 105, 109, 164, 223, 233, 267, 346
Southwest Cooking cookbook, 208
Sovey, William P., 138
Soy protein products, 142
Spartan Bank, 160
Spearmint gum, 13
Special Dark candy bar, 145
Special Dinners pet food, 141
Special K cereal, 103
Special products, 85
Specialty chemicals, 61, 270
Specialty products, 10, 329
Spic and Span cleaner, 274
Sportswear, 50
Sprite, 195
Stafford, John R., 255
Standard & Poor's, 353
Standard smokeless tobacco, 5
Stanhome, Inc., 54–56
Stanley Cup, 210

Star-Kist tuna, 36, 37
Static Guard, 88
Stationery products, 232
Stayfree, 265
Stefanko, Robert A., 228
Steroids, 173, 174, 222
Stiritz, William P., 141
Stix department store, 187
"Store-within-a-store," 51
Stove Top dressing, 2
Strategic Defense Initiative (SDI), 346
Stratton carpets, 136
Streamlined Inspection System-Cattle (SIS-C), 44
Street and parking lot sweeping, 133
Structure, 22
Stryker, Homer H., 299
Stryker Corporation, 299–301
Sugar Babies, 203
Sugar Daddy, 203
Sugarfree Hubba Bubba gum, 133
Sugarless gum, 4
Sullivan, Frank C., 269
Sullivan, Michael P., 296
Sullivan, Thomas C., 269
Sun Flakes cereal, 142
Superbowl, 210
Superfund toxic waste sites, 48, 263
SuperGlue, 246
Super II Schick razor, 203
Super Valu Stores, Inc., 316–18
"Superwarehouse" stores, 199
SupeRx drugstore chain, 332
Supplemental personnel services, 119
Sure deodorant, 274
Sure & Natural panty shields, 265
Surfire hand torches, 138
Surgical equipment, 300
Suter, A.E., 338
Suzy Qs, 141, 142
Sweeteners, 150
Swingline chemicals, 331
Swingline office supplies, 329
Symphony chocolate bar, 145
Syntex Corporation, 173–75
Syrups, 150
Sysco Corporation, 156–58
Systems software, 293
Syva medical diagnostic equipment, 174

T

TAB soft drink, 195
Taco Bell restaurants, 180
Tang, 2
Target, 72, 138
Target paint, 84

Taryeton cigarettes, 328
Tax form preparation, 118–21
TCB hair care products, 88
Teamsters union, 192
Technology-based learning systems, 211
Teenage Mutant Ninja Turtles cereal, 142
Telecommunication products and services, 344–45
Telephone equipment and service, 344–46
Television programs, 236
Temporary help services, 239–41
Tender Vittles pet food, 141
Testor hobby products, 270
Texas Instruments, 116
Textile rental, 248, 249
Theme parks, 16, 235–38
Thermo King transport refrigeration units, 308, 309
Third National Bank, 59
Third World, marketing practices in, 66, 70, 257–58
This End Up furniture stores, 306
Thom McAn shoes, 305, 306
Three-in-One oils, 256
Thrif D Discount Center, 333
Thrift stores, 142
Thrive pet food, 141
Tide detergent, 274
Timepieces, 309
Times Mirror Company, 312
Titan missile, 349
Titleist golf equipment, 329
TM group vending machines, 329
Tobacco industry, 1, 2–3, 4, 5–6, 328
Toiletries, 64, 153, 232
Tollett, Leland, 190, 191
Tools, 339
Torch Energy, 33
Torchmark Corporation, 32–34
Total, 208
Total cereal, 207
Touchstone Pictures, 236
Tower, H.L., 54
Toxic chemicals, 331
Toxic Release Inventory (TRI) data, 4
Toxic wastes, 311
Toy Manufacturers of America, 12
Toys, 9, 10, 11–12, 270, 305, 306
Trac II Gillette razor, 231
Trading services, 284
Treflan herbicide, 214
Trident gum, 202
Triple X pediculicide, 97
Trix, 207
Trojan brand condoms, 97

Tronolane hemorrhoid medication, 68, 70
Tropical Blend suntan products, 221
Turner, Fred L., 251
Turner, John W., 319
20th Century plumbing, 329
Twinkies, 141, 142
Twizzlers candy bar, 145
Tylenol, 265
Tyson Foods, Inc., 190–93

U

Ulcer medications, 61
Ultrex Disposable razor, 203
Underwear, 28, 29
Unfair labor practices, 192–93
UNICEF, 70
Unilever, 116
Union Label & Service Trades Department, AFL-CIO, Labor Management Award, 105
Unions, 52, 78, 103, 105, 192–93, 258
United Food and Commercial Workers Union (UFCW), 78
United Investors Life, 33
United Investors Management Company, 33
United States Air Force, 309
United States Army, 349
United States Fish & Wildlife Service, 237
United States National Institutes of Health, 330–31
United States Postal Service, 217
United States Tobacco, 5
Universal Foods Corporation, 91–93
Univol antacid products, 98
Unix World, 352
USA Today, 74, 312, 313, 315
UST, Inc., 5–8

V

Vaccines, 61
Vagelos, P. Roy, 60
Valspar Corporation, 84–86
Valspar varnish, 84, 85
"Value-enhanced" poultry products, 191
Van Camp's beans, 167
Vanish bowl cleaner, 64
Vargas, Alejandro Diaz, 54
Vasotec blood pressure medication, 60–61
Veg-all vegetables, 112
Vehicle information service, 284
Velban cancer medication, 214
Velveeta cheese, 2

Vending machines, 329
Ventres, R.J., 107
Verifine Dairy, 111
Vets dog food, 35
Victoria's Secret, 21
Victory Veterinary Formula insecticides, 98
Vidal Sassoon, 274
Video industry, 236
Viking Brush, 10
Villa Mt. Eden wines, 6
Vinyl materials, 95
Virginia Slims cigarettes, 2
VISA, 59
Vision care products, 221, 222
Vision desk-top blood analyzer, 68
Vitalis, 64
Vitamins, 69, 70

W

Waddell & Reed (W&R) financial services, 32, 33
Wag's restaurants, 153
Walgreen, Charles R., Sr., 153
Walgreen, Charles R. III, 152, 153
Walgreen Company, 152–54, 333
Walkers Crisp snack food, 180
Wallace, Walter, 320
Wallace Computer Services, Inc., 319–21
Wallace Press, 320
Wall coverings, 108
Wallin, Winston R., 335
Wall Street Journal, 74
Wal-Mart Stores, Inc., 72–75, 100, 138, 281
Walt Disney Company, 235–38
Walter, John R., 280
Walton, Sam M., 72
Warehouse stores, 80
Warner Chilcott Laboratories, 203
Warner-Lambert Company, 202–5
Washington Public Power Supply System (WPPSS), 263
Waste disposal, 46–49, 132–34
Waste Management, Inc., 46–49
Waste to energy program, 46–47
Waterloo tool storage products, 329
Waterman fountain and ballpoint pens, 232
Waterproofing products, 270
WB Cut chewing tobacco, 5
Weapons industry, 263, 311, 348–51
Wear-Ever pots and pans, 138
Weight Watchers, Inc., 35
Welch, John F., Jr., 260
Wells, Frank G., 235

Wendy's, 195
Western Fire Equipment, 287
Westinghouse, George, 309–10
Westinghouse Broadcasting Company, 308–9
Westinghouse Electric Corporation, 308–11
Weston, Josh S., 283
Wexner, Leslie H., 21–22
Wheat Chex cereal, 142
Wheaties cereal, 206–7
Wheelabrator Technologies, 47
White Cloud cleaner, 274
White Rain shampoo, 232
Wholesale Club stores, 73
Willes, Mark H., 206
Williams, Joseph D., 202
Williams, Ted, 206
Williams, Walter W., 9
Wilson, James N., 173
Wilson Jones office supplies, 329
Wilsons leather fashion stores, 306
Windex, 64
Windows software series, 293
Windsor Canadian Supreme whiskey, 329
Wines, 6
Wise Choice popcorn, 109
Wizard air freshener, 256
Wm. Wrigley Jr. Company, 13–15
Wolf chili, 167
Wolfe, Kenneth L., 145
Women
    on boards of directors, 82, 89, 99, 109, 164, 182, 208, 219, 238, 253, 263, 346
    as chief executives, 52
    as corporate officers, 52, 89, 99, 109, 113, 168, 182, 208, 219, 223, 238, 314–15, 346
    as employees, 52, 65, 93, 219
Women's hosiery, 28
Wonder breads, 141, 142
Wood, Richard D., 213
Woodhouse, John F., 156
Woodson, Robert R., 184
Woodward & Dickerson, 43
Woolite, 256
Wooster Rubber Company, 9
Workplace safety and health, 30
World Bank, 331
World Health Organization (WHO), 66, 70, 258, 330–31
World Series, 210
Wright, Michael W., 316
Wrigley, William, 13, 14, 15
Wrigley, William, Jr., 14
Wurtele, Angus, 84
Wyeth-Ayerst pharmaceuticals, 256, 258

Y–Z

Yeast, 92
Yoplait yogurt, 207
York peppermint patties, 145
Young, A. Thomas, 348
Y&S candy, 147
Zaban, Erwin, 248
Zayre, 281
Zelen, Alfred M., 231
Zep Manufacturing, 249
Zest soap, 274
Zig-Zag cigarette papers, 6
Zimmerman, Richard A., 145
Zinsser paints and coatings, 270